Touched by Grace

A Novel Based on a True Story

John Steslow

PublishAmerica
Baltimore

First printing

ISBN: 1-59286-710-3
PUBLISHED BY PUBLISHAMERICA, LLLP
www.publishamerica.com
Baltimore

Printed in the United States of America

*To our grandparents who came from Poland in the late 1800's
and gave us America*

Acknowledgements

To the Breadloaf Writers Conference where I met Jay Parini who encouraged the dream of writing the story, and Jim Torrens, S. J. who elevated its style and became a good friend; to the many Bernardine Sisters in Brazil and the U. S. who shared their experiences; to life-long friends, especially Joseph Walsh, whose letters give the novel a life otherwise impossible to achieve; to my family who will hopefully forgive any infringements on their privacy; to the Holy Spirit whose grace we all share; and finally, to my computer jockey, Linda Schwank, who kept it all in one piece.

PART ONE

"We have gifts that differ
according to the favor
bestowed on each of us."

ROMANS 12:6

CHAPTER ONE

In the summer of 1936, Sister Maria Edmunda, the newly elected Secretary General of her community of sisters stood by the window of the motherhouse and reflected on the scene before her. Mt. Alvernia, named in honor of Mt. LaVerna where St. Francis received the wounds of Christ, or stigmata, was becoming a place of beauty.

Directly in front of the main entrance was the twelve foot, full sized bronze statue of the Sacred Heart of Jesus. His left hand circled a cross which stood a few feet higher and to the left of His head. On the transverse part of the cross was written: *"In Hoc Signo Vinces"* - In this sign you will conquer. The statue rested on a six foot high concrete pedestal bearing the words *"Ecce cor quod adeo dilexit mundum"* engraved on its front. This testament of Christ promised that the heart which He gives to all will transform the world. Beyond the statue a gently sloping hill extended about seven hundred feet to the street below. A macadamized driveway was bordered by three-foot-high privet hedges and divided by a grassy area along its center. When coming up the roadway she always felt she was reaching towards a higher dimension of spirituality and a retreat from the ordinary world. Blue spruce, pines and fir trees grew some thirty feet from the hedges. Within the line of trees, thorny barberry bushes generally reddish in color, enhanced the aesthetic pleasure of the grounds. And beyond the tree line to the left was a large orchard. Apple, pear, peach and cherry trees produced fruit for the convent and their spring blossoms gave a seasonal beauty throughout the years.

To the right of the driveway a narrower road led to the Music Hall originally called Maria Hall. This building was part of the ten acres given to the nuns by Msgr. George Bornemann, pastor of a German parish in the neighboring city. For a time it had served as an infirmary for the sisters stricken with tuberculosis who required a period of quarantine. Along its driveway were Rose of Sharon plants, especially beautiful because of the topiary effect of pruning their branches and allowing a round ball of carefully trimmed flowers to bloom at the top.

To the immediate left of the Sacred Heart statue and driveway was a narrow pathway. This led to the grotto of Our Lady of Lourdes. Built in 1930, it had become one of her favorite places to pray. A small pool of water, fed by a stream, created a very real impression of the grotto in France. A modest, delicate statue of St. Bernadette kneeling in prayer to the Virgin enhanced the grotto's charm.

Sister Maria Edmunda always enjoyed this view from the motherhouse. The scene reminded her of the first day she arrived at the convent twenty-five years before at the age of thirteen. She had always wanted to be a nun. There was something about being a bride of Christ and devoting all of one's energies to a deep spiritual life she could not explain even to herself. She simply accepted her desires as a vocation to the religious life and never doubted the authenticity of that calling. The one thing she had not anticipated was the quick recognition she would receive from her superiors.

While still a postulant, she was teaching students who were not much younger than she. The demand for teachers by pastors of various Polish parishes was too great to allow anything other than on-the-job training to fill that need. Five members of her religious order, the Bernardine Sisters of St. Francis, had come to the United States in 1894 from Poland at the request of a priest in Mt. Carmel, Pennsylvania. By 1911 Sister Edmunda was part of the one hundred members to which the community had grown. Many of the young women came from the anthracite coal region of eastern Pennsylvania. The Polish parish of St. Casimir in Shenandoah, some fifty miles northeast of Reading, was sister's home parish and the school, sponsored by the pastor, was the first elementary school served by the congregation.

Sister Edmunda's elementary school teaching career lasted twelve years. As a teacher she excelled in exactness and discipline. Her students responded generously to her efforts. By 1923 she had received a Bachelor of Arts degree from Catholic University in Washington, D.C. In 1924 she was elected to the general council of the community after the resignation of another administrator. She left that position five years later because her duties as a teacher at Mt. Alvernia High School and as Directress of Studies of the Villanova College Extension, both on the grounds of the convent, commanded much of her time. Meanwhile, Sister Edmunda also studied for and received a Master's degree from Catholic University in 1934. Among her other responsibilities was that of supervisor of schools. She always reminded the sisters to give every ounce of their energy for the good of their students. That summer of 1936 was also her silver jubilee. She had spent twenty-five years in the service of her Lord and savior, and her most adventurous years were about to begin.

Mother Mary Angela had begun to feel the burden of her second six-year term as head of the community and Sister Edmunda became her mainstay of support for most of those years. As always, she prayed that the will of God would be fulfilled in all her undertakings. She entered the office of the previous Secretary General to find all the personal records of the sisters and the community's documents in perfect order. Three items placed on the desk caught her attention: room and file keys; a note from her predecessor indicating that the new secretary would be responsible for the "Community's Customary" which had to be presented to Rome for examination; and two letters addressed to Mother Angela in what looked like a Polish-type script with Brazil as the return address.

Another note indicated the letters had not been attended to nor acted upon. These letters became her main focus of attention. "Is it possible I may be able to teach and work with the Polish immigrants in Brazil?" Despite her years as an administrator she had always found teaching, especially of the poor, an energizing experience. She believed that education would give them the opportunity to grow spiritually and materially.

"This has to be the first order of business." The letters were written in Polish. She eagerly studied their contents. Her Polish was almost as fluent as her English, since both her parents had emigrated to the United States from Poland. Mother Yolanda, a Bernardine originally from the community's cloistered convent in Zakliczyn, was ardently asking for help in the Mission of Dom Feliciano, where she was serving as a practical nurse. Several of the original Bernardine Sisters had decided to leave Dom Feliciano for the state of Santa Catarina to begin another mission there, which left the few remaining sisters in desperate need of help if the Mission of Dom Feliciano was going to survive.

This news was like a dream come true for the newly-elected Secretary General. The Vincentian Fathers of Erie, Pennsylvania, had published a continuous series of articles in their monthly publication *"Skarb Rodziny"* describing the desperate lack of teachers and nurses in the Polish settlements in Brazil. In the evening recreation hours she shared her enthusiasm for the possibility of filling those needs, and if it were God's will, would spend the rest of her life in that distant country.

"How am I going to ask Mother Angela for permission to personally respond to this cry from Mother Yolanda?" The next day Sister Edmunda related to Mother Angela the plea for help from Brazil and at the same time requested that she be permitted to resign her new posts of Secretary General and councillor and go to Brazil as a teacher as quickly as possible. Mother Angela agreed to present the matter to the community's councillors at the first meeting of the new administration. She also emphatically dismissed any ideas of resignation. "You can do more to help the Poles in Brazil in other ways," said Mother Angela.

CHAPTER TWO

Sister Edmunda's family was never neglected in her daily prayers. Her mother, Julia, lived in Shenandoah - a widow since 1921. Her father, Jacob Lojas — the English pronunciation was Woyas — had died in May of that year at the age of fifty-six. Her younger brother, John, had died at the age of fifteen in a coal breaker accident. Her brother Joseph two years younger than she was married to Catharine, whom everyone called Cassie. Her only sister, Maryanne, was nine years younger.

Her father born in Nowy Targ, Poland, in 1864, was a handsome, stately man who had served as an officer in the Austrian army. In the early years of his life Austria controlled the southern part of Poland where his family lived. Every young Pole served a period of two years in the army under the Austrian flag. When he had finished his tour of duty he returned home to a family who insisted he marry a woman whose family owned a good deal of land. He refused to do so and headed for America.

Jacob Lojas was ambitious to do well in his new country. He learned that many Poles had settled in the town of Shenandoah, Pennsylvania, in the anthracite region of the state. Though rather well-educated, he was sure he could be a productive miner in that fast growing industry. At twenty-four, he had no trouble getting hired and quickly learned the skills needed to become successful in his new occupation. He saw immediately that the town was growing in population and many of the newcomers needed housing. He decided to save every cent possible and began to buy houses which could be rented with no difficulty. People respected property owners and his reputation grew as a good landlord. Since he was better educated than most of those around him, they began to ask him for help in their daily dealings with banks, other landlords, and naturalization procedures.

At the age of thirty-one, Jacob married eighteen year old Julia Pyzowska, who had recently arrived from Poland. Since her family was also from the Carpathian Mountain region of the country, this gave them some compatibility on which to build a marriage. The following year he took his oath of citizenship. Now a totally integrated American, he wanted very much to start a family. The first child died in infancy. Their second child, Helen, born in 1898, was a beautiful baby who would eventually become the Reverend Mother of the Bernardines. Joseph came along in 1900, a strong, solid child from the very beginning. John was born in 1902 and Maryanne in 1907. The family lived in a fine townhouse on South Jardin Street with all of their basic needs attended to by Jacob. Julia wanted more than the no-frills attitude dictated by her husband.

"Why are you so tight with your money?" Julia asked him one day.

"There is no other way to get ahead. How else do you think I have been able to buy the houses we own?"

She never asked the question again. Instead she began to rebel against the strict financial regimen he had imposed. The tight rein bruised her vanity because she had always liked fine clothes and better footwear. Out of frustration she began sipping the brandy Jacob kept on hand for harsh winter nights and as a medicinal aid against colds brought on by the dampness in the coal mines. Before long she found the taste of brandy very much to her liking. The warm glow it brought to her cheeks and the mellow disposition it engendered eventually became something she could not live without. An excellent seamstress, Julia was able to earn some money of her own. This gave her just enough independence to buy whatever supply of brandy and other alcoholic beverages she desired. After her early widowhood the habit became a constant in her life, causing a great deal of sorrow to Sister Edmunda and her other children.

To her great sorrow, Sister Edmunda's beloved younger brother, Johnny, had been fatally injured while working at the colliery's coal breaker. When she was notified that he had suffered the deadly accident she had insisted on seeing her beloved brother. His body was at the Ashland State Hospital, where such victims were kept until an autopsy could be performed. The corpse was kept cold on large cakes of ice. She had looked carefully over his entire young body, found nothing seriously wrong and always wondered exactly how the accident had happened. She could never forget this image.

When Joe was nineteen he met and married Catherine Hojnicky. Her brothers wanted a more American sounding last name and adopted the name

Hennessey. Cassie had really hoped they would move to a larger city where Joe could put his carpentry skills to better use. Joe had learned the trade by working on his father's houses. He also decided to change his last name to the more American-sounding Loyes. Shortly into their marriage, Cassie was told by a doctor that she could not conceive a child — a problem she had never anticipated.

His father's death in 1921 had given Joe full control of his father's estate. Cassie's parents owned a fourteen-acre farm some four miles outside of Shenandoah. As each child got married they were invited to build a house on the property. "Joe, let's build a home and start a small business in Ringtown. It may keep you out of the mines." With some reluctance to move out of his hometown, he built the house himself, a raised rancher, which Cassie called her bungalow. The two-bedroom house had all the conveniences and space they wanted. The kitchen was large enough to include a table and chairs for informal dining. The dining room was located next to the kitchen toward the front of the house. The living room included a piano, which she played beautifully. The hallway, from the front door to the pantry in the back of the house, had a large warm-air vent which heated most of the rooms. The bedrooms had their own air ducts.

A narrow stream ran through the property with a very small bridge crossing over the stream to a one-acre garden area on which many vegetables were grown. Potatoes, cabbage, radishes, lettuce, corn, spinach, tomatoes, and many other vegetables presented a delightful sight from the kitchen window. Eggs were collected each day from a few dozen chickens, and colorful roosters crowed each morning at sunrise. Since Cassie had been raised on the farm she knew the daily routine needed to keep the chickens fed and watered. While freshly killed chickens supplied many hearty meals, a cow and young bull were also often added to the livestock to supply milk and meat. A fairly large hill stood to the right of, and behind the house, where Joe decided to build an electric fence around much of the hill so that the livestock could graze on it. Freshly baked bread and pies were Cassie's specialty while she also canned many vegetables for use during the winter.

All of these things became very important because the small hotel and dining room they had opened in Ringtown did not do well. A tall, very strong man of two hundred and twenty-five pounds, Joe began to drink heavily. He terrified Cassie who had never known anyone who drank to such excess and showed so much anger which stemmed partly from the fact that they could not have any children of their own.

Despite their problems of her infertility and Joe's return to the mines to work, an opportunity to have and raise a newborn baby suddenly surfaced. Cassie's sister Elsie, who lived in Reading, had been deserted by her husband, who left her with two young children to provide for on her own. Catherine wrote to her, commiserated with her desperate situation, and suggested a way that she and Joe could provide some financial help until Elsie became more capable of taking care of her two children and herself. The idea made sense to Cassie because she firmly believed that Polish families provided for each other's needs in every way possible. The moral concerns of Joe having sex with someone other than herself would simply have to be overcome in favor of a greater good.

"Joe," she said to him one day, "I have written to Elsie and brought up the idea of her bearing a child by you."

"Cassie, are you out of your mind? How did you come up with that idea?"

"Joe, think about it. We could help Elsie out financially and we would say that the baby was ours. I am on the heavy side. People would have no idea whether I was pregnant or not."

"How many people know about this?"

"No one except the three of us will ever know about this."

"What about my sister Helen? As a nun I am sure she would not think it is the right thing to do."

"We won't tell Sister Edmunda or anyone else about the baby if it happens."

"Oh God, Cassie, I don't know! How do you think I'll be able to live with this?"

"Joe, just think about the good that will come into our lives when we have a baby to love and raise." The whole idea seemed too extreme. He could not imagine the pregnancy happening after just one sexual encounter. Nevertheless, that is exactly what happened.

Cassie had prayed fervently that her sister would become pregnant quickly. She believed her prayers were answered. When the baby was born they brought their son to live with them and thanked God every day for the joy he brought into their lives. They called him Richard. Although Elsie had been resigned from the beginning that this would be her sister's baby, it was still hard for her to part with this beautiful new life she had held in her womb for nine months. In her extreme joy at finally becoming a mother, Cassie went to the parish priest to be "churched," with the special blessing given to mothers after the birth of a child. She wanted to fulfill this custom, even though Joe thought it a hypocritical thing to do. By 1936, when Sister Edmunda assumed her office as Secretary General, her nephew Richard was fourteen, growing strong and well. He helped offset the Depression's effect on the family by delivering the *Shenandoah Herald* to the families in the area. That he had to pedal his bicycle during all kinds of weather, up and down a number of hills, gave Cassie great concern.

Sister Edmunda's younger sister, Maryanne, called Mary by everyone, was now the mother of two children; her first child a girl named Alma, born in February, 1931. Sister Edmunda had suggested the name, for it signified a benignant, gracious, warm hearted and kindly disposed personality. In December, 1932, a son named John was born in the family's apartment in the east end of Shenandoah. His delivery by Mary's cousin Sophie, who acted as a midwife, was a difficult one during which he became bluish in color and Mary and Sophie both prayed he would be okay. After a few hours his color became more normal. Everything would indeed be okay.

Mary had married John Scislowicz, a miner like so many men in the town. They met soon after she had returned to her hometown from the New York area, where she had held various jobs. In New York, she was at first an upstairs maid for a very pleasant Jewish family in Forest Hills. Her very attractive looks brought on some unsolicited attention from one of their sons, but her strong Catholic faith made her resolute in letting him know she was not available to him. At another job, with the Pennsylvania Railroad, she cleaned passenger cars. There she met a friendly and considerate married man, Joe Targonsky, who often invited her to dinner on weekends with his wife Celia. They remained friends for many years, even after her return to Shenandoah. Mary's husband had been born in America; however, he treasured and loved his Polish heritage. At 30 years of age, and many marriage possibilities passed by, he fell in love with Mary. In three months they were married. Happily, Mary had saved some money and still had $2,000 in bonds of the Pennsylvania Power and Light Company from her father's estate. John had never been very good at saving money. His attitude was simply to enjoy life and, like the birds of the air, trust in the good God to see him through his everyday needs. The marriage took place in a quiet ceremony in the rectory of the church because marriages were frowned upon during the season of Lent.

Sister Edmunda was delighted that her family was growing and she plunged into her work and life of prayer with greater energy and trust than ever before.

CHAPTER THREE

In February of 1937 Sister Edmunda and the three other councillors of the order met with Mother Angela. The agenda included the letters of Mother Yolanda and her request for support in the Brazilian settlement of Dom Feliciano. After much discussion and prayerful study, the council decided to send two sisters to Brazil to investigate the positive and negative aspects of such an important venture. In June Sisters Philippine and Adalbert left for Brazil. Sister Edmunda looked forward to their return with the hope that their reports would be favorable.

In the meantime she launched into the compilation of the community's customary which expanded on their constitution. To do so she talked things over with Mother Angela, visited other Franciscan communities, noted whatever customs were inherited from the Polish birthplace of the Bernardines in Zakliczyn, and carefully examined the customs of the sisters who first came to America. The School Sisters of St. Francis of Milwaukee, Wisconsin, proved very helpful. The Sisters of St. Felix of Cantalice, or Felicians, were gracious enough to actually give her a copy of their customaries. This was a real departure from the norm, since communities of women were very cautious about sharing strictly private information about their rules, constitutions, customs, and form of government. The Felicians originated in Poland in the mid-nineteenth century and came to America in 1874, twenty years prior to the arrival of the Bernardines, which may have prompted their generosity. All of the data gathered was carefully considered by Sister Edmunda, however, she knew it would take much more time to reach the decisions needed to produce a customary worthy of presentation to Mother Angela and the community.

Sister Edmunda's zealous prayer life made her especially grateful for the wonderful gift granted to the community by Cardinal Dennis Dougherty of Philadelphia the year before — the privilege of having the Blessed Sacrament exposed daily for adoration on the main altar of the motherhouse. The primary aim for granting the exposition was to inspire continuous prayer throughout the day for God's blessing on the priesthood; the spread of the kingdom of God throughout the world, especially in America; the preservation of the faith; and the return of Russia to the original faith of its fathers. With her office close to the chapel, she never lost an opportunity to kneel before her Eucharistic Lord to seek guidance in everything she did.

At last, a letter arrived from Sisters Philippine and Adalbert describing their first experiences in Brazil. Mother Angela and Sister Edmunda read the letter with great interest since the Brazilian endeavor had become of utmost importance to both of them. The sisters described how they had boarded a bus in Porto Alegre, the coastal capital of the state of Rio Grande do Sul, for Camaqua, a city further inland before proceeding to Dom Feliciano, about 40 kilometers away. With no electricity in the town, they spent the night in the only hotel's lobby because of its overcrowded condition with no rooms available for them. The next morning, the pastor of the small settlement, Father Walter Hanquet, arrived to take them the rest of the way. Father Hanquet and his twin brother, Brazilians educated for the priesthood in Germany, returned to Brazil to minister to some of the Catholic settlements in the region. Father Hanquet had an old car which he used to reach the outer missions and had intended to meet the American sisters upon their arrival in Camaqua. A late emergency had delayed his arrival.

Mother Yolanda and the handful of Polish Bernardines at Dom Feliciano greeted the sisters with prayerful enthusiasm. "Sisters, you don't know how much we have beseeched the Lord that you would join us in this mission. The Poles here are very poor and will not be able to respond as generously as you might like, but they are hopeful that things will get better." Sister Adalbert asked Mother Yolanda how many sisters from the United States could find adequate housing if they came to Dom Feliciano.

"We could start with perhaps a few, maybe six to ten sisters."

"Have you any idea where they might stay?"

"We can't say positively, however, the Army has some buildings they may be willing to let us have for a while."

Mother Yolanda explained how the Brazilian government needed an ambitious, diligent workforce to cultivate the land, promote the economic growth of the country, and populate the "gaucho" territory in the southernmost state of Rio Grande do Sul. They launched a campaign in the agricultural areas of Europe to entice land-hungry farmers to emigrate to Brazil at no cost to themselves or their families. Poland had been the breadbasket of Europe for many years; consequently, many Polish farmers found the prospect of owning larger farms than they could ever hope to have in Poland too attractive to resist. Some Germans, Italians and French were also intrigued by the offer. About 1600 of the early settlers came from Poland, 1900 from the Polish territory under Russian rule and 100 Germans. The number of French emigrants to Brazil was always relatively small, since French Canada had the same language and was more appealing to them. Italians found Brazil very promising. Each family received a colonial lot of 25 hectares and enough reis to construct a home, which was normally made of wood, and provided other necessities. The relatively large area of land granted to each family made it difficult to focus any attention to communal buildings. Most of the families were Catholic and believed that a large Catholic country like Brazil would accommodate and promote their religious beliefs.

In their second letter to Mother Angela, Sisters Philippine and Adalbert described the situation in Dom Feliciano as one of sub-poverty. Camaqua was somewhat larger; however, the housing and food situation would still be a true test of the sisters' vow of poverty. This last communication caused Mother Angela to seriously doubt the wisdom of sending any of her sisters to Brazil. She believed that only a face-to-face accounting from Sisters Philippine and Adalbert would clarify the decision to be made.

On their return to the motherhouse in August, 1937, the two sisters presented all their findings to Mother Angela. The facts were stark enough. Sister Adalbert summarized her own feelings with the statement, "I must say that in all honesty, I think that anyone who goes there will be called a fool." Sister Philippine's sentiments were much more conciliatory. "It is not all bad," she stated, "I'd be very willing to go there if I were sent."

In a human way, Sister Adalbert's attitude was completely understandable. Dom Feliciano and Camaqua were like small outposts in a vast area very much like the American "wild west." True religious zeal and courage would be needed to build a secure future in that region of Brazil. Father Hanquet had told the sisters that no congregation of nuns dared to send its members to open schools in that part of the country of ranches. It was simply considered too dangerous and venturesome, still Sister Philippine's generous heart was enough to convince Mother Angela that the mission to Brazil was worth undertaking. Sister Edmunda was overjoyed by her decision.

A circular letter was sent to all six hundred and fifty teachers and nurses in the congregation notifying them of this newest commitment of their beloved community and asking for volunteers for the missionary work. Fifty favorable responses were received from sisters in their twenties and early thirties. Many were the flower of the community who looked forward to bringing Christ to the people of Brazil. Nothing was too difficult for their young hearts when souls were at stake - not even to part with their parents, brothers and sisters whom they might never see again. After careful consideration, five sisters were chosen as the first missionaries to leave for Brazil — Mother Mary Benjamina, the appointed superior at Camaqua, Sisters Bernadette, Aurelian, Chesla and Herminia. All had their Bachelor of Arts degrees and Sister Herminia was a registered nurse.

Preparation for the trip by steamer began in earnest. Mother Hedwig, one of the council members, wanted to make certain the sisters had the proper equipment for washing and ironing. Sister Adalbert spoke up quickly. "There is no running water; clothes are washed in the river. Washboards are what they will need and those will seem very advanced to the people there."

"Old fashioned irons might be a good idea since there is no electricity," suggested Mother Chesla. Sister Adalbert agreed this might be a good idea so long as the sisters understood that fuel was also scarce and fires could not be started simply to heat irons. Mother Angela made certain that enough warm clothing was included in the trunks, although the sisters felt it would not be needed. Mother Angela had heard that the nights could get very damp and cold and wanted the sisters to be reasonably comfortable in a home which might be unheated. School books were very important since their first priority would be the opening of two elementary schools - one in Camaqua and one in Dom Feliciano. Final visits by the sisters were made to relatives who often had mixed feelings about their loved ones going off to an uncertain future. Convent life in the United States was demanding enough; in a foreign country with a different language and few basic necessities, the sacrifices seemed too formidable.

On December 2, 1937, the eve of the feast of the great Jesuit Missionary, St. Francis Xavier, a departure ceremony was held in the chapel of the Sacred Heart Convent, the motherhouse of the Bernardines. Father Sliwinski, the convent chaplain, blessed the sisters who now wore their missionary crosses, and the *"Ave Maris Stella"* was solemnly chanted.

At the farewell dinner, Mother Francis recalled the leaving of Zakliczyn, Poland with the small band of sisters, to start their own American adventure which had now grown to 650 members. The return God was now making to the same Polish nuns in Dom Feliciano, Brazil, was a momentous reuniting of the American Bernardines with their European birthplace. The dinner closed with Psalm 90, *"Kto sie w Opieke,"* "Lord you have been our refuge" and a heartwarming rendition of *"Szybko Mijaja, Chwile,"* "How quickly time passes."

Psalm 90 of the Old Testament and the Polish farewell song are closely related. A sage's meditation on the shortness of life made still shorter by sin, in Psalm 90, begins with a prayer to the Lord: "Lord, you have been our refuge age after age" It ends with the last two verses.

Let us wake in the morning filled with your love
and sing and be happy all our days;
make our future as happy as our past was sad,
those years when you were punishing us.
Let your servants see what you can do for them,
Let their children see your glory.
May the sweetness of the Lord be on us!
Make all we do succeed.

The Jerusalem Bible, 1966

This melancholy Polish hymn reflects the rapid pace of life.

How swiftly pass the moments
How time flows like a stream
A year, a day, a moment
We'll not be together again.
When the years of our growth
Flow rapidly away
In our hearts will remain
Longing, sorrow and pain.

Mother Angela would not send any of her sisters to their first foreign mission without joining them. She hoped that her presence would be an encouragement as well as a firsthand exposure to their adverse circumstances. The trip was made on a steamer which sailed from New York on December 3rd. Arrangements had been made by Father Hanquet to have the Franciscan sisters of another congregation, the Sisters of St. Francis of Penance and

Christian Charity, receive the Bernardines into their convent and school in Porto Alegre for a short period of time. This would allow the Bernardines to become more fluent in Portuguese and begin to acquaint themselves with their new environment. Mother Benicia, the Superior of Bon Conselho Ginasio, opened not only the school but also her loving Franciscan heart to the new missionaries.

Mothers Angela and Chesla did not remain in Porto Alegre very long. They wanted to acquaint themselves with the mission at Dom Feliciano as soon as possible. They were riding to the mission in a carriage from the town of Camaqua which they had reached by bus when they came to a stream swollen from recent rains. There were no bridges, and as inexperienced foreigners, were sure the carriage would dip into the swollen waters. The driver had no such concern and plowed right on through! Within a half hour they arrived at the barrack-convent of the Polish Bernardines on January 1, 1938.

Mother Yolanda, still wearing the habit of the Polish nuns in Zakliczyn, greeted Mothers Angela and Chesla with the warm traditional three kisses on both cheeks.

"Have you had any breakfast?"

"No, Mother, we wanted to come here as quickly as we could. Whatever you have will be more than enough for us."

The meal was a simple one - *pan de acua,* or water bread, some cheese, and coffee with a great deal of milk called *cafe de leche*, served in a small cup.

Mother Angela brought Mother Yolanda up to date on some administrative matters which were in process. A request had been made to Archbishop John Becker of Porto Alegre for permission to open an elementary school in Camaqua and to help the struggling sisters with their school in Dom Feliciano. Also, Mother Yolanda's petition to have the Polish sisters in Brazil amalgamated with the American Bernardines was also entrusted to Archbishop Becker, since the turmoil of the pre-Second World War years was making it impossible to have the matter transacted by the Franciscan fathers and sisters in Poland.

Mother Yolanda was delighted that the process had begun. She said to Mother Angela, "Mother, you have no idea how relieved I am that you are sending us your educated sisters to help us with the missions here in Rio Grande do Sul. I am sure the cloistered sisters in Poland will be happy to learn we are no longer alone in this endeavor."

"With God's help and the prayers of all who support us we have only to persevere in His grace to see this all come to a successful end," said Mother Angela, with much hope and gratitude that the mission was underway.

Sister Edmunda, working diligently in Reading on the community's customary, was informed by Mother Angela that this work would have to be interrupted because she needed a companion to return to the motherhouse from Brazil. Sister Edmunda was to accompany four new graduates of the Catholic University to Brazil early in February, and return with Mother Angela shortly afterward.

On February 4th, 1938, Sister Edmunda left the United States with Sisters Baptist, Laurine, Terence and Fulgence. While in Brazil Sister Edmunda received news that her mother Julia had died. Deeply troubled and broken hearted, she prayed unceasingly for her mother's soul, and wanted very much to be there for the funeral. That was impossible. Her sister Mary and brother Joe would have to take care of the funeral arrangements. For many years she had felt alienated from her mother because they each looked at life and faith so differently. Her mother's death while Sister was far away touched her deeply. From then on Sister Edmunda began to offer up much of her prayer-life for the souls in Purgatory and the atonement of their sins.

CHAPTER FOUR

Sister Edmunda's nephew Johnny remembered his grandmother for one special reason. Whenever she walked over to their apartment house from her own small basement apartment about three blocks away, she always brought along the biggest, reddest apple she could find. She always made certain to hand it to him directly.

"This is for my Jasiu" she would say. A Polish diminutive of John, *Jasiu*, which in English sounds like Yashew, was a way to differentiate him from his father after whom he was named. Jasiu had just turned five when his grandmother died.

The funeral meant that his grandmother's body would be laid out in the family's living room the day before the Latin Mass for the Dead in the church. The undertaker did the final dressing of the body in the house, including the combing of her hair. Since the living room was between the two bedrooms of the apartment, the house became a quiet sanctuary where everyone spoke in whispers. No one was to go into the room, his mother told him, until the undertaker was finished and the body was in the coffin. Jasiu wanted to peek into the living room soon after his grandmother's body had arrived at the house. His curiosity persisted until, quietly, he opened the door of the living room to find his grandmother's hair being combed by the undertaker's assistant. They had the body out of the casket, which startled him and made him shiver with fright. He quickly closed the door and never looked in again.

The funeral went as planned, except for the impossibility of getting the casket out of the apartment through the kitchen door without turning it on its side, an undignified way to treat the deceased. The decision to take out the double windows of the kitchen and lower the casket to the steps outside overcame the predicament. After that the funeral proceeded as planned. The burial took place in St. Casimir's cemetery, in the older section where his grandfather had been laid to rest in 1921.

"How I wish Sister Edmunda could have been here," said Cassie.

"Perhaps she will be able to visit us this summer," answered Mary.

Joe was his usual tough-skinned self through the funeral proceedings. He loved his mother but never had felt really close to her after he married in 1919.

During the long lunch after the funeral, Johnny's mother suggested he go out to play for a while. After the somber events of the morning, he was happy to get out of the house. He found Mary Jane sitting on the communal bench just up the hill from his house. This was a favorite place for the neighbors to get together during their free time. Mary Jane was his own age and not yet in the first grade of school.

"Johnny, let's go somewhere and 'play house.'"

He walked beside her to an open area away from the neighborhood, to an abandoned car which they inspected to see if the doors still opened. They got into the front seat and for a while watched some older boys playing touch football not too far away. Somewhat quietly she whispered to him, "Johnny, would you like to see how I am down here?" as she spread her legs to let him know what she meant.

"Okay," he said quickly.

With her panties down and her dress around her waist one of her older brothers suddenly appeared at the side of the car. "What are you doing?" he bellowed. They were stunned into silence with no time to react. Her brother grabbed him by the right ear and dragged him out crying until they were in sight of the apartment.

"Now get home and never try that sort of stuff again with my little sister."

With his ear swollen and reddened by the constant pulling, he looked up to find his father waiting at the doorway.

"What's that all about?" asked his father.

"Nothing, we didn't do anything. Mary Jane just showed me her panties!" he cried.

His father, who had never spanked him before, gave him a few good whacks on the behind. "I guess that's a very bad thing to do," he thought to himself and never played with any girls that way again. No one at the house gave him any sympathy after they heard the story.

Jasiu's older sister Alma always enjoyed showing him off to the neighbors. As soon as he had been old enough to walk she would take him on strolls and

26

would say to all, "*To moj brat.*" She was very proud to have a little brother of her own. Alma's playful but careless use of matches had wrenched the family the year before. On a spring day in 1936 she was dressed in a beautiful flossy white dress made by her grandmother for the Easter celebrations. A sudden gust of the April wind caused her to drop the match she was holding against her dress. In a moment she was in flames. In her panic she began to run and tried in vain to protect herself from the fire which began to envelop her entire right side. Little Johnny looked out from the porch window, about twelve feet above the ground, after hearing someone screaming for his father. A neighbor, who had become a good friend of his mother, saw what was happening, but she was too far away to do anything since a seven foot hillside was between her and his sister. His father quickly realized what was happening, picked up some woven rag carpeting on the porch floor, ran down the flight of stairs, wrapped the rug around his daughter, rolled her on the ground and extinguished the flames.

The oldest son of the landlord, in the neighborhood with his father's car, offered to take Alma to the hospital emergency room in Shenandoah Heights, about a mile away. The doctor on duty realized the seriousness of the burns when her dress could not be removed without tearing away some of the skin. Alma's right hand was so scarred by third degree burns that during the healing process she could barely hold a pencil to write. Scars were formed on the right side of her neck and her right breast was seriously disfigured. She spent three months in the hospital recovering from the accident. Her parents were devastated. Mary was pregnant with her third child, due in August.

"Why didn't you watch what she was doing?" shouted their father to Mary on many occasions when the incident was discussed.

"You know we have always told the kids never to play with matches," retorted Mary.

Sister Edmunda bled for her sister Mary and her niece Alma. She prayed that Mary, whose young life had not been easy, would not be tortured by guilt. Sister Edmunda left home for the convent when Mary was only three; her brother John died in a coal breaker accident when she was nine; Joe married when she was eleven and at the age of fifteen, her father died. At sixteen she left her mother, who consistently surrendered many of her days to the intoxication of brandy, to find a better life in New York City. Somehow life had seemed to her a series of departures. She began to feel she would be left alone to make her way through life. Her marriage and family were everything to her. She wanted it to be a success. The terrifying accident with her daughter motivated her to take special care of her son, Johnny. She vowed that nothing like that would ever happen to him.

On the eastern end of the town, the small neighborhood on South Carbon Street where twelve families lived was like an entity unto itself, the neighbors seeming very much like an extended family. The men would gather together on a summer evening, play pinochle under a light if the games lasted into the dark, trump an opponent with great enthusiasm and look forward to the next week's game. The kids played all kinds of games, with rarely a dull moment. Hide and seek was a great favorite with those under nine years old. The girls played jacks. Any boy found playing jacks was considered a sissy. Sometimes a boy would get pressured by the girls to play "house". The girls would bring out their tea sets, "pretend tea" would be drunk and all believed they would very likely actually get married someday.

A young girl named Mary Gobster lived in the apartment next to them in one of the two apartments built above the warehouse. The great attraction was that they both had modern baths and central heat. To the young Johnny, Mary looked absolutely beautiful. In the spring she would place a white veil over her long curly hair, lower herself as much as she could behind a myriad of irises and slowly rise up to look like a princess with all those lovely flowers in front of her. She was at least five years older than he, but the vision always stayed with him, even after she and her family moved to another part of town.

When he was about three or four, little Johnny opened the bathroom door, next to his bedroom, to find his father carefully shaving his face with a straight-edge razor. He had always been impressed by how much bigger his father was compared to his own below-average size, and this day his father had decided to take a bath at home. He normally showered at the coal mine; however, there he stood, without clothes before the mirror shaving. When his Pop noticed Johnny looking at him with a good deal of curiosity, he slowly turned to show his son a little more of himself. Then he said humorously, "If you want to touch it, you can." Immediately Johnny closed the door, ran through the kitchen and onto the porch to play with the canaries caged there. He had simply had an interest in seeing all of his father's body. His curiosity had been satisfied, and ended as quickly as it had begun.

Death came into his young life again after his grandmother's passing. Louis Gregonis was a neighbor who lived just four houses away and they often played together for hours each day. Louis's mother, one of the warmest, kindest women in the neighborhood, was loved by everyone. One day Johnny learned that Louis had the measles. When forbidden to visit him, he wondered why. His mother said, "Measles are contagious. If you go to see him you may catch the measles too. Besides, his mother won't let you go into the house." He waited anxiously for the time to pass until he and his friend could play again. On the third day his mother told him Louie's fever had gotten much worse. She still believed the disease would eventually pass. Measles were simply a childhood illness from which everyone recovered. Louis did not get better. His fever rose to 105 degrees by the sixth day. Pneumonia appeared to be developing. On the seventh day he convulsed into unconsciousness and died. No one in the neighborhood had believed he could die from an episode with the measles. Johnny knew only one thing, his best friend was gone.

The canaries, caged on part of the porch outside the kitchen, took on a special interest to him after Louie died. He began to notice how beautiful they were and how the songs they sang were not always the same. His father could imitate every one of them by whistling those songs exactly as he had heard them. Johnny looked forward to the day he could whistle like his dad, who promised he would teach him as soon as he was a little bit older.

To a coal miner, canaries had a very useful purpose. When taken into the deeper pits, which was sometimes necessary, there was always the danger of carbon monoxide building up to dangerous levels. A canary was very sensitive to the change in air quality and would make distressed sounds before slumping over and sometimes dying. When that happened, the miners would hurry out of the area to prevent dying themselves. His dad sold some of the canaries to other miners for that reason.

One day, when Johnny was absorbed in watching the canaries, his father asked, "Would you like to know what kind of canaries we have?"

Johnny answered with much enthusiasm, "Yes Pop, I would like to know that."

"See the yellow ones? Those are satinettes; so are the bronze and gold ivory-colored ones."

"What are those whose heads are so smooth and clean?" Johnny went on, with excitement in his voice and hands, as he pointed them out.

"Those are golden lizards," answered his father, pleased that his son was taking such interest in one of his own hobbies.

"What are the ones with some red in them?" Johnny continued.

"They are opals. Those three kinds of canaries are what we have, but there are others."

"Do you think we can get other kinds?" asked Johnny.

"Probably not, they're not too easy to buy."

His pop asked if he would like to start going into the cage to pick up the dirty newspapers inside where the canaries had dropped their doo-doo. "Will the birds fly all over me?" he asked. "There are so many of them."

"They won't hurt you," answered his dad. " Let me know when you want me to open the door and go in."

"Let me try right now. I want to do it now."

His dad helped him open the screened door. Once inside, the cage seemed smaller to him and the canaries flew all around his head. "Let me out," he cried to his dad. He did not try to go into the cage again for a long while.

Later that day in 1938, the mailman delivered a letter from Sister Edmunda, addressed to his mother. Her return from Brazil, with Mother Angela, on April 1st, made it likely that she would visit the family in June on her three-day vacation, which she was allowed every three years. This news was a great joy to everyone. Sister Edmunda's presence always brought a refreshing vitality to both Joe's and Mary's families. Sister informed Mary she would stay at the convent at St. Casimir's the first night, visit with the family for the day and spend the next two nights on the farm with Joe and Cassie. Mary was pleased that she would be able to show her newest, ten months old, son to Sister Edmunda for the first time. They had named him Louis Sylvester in honor of her recent silver jubilee in the convent, had considered naming him Sylvester Scislowicz, but that was a mouthful, so they decided Louis would be a pleasant first name, and kept Sylvester as a middle name. Two of the landlord's sons were named Johnny and Louis, and Louis had been Jasiu's best friend before he died.

Mary wished that Sister Edmunda could remain with her for the night, since most of their relationship rested solely on letter writing. How much better and warmer it would be if Sister could spend the entire night and another day with her and the family. With three children in an apartment with four rooms, her sister and the customary nun-companion could not be accommodated. Joe and Cassie's house was more suitable because their son Richard could sleep over at a cousin's house while the nuns were there, which made his bedroom totally accessible to the guests. Also, the farm was always more peaceful and restful than the Carbon Street neighborhood.

In early June, Sister Edmunda and another nun came to the house as anticipated. To her pleasant greeting, *"Niech bedzie pochwalony Jezus Christus,"* came the response *"Na wieki wiekuw Amen."* Praised be Jesus Christ, forever and ever. Amen. The prayer immediately set a tone of reverence for the entire visit. Warm hugs and kisses followed the response. "Adoration" best describes the feelings the entire family had for their beautiful nun. Energy flowed through everyone in Sister's presence. A special liveliness animated their thoughts. They all wanted to say the right things. Words to a nun were not the same as words used in ordinary conversation. Ideas became more elevated.

Sister Edmunda generally treated every member of the family equally. For her little nephew, Johnny, however, she was developing a real fondness. He was so full of joy, alert, awake, quick thinking; she liked engaging him in conversation. On this visit she felt very close to him, as aunt to nephew. Johnny asked her a question to which, not knowing the answer, she gave an evasive one. In a short while he asked it again, the same question worded differently. Sister gave another evasive reply. Then came a third question, worded differently but meaning the same. She finally answered, "Oh just because." He thought a while and said, "Oh, the why is the just because." "Yes, that's it," his aunt said, happy to close the exchange.

The visit also gave her a first look at Alma's burns, and the resultant disfigurement to her right hand. Alma was now seven years old, in the second grade, and very much captivated by her aunt. She wanted so much to show Sister she could write with her right hand and was beginning to recover completely from her accident. Unfortunately, she had begun to limp because her right hip had developed an unknown problem. She was under a doctor's care; however, he was unable to pinpoint the exact cause of the discomfort she felt. Sister asked, "Mary, do you think her hip problem is a result of the burns she suffered?"

"I really don't know, Sister. We will watch her carefully."

"Perhaps a more experienced doctor could help."

"Sister, we will do everything we can for Alma. Please say some special prayers for her," answered Mary's husband. They both hated to tell Sister the added medical expense was something they could not afford.

A joy to watch, Louis was a robust eater whenever Mary nursed him. Delighted that she had this second boy despite the rough economic times of the Depression, Mary began wondering about the number of children they should have. She accepted the official Catholic position on artificial contraception, still she pondered how she might need to deal with the Church's stand on the matter. Perhaps if her husband could refrain from getting drunk every payday she would feel more secure. She kept hoping he would finally realize he could not go on with his wasteful spending and his financial irresponsibility which caused continuous arguments between them. Sister Edmunda sometimes spoke to him directly about the situation. With unaccustomed shyness, he always promised to "reform."

After a pleasant meal, Joe came for his sister to take her to Ringtown. He had just finished his day's work at the colliery; this was merely a stop on the way home. Joe wanted to be the kind of brother Sister Edmunda could be proud of, which meant he would have to cut back on his payday drinking as well. This was a tough challenge for him. From time to time, especially during the winter, he would stay sober for six or seven weeks. Longer than that, and he would become edgy, unsettled, and often bite his nails. Sister Edmunda felt he might have inherited his drinking problem from their mother, Julia. The best she could do was pray fervently for a breakthrough from the habit. She also depended on Cassie's continued respect for their marriage vows, hopeful that she would find other satisfactions in their relationship.

When they reached Ringtown the same ejaculatory prayer was pronounced respectfully. Cassie's response echoed the deep feeling she had always had for her sister-in-law. Cassie called the nuns "holy women," considering their lives were wholly dedicated to spiritual growth and perfection. Cassie's own intense prayer practices intimated her own desire to follow the same path in life. There was no doubt that she had developed a truly close relationship with Sister Edmunda.

Richard was always happy to see his aunt. She asked him about his schoolwork and what his plans were after graduation the following year. He told her his cousin Victor and he were pretty certain they would go into the CCC's. In the Civilian Conservation Corps they would have a job and earn some income for both of their families, plus have some spending money of their own. Sister told him she liked the idea and wished him the best of luck.

The house smelled of freshly baked bread and warm apple pies. "Cassie, I can't get enough of the wonderful smell of your bread and pies. How do you manage to make them so perfectly every time we come to visit?" commented Sister Edmunda.

"Oh, it's nothing. I just do it," said Cassie. "Would you like some pie now or wait until tomorrow since you've already eaten at Mary's?" asked Cassie.

"Well, perhaps a small piece tonight, since it looks so good. How about you, Sister?" Sister Edmunda asked Sister Imelda, her companion.

"Oh yes, I'll have some," Sister answered. After the little treat they went into the living room to hear Cassie play the piano. Sister Edmunda liked good music. She was especially fond of Chopin and Paderewski. She often mentioned that Chopin had died at thirty-nine, and in his relatively short life he had become "the poet of the piano," composing hundreds of pieces as well as two piano concertos. Paderewski was especially respected by Poles everywhere. In 1919 he was prime minister of Poland. In his eighty-one-year lifetime he had become one of the most renowned pianists of modern times. His many piano works included an opera, a symphony, a concerto, and well-known songs. Cassie did a passable job on compositions from both Chopin and Paderewski. They all sang along when she played Verdi's "Ave Maria." Before long, however, the loud chirping of crickets could be heard throughout the house. The time for bed had definitely arrived.

The next day, after a restful sleep, Joe asked Sister Edmunda if she would be willing to pose for a special photograph he wanted to keep as a remembrance of her visit.

"All right, Joe. Where?"

"The front of the house would be the best place. You can sit on the cement railing at the bottom of the steps and then turn to the camera. But please be careful as you walk down. I don't want you to trip." He never forgot the day young Richard came rushing out of the front door to greet him and Cassie. In his childish enthusiasm he fell down most of the cement steps, hit his head, and developed a vision problem which required him to wear heavy glasses throughout his boyhood.

Sister Edmunda always walked with grace. She also made certain her habit was spotless. Her bib-like, rectangular, celluloid breast cover was always kept carefully in place. This cover reached upward to a celluloid collar which helped to keep her stiffly-starched headwear in place. The front of her face alone remained visible. A starched white veil liner gave shape to the black veil covering it. She wore a four-inch-long crucifix, held on a chain, directly below the white breast cover. A full-length scapular, made of the same brown material, draped neatly over the ankle-covering dress of her habit. The brown wool habit was belted by a long white cord with three knots signifying the three religious vows of poverty, chastity and obedience. A large rosary with heavy beads hung on the left side of the cord — eighteen inches on each side of the cord. Black stockings and black oxfords completed her habit. With her head held slightly to the right, her hands folded gently across her lap, and a pleasant smile on her face, the picture became one of the family's favorites. The picture, which Mary had enlarged to eighteen by twelve inches, always hung on the parlor wall for everyone to see. On the second day Joe and Cassie drove the sisters back to Reading and their beloved motherhouse.

CHAPTER FIVE

With their lives totally concentrated on things spiritual and Catholic, the sisters rarely read newspapers or periodicals. In the year 1939 however, the threat of all-out war became more ominous and the invasion of Poland by Nazi Germany in September keenly affected the American Bernardines because most of them had Polish backgrounds. Sister Edmunda found herself reading the local newspaper more carefully to stay attuned to worldly matters. The church in Poland and the effect a German occupation would have on her relatives and on the Bernardines in Zakliczyn troubled her greatly. She also worried about her nephew, Richard, who would soon be of draft age, if the United States became involved in the war.

Sister had received a letter from Richard postmarked Montesano, Washington in the spring of 1939. He told her how he and his cousin Victor had signed up for the CCC's in Pottsville, the county's capital, and had gone immediately to a military base near Harrisburg for two days where clothing items like fatigues, shoes and hats were distributed, and then, transported by bus to Camp Roosevelt, Virginia for assignment. He mentioned how happy they were when told they would be going to Washington, which they were sure meant Washington, D. C. Instead they traveled by rail across the country to the state of Washington, assigned to Fort Lewis, about 25 miles from the capital city of Olympia.

"It is like the Army," he wrote. There were fifty men to a barrack, breakfast was served at seven, a lunch was packed for each of them and they were driven by truck to a soil conservation project. No question, they were there to work. Victor was so efficient at the job of planting tree seedlings they quickly made him a foreman. He said his expertise came from planting cabbages for farmers around Ringtown.

Sister was happy Richard had found something useful to do which helped his parents through the difficult economic times. Every month the government sent twenty dollars directly to his family and he received five dollars for his own use. Sister always replied almost immediately to every letter she received. In her return letter she told Richard how delighted she was with all that he was doing. She also told him of her concern about the possible war the country might enter and promised her continuous prayers for his safety.

In the meantime, Sister reserved much of her time for the compiling of the customary for her order. By 1939, the first draft of the customary was ready. The councillors studied the document meticulously, with matters either deleted or added. Sister Edmunda, with her democratic tendencies, persisted in her strong belief that the customary should be accepted by the whole community and not only by the administration. An Extra-Ordinary-General Chapter was considered by the councillors to be the best way to present it to the other members of the order. According to the constitution, this general chapter could not be convoked without a special permission from the Holy See. Permission from Rome was sought and granted.

To prepare for the chapter, copies of the compiled customary had been sent to the local houses for study. Remarks had to be returned to the motherhouse by the spring of 1939 and requests for changes presented as proposals.

Mother Angela was the presiding officer of the chapter. Sister Edmunda, at her request, conducted all discussions, for she had compiled, studied and organized the customary. She had studied the Canon Law for Communities on Pontifical Right and made many inquiries on the more intricate matters governing the daily lives of religious and management of communities as a whole. She was the best prepared of all the councillors to answer those and explain the importance of the sisters' questions or perhaps, the unpleasant demands that would be made on the sisters once the customary went into effect.

Proposals sent by members of the order guaranteed that there would be some difficult, crucial moments relative to some of the articles and could be met with outright opposition. One article that was strongly debated in the chapter was the term of office held by local superiors. Sisters who had become superiors as soon as they had left the novitiate, and had never known what it was to be a subject, found it very difficult, almost impossible, to step down to the ranks. Some of the sisters had been superiors for some forty years.

When finally, after much discussion, the long debate on this particular proposal closed and the votes were taken and counted — the result was a complete deadlock — fifty percent of the delegates approved and fifty percent dissented. Perfect silence, a dramatic silence, followed the announced result. After a long moment, Mother Angela stood up and said bravely with perfect courage, "My vote is 'yes.'" More silence. No applause. The 'yea' voters respected the pain of the "nay" voters. Unity in the community dominated the overall scene. The proposal went into effect without any serious consequences. Of course those who had voted against the proposal, despite broken hearts, accepted the will of God because they were convinced that only in His will is there salvation of souls, of individuals and institutions. For a long period of time both sisters and pastors of schools found this new custom difficult to accept. Mother Angela's patience with her sisters proved a blessing.

The Chapter of 1939 gave the community its first customary, not a perfect or closed set of articles.

Sister Edmunda fervently believed that in the end there might never have to be one. At the entrance to eternity, St. Peter (or perhaps St. Francis for all Franciscans) would hand them a single rule which would prevail — the Rule of Love.

Sister Edmunda's first major assignment, the customary, had required three years for its completion. The next important task was the advancement of the mission in Brazil. Father Hanquet, the pastor at Dom Feliciano and Camaqua, ministered to the Poles there and the entire surrounding area. He supported the sisters' efforts in every possible way during the very difficult early years of missionary life in that distant country. There was an old Polish adage, "*Jak dlugo swiat swiatem, Niemiec nigdy nie bedzie Polakowi bratem*" (as long as the world is a world, a German will never be a brother to the Pole). In the Americas that saying no longer held true, especially among Catholics.

Sister Edmunda's passion for the Brazilian missions dominated her activities now that the community's customary was ready for presentation to Rome. Health care and hospitals became important new responsibilities both in Brazil and the United States. As Directress of Studies of the Villanova College Extension, also located in Mt. Alvernia, she was totally involved with ever-widening educational requirements and acquisitions of or construction of hospitals. By 1942 the new school in Camaqua was near completion, with room for 300 day students and some boarders. The school gave Camaqua special standing in the region west of Porto Alegre. The town grew and prospered because of the Bernardine's presence. Among all the other small missions Camaqua remained the largest.

CHAPTER SIX

Johnny's elementary school years at St. Casimir's always interested his aunt. A very ethnic parish, the pastors and parents wanted the children to know something of their eastern European heritage, therefore, the reading and writing of the Polish language was included in the first three grades. This made the students aware of the differences in the alphabet and the pronunciation of words. Sister Edmunda knew the sisters who taught at the school each year and sometimes asked them about Johnny's grades. Invariably the sisters found him a good student. Sister Liberta taught him in the third and fourth grades. He was completely in love with her. No other teacher could come close to the rapport they had together as teacher and student. She delighted in the way he participated in each subject every day and participated in the plays the Bernardines always fostered in their schools.

One day she asked the class, "Can anyone tell me where high C is on the piano?"

No one seemed ready to respond. Johnny remembered the scales his aunt had taught him and he finally spoke up. She was delighted. This placed him in greater favor with her. His marks were always at the top of the class.

During those late years of the Depression and the war years, the sisters were very helpful to his family. The government distributed some food items such as American cheese in five-pound blocks and other staples which were bought from dairy farmers to support their prices. Whenever the nuns received a distribution they always invited Johnny to stop by for some, which he did gladly. The family always had plenty of toasted cheese sandwiches.

Sister rarely initiated the exchange of letters with family or friends. Despite all her community and spiritual activities, Sister normally replied almost immediately to her correspondents. In the spring of 1942 Sister Edmunda's sister Mary received a letter in response to one she had written.

D. M. & O. (Deus Meus et Omnia)
Friday a.m.

Dearest Mary,

A "thank you" for your letter - I was waiting for it, because I'm constantly thinking of Alma.

Cassie's letter came in a day or two before yours and she mentioned that she was down to see you and the kiddies. She included a mention about Alma and Jasiu coming in from school. Since she made no notice about the crutches, I hoped joyously for a while that these were discarded. Well, your letter assures me of the contrary. Yet, may the will of God be praised! He knows best what is good for us.

Is the diet's purpose a loss of weight with Alma? You know I spoke of this to some of our sisters here some time ago, and I thought of it ever so often, but I hated to say it to you for fear I may be making a mistake. I often thought that she was too heavy for a weak hip and leg to carry her. Whatever was and is the purpose, please see to it that she lives up to doctor's orders. Don't be soft and easy in this matter, for it may be detrimental to Alma in the end. Had I known of the diet, the box would have never been sent to her.

Are you still trusting in doctors and clinics? I have said a final adieu to them by this time. Mary, I think that we must now turn entirely to the Heavenly Doctor, for I'm sure that only He can help her. I really do not know why - but for the last few days I have been thinking of some sacrifice that must be made that Alma does not remain a cripple, handicapped for the long life that may be before her. Does Alma ever hint or show any signs of a religious vocation — that is, does she ever speak of desiring to be a nun? She is only 11 years of age, but she is well developed for it, and certainly can understand her plight of being a cripple for life — and at the same time, she also understands in her own way what a nun is. I was 13 when I entered and long before that I wanted to be where I am — and believe me I understood my life then just as I understand it now — 30 years later. I have never yet said to myself or others: "Had I known this before, I would never be where I am" — even though there are troubles galore at times, for there is no place, no person without a cross.

Alma did say to me once that she would like to be a nurse. Now what about a nun nurse?

But, I suppose by now you are wondering what am I driving at? Well, to attack the problem, I repeat that for the last few days, I have been continuously returning to the thought of a certain community — the Sisters of St. Dominic of the Congregation of St. Rose of Lima of Hawthorne, N. Y. They were founded in about the same time as our Mother Foundress came from Poland - that is in 1896, I think. Their Mother Foundress was our American writer's Hawthorne's daughter, who was converted from Protestantism and later gave herself up entirely, as a nun, to the care of God's poor sick. They take care of the poor sick who are victims of an incurable cancer. There are two conditions necessary for being admitted to their hospitals:

1 - it must be a case of an incurable cancer.

2 - the person must be so poor that no other hospital will take him, because of lack of funds.

You realize that taking care of these sick is a sacrifice. A sister of our Sister Columbine, who went to Brazil, is there, and that is how I first heard of them.

Now, not knowing why — perhaps, it is God's will — since I ceased to think that doctors, casts or crutches will help Alma, I'm thinking of trying once again a storm of prayers with the promise that if Alma does grow well, she will offer her life for the service of these poor sick who are crippled for the rest of their lives by a disease, whose pain is greater than any other, and who often are forsaken by their own, because of the stench, pitiful appearance when it attacks the nose, lips, cheeks, etc.

I received a dollar which I'm sending to those sisters asking them for prayers, especially of some of their saintly patients. I am also asking them to send Alma some medal or other religious article which she may wear. You yourself promise the Lord that you will let Alma go to take care of these sick, if her returned health will show that such a sacrifice is pleasing to God. It may be that all this is only a good thought and not the will of God, but let us turn to Him with full trust and wait for His fatherly will to show in us.

Speak about this to Alma privately. Tell her to pray hard these days, to wear the medal or whatever the sisters send her with loving faith and to keep offering herself for these sick if God returns her health. But don't speak about this to anyone else. God's ways are covered with a veil of secrecy, as we read in the Bible that Mary kept all these things in her heart. Tell Alma to keep the secret, too.

Please let me know how you feel about this promise, and how Alma looks at it. I'll have more confidence in prayer, if you two are ready to use the power of prayer and sacrifice.

I don't like those repeated headaches of Jasiu. If it's really due to carelessness in eating, please direct him promptly; headaches may be symptoms of some other serious trouble. It would be wise to see some good doctor.

I'm glad to hear that you are feeling rather well. Thanks to God! I'm just disgusted with the big man's record; I just hate to think of him and his lack of consideration for his own. Cassie wrote that Joe said "good-by" to it since New Year's Day. May God help his good attempts! However, I'm so disappointed about the last break of good will that I cannot trust him now or rejoice. I'll simply pray that God gives him the strength to forego the evil habit permanently.

Loving regards! I'll be waiting for your next letter!
Lovingly,
Sr. M. Edmunda

Mary was delighted, as always, to read the thoughts of her sister. She knew that her sister, Helen, as she sometimes referred to her older sister, meant only the best for her and the family. Alma was hurting so much from her scarred hands and consistent ache in her right hip it was impossible for her to even think of relating the ideas suggested by the letter. As for her son, Jasiu, she felt only the greatest sympathy. With two younger children, Louis and Sylvia, she had little time to spend on her two older ones. And her husband, the "big man", who continued to buy drinks for everyone at the neighborhood bar every two weeks on payday, she felt helpless to get him to quit. He had drunk before they were married, and the hope he would stop because of the growing needs of the family seemed a distant dream. On many of those paydays she would send Jasiu to the bar to bring his father home. He glanced at the men sitting at the bar until he found his dad.

"Jasiu, what do you want?"

"Mom says you must come home — dinner is ready."

"I'm not ready yet. Come and sit here at the bar and have a birch beer." His father, by now speaking with a drunken slur, would tell all the people in the bar how smart his son was.

"He gets 100's in school! Maybe we can make a priest of him."

After what seemed like a long wait, his father would stagger home with him — sometimes placing an arm on his shoulder. The twelve stairs leading to the apartment were always a challenge in his condition. When he reached the closed-in porch he would open the door to the kitchen and wait for the invariable tirade from Mary.

"Mary, what do you want from me?"

"I don't want anything from you. I want nothing. How much do you have left this time? The bar owners don't need your money — we do!" Reluctantly, he would pull whatever money he had left and place it on the kitchen table. In desperation she asked him how much money he had before he went to the bar.

"Oh, I didn't spend that much. I can't even remember how much I made."

"How am I going to feed the kids, pay the rent and the insurance?"

"There'll be enough." Of course, he never paid the bills, went shopping for groceries or saw the insurance man who collected premiums in a monthly visit to the house. There wasn't that much insurance and the little there was would pay for funeral expenses and not much more.

On some of his drinking days he would arrive at home in a happy mood, play pony-ride with the youngest boy and pretend he was going to crawl down the outside steps of the apartment. Jasiu had always loved those rides, had held tightly onto his Dad, who was on all fours, and laughed until the ride ended. Mary would shout at her husband to be careful. She didn't want anyone of her children hurt by a fall or other careless accident. The drunken paydays never came to an end except during the six weeks of Lent. Those weeks seemed like paradise to Mary and the family. She could then pay off any debts still outstanding at the butcher shop; the owner gave credit to his customers until the next pay. They would also fill the coal bin for use in the kitchen stove. Throughout the Depression years of the Thirties, the family never missed a meal or lacked fuel for cooking.

In April of 1942 Mary wrote to Sister Edmunda about the continued pain in Alma's right hip. Their landlord, Frank Twardzik, had seen Alma's inability to walk without crutches and offered to get her admitted to the Shriner's hospital in Atlantic City — for crippled children. There would be no cost to the family. It seemed like the best thing to do and accepted his kind offer.

Sister Edmunda's reply was written on the Feast of Our Lady of Good Counsel — April 26, 1942.

My dearest Mary:

A propitious day to write on, isn't it? I do hope that with the help of our Heavenly Mother I can give you a few thoughts capable of a spiritual booster to struggle on the path to Heaven.

Your letter has explained in a way why I was so depressed throughout last week and especially on Friday and Saturday when the sky just seemed to turn a dark gray and heavy with leaden droops of spirit. When trouble comes, it is just impossible to feel cheery and even the Lord does not expect us to act against our nature. I am not surprised that you have lost all ambition for a while when the news of Alma's progressing ailment was brought to you. I really expected that all along and that is why I have written the letter about turning our hearts entirely to the Mother of God. I'm convinced that only Her intercession with her divine Son can bring about a turn in Alma's trouble. Perhaps Alma did do herself damage by being too free in the use of her leg. She is willful and one cannot beg her enough to do the right thing once she makes up her mind to do something else. But, after all she has been pretty young all this while and because of this she could not fully understand the consequences of her disobeying of orders and suggestions. We adults know much better what to do but do we do it always? Please try to explain to her now before she goes to the shore that she must be very careful about the use of her leg. Give it a perfect rest if you want it to heal. If we had a wound on our finger and kept continually opening it by inadvisable use of the hand, we couldn't expect the finger to heal, could we? Well, the same is true of bones — only that it takes them a mighty long time to heal. Then, let her make good use of the sun. These baths may not be too pleasant at first; they may even cause pain, but let her be ready to do all that health may be restored to her. But, above all, please tell her to pray incessantly and with perfect confidence that the good Lord through the intercession of the Blessed Virgin and our other patrons, will give her what we are praying for. Let her pray hard despite all that is being said by the doctors and nurses and let her pray a hundred times a day and more saying to the Infant Jesus and His Mother that she trusts them and that she is sure that they will cure her leg. You do the same at home. Miracles do not come only when all help here below is gone, and yet, despite that, we do not lose hope and faith in the Almighty. I really see that now is the time for help from Heaven — for now more than ever do we see that doctors and clinics and hospitals are all in vain. We should keep doing all that is advised and doing it to the best of our ability, but at the same time have faith that through these remedies the Lord will act for the remedies are ineffectual.

Alma mentioned in her letter that the nurse explained how the disease is spreading — is it T.B. of the hip bones, as the doctor suspected?

Before I go on, let me also ask about your brace. Is it of steel? Where worn? Then about your failing in weight. Do you eat as before? Perhaps, you are worrying too much? That kills more than anything else. Alma also wrote that Louis went to the clinic to get measured for shoes. What did she mean by that? There's nothing wrong with his feet, is there? Then, our Jasiu. You know I often wondered whether his head trouble isn't a consequence of his head trouble as a baby. Right along he wasn't physically what he should have been. A little mosquito without a sting — that's what he was and is. What did the doctor tell you Monday? Maybe an X-ray would show the cause of his trouble? After all, it may not be his stomach at all; or just the opposite, the whole trouble may be in the stomach, and his head.

In all truth, I must confess that the Lord is trying us a little too much at times — I mean too much according to our measurements and standards. However, dearest Mary, you have been a good soldier thus far. Keep it up, begging for strength for the day every morning when you rise and whenever life appears too thorny. My life isn't rosy, either. I feel the same way as you do many a time. Of course, mine is entirely different than yours — for one thing, the worst of all thorns - I have no husband to drain blood out of my veins and heart, as you poor wives have. Yet, I do suffer with you, but this suffering is a pleasure for by it I hope to help you a little. You know when one loves dearly, the very pain for the beloved becomes sweet. I would feel much worse if you didn't trust me enough to share your troubles with me.

This past week, as a preparation for today's feast of Our Lady of Good Counsel, I meditated each day on the sorrows of our Heavenly

Mother. Friday, I meditated on the fifth sorrow — the death of Christ on the cross. Suddenly, from the clear sky, came an answer to my often repeated question: "Why are you and I tried so much — one trouble ends when two or more come?" You see I often ask this question, but never with any bitterness. I know that Jesus gives crosses to those whom he loves and the more he loves them, the more and the heavier are those crosses. After every pain that I experience I thank the Lord for it — if not with anything else then at least with a very cordial hug and kiss of His cross. After I read your letter yesterday, I went to the chapel and said a rosary of thanksgiving for His love in crucifying us, even though this love doesn't appear very gracious and sweet. But, please do not think that I do not feel the pain. I'll say the rosary, hug my crucifix and kiss it while at the same time tears bedeck my eyes and cheeks and my heart is torn to pieces. So, as I started to write, the answer came suddenly: "My Holy Mother and I suffer so dreadfully, because I have taken upon myself the sins of all sinners. I suffered innocently for the sins of others and that is what I want you to do as my chosen ones. You are not innocent, for you are sinners like all people, but I want you to help me suffer for the sins of your near ones." Mary dear, when I stopped for a while, for I was really astounded — the thought came as a flash and with such conviction, with such a sweet satisfaction, and when I began to reason out the meaning of these words, I really agreed that there is much in our past for which we have to help our dear ones to suffer. Let us cheer up then and take the crosses with love, for we are helpers of Christ in wiping away the sins of our own. Let me give you just one example: Mother was healthy and was blessed with a number of healthy children; there was enough of money for many years. Has she been grateful to the Lord for her health? Hasn't she ruined it herself? Did she act as a mother to her children? Was she devoted to them as was expected from her? Was she grateful for the home, food, etc. that was her daily lot? What example did she set to us? Now, please, Mary, do not take me wrongly. I wouldn't say this to anybody but you and Joe, for she was our mother and I respected her to the best of my ability and I still do respect her memory — but this is just to show you what I understand by the thoughts which the Lord gave me so suddenly. Now, we are her children and since we must help her to pay her debts to the Holy Justice of God, we must suffer. You are a loving devoted mother, but the Lord is trying your devotion in a hundred ways. You are not well — this is a big cross, but won't you try to love it for the sake of the Lord who wants you to help Him in washing away the sins of mother? Your children are having the best of attention, for you are with them from morning till evening and next morning — but they are tried and you with them. Isn't this to pay up for mother's neglect of us? Aren't the little ones who have been denied the right of life and health, because of her, demanding a retribution? Yes, the sins of the parents must be paid by their children, but the difference? What a difference? All these sufferings of ours are very meritorious. We cannot understand them here below; if we bear them patiently and with a love of the Divine Will, our reward in the life hereafter will be great. So let us console ourselves that in a way we are suffering innocently, we are helping our Lord to suffer for the sins of our nearest ones, and as such we will merit the great joys of Heaven. Let us not give in to discouragement, let us not complain, but let us pray for help, for strength, and all will be well for our souls. After all, what is this life worth — even though it was spent in luxuries and good health, with no pain. All comes to an end very soon, and if there is nothing for Heaven earned, what about eternity? What joy did mother get out of her living? She couldn't see the need of mortification, refusing herself all that she craved for and how is she looking at it today? Take the wealthy people, the millionaires — are they happy because they are enjoying all that life can give? Most assuredly NO, for why so many suicides among them? Mary, you are brave, you are a soldier, you're not like mother seeking pleasure in sin to forget your troubles; you are bearing your cross valiantly to share your troubles with me or somebody whom you trust, as you trust me, is all OK. That is why we live in the company of others — we should bear the burdens of each other. Even Celia Szal said to me last Sunday, "Your Mary is to be marveled at how she can keep up her spirits amid so many troubles?" This is the grace of God. He is trying us but He is also giving us the help we need, and in eternity won't He reward us? So, Dearest, go on bravely; pray for help each day and all will be well, according to the will of God. You will be a good mother as you have always been; your children will be proud of you, love you, and revere your name here and in eternity. If you continue being a soldier as you are, you will bring your children no disgrace, you will not be the cause of any of their sufferings.

Then, as to trouble, Mary, it finds its way everywhere. Our Sister Daniel's nephew has been working for the convent. Something happened, a toothache apparently; he went to the dentist, had the tooth extracted, then his face swelled up dreadfully; he was sent to the hospital about 11 weeks ago, had one operation after the other — the last one last Thursday, when they took out his cheek bone and cut his face above and alongside the eyes to permit the pus to drain. There is danger of his eye falling in. For a while nearly the whole eye was lying on his cheek, pushed out by the pus. What will happen - only God knows. A boy of 17 years, handsome, humorous, promising.... Then, the directress of nurses in St. Joseph's Hospital, a sister of Father Klekotka, was for a few days to her sick mother. She wanted to come to the hospital last Tuesday to do a little of her work, for in two weeks they have the graduation of nurses, and this past Friday she was planning to return to her sick mother. As a nurse, she was nursing her mother. A graduate nurse went for her; on their way back, to avoid a truck, they ran into a bridge — Sister Laurencita, the directress, is hovering between death and life: chin broken, collar bone and ribs broken, her both legs, especially knees so smashed that even tho' she lives, she will never be able to walk — unless some miracle happens. She never returned to her very sick mother and now the family has two nearing death.... I could give you so many examples, Mary, where others are tried very painfully also. But, you know of these cases just as well. So, once again, please continue to be the soldier that you have been so far.

What about your debts, Mary? Do you have much more than the rent and the $100.00 at the butcher's, of which you spoke to me? Well I realize how you feel. I can imagine how I couldn't stand them myself; but even here, it wasn't because you didn't want to pay them; you want to, but if the pays are insufficient, if the unthoughtful father of the family loves the bar more than his wife and children — you are not responsible for them. Try your best and leave the rest to the good Lord. Be thrifty, Mary, we must practice economy ... e.g. when I read of daily fruit for the children, esp. oranges, I must say that I don't think they are necessary. They are expensive, but we can do without them easily and suffer no consequences in health. Years back, *we hadn't heard of all that and we were well. Then, meat isn't wholesome for children and yet it is expensive. Beans are very nutritious, cereals of various kinds, vegetables - pancakes where only an egg or two are necessary.... They may not like them at first, but they'll get used to them. Don't give in to their whims too much; that will be bad for them in their future life. They'll expect everybody to give into them and you know that isn't true to life. So deny them some of their desires and they will bless you for it in the future someday.*

Well, this is a very long letter, but I just couldn't write less. In fact, I could write and write without an end. This is for you only.

God be with you and give you strength and joy. Today's Gospel was for us: "You will cry and lament when the world will rejoice; but do not despair; your tears and sorrows will be turned into joy, which nobody will take away from you." Let's trust Him and He will not forsake us. The harder it is for us to trust, the greater will be His mercies here and hereafter.

Loving regards to yourself and to all. I shall pray for you all very fervently. The enclosed stamps are my own; I'm including them that you can have them on hand to write. I'm also sending some pamphlets. Read them from time to time, just a sentence a day and it will keep the blues away.

Love,

Sister M. Edmunda

When Mary read the letter her spirits revived. She always loved her sister who was always her greatest support. It was hard to be a soldier in a seemingly never-ending battle with her rheumatoid arthritis which now threatened to bend the top of her spine forward in a way which made it impossible to raise her arms to their full length. The back hem of her dress now rose higher than the front so that clothes-buying became an unhappy task. House cleaning became difficult despite her desire to keep the apartment as clean as possible. Her son Jasiu, or little Johnny, became her best, if reluctant, helping hand. She had him do all the things she found difficult to perform. Every Monday she washed clothes in the electric washer which they kept in the kitchen. (Some neighbors still had to use washboards and tubs.) They hung the wash on two movable lines stretching from the porch windows to an electric pole across the back yard. In the winter the clothes would freeze, which made washday an even greater chore. Tuesday she ironed — pressing sheets as well as underwear along with the other clothing. Mary prepared three meals each day, which made her days always active. She really did try to stay up emotionally. The thought of Alma in the hospital in Atlantic City, the recurring headaches of her son and the need to watch her two youngest prompted many more down days than she would have liked. Mary would sing Polish hymns as a form of prayer. The children liked them so much they sometimes asked her to sing them.

The family spoke English in the home; prayers were said in Polish. By the age of five the children knew how to bless themselves: "In the name of the Father, the Son and the Holy Spirit," could recite the Our Father, the Hail Mary and the Apostles Creed, and did so on their knees by the bed each night. As a good Catholic mother, Mary took great care the prayers were said with devotion. Religious belief, carefully fostered, became part of the family's life.

CHAPTER SEVEN

As Secretary General of the Bernardines, Sister Edmunda became focused on the general council which was called in the summer of 1942 to elect the successors to Mother Angela and the four councillors. Cardinal Dougherty, the Archbishop of Philadelphia, presided over the council. His presence was a great show of recognition that the Bernardines were becoming an important congregation in the educational and other needs of the diocese.

On the second ballot Sister Edmunda was elected the Reverend Mother — the third Superior General after Mother Veronica, the foundress. With great humility she received the religious embrace of each of the eighty-two delegates. This traditional show of obedience filled her with the undying resolve to devote all her energy to the sanctification of the sisters under her tutelage. The congregation had always meant everything to her - now it took on greater significance. Through her leadership and the assistance of the new councillors, Mothers Angela, Adalbert, Gabriella, Bridget and Victoria, the sisters would follow in the steps of St. Francis, or be diminished by a departure from his teachings.

"*Ma cherie*," Mother Angela said to her in a private moment, "now the congregation is yours to lead. You have been such a help to me these past six years, I am confident you know where to take us. Now you can attend to the dear Brazilian missions you have loved so much."

"Yes, Mother, Brazil shall be one of my highest priorities! Meanwhile, there's one minor change I want to see implemented in the community's dining habits. I have thought about this for a number of years. Please tell me how you may view my idea."

"Of course, tell me what you wish to do."

"I want each of the sisters to place her dishes and utensils in a central location after she has finished her meal. This will make the work of those in charge of the dining room much easier and create an atmosphere of greater consideration. There may be nine choirs of angels in heaven , with greater or lesser ways of honoring God, but on earth we are all servants of one another. This would be a daily way of showing it." A small matter, however, reflective of the care the new Reverend Mother had for all members of the community whatever the level of their talents. Mother Angela agreed the practice would be a good one. She wondered why she hadn't thought about it herself.

Soon afterwards the Reverend Mother reviewed in her thoughts the status of the Brazilian endeavor. In Dom Feliciano the first year of school had a registration of 140 pupils, and about 50 patients had been cared for in the temporary hospital. Unexpectedly, the Brazilian government passed legislation outlawing the use and teaching of any foreign language. Portuguese alone was to be the language of its citizens. The Polish farmers believed this legislation crippled their Catholic school run by Americans so that the number of students enrolled varied from year to year. Instead, the parents sometimes enrolled their children in the government schools. The sisters prayed that some agreement with the government could be reached which would allow them to exert the best possible influence on the greatest number of students. The town of Camaqua had become very proud of the Nossa Senhora Aparecida Hospital, the Sao Joao Batista Escola and Ginasio. Encruzilhada, also in Rio Grande do Sul, had a hospital and kindergarten. In March, 1942, a school with a kindergarten and a one-year commercial course had been established at Canela, Rio Grande do Sul, at the request of the pastor of Sacred Heart Parish. In the state of Matto Grosso, many kilometers northwest of Dom Feliciano where the climate was much hotter and more humid, three missions became the responsibility of the Bernardines: the Immaculate Conception School at Dourados in the diocese of Corumba, the Sacred Heart School at Rosario Oeste in the Archdiocese of Cuiaba, and Santa Clara School in Paranaiba.

The Reverend Mother was grateful and appreciative of the truly Franciscan spirit of the sisters stationed in Brazil. At Rosario Oeste, Sister Mary Roberta, R. N. acted as the superior, the doctor, the nurse, the mother, the master of all trades among the poverty stricken people. Sister helped the other two sisters, Marceline and Gaudenta, in school and church, visited the sick in their homes, took care of them in the clinic and did all around medical and even surgical work which would normally be done by a licensed doctor in the smallest towns in the United States. Sister was paying a high price for the toll exacted by this strenuous life. Despite her own chronic heart and kidney ailments, she was eager to go on. The school enrollment generally had forty to fifty pupils. The nursing involves hundreds of cases each year. In Dourados the sisters conduct a five-grade elementary school and teach handwork, domestic science, and Christian doctrine to the older girls of the parish. The annual enrollment is close to one hundred pupils.

A letter from Sister Benjamina exemplified the fidelity to Franciscan fortitude of all the Sisters: "In Camaqua," she wrote, "we have been celebrating our Easter in grand style. The dinner was eaten under spreading umbrellas amid peals of laughter. Did we try to shut out the heat of the sun? No! We were outwitting the rain trickling down on our festive table through a leak in the "dach" (roof)!" Their joy was as pure as the hearts that beat for God and His little ones! Another sister wrote, "We are rich! Imagine! We have a cow, a whole cow, milk and all! The mother of one of our boarders brought the cow along with her daughter because she wishes to make sure her pet will have all the milk she can drink. The remainder of the daily milk feast is ours! How is that for an example of the generosity of our people and the loving care of Divine Providence?" The dominant note in almost all of the letters from the sisters in Brazil is deep faith, childlike confidence, and joy. "God is good to us!" is their favorite expression.

But amid all the joyous tones were overtones of tearful courage and courageous tears came through. In Dom Feliciano, on June 10, 1942, the sisters lost their beloved pastor and friend — lost him by an assassin's bloody knife. Father Victor Devor, C.M., died before the eyes of the sisters who rushed to the aid of this saintly priest from their post-Communion prayers. The communistic teachings had to be counteracted; the sisters were there to do this by prayers, sacrifice and deeds of charity. "God is Good; He will take care of us and our work." This was true missionary spirit.

Catholic Action played a significant role in the religious education of the young. Every school in Brazil, taken over or established by the sisters, took part in the Eucharistic Crusade movement. There were now seven altar fires lighted from the original fire at the Sacred Heart Motherhouse in Reading. The children's response to the sisters' appeals and instructions transformed these little crusaders into marvelous examples of piety, fidelity to duty, and sacrifice respected greatly by the adult members of the parishes. The sisters placed very great confidence in the Crusade Movement, considered by them a real apostolate - an apostolate of the little ones. The fruits of the work of the crusaders were truly unprecedented. They studied, read, prayed, delved deeply into the mysteries of our holy faith in order to foster it among their relatives, neighbors and fellow countrymen. They organized dramatic clubs, movies, debating clubs in which, using pictures, pantomime, and argument they tried to portray and make concrete to their little brothers and sisters, and to the illiterate adults, the truths of our faith, the life of Our Lord, the lives of saints. All of this was done to counteract the influences of Protestant organizations such as the YMCA, Salvation Army, Spiritists, and many Communistic and Nazi-supported propaganda centers.

The zeal of the children at Dourados was shown by their request to have the Sunday Mass said at 4 A.M. since picnics and outings were often planned as all-day affairs on that day. Nylda, one of the crusaders, begged the Padre for this early morning Mass, and he agreed, if enough people attended. The crusaders informed the entire parish by personal visits and received promises of cooperation. Nylda received Communion at the early Mass along with many other parishioners. She was overjoyed by this show of faith. She was ready to die of love for her Eucharistic Lord. The Lord received the oblation of this pure lily. That very afternoon Nylda was drowned in the waters of the river where she supervised the swimming of her younger companions. The following day her body was found, in a kneeling posture, with hands folded over her heart. What a wonderful example for all!

The Reverend Mother also looked forward to the year's novices entering the congregation in the late spring of 1943. A very moving ceremony — the nineteen young women, in their late teens and early twenties, dressed as brides in white gowns and veils wore a green and white wreath on their veils to signify the vow of Chastity, a gold coin placed in a container represented the vow of Poverty and Obedience was denoted when the constitution, new name in religion and Rule of St. Francis were given to them at the altar. The choir and the organist gave their best performances. To the parents and those present the music and singing sounded as close to heaven as they could experience in this world. The choir of nuns were trained meticulously by a very disciplined organist and director - Sister Mary Chrysostoma.

The "Brides" came to the Bishop, or his representative, to ask for the habit of St. Francis while the Reverend Mother stood at his side. Their hair had been cut the night before and a strand of hair was also cut at the altar to show total dedication to their new lives. After the presentation of the Rule of St. Francis, they left the convent chapel and returned, clothed in a brown habit and scapular, a white veil and a completely new look. They now appeared so alike, the congregation had to look carefully to see who was "their" nun.

The novices were then interrogated as to what they sought in the religious life. A very pertinent homily followed. The novices were filled with joy and zeal to follow Jesus and St. Francis — to love, pray, and suffer for self, family and the world. After this ceremony the novices began a year devoted to preparing for their lives in the order. There was no contact with anyone or anything which was not directly relevant to their path to holiness. A novice mistress became their sole guide during the year.

In the same year, the Reverend Mother and her councillors agreed to divide the congregation into three provinces: the Holy Name Province in Philadelphia, the Saint Francis Province in Scranton, and the Immaculate Conception Province in Brazil. The Philadelphia province included institutions operating in Boston, Pittsburgh, Altoona, Harrisburg, Fall River, Hartford, Providence and Trenton. Located in the suburb of Mt. Airy, the provincial house had been the former residence of the papal chamberlain James Sullivan. Mother Hedwig, the Superior General prior to Mother Angela, became the new provincial of some 420 sisters. The Scranton Province had 239 sisters working in the Diocese of Scranton. Miss Pauline Casey donated her fully furnished home for use of the provincial, Mother Zygmunta. In Camaqua, Brazil, the 52 sisters with Mother Benjamina as provincial, were delighted to have their own province, novitiate and provincial head. This division helped Mother Edmunda to administer the Bernardines more efficiently.

CHAPTER EIGHT

The Reverend Mother's nephew, Richard, wrote to her from his Army base shortly after his draft notice and induction in the late summer of 1943. The war against the Germans had reached the critical turning point of eliminating them from North Africa and looking toward the invasion of their European domains. Cassie had already written to her of the arrival of the draft notice and the certainty she felt that Richard's eyesight would keep him out of the armed forces. His cousin Victor had joined the Navy after his release from the CCC corps and had been in the service some eighteen months. Richard went to work for a shipyard in Delaware with no intention of enlisting. Cassie was in a state of panic regarding her only son. "How could they accept him with his fragile eyesight?" she wrote to her beloved sister-in-law. Richard said in his letter to her that he might not have to be an infantryman and was hoping for the best. He asked for her prayers.

In just a few short months he was on the beach at Anzio, Italy. His letters to his mother and father were full of hope that their prayers would see him through. To his fiancé, Alice, he admitted he was afraid of the way things were going. The wet terrain in early 1944 brought a severe case of trenchfoot. Another infantryman and he shared a foxhole which was easily dug through the sandy soil. The water unfortunately was only a few feet down which kept them in a perpetual state of wetness. He wrote to her that he wished he could have a warm meal after all the canned food, or a hot bath since the only washing he could do was from water in his helmet.

In February a letter came to Cassie and Joe letting them know Richard had been killed while on a night patrol on the 22nd of the month. The sorrow and pain Cassie felt would not go away. She begged Joe to sell the house in Ringtown and move to Reading to be closer to the Reverend Mother, and the possibility of working, to get her mind away from the grief she was feeling. Within a year they did that, found a house one block away from a Catholic church which she attended each day.

When Johnny had heard the news of his cousin's death he went into a bedroom and shed some tears for Richard whom he knew only from a few brief visits home. The whole episode brought the war into their own lives with greater impact than all the newspaper stories which showed the battle lines each day. As a young eleven year old he felt more deeply the death of Richard because of the many summers he had spent on the farm with his Uncle Joe and *Ciocia* Cassie. From the time he was seven years old he had always been invited to spend five or six weeks of his summer vacation on the farm, the only one in the neighborhood to spend that much time away from home during the summer break from school.

A look through the Montgomery Ward catalog was the first priority for his *Ciocia* Cassie, who sent an order to the company for all the summer clothes he would need, including swimming trunks for the daily swims in the "sulphur" creek. No fish could live in this water because of contamination from some coal mines several miles away, but there was no danger to swimmers. The enclave of six families became an extended family to him. Johnny called every adult "aunt" or "uncle" and their children were his cousins. At age seven Aunt Martha taught him to swim. Married to Cassie's brother, Ziggie, and childless, his mother lived with them until she died. There were times of the day when no women went to the creek to swim or sunbathe. It was understood that the older boys swam there in the nude; dove from some trees and generally had a great time. Johnny enjoyed the sense of adventure. Shortly after he had learned to swim he decided to try to swim to a rock on which he could stand. After swimming a short distance he found he could not locate the rock and began to panic. He splashed around looking for help but no one realized he was in trouble. After a few minutes he began to go under. Only then did one of his cousins come to his aid. The feeling of having almost drowned made him cautious about swimming in deeper water for many years afterward. He always wanted to be sure he could touch bottom.

Very good at math, his Uncle Joe began to teach his nephew as much as he thought Johnny could understand each summer. The lessons always put him ahead of his classmates when he returned to school. His Uncle Joe sometimes sat by him on the swing on the front porch and told long stories which were always interesting. When his uncle was in a good mood everything went so much better around the house.

One summer evening his uncle said, "Jasiu, go down to Stasun's and get me some draft beer. Cassie will give you a can to carry it in." Stasun's was a bar on the first floor of a house about a hundred yards down the highway. They were not related to Cassie's family.

"Cassie, get that two-quart can for the boy."

"Oh Daddy, why do you need to drink while the kid is here?" Joe had already been drinking some whiskey he had in the house and wanted some beer to chase it down. A whiskey and chaser was a common way to drink in the coal regions. He looked at her impatiently and said, "Just get it!" Cassie always hated the way he got when he drank too much. He never became relaxed or mellow; he just got angry and ugly and mean.

Johnny took the can from his aunt along with two quarters to pay for it. "If it costs any more," Joe said, "tell them I'll pay later." When he returned with the beer he and his aunt went to the living room to play the piano and sing one of her favorite songs, "Ramona." He learned the song and liked to sing it when alone — he could almost see and hear the mission bells mentioned in the song.

Suddenly they heard a loud shouting from the kitchen. His uncle was brandishing a knife and threatening to "kill somebody." "Johnny, let's get out of the house," she said quickly. They hid outside behind a large crabapple tree. From there they could see Joe and prayed the madness would pass. She could not forget the time in their marriage when he had to enter a treatment center to control his irrational temper and addiction to alcohol. She hoped that would never be repeated again. In a short while, which seemed like forever to Johnny, his uncle collapsed into a drunken sleep. The crisis, at least, had passed, an incident he would never forget. His own father drank heavily at times, but he never became angry or threatening.

The next day life went on as usual. Nothing was mentioned by his aunt or uncle. His Aunt Cassie said to Johnny, "Let me show you how to pick up the eggs from under the hens." There were about a dozen good layers; the eggs had to be gathered every day. She showed him how to place his hand behind and under the chicken as she laid in the nest.

"They feel so nice and warm," he said to her.

"Yes, Jasiu, when they are freshly laid the eggs feel that way. Sometimes the hen doesn't want to part with the egg she has lain so you have to be persistent. Don't worry or get frightened if she makes a noise or wants to peck at you." They gathered about ten eggs that day and very happily placed them in the refrigerator.

"Now I'd like us to go over to the garden and do some weeding and other things."

"Okay!"

Along with the weeding she showed him how to shake lime over the potato plants to protect them from potato bugs and other pests. He decided he liked to do this because he knew the job was done when the white lime spread over each plant and stood out against all the other plants. After lunch he told his aunt he was going over to visit Sainksa who lived on the same side of the highway and was just a short pathway from Joe and Cassie's. Her sister Victoria had been a widow since 1928 when the youngest of their five children were two years old - twin boys. He liked to spend time with Sainksa and the children who were not busy working on other farms.

"Let's milk the cow, Jasiu. It's time for the late afternoon milking," she said when he arrived.

"Sainksa, let me milk the cow today. Please show me how to do it."

"Okay, let's see if you're able to do it." In his enthusiasm he got very close to the rear end of the cow. "Don't do that! Always stay to the side of the cow or she might kick you and hurt you badly. We don't want to send you back home with a broken leg." He took her warning seriously and stayed to the right side of the cow, next to the little stool she was using to prepare to milk.

"Let me show you how to do this. Take two of the cow's teats and pull down in a steady regular motion. See how the milk comes out? You have to put some pressure on it, otherwise nothing will happen." Very excitedly, he sat down on the low chair and did as she had said. Nothing happened!

"What am I doing wrong?"

"Just be patient. It takes some time to get the feel of the teats, how to hold them and exactly how much pressure to use." She showed him again exactly how it was done.

When he began to pull down on the teats again he reached up a little closer to the cow's sac, came down the length of the teats and succeeded in getting some milk. It did not come out as strongly as hers, but at least he was learning. "I'd like to let you go on but I have to get supper ready. You can try again some other time." His summer vacations on the farm always boosted his spirits. Cassie always treated him with great affection, he never had any headaches while there and wondered why she told him he would be a heartbreaker when he got older. Sometimes she called him Tyrone, referring to Tyrone Power, the actor. He simply accepted the remark because he had no idea how he would look when he got older. With Richie dead he was not sure he would spend his summer on the farm anymore.

CHAPTER NINE

Later in that sad February of 1944 the Reverend Mother undertook the risk of making her first canonical visit to the Province of the Immaculate Conception in Brazil. Sisters Scholastica and Bertilia accompanied her on the hazardous trip in the only way possible for them to travel, a western plane route with various stopovers. The Second World War forced all steamers to cancel trips to South America for fear of mines and Nazi submarines in the Atlantic Ocean. All eastern plane transportation was reserved for men in the armed forces. The travel agency planned for a two-week trip from Reading to Porto Alegre. They went by train to Miami and were to proceed to Colombia, South America, via Jamaica. From Colombia they were to fly to Ecuador, Chile, Bolivia, western Brazil, Sao Paolo and finally, Porto Alegre. In Miami their sea plane was delayed some 25 hours, for repairs, which interrupted the rest of the schedule. The trip took more than a month to complete.

"Sisters, I knew this would be a risky journey. Let us pray for the community during these delays, especially for our sisters in Brazil." They were able to keep their spirits high throughout the trip and trusted that the Lord would see them through.

The missions in Brazil had grown both in number and distances away from the provincial house in Camaqua. The Escola Brasileira Americana de Menino Deus opened in Porto Alegre, the capital city of Rio Grande do Sul. At the request of Archbishop John Becker, the school offered its students the opportunity to study English and the arts in a Catholic institution operated by American sisters. The school delighted the Reverend Mother; however, she was not completely happy with some of the reports given to her by Mother Benjamina. She now knew for certain she needed to visit all of the localities where her sisters were stationed, especially in Matto Grosso.

When she arrived at the three houses in Matto Grosso she was appalled by the unbearably hot and humid weather the sisters had to endure.

"My dear sisters, how do you live under these conditions? Are all of you well, how is your health?" she asked the sisters at Rosario Oesto which was the most distant of the missions, in the very heart of Brazil.

"We have the priest and the Blessed Eucharist. This is our support. The weather conditions unfortunately are almost impossible," replied Sister Gaudenta. Sisters Roberta and Marcelline agreed.

The people were really poor. Sister Roberta, a trained nurse cared for the sick who came to the house for treatment. She would sometimes spend a night in a family's hut when the patient was very sick, sleep in a hammock and eat from a communal dish they all used. At times they saw naked children eat dirt to satisfy their hunger. The people paid for the sisters' services by gifts of corn and bananas; money paid for the embroidery lessons.

Ants were a never-ending problem. "We have seen them strip a tall tree of all its leaves. One morning they feasted on a breakfast prepared for some First Communicants," said Sister Marcelline.

"Sisters, I am convinced you cannot go on in this part of the country. Changes will be made." Upon her return to Camaqua the Reverend Mother told the provincial she was closing the houses in Matto Grosso and asked her to assign the nine sisters to other stations. "Three years in Matto Grosso are quite enough!" The bishop accepted her decision. Overall she was delighted with the progress and good works being done in Brazil by the 52 American sisters stationed in this her much loved province of the community.

In early summer another vestiture of novices would take place. Cassie's niece, Frances, would be in the group of postulants. Victoria's daughter, Frances, had been quite certain of her vocation at the age of 13, very much like the Reverend Mother's experience as a young girl. Frances initially entered as an aspirant, enrolling in the high school for girls at Mt. Alvernia. The aspirants boarded in the same building as the orphans. After four years she became a postulant and one year later was prepared to take her temporary vows as a Bernardine. All of the relatives attended the inspirational rite of investiture. The Reverend Mother knew all of them from her visits to Joe and Cassie. Victoria was in heaven! This was the moment she had been awaiting these past five years. On occasions such as this those who greeted the Reverend Mother usually handed her a monetary gift for the good of the order. Her gracious way of accepting these gifts made it an added joy for the giver.

"Victoria, what a wonderful day for us all!" she said to her after the ceremony. "Yes, Reverend Mother, the chapel and the singing and the beautiful name of Rosemarie which you gave Frances will make me forever grateful that I could see this day." Cassie was always her reverential best and treated the Reverend Mother as a jewel to be loved.

This was the first time Johnny had seen this transformation of "brides" into white-veiled nuns. The ceremony, the homily, and the unbelievably beautiful singing made him think how desirable the religious life might be. His very next year at school he wrote an essay about a vocation to the priestly life as a missionary in some distant land.

The golden anniversary of the order in America was to be celebrated in October. The councillors and the Reverend Mother were finalizing the necessary preparations, a three-day celebration beginning on Sunday, the feast of Christ the King, with solemn Pontifical Masses celebrated each day in the chapel. Cardinal Dougherty said the Mass on Sunday in thanksgiving for the many graces received by the community; Monday, Bishop Hafey of the Scranton Diocese prayed for additional blessings in the future; and Tuesday, Bishop Woznicki of Saginaw, Michigan, offered the Mass for all the community's benefactors.

The Vatican sent its recognition of the event. Archbishop Cicognani, the papal delegate in Washington, Cardinal Salotti, official protector of the sisters, Archbishop Becker of Porto Alegre, Dom Antonio Zattera, Bishop of Pelotas, Brazil and many priests in the United States and Brazil also sent theirs. Many religious sisters attended - the Sisters of Mercy, Sisters of Charity, Sisters of St. Joseph, Sisters of the Holy Family, and also Sisters of Saint Cyril and Methodius, Trinitarians, Servants of the Immaculate Heart of Mary, Felicians and Glen Riddle Franciscans. Young women preparing to enter the order presented excerpts of the community's progress. Some fifty priests also joined them at a festive dinner. Cardinal Dougherty of Philadelphia sent a letter especially dear to the Reverend Mother.

> *Rev. and dear Mother Edmunda,*
> *Because you are celebrating by the mercy of God, the Fiftieth Year of the advent into this country of the Sisters, styled the Bernardine Sisters, I beg to join the many admirers and friends of your community, who rejoice with you on so happy an occasion.*
> *I confess that I have been struck by the activity of your Sisterhood, founded as far back as the year 1457 in Poland, and now, after so*

long a stretch of time, spread over diverse parts of the world.

The development of your community is most striking, and no less striking in the variety of your charitable undertakings.

Remarkable is the expansion of your community in the western hemisphere during the last fifty years, since October 24th, 1894, when a band of five of your Sisters landed in New York and, without delay, came to the State of Pennsylvania.

As an evidence of God's blessing on you and your work, may be cited the fact that, in short space of five decades, the little band of five Sisters has increased to 715 Professed Sisters, 17 Novices and 20 Postulants, that your Sisters teach in 71 schools, 3 Archdioceses, and 12 Dioceses, as well as in three academies; that you conduct a teachers' normal school; and in the line of charity, you have charge of 3 orphanages; that your Community has grown to such an extent in this country and South America that it has to be divided into 3 Provinces; and, that among your works, must be counted that of conducting hospitals in different parts of the United States and South America.

Although you do not look for a reward in this life, such a growth, such an exhibition of religion and charity, such unbounded zeal should be, even in this world, some compensation for the sacrifices that you have made.

Hence, in congratulating you, my dear Sisters, on your Golden Jubilee in this country, I do so not merely because of the many years that you have worked here, but also, especially, for the marvelous good that you have accomplished; and I pray God to continue to bless you and to fructify your labors, as He has done up to the present.

In my place as Archbishop of Philadelphia, I take this opportunity to thank you and all your Sisters for all you have accomplished here both by your good example and the help you have afforded Religion in this section of God's vineyard.

With sentiments of the highest esteem, I remain, my dear Mother Edmunda,

Very devotedly yours,
+ D. Card. Dougherty
Abo. of Phila.

Before the year ended the Bernardines also noted and celebrated the 500th anniversary of the death of Saint Bernardine of Siena, close follower of the beloved St. Francis, and patron of the Bernardines.

CHAPTER TEN

The Reverend Mother's sister Mary and her family always looked forward to the Christmas season. In her Christmas greetings the Reverend Mother always included a large rectangular wafer or two of different colors which were to be used by the family at the Christmas Eve supper. Mary spent a number of days preparing for this solemnly celebrated occasion so closely connected to family life. Members of the family who were away felt their absence from home deeply.

"Remember, we must not eat anything during the day," she said to the children. "This is a day of strict fast and abstinence. When the first star appears in the eastern skies we will all gather at the table for our *Wigilia* supper." At eleven years of age Johnny found it a challenge to observe the fast completely. Six-year-old Louis and four-year-old Sylvia obeyed their mother's will and looked for the first star they could find.

"There is the star!" Louis called out at around 5:00 PM.

"Let us all kneel and pray," she said. A heartfelt Polish prayer carefully followed her gentle directive. Always tearfully fragile at this meal, their father felt the family was not really whole with Alma absent from the table.

After the prayers they all eagerly took their seats at the table to begin the commemoration of the birth of the God child. Their father passed a piece of blessed wafer, or *oplatek*, to each one. As they received the wafer, sweetened by some honey, an exchange of good wishes followed. They then turned to one another and did the same thing. The family celebrated their togetherness on this evening as never before. A lighted candle had been placed in the window symbolizing the hope that the God child, in the form of a stranger, might come to share the *Wigilia* supper. They set an extra place at the table for the expectant guest. When their father saw this empty place setting he always thought of his missing oldest daughter. Before the eating started everyone looked to see if they could see their own shadow. The absence of one's shadow, according to an old tradition and belief, meant another Christmas would not be seen. Happily everyone saw their shadows!

Mary had seven courses planned: fried fish - usually small smelt - cabbage soup, dried fruit compote, potatoes, rice, pierogi and pastries, coffee, nuts and candies. The supper seemed very long to the children who were impatient to see the lighted Christmas tree. A carol was sung and the gifts opened. The real spruce Christmas tree was always beautiful! Though not very numerous, every gift was appreciated. At eleven p.m. they went to church for midnight Mass. Many beautiful Polish carols, *kolendy*, were sung before and during Mass.

Johnny had been invited to become an altar boy and he looked forward to serving Mass one day. His mother and father told them of the belief in the villages in Poland that while the congregation is singing, peace descends on the snow-clad earth, and that during the night the humble companions of men, the domestic animals, assume voices, that only the innocent of heart may hear.

St. Casimir's looked beautiful that Christmas eve. There were poinsettias and Christmas trees at the altar, with every candle lit. On both sides of the church were stained glass windows, one of them donated by Johnny's father's parents, Jozef and Kunegunda. The "Holy Trinity", painted atop the ceiling of the altar pictured God the Father as an old man in a long gray beard. Our Lady holding the child Jesus was found in the center of the altar with St. Casimir, in princely dress, painted above the Lady and child. Statues of Saints Stanislaus and Adalbert stood on either side of the golden tabernacle, whose red and gold doors dominated the altar. Two large angels held shafts of twelve brilliant lights. Faces of the twelve apostles circled around the church balcony on either side, while fourteen large, beautifully painted stations of the cross covered the church walls between the windows. The pulpit stood at the left front of the congregation, away from the altar which brought the preacher closer to the people. The older parishioners always enjoyed the sermon given in Polish. The church holding hundreds of people was always standing-room only on Christmas Eve.

In the third grade, after Johnny received the sacraments of Penance, or Confession, and Holy Communion, he next received the sacrament of Confirmation, in the sixth grade. He was then old enough to more fully realize the sacredness of his Catholic Faith. By accepting the gift of Confirmation he would more totally understand what it meant to be a Christian. The Auxiliary Bishop of Philadelphia was to come to St. Casimir's Parish to confer this blessing of the Holy Spirit. He wanted to have his godmother as his sponsor whom he had come to know so well because he had never met his godfather who lived on the west side of town and had become estranged from Johnny's father. At school, Sister said he had to have a man as a sponsor just as every girl needed a woman to sponsor her.

"Who am I going to have as a sponsor?" he asked his mother. "Dad says your godfather would probably have no interest. Why don't you decide on someone to ask?"

He thought about all the men in the neighborhood and finally decided to ask one of the landlord's sons who lived in an apartment close by. Walter looked like someone he would be proud to have as his sponsor because of the self confident and well-to-do air about him.

"Do you think he would be willing to be my sponsor?" he asked his mother shortly thereafter.

"Well, just ask him and you will find out."

The next day he went to Walter's apartment, about two houses away, knocked on the door and was greeted by his wife. "Hello, what can we do for you? Is there anything wrong with your parents' apartment?"

"No, I'm here to see Walter. I need a sponsor for my Confirmation at St. Casimir's in about two weeks. Is he at home?"

"Yes, he is in the kitchen. I'm sure he will be happy to do that for you. Let me get him."

"Walter, come in here, you have a visitor."

"Hello Johnny," Walter said, "What can I do for you?"

"Hello! I have my Confirmation coming up pretty soon and I need a sponsor. I have never met my godfather so I was hoping you would sponsor me."

"OK! When is it and what do I have to do?"

"There will be a practice for all of us next week and then the Confirmation will be a week after that, is that okay with you?"

"Yes, just let me know the day and time, and thank you for the invitation."

When the day arrived, the bishop's presence made it all seem very sacred. "Confirmation is the powerful sacrament you are receiving today," said the bishop. "The Holy Spirit will shower you with many graces and strengthen your faith in ways you cannot conceive of now." He then asked a number of questions regarding the faith Christians held from the very first days of the

Lord's presence on Earth. Sisters had prepared them well and each one who responded to him generally responded correctly.

The bishop then prayed that the Spirit of wisdom and understanding, the Spirit of counsel and fortitude, the Spirit of knowledge and piety be granted to all through this new birth through water and the Holy Spirit. He next asked each candidate the name by which he wished to be confirmed and Johnny said, "Joseph". This was his other grandfather's name, since he had been baptized John Jacob. Jacob was his maternal grandfather's name. Then the bishop dipped the tip of his right thumb in the chrism, or blessed oil, placed his right hand on Johnny's head and with his thumb made a sign of the cross on his forehead. He then prayed "I confirm you with the chrism of salvation. In the name of the Father, and of the Son, and of the Holy Spirit, Amen." He then gently stroked Johnny on the cheek and said, "*Pax tecum,*" Peace be with you.

After washing his hands he prayed the antiphon in Latin: "*Confirma hoc, Deus, quod operatus es in nobis, a templo sancto tuo, quod est in Ierusalem.*" Strengthen, O God, what you have wrought in us, from your holy temple, which is in Jerusalem.

Walter, and the other sponsors, stood behind the candidates with their right hands placed on their right shoulders to indicate their witnessing of the sacrament.

Johnny's parents and family were happy to see this day and they congratulated him afterward. Walter gave him a roll of nickels amounting to a dollar. The way he gave them to him felt like a disparagement of his status as the son of a renter of one of his father's apartments. This deprecating gesture deflated Johnny's remembrance of the day.

The summers when he remained at home were full of activities. Huckleberry picking not only meant great pies made by his mother; if enough were found he was able to sell them to the bakery at 30 cents a quart. His father, when he was not at work, took him into the hills around the town , often a mile or two from their neighborhood.

"Johnny, don't forget to look under the branches; that's where they are a lot of the time."

"OK Dad!" He really enjoyed being out in the hills with his father who often whistled while he picked or walked from bush to bush.

"Dad, how come I could never whistle like you?"

"I don't know Johnny. Remember we tried a few times but you just couldn't get it. Some people just don't learn how, you are probably one of them."

On another day his father said to him, "Let's go out and throw a while." His father had been a really good pitcher in his younger days and hoped his sons would follow in his steps. They had tried throwing every now and then without much success. Now his father wanted to find out whether Johnny had any baseball talent at all.

"Look, I'm going to show you exactly how to hold the ball and how to throw it." As much as he tried, Johnny just couldn't do the things his father tried very hard to teach him. "Maybe Louie will take after me," he finally said.

The canaries had been sold off so that the available porch space would be larger. His mother was also concerned that they might be a health danger to the family. With her own arthritis, Alma's illness and Johnny's persistent migraine headaches, she hoped the younger children would stay well and healthy.

Johnny had become used to going away for part of the summer, and one day while visiting Shenandoah, his mother's New York friends invited him to return with them to Maspeth, on the Long Island side of Manhattan. This made him really excited about traveling that distance from home and getting to know something about New York. Louie also wanted to go, climbed into the trunk of the car and was very unhappy when told he could not go along.

Joe and Ceil Targonski always had a contented way of living each day. They made Johnny feel wholly comfortable during the trip and told him all about the Holland Tunnel as they went under the river. He almost felt the river surrounding him as they proceeded through the seemingly long distance until they entered Manhattan. He found it exciting to see and feel this largest city in the country. "Do you think I'll be able to see a ball game?" he asked while riding across the city to the expressway which would take them to Maspeth.

"I think the Dodgers and Giants are playing sometime this week. Maybe Teddy could take you one day," answered Joe. "Remember we also want you to see Coney Island and do some clamming at Long Beach. There's a lot to do here." Teddy, their oldest child and already married, had a lot of musical talent. He played in a band at many of the weddings and a few of the dance halls. There were many Poles in Queens which also kept him playing his drums at polka parties.

"Teddy, here's our friend from Pennsylvania," said Ceil to Teddy when they met the next day. "He would like you to take him to see the Dodgers. What do you think? Could you take the time to do that?"

"Yes, Mom, I'll be off on Saturday. That could be the best day if we can get tickets," answered Ted.

"That would be great!" shouted Johnny.

During the week Johnny practiced some handball on an open court not far from the house. There were no handball courts in his home town, therefore, he found the new game different from his usual experience. No one seemed available to play at his level. He watched how some of the better players attacked the game. That was enough for him because he knew it was just for this short time with the Targonski's.

"Today we will take you to Coney Island," said Joe, "when I return from work."

"Where is Coney Island?" he asked.

"Coney is on the waterfront in Brooklyn. It shouldn't take too long to get there."

They headed for Coney Island at around 4:00 in the afternoon. The sight of the giant ferris wheel and the roller coaster, which looked intimidating to him, made Johnny feel he was in a really different part of the world from his neighborhood.

"Let's get a hot dog from Nathan's Famous before we go on some rides," said Ceil. "These are the best hot dogs in the world." The hot dogs were good!

"I'd like to try the giant ferris wheel so I can see the whole island," exclaimed Johnny in an impatient voice.

"That's a good idea, let's go," answered Joe.

The ferris wheel was higher than he had imagined from the ground. He held onto the handlebars on his seat to keep it from rocking. He could see the waterfront, the sand, and much of the rest of Coney Island.

"How about the roller coaster?" Johnny asked.

"You know they call it the Cyclone. Take a closer look at it before you decide to go," said Joe.

As they drew closer to the Cyclone, Johnny could feel the queasiness hitting his stomach as he looked at the sharp plunges the coaster was taking as it dropped from the top of each incline. "Maybe I'd better wait till I'm older," he said to Joe and Ceil.

"Whatever you want. Perhaps we can go to the freak show before we go home."

The freaks were incredible! The tallest woman in the world at seven feet, a girl who could twist herself in every direction, Siamese twins joined at the hip, and others.

"I guess we've seen enough. Time to go home," said Ceil.

On the way back to Maspeth he talked excitedly about the visit. He was having a great time. "Wait till I tell everyone at home about this!"

Their next outing was a trip to the southern end of Long Island. Long Beach was near the barrier islands and its white beaches gave him a feel for the ocean as he had never known in Atlantic City on visits to his sister Alma.

"We are going to see how many clams we can get today," said Joe. "You can do some clamming yourself."

Johnny worked for a couple of hours in a shallow bay and was not very lucky that day. He couldn't find any clams. The time spent near the ocean was exciting for him and that is all that mattered.

"I got the tickets for Ebbetts Field. A lot of the best players are in the service now so it's easier to get into the ballpark these days. I really liked it better when I could get to see Pee Wee Reese at shortstop," Ted said to Johnny the day before the game.

"That's great," answered Johnny. "This will make the trip to New York better than I expected." It was a good game with fans, almost all New Yorkers, rooting either for the Dodgers or the Giants.

"Tomorrow we will be taking you back home. Our daughter and her husband have wanted to visit Pennsylvania as well. You will be safe with them," said Ceil.

When he arrived at home he told everyone how exciting the trip had been and showed them his Brooklyn Dodgers baseball cap.

CHAPTER ELEVEN

From the beginning of the Reverend Mother's first year in office the number of requests from the pastors of ethnic Polish parishes began to diminish. Very few new parishes were established by the bishops, limiting them to one heritage or another. Immigration had slowed and second-generation Americans were amalgamating into a larger Catholic community where backgrounds were becoming of secondary importance. Requests began to come to the Reverend Mother from pastors, and some bishops, to staff small hospitals in the East and Midwestern United States.

In 1943, the pastor of St. Anthony's parish in Hoven, South Dakota, asked the Bernardines to administer and staff a newly built hospital in the city. The Reverend Mother and her councillors accepted the invitation, sent Sister Dolores as administrator and a group of sisters to undertake this mission in the medical field. Within days after their arrival the Hoven Hospital opened its doors, two babies were born the first day, and an appendectomy was performed. In 1946 the city transferred ownership of the hospital to the Bernardines.

"Reverend Mother, we need to expand the hospital. The demand for our services is growing very quickly" wrote Sister Dolores. The Reverend Mother, always careful to keep the community's financial obligations sound (a trait she had very likely inherited from her father), added a new wing to the newly renamed Holy Infant Hospital.

Also in 1943, the Bernardines purchased the Corrigan Maternity Hospital in Hazleton, Pennsylvania with Sister Wilhelmina as the administrator. War conditions delayed the Reverend Mother's and her council's intent to establish a general hospital in this city which was part of the coal regions of the state. In 1946 construction began on a new two-hundred-bed hospital named after

St. Joseph, in full operation within two years. The doctors and the people in the area contributed much financial help to the Bernardines. Within a short time the American Medical Association approved the hospital for the training of interns. Sister Ernestine was appointed superior and administrator of the new enterprise. The Holy Infant Hospital in Hoven and the St. Joseph Hospital in Hazleton, added to the six hospitals in Brazil, reflected the growing commitment of the sisters to hospital services.

The Reverend Mother's fondest moments were those spent at Mount Alvernia where she felt completely at home, especially with the chapel close by. The novices were in the same building as the motherhouse, and the aspirants were in St. Francis Hall, built primarily as an orphanage in 1924 and dedicated by Cardinal Dougherty of Philadelphia in 1926. Soon afterward a wing of the building housed an academy for young aspirants to the Community, of high school age.

"What a pleasure it is to see these young aspirants!" she often thought. They reminded her so much of her own early entrance into the community which now numbered hundreds of members. Now in position to lead all those under her care, the need to fully educate these new Bernardine candidates became even more paramount. Talents were needed to fill many positions in education and hospital care. The Reverend Mother's tranquil face and demeanor were a magnet to all who met her.

"Is the Reverend Mother always this pleasant? asked one of the new aspirants.

"Yes, especially when she notices that when you agree to do something you follow through. She really prefers that when you say 'yes' you mean it and when you say 'no' you also mean it. She is not a 'maybe' kind of person," answered the nun assigned to their care.

In late September of 1946, Mother Hedwig, the superior of the Bernardines' largest province and the Superior General for 18 years prior to Mother Angela, died in Philadelphia. At the age of 24 she had been declared the new Superior General by the Polish Franciscan visitor, Father Zygmunt Janicki, at the first convocation of the American foundation. He did this despite an overwhelming majority of votes to continue Mother Veronica in office. Mother Hedwig had been stunned by this nomination; however, for three terms she led the order as the first American-born Superior General. When she died suddenly at the age of 59 the Reverend Mother ached at the thought of having to cover the face of Mother Hedwig prior to the closing of the casket. Despite the hopeful prayers of the Latin Mass for the Dead, the departure of one of her sisters to, hopefully, a heavenly reward and face-to-face meeting with their spiritual spouse still caused her heart to suffer. Gratefully, only twelve of her daughters in Christ had died during the years 1943 to 1946.

December of 1946 brought an unexpected visitor to the motherhouse. A priest from India told the Reverend Mother and her council the distressing story of a number of displaced Poles whose temporary refuge in India had ended. They had left Poland in 1942 after a pact had been signed by Poland and the Soviet Union. These "free Poles" were really exiles who were first transported to Siberia and later found their way to Turkey, Africa, England and finally India. The Polish government in exile took care of Polish nationals from their headquarters in London. Some of the men followed the free Polish army, led by General Sikorsky, and fought with the allied forces in Africa and Europe.

After the war some of the refugees returned to Poland. Others wanted to stay free of the Communistic Soviets who controlled Poland. The priest hoped he could persuade the Bernardines to sponsor some of them. Despite the expense it would entail, the decision was made by the Reverend Mother to offer a home to fifty girls who believed they might have a vocation to the religious life.

"Let's decide the various ways we might solicit support for this project," said the Reverend Mother.

"We should certainly ask all the Polish parishes we serve to become involved," suggested Mother Adalbert, one of the councillors. The response was immediate from the various pastors and their congregations. Enough funds were raised to cover all the necessary expenses. When told by the priest of their immediate immigration to America, the girls wrote their thanks to the Reverend Mother. They were so happy about the opportunity to, at last, find a permanent home in a country so well known for its hospitality to new prospective citizens.

The Reverend Mother, Mother Adalbert and Mother Victoria welcomed them in San Francisco after their long voyage from India via Singapore, Hong Kong and Honolulu. Mother Adalbert, especially, took a special interest in looking after the welfare of these 15 to 19 year old girls. The San Francisco Catholic Charities organization made all the necessary arrangements for their ride to the railroad terminal and provided box lunches for them as well. In Salt Lake City, Bishop Hunt came to the station to give them his blessing. Sunday Mass was available for them in Chicago, and in New York the National Catholic Welfare Council provided a warm welcome. Stamford, Connecticut, was the first Bernardine home to accommodate them.

After a brief stay in Stamford, twelve of the girls were admitted into the postulancy — a brief introduction to the religious life prior to the novitiate. Within eighteen months they were wearing the habit of the Bernardine Sisters, sent to colleges for further education, or went into training as X-ray technicians and other specialties. The younger girls lived at Mt. Alvernia, attended high school with the aspirants and later received scholarships to colleges or nursing schools. Of the fifty girls, twenty-five pursued their stated intention to become nuns, half of those remained in the order and the others went on to other life experiences. Grateful to the Bernardines for rescuing them from their life of exile, many returned for visits to the motherhouse.

"Trust in God, I'm praying for you," the Reverend Mother wrote in a short note to one of the postulants who was heartbroken because her father was not pleased with her decision to become a nun. In her distress she had begun crying while making the Stations of the Cross in the chapel. The Reverend Mother, not far behind her, also praying those fourteen stations of her blessed Lord, had not said anything, but wanted her to know how much she cared. A special bond had developed between them when she had told the Reverend Mother of her older brother's death at Monte Cassino in May of 1944 — three months after the Reverend Mother's own nephew, Richard, had given his life on the beach at Anzio in sight of Monte Cassino.

The year 1947 was the fifth year of Reverend Mother Edmunda's term as head of the order. A new election would be held the following year; there was no special date set for a general chapter and no one seemed hurried about determining when the chapter would be held.

CHAPTER TWELVE

"Somebody is going to die!" Johnny's father declared dramatically when he returned home after one of his long sessions in the barroom. Johnny tried not to take this dire notice too seriously. After all, his father had been a popular local actor in ethnic plays and could be melodramatic when the spirit moved.

"Don't listen to him, it's just the booze talking," said his mother.

"Somebody's not going to live to see their eighteenth birthday!" continued his father. Johnny remembered the day he had almost drowned in the creek. He also thought about his young friend Louis who died at five. And most recently an older altar boy had died before his eighteenth birthday, despite having three sisters in the same order as his aunt. A fourth sister was considering doing the same thing. Why hadn't he recovered from his illness with all those holy women praying for him? Alma was still in the Shriner's Hospital in Atlantic City, and he was this skinny kid who got those horrible headaches. At times his father would look directly at him when he made the ominous prediction. He began to feel his future prospects were not too good. Maybe he would die before he reached his thirteenth year. His fear of dying kept him from falling asleep peacefully, for he was afraid he might not wake up after he closed his eyes. He kept his fears to himself.

School always went well. He learned eighty-five percent of his subjects in the classroom. Some homework made up the rest. Besides, the nuns always seemed to give him better grades than he expected. The Bernardines who taught at St. Casimir's usually knew that his aunt was the Reverend Mother. He also was an altar boy, which seemed to make a difference with his teachers. After he wrote a contest-winning essay about his desire to become a missionary, even the pastor thought he should attend the local Catholic high school when he finished grade school.

"I'm not going to spend any money sending you to the Irish high school. Public school is good enough," his father stated emphatically. "You're Polish and don't ever forget it!" That's the way it was and that's the way it would stay, Johnny thought.

In eighth grade, their teacher and school principal decided to do a class play based on Dickens' Christmas Carol. Sister Camila said she would like him to play Scrooge — a very long part with a good deal of dialogue. There would be three weeks to practice. Having taken part in almost every play throughout the prior eight years, he made up his mind he could do it. And he did. He also had reached his thirteenth birthday that December and was still around. Perhaps he would somehow survive.

Valentine's Day came quickly enough after the Christmas holidays. In their very early teens, his classmates had become more selective about who got a Valentine. Sister decided the time had come to make certain that the class knew something more about Valentine's Day.

"Who knows how Valentine's Day began?" she asked.

"Was he a saint?" questioned one of the girls. "We know that St. Nicholas was the first real Santa Claus; was there ever a St. Valentine?"

"Yes, the first Valentine was a saint. Class, here is the Legend of St. Valentine as it was told to me."

It all began in the third century. The emperor of the Roman Empire, Claudius II, had ordered all Romans to worship twelve gods, with the death penalty inflicted on all those who refused. Valentinus was a Christian dedicated to the ideals of his faith. When he refused to worship no gods but the one true God he was arrested and imprisoned.

During the final weeks of Valentinus's life, the jailor, seeing that he was a learned man, asked if Valentinus would be willing to teach his blind daughter some lessons. She had been blind from birth and had received no education in any subjects. A very pretty girl with a quick mind, she trusted everything Valentinus taught her. He spoke to her of Rome's history, described the world of nature, taught her some arithmetic and told her about God. She found great comfort in his quiet strength.

'Valentinus,' she asked one day, 'does God really hear our prayers?'

'Yes, my dear child, He hears each one.'

'Do you know what I pray for every night? I pray that I might see. I want so much to see all the things you've told me about!'

'God does what is best for us, Julia, if only we believe in Him.'

'Oh Valentinus, I do believe, I do!'

She knelt and grasped his hand and asked if he would also pray with her. They prayed together with great faith. Suddenly a brilliant light filled up the cell and Julia cried 'Valentinus, I can see! I can see!'

'Praise be to God!' Valentinus exclaimed.

On the eve of his death, Valentinus wrote a last note to Julia, urging her to stay close to God, and he signed it 'From your Valentine'. He was executed the next day, February 14, 270 A.D. near a gate of the city of Rome that was later named Porta Valentini in his memory. He was buried by his Christian friends in an area now known as the Church of Praxedes in Rome. It is said that Julia planted a pink-blossomed almond tree near his grave. Today, the almond tree is a symbol of abiding love and friendship.

"That is the reason why, on February 14, the Feast of St. Valentine, messages of affection, love and devotion are exchanged by many people around the world."

Sister's story impressed most of Johnny's classmates. Each year thereafter he sent Valentine's greetings only to the one girl he really liked at the time.

In early May, Sister told the eighth-graders that the graduation address would be given in Polish. Johnny wished she would choose Anne to give the speech. Anne was certainly one of the brightest students and had three sisters in the convent as Bernardines. Instead, she announced that he would be the one to represent the class. His one hope was that he could pronounce the words properly since the pastor and all of the parents would be in the audience. He especially wanted to please the pastor who had informed him that the parish would pay his tuition to the Catholic high school in the town, with the understanding it would be a better preparation for his entrance into the seminary for the priesthood. The speech went well enough, despite his nervousness. He was very happy to have it come to an end.

The following summer Johnny delivered the *Shenandoah Herald* to seventy-five customers on the west side of town. The income, and Christmas tips, meant a chance to buy better clothes during his freshman year in high school. An older altar boy had invited him to take over the paper route - an invitation he greatly appreciated.

When he began his first year at the high school, he realized he was the only boy from his Polish parish to attend the Irish high school taught by an order of mostly Irish-American nuns. The Immaculate Heart of Mary Sisters, or IHM's, were mostly from the Philadelphia area. They brought to the much smaller coal region town a big-city attitude which encouraged the students to look to the larger world outside the coal regions. He would be fourteen years old in December and was beginning to feel the need to become free of the confines of his family and town. The teachers' attitudes confirmed his own feelings.

Johnny's sister Alma had finally been released from her hospital stay in Atlantic City. Her right hip was fused together to eliminate the recurring pain; however, the procedure resulted in an exaggerated limp. Although twenty-three months older than her brother, she had to join him in the ninth grade because of her limited education at the hospital.

"Mom," said Alma to their mother, "Johnny says he has to walk too slow when we go to school together. I met a girl, Dolores, who lives only a block from our house, who said she would be happy to walk with me."

"Johnny, what's your hurry? Are you ashamed of your sister?"

"No, I'm not," he replied very quickly.

The truth was that he was somewhat embarrassed to have a sister who had a burned hand which was always visible and who limped like a cripple. He was also distressed to have a mother whose head was always tilted forward and down, with the back of her dress or coat always looking uneven. Every two weeks his father got ludicrously drunk. He was beginning to wonder what his own future would hold. Would he actually live to see his eighteenth birthday? Everyone said he was too skinny and the headaches didn't stop. They were never severe enough to keep him from going to school; nevertheless, they did seem to cast a pall over him, which sometimes remained after the headache was gone.

In October, the freshman class was given an IQ test in which he scored 140. This placed him in the top five percent of nationwide results. He had always felt he was an above-average student. This score showed he had a real ability to do well with his high school courses.

"Have you given any thought to playing a musical instrument, Johnny?" asked Sister Cecile, the music teacher. She had noticed that he seemed to know something about musical notes during one of the sessions she gave to the class. "We could use a good tenor sax player in the school band. One of my former students is selling his and buying a new one. I could give you lessons each week."

"Sister, let me ask my parents," Johnny answered.

"How much will this saxophone cost?" asked his mother when he mentioned the idea to her.

"I don't have the price yet. How much do you think we can afford to pay?"

"Johnny, you know we recently won that $700 pool, but I don't want to throw the money away. You know what happened to the new bike I bought for you. On the second day, you smashed it up against the sidewalk after coming down the hill on Center Street. You shouldn't have had Louie on the handlebars with you."

"Mom, if that ice truck hadn't come across the street in front of us nothing would have happened. I had to get out of its way." Both he and Louis had scraped up their faces against the shingled siding of a house after the bike's front wheel collapsed against the sidewalk.

"You're lucky you didn't break your necks," his mother added. "Anyway, let me know what the saxophone will cost and we'll talk about it."

The sax cost $125 and lessons were a low $2 each week. He practiced each day except for those days he had a headache. Their dog, Tiny, a small rat terrier began to howl at the sound of some of the high notes. The howling at first sounded funny; later he began to fear the dog sensed something more ominous. In the neighborhood there was the imaginative notion that a dog's howling in a certain way almost always predicted the smell of death. He began to hate the dog's continued response to his practices. When he played "The Indian Love Call" the dog went almost demonic with his howls. He finally said to his mother, after about six months, that the size of the tenor sax was too big to be lugging around and he quit practicing. He told Sister Cecile he no longer had any interest in playing.

"What are you going to do this summer, now that Joe and Cassie are no longer on the farm?" asked his mother.

"You know there aren't any job possibilities in town. Why don't I ask them if I could go to Reading and work there? Louie could deliver the papers while I am away." His Aunt Cassie answered his letter immediately and said he was welcome to come. They would be happy to have him. He found a job at a jewelry store cleaning the shelves and merchandise. At the end of the day he vacuumed the floor; each morning he swept the pavement and entrance to the store. The manager, Mr. Tuck, and the bookkeeper, Frances, liked him immediately. Each lunch day he went to a Jewish deli close by and bought a corned beef on rye for the manager who sometimes treated him to one as well, especially if business was good. Frances introduced him to some of her nephews and nieces. She was extremely pleasant and, although married, had no children of her own. The summer went well and he arrived home with enough money to keep himself in first rate clothing and shoes.

"Mary, I think we're raising a little Jew," declared his father one day during his sophomore year in school. "All he cares about is clothes and getting jobs to have money."

"Leave the boy alone. He has his own idea about things. They may not be the same as yours, so just let him be," answered his mother.

After his return home, an ice cream parlor owner invited him to work a few hours a week. The business was a few blocks from his own home, so he agreed. The owner believed that he needed someone good looking behind the counter to attract the young girls on the east end of town. The job was not too bad. He learned to make milkshakes, ice cream sodas, grill hamburgers and wait on some of the customers who sat in booths rather than sit at the counter. The owner was a Syrian who liked to listen to Middle Eastern music. He was short and dark. His wife was much taller and rarely came into the store. On one of the evenings he was at work, one of the owner's sons sat at the counter, looked at Johnny's hands and said, "I wish my skin was as white as yours." He was no more than seven years old and the remark stayed with Johnny whenever the boy came into his presence. The hot sauce the owner made to put on the hamburgers was the best he had ever tasted. The paper route and the ice cream parlor gave him some sense of freedom from the financial problems at home.

CHAPTER THIRTEEN

The Reverend Mother remembered 1946 as the year the first Bernardine sister in Brazil went to her heavenly reward. Sister Gaudenta's burial in Camaqua in August of that year was celebrated by many of the people who brought flowers which covered her coffin and the floor around it. The tiny convent chapel was much too small to allow all the mourners in at one time. Father Hanquet and the sisters sang the "Salve Regina" on the way to the cemetery. Lilies planted on her grave around a marble cross indicated the perennial care she would receive for many years to come.

In early 1947 the Reverend Mother approved the purchase of an eighteen-acre property in Stamford, Connecticut. Mother Regina, Provincial of the Holy Name Province, had discovered the estate available for a very reasonable price. A retreat house named Villa Maria in honor of Mary Immaculate, Patroness of the Bernardines, became a wonderful place of grace for many people as well as the sisters.

In January, 1948, the sisters in Brazil celebrated their tenth anniversary in that distant country, with a Solemn High Mass celebrated by the Bishop in Camaqua. In March the Sao Joao Batista Normal School was opened in Camaqua and in December, twenty-two sisters returned to the United States for their first visit home since leaving for Brazil in 1937 and 1938.

In 1948, the provincial of the St. Francis Province in Scranton, Pennsylvania informed the Reverend Mother that the bishop wanted the Bernardines to staff an orphanage in Elmhurst. He had purchased a two hundred and eighty acre property with a large brick building, originally a home for Greek orphans. Bishop Hafey simply said to the provincial, "I want the Bernardines to take care of it." She told him she had no nuns to spare. "I would love to take it," she said, "but I really do not have the staff." The bishop would not take no for an answer. She found the staff.

The orphanage in Elmhurst was named Our Lady of Fatima Home. Sisters who had been trained at the Catholic University of America in Washington were some of the same sisters who had been trained originally with the intent of working in Poland after the end of the war. The sellout of Eastern Europe by America and England to the Soviet Communists negated their going to Poland. Their training in social work would be invaluable at Elmhurst. The intent was to make the home a snug harbor for those who had been in other orphanages as well as those who were also emotionally disturbed.

The fourth general chapter took place on December 29, 1948 with Reverend Mother Edmunda re-elected on the first ballot. She prayed to Her Lord that the next six years would be as fulfilling as the years of her first term.

PART TWO

"And some seed fell
into rich soil and grew
and produced its crop
a hundredfold."

LUKE 8:8

CHAPTER ONE

"Sister, now that the orchard has been cleared away, I am thinking of having my brother Joe erect the Stations of the Cross along a pathway starting at the driveway and ending just below Our Lady's Grotto," remarked the Reverend Mother to the always cheerful portress, Sister Imelda. She said this while looking out the window of the motherhouse.

"What a beautiful idea! How is Joe these days?" answered Sister Imelda.

"He's not in the best of health. Still, I believe this is a project he could do very well. He has always been a perfectionist. I don't know anyone I would trust more."

The Reverend Mother instructed the new Secretary General, Sister Chrysostoma, to place the proposal on the agenda for the next councillors' meeting which would take place after she and Mother Daniela returned from a visit to Cardinal Micara, the newly appointed Cardinal Protector of the congregation.

The Reverend Mother, in late January, had extended a fervent goodbye to the sisters who were returning to Brazil after their six-weeks' vacation in the United States. She held them in the greatest esteem for the missionary work they were doing and promised her unwavering support during the rest of her tenure as Superior General of the order. They gave her a promise, in return, to continue their efforts to serve the Lord and His mother among the Brazilian people whom they had come to love.

The Reverend Mother and the four councillors carefully discussed the construction of the out-of-doors Way of the Cross at their next meeting.

"What is the best way to finance the cost of material and labor?" asked Mother Daniela.

"The work will be done by my brother Joe, I am certain, who has lived in

Reading these past few years. He knows construction as well as any professional. Sister Maxentia will be able to share one of her workers to help with any lifting that may be required," offered the Reverend Mother.

"Any idea what he might expect as his pay?" asked Mother Duclane.

"I am sure he will be happy with whatever we decide to pay him," answered the Reverend Mother.

Mother Angela then suggested this could be a wonderful way for some of their benefactors to participate in this beautiful addition to the convent grounds.

"Let us offer each donor of at least one hundred dollars a plaque to appear on each of the stations," she said enthusiastically. They all agreed the project would be welcomed by many of their supporters.

The Reverend Mother's brother accepted the challenge of putting in place the fourteen Stations of the Cross, which would surely last much longer than their own lives. One of the stations carried the name of "Deceased Members of the Loyes Family" as an added reward to Joe for his efforts. Many of the Polish pastors and relatives of the sisters covered all of the expenses. Soon after the completion of the stations, the chaplain, whose newly-built chaplaincy stood close by, conducted a blessing ceremony attended by many of the sisters stationed at the Sacred Heart Motherhouse.

The Reverend Mother's nephew, Johnny, would complete his junior year in high school in the spring of 1949. She invited him to work on the grounds of the convent for the summer since no job prospects were available in his hometown. She had run the idea past Mother Daniela, the treasurer, who believed the money was available. "I think we should, at least, inform Sister Maxentia that he will be one of her summer crew," said Mother Daniela.

"Do you know anything about him?" asked Sister Maxentia, who was in charge of maintaining the grounds, when Mother Daniela spoke to her of the Reverend Mother's request.

"Not really. He is in his junior year at Shenandoah Catholic and is considering going into the seminary."

"That's very well, but is he reasonably strong? Can he do all the things we do around here every day for six days a week? I really need someone who can drive the truck around the grounds and run the tractor."

"You can take all that up with him when he gets here," concluded Mother Daniela.

The Reverend Mother was delighted to be able to give this opportunity to her nephew. She hoped Sister Maxentia would keep him busy and productive on the convent grounds while he earned some funds for his future education or perhaps to help the family when he returned home.

Maxie, as Sister Maxentia was fondly called, welcomed him the day he arrived in early June, and shrugged somewhat at his boyish looks. She had been raised on a farm and was a tremendous asset to the Bernardines because of her acquaintance with farming, cultivating fruit, and raising crops on the large open fields which were part of the convent grounds. She also dealt with a nearby bakery where she could pick up day-old bread. She rarely looked like the other nuns who kept their habits reasonably clean and never missed any of the required prayers during the day. Maxie was too busy, for the convent grounds were quite extensive. The Reverend Mother sometimes cautioned her about the need to be faithful to the spiritual rules of the order. After a few days Sister Maxentia found Johnny was able to cut grass, trim hedges, and weed flower beds as quickly as the others. One day she showed him how to drive the tractor. He felt like he could walk on air when she left him alone in the large, slightly sloping field with instructions to plow the field for a planting of winter wheat. At one side of the field, where he needed to turn around, the tractor almost overturned. Badly shaken, he told her he didn't trust doing that anymore.

The two cooks became his best friends. He would stop in to greet them and usually came away with a satisfying snack. Sister Imelda, the portress, would let him know if his aunt had some time to see him, which was seldom because of the many duties she had to fulfill. On many occasions sister would give him a Mounds bar of shredded coconut covered with dark chocolate. He always enjoyed her smiling face and warm greetings.

A book salesman arrived one day at the academy adjacent to the orphanage where the aspirants, some postulants, and a few neighborhood girls studied. The Reverend Mother wanted to personally inspect his textbooks, along with the school's principal, and for some reason invited Johnny to meet the gentleman as well.

"Johnny, I'd like you to meet Mr. Jacoby," she said as she introduced him.

"Hello Johnny," he said, and shook his hand.

"Yes, sir, how are you?" answered Johnny after he tried to shake the man's hand with some enthusiasm. The man's handshake was so limp and his appearance so effeminized he excused himself immediately and returned to his work.

The next day the Reverend Mother asked him what he had thought of the textbook salesman. "Not much," he answered. "He doesn't shake hands very well."

"Well Johnny, that's why I wanted you to meet him. I trust you will want to become more polished than that. Do you know what I mean?"

"Yes, I think I know exactly what you mean." She loved her nephew very much and wanted to protect him from moving in any wrong directions in life. With his good looks and happy disposition she was not oblivious to the seductions that might await him as he grew into manhood.

"Have you had any headaches lately?" she asked.

"Not really. When I'm here I don't seem to get any."

"Sister Maxentia says you're doing very well. Do you like the work?"

"Very much. She keeps me going all day. There's a lot of grass to cut, the hedges have to be trimmed just right and I've driven the truck a few times."

"How is the food? Is there enough?"

"Sisters Macrine and Perpetua are wonderful. I not only get three good meals, they often give me a snack some days if I am around the kitchen."

"What are you doing about Sunday Mass?"

"I usually go down to St. Anthony's in Millmont. When I attend Mass at the convent chapel I feel I am intruding."

The summer went by quickly. When the time came to return to school Sister Daniela gave him all the money he had earned.

In October of 1949, on the feast of Christ the King, Bishop Hafey presided at the services dedicating the newly built St. Joseph Hospital in Hazleton, truly a great satisfaction to the Reverend Mother who had spent much of her time monitoring its construction.

CHAPTER TWO

The Reverend Mother's sister, Mary, began to feel happy about the family's progress. The two oldest children would be finished with school by June of 1950. They had done very well at the Catholic high school. Johnny was seriously considering entering the seminary and that would keep him out of the draft if a war in Korea developed. Alma had good enough grades to allow her to train for a profession that might reduce her need to be walking while at the job. Louis was a challenge. His red robust face was always full of a sparkle, which made her wonder what he would do next. She loved him unconditionally. The Reverend Mother believed she was too easy with him. Many times Mary chased him around the house to try to catch him and punish him for some misdeed. She always believed the sisters at St. Casimir's were flawed in their expectation that this young son of hers should be as well behaved and studious as her other son. She wanted him to succeed in his own way and at his own pace. Her children loved their mother. Sylvia, her youngest daughter, had been a beautiful blond, blue eyed, loving girl from the day of her birth. Her blue eyes seemed to prove that the fourth child usually exhibited the family's recessive genes. Both of their grandmothers had blue eyes. Everyone else in the family had brown eyes.

In early March a letter from the Reverend Mother arrived for Johnny in answer to one he had written to her explaining his decision to enter either the Maryknoll Fathers or the new Glenmary Society dedicated to the home missions in the United States.

Dearest Johnny,
Thank you for the letter. It portrays your soul all aglow with
God's love and a desire to spread His kingdom in your own and the

souls of others — a noble calling and sublime desires, indeed. The path to its realization is not easy, dear Johnny; there will be many a stumbling block, many a hardship to overcome — but the distant horizons are always wrapped in warmth and light of God's Love as long as we hold ourselves close to His Sacred Heart. Would that I could share with you the love which I have always cherished, and do cherish, for my vocation, as one of Christ's choice plants.

Hold on to the love of Jesus and Mary — keep company of St. Therese and your heavenly friend, Blessed Theophane Venard. Do you know he was St. Therese's specially loved saint? She loved him because he was such a warm soul, with a heart that was very much devoted to his family - but at the same time a courageous heart, that was capable of sacrificing all for Jesus' sake.

I received an answer from Maryknoll and Glenmary this morning. What a coincidence?! The two which are first choices with you!

Say a fervent prayer. Better, make an hour of adoration in one of the churches before you answer their inquiries regarding your qualifications and state of health. The Maryknollers have grown into an impressive army of missionaries with 436 priests, 75 brothers and some 750 students preparing to become missionaries. The Glenmary missionaries are very new with 18 priests, 5 brothers and 25 in preparatory seminaries.

Personally, I do not wish to have any influence in your choice. Johnny — it is your life and you will live it. whatever you decide will be fine with me. Missionary work is important. This month's intention of the Apostleship of Prayer is for the conversion of the Negroes of the U.S.A. Only 3% of them are Catholic.

God bless and love you. May you be settled in your decision by May 15th, when I'll be ready, God willing, to hear whatever Bozia wants of you.

Lovingly,
Mother M. Edmunda

Within a week he wrote to his aunt again. Maryknoll would be his choice. She replied that she was not disappointed in his decision.

"The greatest mistake parents and families can make is to impose the choice of some path of life upon their young members."

She also thanked him for his good wishes on her trip to Rome for the Holy Year. The M. V. Conte Biancomano would leave New York on March 21st and she expected to return on May 15th.

"When do you expect the priest from Maryknoll to come for that interview you've been talking about?" his mother asked Johnny. She was very excited about the idea that her own son might become a priest. She knew this would make her sister very happy as well.

"The last I heard from him he said he expected to visit a number of candidates in Pennsylvania sometime this spring. He said I can expect a letter from him about a week before the interview," answered Johnny.

"Please let me know when it is. I'd like to have the home spic and span when he arrives."

This meeting with the priest from Maryknoll had become a real priority in his life, since three of his closest friends had already shared the news that they were headed for college right after high school. One of those friends, Joe, was entering a novitiate in Oak Ridge, New Jersey with the Paulist Fathers. The Paulists were a totally American order founded by five Protestant ministers who had converted to Catholicism in the middle of the 19th century. Preaching was their strong point. They primarily preached missions at Catholic churches around North America and published a magazine and books. Dick was headed for Mount Saint Mary's in Emmitsburg, Maryland, as a biology major. Walter had received a football scholarship to the University of San Francisco. He expected to major in business or accounting.

One late afternoon in April the Vocation Director from Maryknoll arrived outside the apartment. Johnny had been awaiting his arrival when he heard the slurred, incoherent sound of his father who had become drunker than usual. The priest was attempting to introduce himself at the bottom of the steps where his father lay completely boozed up.

"Father, sorry about all this. Today happens to be payday," Johnny quickly said to the perplexed missionary who had come to see a promising candidate and found an angry, embarrassed young man uncertain of what to do.

"Hello, I'm Father Carroll from Maryknoll. Why don't we help your father up the stairs."

"Father, I don't know what to say. I can't go through any kind of interview today. Please, let's just forget about it."

"I think I know how you feel. Perhaps we can get together some other time." He drove away immediately. Johnny's missionary calling ended in that crucial moment. He never thought seriously about Maryknoll again.

At school Johnny was doing exceptionally well in his senior year. He was competing for high honors at graduation. There was a possibility that Sonny (Walter's nickname), Joe and he could finish as the top three students in the class - a rare occurrence. Usually the girls led in the running for top honors.

Every Friday afternoon all the students went to confession. Father O'Brien, the pastor, often sat in the confessional on the side of the church where the boys were lined up to enter. In the privacy of the confessional, with a narrow screen separating the priest from the penitent, Johnny hoped the priest could not identify him personally from the others. The biggest hurdle in his examination of conscience was the virtue of purity. Had he acted in any way to desecrate his body or allowed his thoughts to dwell too long on impure desires? His hope to enter a seminary, and possibly become a priest, which required a celibate way of life, meant he really had to live that way during his teenage years as well. His turn to enter the confessional had come. He walked quietly to the door, knelt down and waited for the priest to open the small screen. Father was hearing the confession of the boy on the other side of the confessional and the wait this one day seemed very long. When the screen was opened Father said, "The Lord be on your lips and in your heart that you may properly confess all your sins, in the Name of the Father, the Son and of the Holy Spirit."

"It has been one week since my last confession, I said my penance, received absolution and accuse myself of the following sins: I abused myself sexually eight times. I was careless with the Lord's name, three times. For these and all the sins of my past life I beg thee Father for a penance and absolution."

No penance or absolution came from the confessor. He asked Johnny if he realized the importance of restraining himself in these acts of self abuse.

"Do you think you can make an act of contrition with the intent of keeping away from these sins?"

"I've tried, but I don't think I can."

"Then I cannot give you absolution. Your attitude will have to change. Come back to confession when you can promise a real effort to do something about your impure actions."

This was the first time he had ever been denied absolution by a priest after confession. How could he receive communion on Sunday without being absolved? On the way home he passed by the Slovak Parish of St. Stephen's and stopped in to pray. After a few short moments he decided he would return to St. Stephen's on Saturday afternoon and go to the priest there. Absolution came as it usually had before, even though he eliminated the information that he had been refused absolution the day before by another priest.

"Please say 10 Our Fathers and 10 Hail Mary's and say your act of contrition," said Father.

Total relief came into his spirit and he vowed he would never again tell or confess that he would not be willing to try to overcome his sins.

Sister Eymard, the seniors' homeroom teacher, spoke to them with great conviction one day while in one of her philosophical moods. "There are pleasures in life and there are treasures in life. When you are out there in the great big world don't get lost in the pleasures, pursue the treasures as well." Not young anymore, sister was very spirited and seemed larger than her small, thin physical size. Though the English classes she taught were sometimes tedious, she made certain all the material was covered. A calling to the religious life was one of her greatest treasures. Nothing made her happier than the news that one of her students was joining a religious order or going into a seminary. Two of the girls, Annemarie and Bernadatte, had let her know they were going to be novices in the Order of Sts. Cyril and Methodius composed mostly of women with Slovak backgrounds. And Joe informed her he was going to be a Paulist. There were some rumors that Johnny was entering a seminary. He never dispelled the talk because he got the impression that his grades on the quarterly report cards seemed to be going higher with the rumor. He did not know the Maryknoll idea would fail so quickly.

The senior play was always a major event at the school. Johnny was cast as a stockbroker. When he appeared on stage in his new double-breasted, blue serge suit everyone said he looked the part.

"Aristocratic, that's the way you looked," said his Aunt Cassie. She and his Uncle Joe were visiting and decided to stay long enough to see the show. Her comment was the ego-boosting way she had always talked to him.

"How do you like Reading by now?" asked his mother.

"Much better than being on the farm. I work as a seamstress and Joe was very busy building the Stations of the Cross on the convent grounds last year."

"I sometimes wish we could move to a town where jobs were more plentiful," said Mary.

"Maybe someday you will move to Reading as well," answered Cassie.

"I doubt I could ever get John to move out of this town," lamented Mary.

"Will you be working at the convent again this summer?" asked Joe as he looked at Johnny.

"As far as I know, they are still holding a place open for me. By the way, that was a big project building those fourteen stations."

"Yes, on top of the cement subbase there is the three-foot stone base and the two-foot-high stations. Mother Edmunda told me the particles of stone which I deposited under each station came from the Holy Land."

"The dedication of the stations was on the Feast of St. Francis last October. I understand we gain special indulgences when we make this Way of the Cross," said Cassie with great piety. She was very proud of Joe for his coming through for the Reverend Mother.

Johnny carried newspapers on his route each day after school and worked at Khoury's ice cream parlor. The year came to an end quickly. Anne had become the third highest-ranked graduate after Sonny and Joe. He did take honors in French during the graduation ceremony. Sister Maxentia was happy to have him return for the summer. Alma enrolled as a student in medical technology in Philadelphia. Louis was developing into an all-around athlete, which made his father very proud. Sylvia helped Louis deliver the paper route which he took over when Johnny left for Reading.

CHAPTER THREE

"What are you going to do after the summer comes to an end? Do you have any plans?" asked the Reverend Mother soon after her return to the motherhouse from a visit to Watertown, South Dakota.

"I don't have enough money for college. Perhaps I could get into the Air Force," answered Johnny dejectedly.

"Johnny, God will lead you in the right direction if you just stay open to His voice." She tried to raise his spirits in the one way she knew best. "Pray to Our Lady and Jesus for some guidance and you will do the right thing."

"I am sure there must be some way for me to eventually go to college. By the way, how was your trip to South Dakota?"

"Sister Edmundine did a truly wonderful job of helping the bishop raise money for St. Ann's Hospital. The Catholics had been wanting to build a Catholic hospital for quite a few years. When we agreed to staff the hospital, Bishop Brady of Sioux Falls began a public subscription drive. We now have a first rate facility, four stories high with a chapel. The doctors are very enthusiastic for its success and I have appointed Sister Edmundine as administrator. Overall, everything went very well. We are blessed."

"Do you expect to go to Brazil again?"

"Not this year. I have asked Sisters Lauretta and Chrysostoma to conduct a summer school for the Brazilian sisters. Sister Lauretta, our Supervisor of Schools, will share with them all the new methods she has learned in her position. Sister Chrysostoma will teach them a course in Gregorian chant and modern music now popular in the States. Two of the native Brazilian sisters will be coming to the U. S. to further their educations. It will be a new experience for the Brazilian province, since they will be the first sisters to do this."

August arrived very quickly for Johnny. He told the Reverend Mother he was going to enlist in the Air Force. The Korean War had started in June and he would have to sign up for the draft when he reached eighteen.

"I will not sign anything to allow you to enlist!" exclaimed his mother when he told her he needed his parents' signatures to join the Air Force at seventeen.

"What do you want me to do for the rest of the year? There are no jobs here in town." He was very unhappy about their attitude. Nothing he said would change their minds.

"Why don't you ask Mother Edmunda if you can stay on at the convent for a while?"

"I don't know how much work there is during the fall, but I guess I can ask."

The next day his parents discussed the whole idea.

"What can we do to keep him out of the war? Richard was killed in the last one and now we may be losing Johnny in this one."

"Mary, don't worry about him so much. He probably won't even pass the physical exam. He's so skinny and he gets those headaches."

"How did we get into another war so soon after this last one?"

"Mary, I don't know. All I know is I was too young for World War I and too old for World War II. I really wanted to get out there and fight and never got the chance."

When he returned to the convent Johnny asked his aunt if he could continue to work until December when he would be eighteen and could enlist in the Air Force on his own.

"Let's ask Sister Maxentia if there is enough work for you. " Maxie said 'yes' to the request.

"You are probably making a wise decision. The GI Bill has seen many veterans through college since the war ended. It may also be your key to a degree," his aunt added encouragingly..

"That's the way I feel. I don't understand why my mom and dad won't sign for me."

"Johnny, just be patient, December 4th will be here in no time. By the way, I will be away most of the fall. Mother Jerome and I will be visiting all of the Bernardine convents in the United States. Thank the good Lord the order continues to grow. We are now becoming more active in the midwest. Our first school there, St. Clement's in Dearborn, Michigan, will open in September. We are broadening out in so many directions the visits take up much more time than when we were concentrated in the northeast."

"You know, Mother, I always thought nuns spent most of their time in convents."

"Johnny, travel is part of the administrative duties of a Superior General. This year was unusual because of the two months I spent in Europe for the Holy Year. My summers are usually spent here in the motherhouse so that I can have some time with the sisters when they come for a retreat or simply a visit. These times are special for me for it gives me an opportunity to encourage each one of them to develop their spiritual lives as fully as possible. Some of them prefer to discuss their own requests and ideas personally. I can't always agree with their interests for so much depends on their proven talents."

"I guess that's why I have sometimes seen a number of them waiting in line to see you. Their comments about you have always made me feel happy to have you for my aunt."

"And I have always been delighted to have you as my nephew. I do hope you've enjoyed your time here with us."

"I certainly have, and I've always gotten a great tan."

CHAPTER FOUR

Johnny enlisted in the Air Force on his birthday, excited about what lay ahead.

"Dad, I passed the physical, and I'll be leaving for Lackland, Texas, on January 2nd," he proudly told his father when he went home for the last few weeks of 1950.

"Well, I don't know how you did it. They must be taking anybody who shows up," chided his father. Mary was pleased that her son was getting on with his life. She had found it difficult to forgive her husband for his drunken behavior when the Maryknoll priest had arrived at the apartment for the interview. Her son might be in the seminary instead of the Air Force if the priest had been able to get to know her son. Louie and Sylvia were thrilled to know their brother would be going to the biggest state in the country many miles away. Alma was enrolled in a medical technician school in Philadelphia and would not be home until the Christmas break.

"Did they tell you how to dress for the trip?" asked his mother.

"Don't dress up is the way they put it. They also said we would be getting military clothes when we arrived at the base. I guess I'll do as they say."

Christmas arrived quickly. The *Wigilia* supper was more poignant. As pleased as he was to be getting away, he still felt a great love for everyone in the family. His father cried as they broke the *oplatek* and shared it with each other.

He was sworn in as a member of the Air Force on January 2nd in Philadelphia and boarded a train with the other enlistees for the long trip to Texas. When they arrived at Lackland AFB near San Antonio they found themselves assigned to a small tent city set up to accommodate the thousands who had enlisted in the Air Force to avoid the draft. No one with any brain power wanted to end up in the Army or Marine Corps.

"We have no clothes for you at this time," shouted the sergeant when they arrived at the base. "You will be assigned to a tent which we expect you to take care of because that will probably be your home as long as you are here."

Twenty enlistees gathered in their basic training tent, found one cylindrical stove in the center of the tent and canvas beds to sleep on. The first ones in the tent claimed the beds closest to the stove. They had all been on the train for at least fifty hours without a change of clothes and with no promise of when the military would distribute their clothes to them.

"What are we supposed to do about showers?"

"There are some barracks you may be able to get into for your personal needs. Make certain you leave them in the same condition you find them in," answered the sergeant. "For now, make yourselves as comfortable as you can. Reveille will be at six."

The next morning they woke up to the coldest weather Texas had had in sixty years. Everyone had slept in their clothes just to keep warm. After another three days they finally went to supply for their military clothes. Then came the marching drills.

"At least the drills keep you warm," Johnny said to the recruit next to him. He and the others were from Pennsylvania or New Jersey. Their drill sergeant from Little Rock was not impressed. Next came the tests. Verbal and technical marks would determine the assignments they might get. Johnny's college prep course looked good to the examiner, since he had completed 4 years of Mathematics, English and Science and 3 years of History. His scores of 10 for verbal ability and 9 for technical ability placed him in a position for a good school assignment.

"I wonder where we will be going," was on the minds of the last four airmen who had not yet received their orders.

"Looks like you guys are heading for Keesler AFB in Biloxi to become control tower operators," announced their sergeant.

"All right!" shouted Johnny when he heard the news. He had no idea he would be given this kind of opportunity in the Air Force. The wait had been worthwhile. The others had been assigned to radio school, ground control approach, or aircraft maintenance. This school sounded best of all.

"You will complete your basic training at Keesler. Six weeks was not long enough. Since we're getting you out of here early there will be time for the additional weeks before your school begins. Good luck," added Sergeant

Wilson.

Johnny wrote to his family and the Reverend Mother about his good fortune.

Keesler AFB near Biloxi, Mississippi brought him a few surprises. The dentist removed a small particle of a tooth which protruded above another tooth and had a way of showing if he smiled too broadly. He felt like he now had the freedom to smile more comfortably. Control tower operators were given meticulous eye examinations to make certain of 20/20 vision. A pair of glasses corrected his slightly imperfect distance vision. He had never realized that was necessary. Basic training continued until the next session began for control tower operators. After twelve weeks he completed the course successfully. The airman who finished at the top of the class was promoted immediately to a corporal. Johnny came in second.

During his stay at Keesler, Johnny became a godfather for the first time. A neighbor from his home town was living in Mobile with her husband Charlie, who was a teacher and coach at a Catholic high school in that city. He had also come from Shenandoah which was a considerable distance for both of their families and friends. His wife, Mary, decided to invite Johnny to become their baby son's godfather since they had known each other all of their childhood years. He was surprised by the request and happily consented. A swim in the Gulf of Mexico added pleasure to his several visits to his hometown friends.

"Queer bait is what you are, Johnny," was the response he got from a fellow airman when he told him of his unexpected experience on a return bus trip from his last visit to Mobile. He was sitting in a seat next to a window when he dozed off after a full day of activity. On one of the stops a man in his twenties entered the bus and sat next to him.

"I've just returned from San Francisco," he said as he introduced himself.

"I'm just going back to Keesler after a visit to Mobile. I have a friend who plays football at the University of San Francisco. Some day I hope to get there myself. If you don't mind I'm going to get some sleep," Johnny answered quickly.

At eighteen, the movement of a bus was sometimes enough to arouse him when he suddenly realized how aroused he was getting. He moved toward the window as he felt the man's hand playing with the opening to his front pants pocket. Before he realized it he was climaxing right there in the bus. "What the hell is this guy doing?" he thought to himself as he wakened from his sleep. Just that quickly the bus had come to its next stop and the fellow exited quickly. This was the first time he had ever found himself in such a sticky position, did what he could to relax under the circumstances, and was relieved to get back to his barracks.

A letter from the Reverend Mother arrived around the time of his graduation from the control tower operator school. As usual, it was in answer to one he had written to her.

> *D.M. et O. Feast of the Visitation, B.V.M.*
>
> *Dear Johnny,*
>
> *Your letter was forwarded to me. I received it this morning. As busy as I am here in Watertown, S. D. at St. Ann's Hospital I cannot let letters go unanswered.*
>
> *Today is the 9th anniversary of my being in office. God, only God, ordained that on the day of Mary's "Magnificat," I became the "servant of God's servants." There was a Mass of Thanksgiving today in our chapel, the sisters sang beautifully; for the next three days, there will be masses petitioning blessings for the next three years, which, God willing, I must spend in the same capacity. The sisters baked a beautiful cake and made a table favor a clock, with the hands pointing to "nine on the dot." The dinner was a banquet and this evening there will be a party. All in all, the sisters could do no more to make the day a memorable one!*
>
> *Yet, how little they know what's transpiring in my soul, where nothing but God is of importance and meaning anymore. This morning after Mass, especially after Holy Communion, I thanked him for all graces received in the last nine years — not for the hospitals we built, not for the improvements made — no, not for anything material, transitory — but for what He has done within me — I renewed my consecration to Mother Mary and begged her to give me to her Son, that in union with Him, through the spirit of Love, I may belong entirely to the Eternal Father. I chanted the "Magnifcat" in the recesses of my heart several times — yet, little did I suspect that Mary would send me within the next three hours a seal of her complacency with my gift of self: your news of the cancer. From a full heart, I added one more "Magnificat." A cross? Yes, but what can compare with it in meaning? Eternity is for our enjoyment of the Triune God. How can a soul of any noble feelings think of this and not rejoice when she can earn at least a few copper coins to*

make returns to God for His eternal gift of Self? How can we prove to Him our love and confidence more than by accepting whatever He gives with a loving "Deo Gratias."

However, please do not misunderstand me. It isn't easy to take bad news and I accepted yours with a lump in my heart. But, you said so little. Cancer? Where? How do you know? Did the doctor say so? Any lab tests? I'll await more explanation.

July 8th, I'm leaving, God willing, to visit Salem, S. D. and Osceola, Nebraska. Then Sister Edmundine begs that I continue to Colorado Springs, Col., and by way of Cheyenne, Wyo. return home. I'll be in Reading, again God willing, about July 24th.

In prayer and love,
Mother M. Edmunda

The letter Johnny had written to her reflected his own suspicion that some white marks on his left hand appeared to deviate from the norm. Later he did find out that those marks were not an indication of any kind of cancer. His mother, of course, had been frantic with worry. She had wanted to come down to see him immediately. Fortunately the crisis passed. What he never realized, and would never realize for many years, was that he had been through another incidence of a cyclothymic disorder which had colored much of his life.

In late July he received orders for his next duty assignment. Japan is where he would spend the next 30 months of his Air Force career. As exciting as it sounded, there was always the possibility of ending up in Korea where a control tower operator faced extreme danger in any attacks by the enemy. The estimate was that in an air attack the tower would be destroyed in 30 seconds. At least he would have a seven-day furlough before leaving the States.

His mother already felt the loneliness gripping her as she hugged and kissed her son goodbye. She kept asking him why he had ever enlisted. Now he was heading off into the war zone with a good chance he could end up in Korea. Johnny always had that mixed feeling of wanting to show deep affection for his mother without surrendering his desire to get away. His father could not believe his son was actually doing what he himself had always wanted to do. They never had been able to develop a real closeness and the warmest his father got was a very congratulatory handshake and a pat on the back. Louis was in Reading for the summer working on the grounds of the St. Francis orphanage. Alma was at school in Philadelphia. Sylvia kissed her big brother goodby and said she would pray for him.

When Johnny reached Camp Stoneman, an army base near San Francisco, he learned the U.S.S. Bayfield would not leave for Japan for at least a week. He went into the city to see the university where Sonny was enrolled. A Jesuit priest greeted him and spent some time telling him that Sophia University in Tokyo was run by the Jesuits as well. He gave Johnny the name of a priest there and suggested he stop in to say hello when he was in Tokyo. The visit was worthwhile despite the absence of Sonny who had not yet returned to school.

The U.S.S. Bayfield sailed from San Francisco Bay with 500 airmen and 1,500 army combat troops at 2:30 p.m. on the 18th of August. The first few days the rough sea had many of the 225 men sleeping in Johnny's compartment throwing up everywhere.

"I've got to get out of here," he said to the guys lying in the cots around him. They all slept four high on beds of canvass cloth attached to iron poles with heavy cord. He walked as carefully as he could across the vomit-strewn floor, climbed up the metal ladders which were also covered in puke, to the deck. The fresh air warmed by the summer heat was his best antidote to the stale air below decks. Every morning sailors would hose down the ladders and the compartment to clean up the mess. By the fifth night Johnny decided to sleep on the deck. The chilly air and harder sleeping surface were a thousand times better than the smelly hold. His blanket helped.

The Navy gunners had some target practice when the ocean calmed down.

"Now I know what a cannon sounds like. My ears cleared up after about twenty minutes," he said to his pinochle-playing friends the day after the display of rockets, tracers, 38 mm cannon. At one point he had been just five feet away from one of the cannons.

"Anybody else see the flying fish this morning?" asked one of the players.

They all agreed the fish flew as much as two feet above the water. The fish were silvery in color, 2 to 8 inches in length, and were always fun to watch. They all hoped to one day see some porpoises or sharks.

After a week at sea, shots were given for the Japanese Beetle which no one seemed to know exactly what that meant. The chow was consistently good although one of the sailors told him the food was always better when no troops were aboard. One night he tried sleeping in the hold again. The sweat rolled off so heavily it was like sleeping in a Turkish bath. From then on he slept on the deck almost every night.

On August 28th they crossed the International Date Line. They went to bed on Sunday night and got up on Tuesday morning. There was now a 32-hour difference from the U.S. Captain Jordon, the Navy Commanding Officer conferred membership in the "Order of the Golden Dragon," the Ruler of the 180th Meridian, to all the non-sailors on board.

During the trip an Air Force Staff Sgt. suddenly died of a heart attack. Johnny saw his very overweight body in the medical station. They were to take his body to Japan and then ship him home.

On Sunday a Catholic Major led a small group of Catholics in the rosary and gave them a little talk with the announcement that he would lead the rosary every day until they reached port. Johnny thought that was pretty good of him. His leadership showed there were still plenty of good people in the world despite the evil influences around. One day he met and talked to a light-skinned, colored airman who had two rosaries, one a really big one, around his neck. Certain that he was Catholic, Johnny wanted to commend him on his spirit. "I am an Episcopalian," he said. "More important, I don't consider myself a Protestant." Surprised by the comment, Johnny finally realized that some Episcopalians have liturgies so close to the Catholic church they really don't believe there is any difference in their beliefs, except for the papal connection.

Johnny introduced himself to the American Baptist chaplain, the only clergyman on the ship. He attended his Sunday services, exchanged friendly smiles at some of his remarks. He wondered how one converted a good Protestant who does no apparent wrong and has Christ as the banner of his faith. Still, he was also thankful that he was living the one religion taught by Christ himself and not someone else's interpretation.

Soon after chow one morning the "PA" system's attention signal pierced the air: "All Air Force personnel whose last names begin with the letters from P to Z lay to the forecastle." Johnny made his way to the available space about the anchor chain and minutes later a young, studious looking officer stood before them. His manner was brisk and unpretentious.

"As you may have noticed by the medical insignia, I am a doctor. I've been asked to lecture on venereal disease. You are all familiar with the term. You've been lectured on it before since enlisting. There is little I can add. But let me tell you this from personal experience..."

He said he was returning to the Far East after an emergency leave and knew too well the absolute need for restraint in certain social activities if we didn't wish to return home with bodies weakened from constant combat with infections.

"Each of you has a responsibility," he said, "to your wife or future wife, and children. If you abstain, you will be able to face those kids with a clean conscience knowing you gave them the best start in life possible. If you choose not to abstain make certain you are protected."

He then dramatized some of the effects of syphilis, gonorrhea and herpes.

"That is all, gentlemen. I thank you for your attention."

In the enlisted men's lounge that night Johnny finished a long fifteen-page letter to his parents. With Japan so close and Korea a real possibility he wondered if perhaps they might have been right in their objections to his enlisting.

Why did I join? he asked himself.

"Hell, I don't know. Why did you join?" Smiling, his friend Jim Blake sat down beside him.

"Well, I guess I just wanted to ... But wait a minute, I was asking myself that question."

"You were. I took one look at you and decided you couldn't be thinking about anything else. My guess was right." We laughed.

"Why did you enlist, Jim?" Johnny asked.

"Why does anybody enlist? The draft call gets a little too close for comfort and you enlist in the Air Force or Navy. Simple."

"Yes, I guess so."

"Well, it's too late to worry about it now. I just hope I get assigned somewhere near Tokyo."

"I'll be satisfied anywhere in Japan. I'm not too sure about Korea."

"Well, Johnny, it won't be long before we find out. Right now it's time to hit the sack. See you in the morning."

"Good night, Jim."

The next day Johnny could hardly believe his eyes. The boat trip had taken so long he was totally enraptured to find the ship in gently rippling waters heading into a bay. A narrow strip of land stretched far to starboard on the horizon. Soon the blue Pacific was left for the velvety green waters of Tokyo Bay. Although they reached Yokohama harbor at dusk they could not get off the ship until noon the next day. The next destination for the airmen was Tachikawa, forty miles north of Yokohama. A rickety, toy-like train took three hours to reach the replacement depot. The small size of the train was a culture shock along with the narrow-gage tracks on which it rode.

At Tachikawa they were served a meal which sent Johnny's spirits soaring:

pork chops, french-fried potatoes, fresh vegetables and dessert — a really good American meal. The Japanese girl serving them was a whole new sight. He looked carefully at her dark brown slanted eyes, black hair and near white complexion, and when she smiled, protruding teeth with more gold than white showed. Sometimes just parting her lips would produce them. She was about five feet tall, waddled on stubby legs, and paraded her full breasts. For some reason she wasn't unattractive. He figured she was the sort of woman he would have to look at for more than two years.

The night was spent in a tent, one that was far superior to the one at Lackland AFB. There was a wooden floor, electric lights and the warmth of early September. A Catholic chaplain Johnny had met at Camp Stoneman was at the base. Too late to attend Mass, he did go to confession. While at the chapel he met a Japanese woman who spoke English and was the secretary to the base commander; unexpectedly she was also Catholic. In the late afternoon he went by bus to Tokyo. After a twenty-hour train ride he reached Misawa, on the northernmost end of Japan's main island of Honshu. Five of his friends from Keesler were already there. Although he made friends easily, these familiar faces helped.

The chaplain was an Irishman from Tennessee and a typical southerner. The chapel was a short distance from his barracks which would make it possible to for him to attend Mass several days a week.

"So here's our newest man," announced the tower chief when they met the next day.

"Yes, fresh out of school. Put me to work," he answered the Staff Sergeant who seemed easygoing and would probably be good to work with in the coming months.

Misawa AFB was two miles from the ocean, one hour flight time from Russian territory. Korea seemed very close. The base was home for F-84 and F-94 jet fighters which often flew to Korea. At least twice a month a jet cracked up on the runway. That brought out the fire trucks and ambulances and always intensified the pace of work in the control tower.

"How long do I have to stay in the "B" position before I can work the mike?" Johnny asked Dave Bowers, the trick chief who usually performed the primary position of controlling traffic on the mike.

"Give it about eight weeks. By then you should be on top of all the paperwork and have some expertise on the direction finder. In the meantime, keep memorizing every instruction I give to pilots. You have a copy of each procedure. The better you are at it the easier the mike job will be. And always keep your eye on what's going on around the field, including the taxiways. Keep the weather reports up to date."

"How about the light gun? That can be a little tricky as well. Perhaps I can do that sometime."

"Okay, but don't crack anybody up on the taxiways or somewhere else. Vehicular traffic is part of our responsibility as well."

Johnny knew he was going to love this job as a control tower operator. The 114-step climb to the operations area made him feel he was on top of everything. His world was falling into place. He began his first college course, General Biology, from the University of California at Berkeley Extension within a week after reaching the base. The cost for three credits was $13.50. Two classes each week were three hours long and lasted eight weeks. Forty percent of the thirty students were officers.

Professor Danforth believed in evolution. Although Johnny was familiar with the term, he never had any exposure to a teacher who taught it as more than a theory. The first test was a disaster - sixty percent of the class had failed. The professor said this one time he would scale the grades by adding ten points to everyone's grade. The ten points gave Johnny an "A." In the remainder of the course he continued to score well and ended up with an "A." He was delighted to know he could do so well at the college level.

Military life in Japan was far easier than in the States. Houseboys or "boysans" did all the cleaning, made beds, shined shoes and cleaned clothes for $2.00 a month. The inspection each Saturday morning meant getting dressed in class A uniforms, standing at attention and hoping the MI rifle was cleaned to perfection. For control tower operators the work schedule was divided into two five-hour shifts during the day and two seven-hour shifts at night. After each rotation a sixty-hour break followed, which allowed a great deal of recreation time.

One day some fifteen letters arrived for Johnny. The Reverend Mother's charismatic letter offered many good points on living a good Catholic life. She also noted his mother's loneliness about his being so far away as well as her dread of his possibly going to Korea. Then she told him of a visitor to Mt. Alvernia who was not only a major philanthropist to the southern missions, he also was capable of having boys released from the service in order to enter the seminary. She gave Johnny's name and address to him since she knew he still had hopes of becoming a priest. In a return letter to his mother he told her of the new confidence he now had that his hopes and dreams of the past few years might yet be fulfilled. He also apologized for not sending more money home.

Johnny wrote to his family and his aunt about the French Canadian missionaries active in Misawa and Hachinoke, about 12 miles south. An American Air Force chaplain, Father Maulier, had been stationed in Misawa for eighteen months and helped to establish the mission in the town adjacent to the base. He had recently been killed in a plane crash near Tokyo. A French Canadian missionary, Father Gaudry, was assigned to develop the mission Father Maulier had started. He often said Mass with no one in attendance. John went in to visit him one day. Father told him two Japanese nurses were in to see him and asked about the Catholic Faith. Johnny prayed they would be given the gift of Faith regardless of the missioner's early faulty attempts at communicating in Japanese which he still did not know very well. The chapel was a real beauty and his rectory was under construction so that in time conversions might develop.

By contrast the mission in Hachinoke was flourishing and the parishioners opened a school. The priest there was also a French Canadian from one of Canada's wealthiest families and was a zealot for the church. Johnny was beginning to believe the church in Japan was growing fast and if that growth continued the country would be a true daughter of Rome in no time.

In answer to one of his mother's letters he informed her the typhoon that the papers were reporting did not affect northern Honshu. The 100 mph winds had hit southern Japan. Misawa was affected only by all the planes that had been flown north to avoid the threatened devastation.

"Hey, is that the earth moving?"

"Johnny, if it isn't then we're both drunk," answered his friend. "Let's go into the next barracks and find out what's happening."

When they entered the hallway a light which hung on a long wire cord was swaying from the motion.

"We'd better stay outside. This could be an earthquake." Just that quickly the disorienting motion stopped. Later they learned it was an earthquake. It was not the only one he would experience during his tour of duty in Japan.

The weather was identical to what he had experienced growing up except for the closeness to the ocean. The typical fall mornings had a brisk breeze blowing and a chill in the air which really woke you up. The sunrises and sunsets were spectacular! Some sunsets left him spellbound. The incredibly beautiful rainbow-like colors, sometimes muted by a few clouds, made him believe Japan was truly the land of the rising sun. A walk into the nearby town gave a distinctly different aroma to his senses. The rice fields separating the base from the town were a challenge to one's nose. Honey pots, full of human excrement specially prepared for application to the fields, cast a reeking, pungent smell whenever a farmer passed by. The already-manured fields treated with this human waste were a constant affront to overcome during the growing season when airmen went into town.

On a recent trip into the small town of Misawa Johnny bargained with a shopkeeper for a reversible jacket for his brother Lou for 2500 yen or $6.50. He sometimes passed by the bars which always seemed to have somebody in them. By the end of October he had never spent a cent for beer.

"Sarge, how's it going this morning?" he asked Sgt. Gaffin who was on a binge and drinking like mad.

"Johnny, how are you, here, have a beer on me."

"Thanks, I will. These days off are like a three-day pass every week. Things couldn't be better." These beer treats came often enough so that he had no need to spend any of his own money.

That same late afternoon another earthquake hit and seemed to shake the barracks from its foundation. Everyone ran for the door to get outside. Then the lights went out, scaring the devil out of everyone.

"How often are we going to have these things?" Johnny asked.

"The Japs are used to it. We'll all be nervous wrecks if we get too many more," answered one of the airmen who had been there two years.

In his next letter to the family he shared the news that his friend Joe was happier than ever in his second year in the seminary. Johnny hoped that he would continue on to the altar. What a great day it will be for his family, he concluded. Johnny led some fellow airmen in the rosary at 5 o'clock Mass one evening since the chaplain's assistant wasn't present. There was a movie on chemical warfare one morning as part of their ongoing training. The work schedule changed — six hours on and 24 hours off. Five new tower operators arrived in October which meant the schedule could change again.

Ten months had passed since Johnny enlisted. A letter from the Reverend Mother took him by surprise. She had met the vocation director from the Society of St. Edmund at Notre Dame where a conference was held for superiors and directors who wanted to improve the quality of their vocation information. She had told Father Galligan of Johnny's continued desire to become a priest and to enter an order which did some missionary work in America or in foreign lands. Father told her they had a men's college near Burlington, Vermont, where he could enroll when he finished his term with the Air Force. If he got an early release, the Edmundites would simply require a physical examination, a letter of recommendation regarding his character, and his high school record. At the Reverend Mother's request, a priest who was the brother of one of the Bernardines, who knew him briefly in his hometown, had already written a letter of recommendation to the Edmundites who were apparently willing to accept him as a student. The priest who wrote the letter had not impressed his father because of his "cream puff" appearance and character. Although Johnny had the same opinion, he still appreciated the priest's willingness to meet his needs. He promised his mother that if everything went well she would be seeing him sooner than expected. He ended the letter with a description of a joke three tower operators pulled on his shift just prior to relieving them.

"Let's see if we can rattle Dick and his crew before we climb the stairs."

"What do you have in mind?"

"See if we can shake the tower enough to scare the hell out of them."

All three shook the wooden tower enough to send them scurrying out of the tower. Johnny laughed like mad when he found out what caused the panic. Dick was really burning. As a trick chief who was a stickler for regulations, he already had his college degree from Colgate and had made sergeant in one year. Johnny had great respect for him.

In the current *Stars and Stripes* he saw a picture of his friend Sonny along with Ollie Matson. In Sonny's last letter he said he was going to try his best to make the traveling squad. The game was at Fordham, so he obviously had made it. The University of San Francisco's football team was having a spectacular year; probably the best college team in the country.

In November Johnny took the physical examination for the Edmundites. Everything seemed to be working well in the effort to get an early release. His interest in the missionary effort in Misawa led him to visit the missionary one Sunday afternoon where they had a long talk.

"Father, when do you expect to move into the rectory?"

"It should be ready by the end of the month. Johnny, I was wondering if you would like to visit the mission at Hachinoke for a meeting with the missionary there whose parish has now grown to 250 people."

"That would be just great. Father, what do you think about my teaching an English course here at the mission?"

"I don't think I'm quite ready for that. I really would like to have the people get acquainted with me first. When the time comes a class in English would probably bring the people in by the dozens. I'm happy to know you are willing to take the time to do this. By the way, another French Canadian missionary will be here soon along with a woman catechist."

"Father, if the missionaries keep up this effort in about ten years half of Japan will be Catholic. As for me, I'll never be content until all America is Catholic."

"Johnny, it's good to have someone around with your optimism." The missionary thanked him for stopping by and wished him well.

"Johnny, let's take in the Service Club dance tonight. I went last week. The women aren't bad, not bad at all," called Jim Blake from the steaming shower room.

"OK Jim. Why not? I was a good dancer in high school. It might be fun," Johnny shouted back through the whir of his electric razor.

"I met a real beauty there. Took her in town for the night."

"So, I've heard," Johnny said with a laugh. There was always the chance he got more than he bargained for.

A familiar waltz greeted them at the club entrance.

"Sounds good, doesn't it? These Japanese can play," observed Blake.

The airmen who weren't dancing stood about the outer edges of the floor talking in groups and looking over the women. On the bandstand five Japanese musicians with greased, shining black, pompadoured hair tried their best to imitate their American brother musicians. They were doing a good job of it. "The Tennessee Waltz" filled the room as they reached the edge of the dance floor.

Johnny found himself staring into the bright soft brown eyes of one of the dancers. He couldn't turn away from them. Suddenly her partner whirled her into a step which took her out of his sight.

"Jim, do you know that one?" Johnny asked, trying to appear nonchalant.

"Which one? I didn't notice."

"That one, in the tight green dress."

"Oh yes, I see her now. Yes, I know her. I danced with her a few times last week. She's about the best I've seen over here so far. I think her name is Linda or something like that."

"Ah so," Johnny answered. It was an expression they had picked up from the Japanese. The dance ended. With a little uncertainty Johnny walked toward the chair she was about to take. She noticed his approach and smiled. What a surprise! No buck teeth and no gold.

"The next dance?" he asked. She nodded approval. Johnny stood before her a bit perplexed. This was something new. She probably spoke no English and he knew next to nothing of Japanese. The disturbing silence was broken when the band swung into the next dance, a jitterbug. He had been one of the best jitterbug dancers in high school and wanted to show her how good he was. She deferred the opportunity. She didn't want to jitterbug.

He took the seat beside her to wait for the next waltz. After watching the dancers awhile, he turned to her. She was looking at him with those warm bright eyes and smiled again. When she turned away he continued to look. Her nose disappeared between her eyes with just enough to form nostrils, full lips parted slightly and her chin squared sufficiently to save her face from becoming a full moon.

"At last," he said as the band moved into a waltz. He held her close, her forehead barely reached his chin.

"How long you stay this base?" she asked him in her halting English.

"Only a few months," he answered. "And you, how long you stay this base?" he mimicked playfully. His fingers went to the back of her neck beneath the curled edges of her well brushed hair.

"Oh, I work for captain and family one year."

"Your name is Linda, isn't it?" His eyes fell to her breasts momentarily.

"My name? My name Linda. How you know?"

"Oh, I just know. You have a Japanese name, no?"

"Yes, my Japanese name Masako. But you call me Linda. What your name?"

"Johnny," he answered. "Only I like Masako better. I'll call you Masako." The dance ended and they returned to their chairs.

"Do you like working for Americans?"

"I like you," she answered.

"Ah so," he said. They both smiled. They danced all that night and for several weeks Friday's dance became a standing date. Meanwhile another roommate took the place of an operator who had been assigned to Korea. One day at noon, after working in the tower Johnny returned to his room and found his new roommate unpacking his duffel bag. He then learned that Dave, his new roommate, had begun keeping a girl in town. One night, as Johnny was leaving the room Dave grilled him a little bit.

"When are you going to start enjoying life, Johnny?"

"I'm happy."

"Maybe, but you'd better get some while you're here to get it. There's nothing like it." He sounded like a contented husband.

"I'll get around to it one of these days." That night Masako looked even more terrific. When he took her hands in his he realized how much he had been yearning to see her. She responded to his close embrace by moving in closer. His blood warmed to her nearness. She was tender, hopeful. He began to feel he just had to have her.

"Tonight, you go back to barracks?" she asked.

"That's up to you, honey," he said confidently. Her eyes gave the answer he awaited. Slowly they walked the half mile into town. They were in a different world outside the gate. They could see it, and they could smell it. Ten o'clock. The souvenir shops, with their already familiar cheap silks; richly embroidered, though sometimes gaudy kimonos; photo albums, chinaware, and an endless assortment of trinkets had their sliding doors open for the remaining hour's business before the invading Americans hurried back to the base to make curfew.

"Mamasan's," the "Star," the "Shamrock," and countless other beer halls rocked with the effects of Nippon-saturated airmen and women hustlers. Besides the souvenir shops and beer halls, the remaining structures could be counted upon to accommodate a yen-spending Yank with other ideas. Girls, reeking with cheap perfumes, patrolled the street or stood in the shadows, waiting to "ketch GI." In every available patch of ground something was planted. The overwhelming smell of freshly fertilized rice paddies came from behind the small houses. Also, a few merchants could always be counted on to add some fuming fish to the pungent-smelling air.

Despite it all, they found a room. As they stepped inside the tension grew.

"Shoes, Johnny!" she exclaimed, smiling at his ignorance.

"Oh, yes, I forgot." Promptly he took off his shoes and placed them outside beside hers. She turned to him. His arms encircled her as he kissed her with a tenderness he had expected to have only for the girl he married.

"Johnny," she whispered. Lost in the desire of wanting her, it mattered little that no bed furnished the room. They sank to a quilt spread along one of the cardboard-thin walls. He hovered a moment as her lips brushed his chest while his heart pounded furiously. Her fingers dug into his back, she whimpered, and the beat of never-ending time was theirs. Whatever moral doubts he had were drowned in the moist sweetness of unrestrained lovemaking. In the morning they made love again, without any protective prophylactic as they had used earlier. He felt totally entranced by her.

Johnny could not wait until the following Friday night dance at the club. His roommates knew he had hit pay dirt with his girlfriend and were happy to know he could now really enjoy his time in Japan.

"Friday night is here, Johnny, let's go get 'em." When they reached the club all he could think of was holding his Masako once again. He couldn't spot her anywhere.

"Are you Johnny?" asked a girl he had seen with Masako on other nights.

"Yes, where is Linda?" using the name most people called her.

"Linda say I tell you her mamasan very sick. Papasan say come home."

"Any address or telephone?" asked Johnny.

"No. She say she very sorry, she love you, and *sayonara*."

Disappointed by this news, he left the club, stopped by the chapel and tried to make sense of all that had happened. He prayed before the tabernacle which was kept in a smaller room where he always felt especially close to his Lord. One thing he had done all of his life was to pray for forgiveness of all his sins, the discipline to live his life better and to do whatever God wanted of him no matter how imperfect he might be. He also realized that if he never met Masako again he had known a deep sexual love he had never experienced before. He thought about Sister Eymard's pleasures in life. This undoubtedly was one of the big ones. Perhaps he would yet find the treasure which would replace it.

Psychology 101 followed immediately after General Biology. Johnny plunged into the study of a subject he believed would shed some light on his own emotional makeup. The Biology course was a perfect intro, since he felt more familiar with the physical functions of the body also covered in Psychology. The professor was not as likeable as his General Biology teacher; however, he was so pleased about continuing his college courses he didn't really care about the man's personality. The course was very helpful. He believed he was getting a great deal of insight into his feelings and attitudes which made him feel like he was growing in ways he had not known before. There was a freedom which lightened his thought processes. He could almost feel the growth and maturity developing within him. The course was somewhat more difficult, or perhaps it was the professor's methods, that he ended up with a "B". In his next two courses in first year Reading and Composition and an English Literature course he passed with A's.

"Johnny, you must have an IQ of 140. You're beating the pants off most of the other students," his trick chief said to him one day.

"Dick, maybe it's because I like the idea of getting my first college credits from Berkeley."

"Whatever it is, you're doing very well."

He always had a lot of respect for Dick and appreciated his comments about his classwork.

Johnny's first birthday away from home gave him much to think about. His mother wrote a letter, among her many others, that she and the Reverend Mother were offering a Mass in Poland for his intentions. The Reverend Mother had always kept in touch, by mail, with her father's family in Nowy Targ and Krakow. The Mass would be said in Nowy Targ, her father's birthplace. Johnny thanked his mother for remembering his birthday in such a special way. The Reverend Mother had visited his parents' home recently and commented to Johnny that the apartment was taking on a new look with the new furniture bought primarily by the money he was sending home.

The work in the tower was losing its glamor. He and many of the other operators had 26 months left of their tour of duty in Japan. Everyone wanted to get back home to get on with their lives. He was becoming more confident that his own wish would still come true and prayed to see his family again much sooner than scheduled.

Of course, work in the tower still had its exciting days. In early December, after three days of snow, the traffic was the heaviest since he had arrived at Misawa. With only two operators on the shift in zero-zero weather the visibility was miniscule. Coordination with GCA, the ground control approach operations, was of paramount importance. Suddenly, right before he and his fellow operators were about to finish their shift, a C-54 made a missed GCA approach and came within ten feet of the tower. The plane just loomed up in front of them. How it missed the D.F. antennas they would never know. The experience convinced them that those who said the tower work wasn't really that important and doesn't really have any danger or thrills simply didn't know any better. It made him determined to become as good an operator as possible for as long as he was in the Air Force.

Father Eymard Galligan sent him a letter right before his birthday officially accepting Johnny into the Society of St. Edmund, and St. Michael's College, as a first year student. He wondered how long before the dream would become a reality. He would also become more serious about saving for his college expenses, which would mean less money for his family. He decided to send his mother $25 a month for the household and would put the rest of his pay in bonds. He told his mother she could keep the bonds in a bank deposit box. In that way, if anything happened to him she would have the money for her own use. He also decided it was time to challenge his father to become a more disciplined husband and dad by writing a personal letter to him.

> *Dear Dad,*
>
> *I don't know if this letter is going to do any good but I must write it and pray that it is not in vain. Whatever your opinion, please answer me because our lives just can't continue to go on this way.*
>
> *As a father I love and respect you because of the gift of life you've given me in conformity with the will of God, but frankly, as a man I've found nothing in you to make me really proud so that I might say, "that's my old man," and "what a guy!" You know Dad about my plans for the priesthood and yet you continue in the same old way. You let me down once, I hope you don't do it again.*
>
> *What is it that keeps you from bestowing all your loyalty to your family? Mother wrote a pretty discouraging letter and I don't think you're being fair to us. She never says much and always taught us to respect you whether you knew it or not. Just how much suffering you've caused her is known by God alone. It's about time you started living up to our religion and make a little up to her.*
>
> *Why don't you wake up to the fact that people lose respect for those who can't control their passions, whether it is for drink or lust? Look at your own life! George Osinski gave up hope in you, Uncle Frank surely has asked you to wise up, and now Mr. Wiernicki couldn't even find room for you at his daughter's wedding. These are cold facts, dear Father, and they must hurt you deeply. I have made some close friendships with Sonny, Joe and Dick. If I knew that in my later years they would be disappointed in my record, I wouldn't feel very great about it either.*
>
> *You have two kids who are now at an age level where impressions last longest. Louis needs someone he can look up to with respect and admiration. I always wanted to have someone I could esteem and cherish. I'm sorry but you fell far short. There was only one incident in our lives that made me stop and think about you with a certain amount of respect and that was when you'd kneel down to say some night prayers...on the other hand, the many times I've seen you drunk, miss Mass, never have I seen you take Communion or maybe I'm mistaken. There were a few Christmas morns and Easter confessions that I do remember.*
>
> *Why not start anew from this blessed Christmas and really get*

on excellent terms with God and your family? We are more than willing to forget the past for the promise of a bright future. Tomorrow I'll be nineteen, Dad, and we've come a long way together. Maybe the reason for our spiritual ills has been a lack of prayers. From the fourth of this month to Christmas my intentions at Mass, Communion, etc. will be for you, Dad. Please try to cooperate with the grace of God and all evil longings will be subdued. Will you not pray for my intentions for a like period of time because it isn't the easiest thing in the world to be good even in the service?

Try reading some good literature on the saints during these long winter evenings, it still isn't too late for all of us to be saints if we only try a bit. It's only because I love you, Dad, that I'm writing this letter, please don't let it go unanswered and keep it between you and me if you wish. All the others have to see is good example.

I've been accepted by the Edmundite Fathers but I doubt that it will mean much since little has been said about the case for a time.

God keep you near and dear to us,
Johnny

P.S. Please write to me and give me the low down on everything.

On December 16th Johnny flew to Tokyo to take an examination to be a certified civilian control tower operator as well as military. Another operator was also going down for three days. In Tokyo they went to Sophia University to meet Father McCoy, S. J., who greeted them in place of Father Miller who was away.

"Father, my name is John. Father Miller's friend at the University of San Francisco suggested I stop by to see him when I got to Tokyo. We are here to take an examination for the CAA to qualify as civilian control tower operators. This is my friend from Misawa."

"Good to meet you. I'm glad you took the time to visit us. Sophia is doing very well these days."

"You know, I was surprised there was a Catholic University in Japan. How long has it been here?"

"Well John, the idea for the university dates back to 1549 when St. Francis Xavier arrived in Japan. Admiring the Japanese temperament, he wrote to Rome of his wish to establish a university in the Japanese capital. It was 1908 before three Jesuits arrived in Japan to prepare the establishment of the school. The first classes, for men only, began in 1913. We've been here ever since. If you like, I can take you for a look around the site."

"Father, thanks very much. I just wanted to make certain I said hello. And thanks very much." The Jesuit could not have been more gracious during the visit.

Johnny and his friend took a walk along the Ginza, stopped at the Mikimoto pearl store and took pictures of the moat around the emperor's grounds. The Diet was very impressive. A large, long line of communists were demonstrating outside waving red flags. They stayed away.

The Midnight Mass at Christmas was standing room only in a beautifully decorated chapel. Johnny was very happy that night for he knew he would possess in his heart, as many Christians, especially Catholics, the Christ who was born so long ago, yet lived with them in the Eucharist. He believed Catholics had so much to be thankful for and hoped that one day the whole world would worship in the same way, Christ's way.

The squadron's commanding officer hosted a Christmas party for them. Johnny danced with the officer's wife. It was good to be near an American woman again. Major Parker knew him well since he also took the courses from Berkeley.

New Year's eve was a good reason to have a party in the barracks for those who did not want to go in town. With curfew at 11 PM there was no sense in leaving the base. Six guys decided to play poker and drink Scotch. Johnny had never drunk Scotch before. His poker expertise was minimal.

"Come on Johnny you have to help us with these bottles of Scotch."

"Well I'll give it a try," he said. By midnight he was totally drunk. When he got up to try to go to his room his head began spinning. He wanted to get to the latrine before he threw up everything in his stomach. Dick realized what was happening, ran to his aid only to get messed up from Johnny's vomiting. Dick decided they both needed a shower, undressed Johnny and dragged him to the shower before putting him to bed. Johnny barely felt the cold water hitting him and only the next morning realized what a good friend Dick had been. He never drank Scotch again. Perhaps that was one pleasure he would forego.

The family missed him that first Christmas season away from home.

"Oh, Blessed Mary, why did he have to enlist?" cried his mother as she prepared the Christmas dinner.

"Mom, he likes what he's doing in the control tower. I wish I was as happy as he seems to be. My school work is almost impossible. They crowd so much into the courses I wonder if one year is long enough to learn it all," remarked his sister Alma who was home for the holidays from her school in Philadelphia.

"Mary, you worry too much. He's in Japan. He'll probably stay there," his father exclaimed.

"Mom, he goes to Mass a lot. That should help him get ready for the seminary," commented his young sister Sylvia.

"Seminary? I think we can forget about that. If your Daddy had tried to stay sober Johnny might be at Maryknoll now. Look at all the things he tells us he is doing which sound like they're getting him ready for Korea."

"Yeah, I think he's going to be fighting there," announced Louis, who liked the idea of his brother's getting into the war.

"See that last letter he wrote? They were digging foxholes four miles from the airfield," continued his mother. "What's that all about?"

"Look, he has the right attitude. He told us how a tower operator might have to direct traffic from a jeep when at an advanced base and he had no trouble with that. He told us directly, 'what would I be doing in the service if I didn't want to get to the front line or have some part in doing the job cut out for us?'" observed his father.

"I know only one thing, if he doesn't come home safely I don't think I'll be able to take it! I have told Mother Edmunda to keep trying to get him out of the Air Force early."

CHAPTER FIVE

The Reverend Mother continued to pray that the philanthropist from Washington and the Edmundite Fathers would facilitate Johnny's release from the service. She also steadfastly believed that whatever finally developed was not in her hands alone. The Holy Spirit would move in its own direction, with her own 'Amen' given to the result.

The common prayer life of the community was central to each of her days. Morning prayers were said from the Seraphic Manual which included the Little Office of the Blessed Virgin Mary. Since many of the sisters were conversant in Polish that language was used although an English version was included in the same manual. Prime, Sext and None were all read at this time followed by a one-half hour of meditation.

The chaplain then offered his daily Mass from which the Reverend Mother found the strength for her usually long hours of work. She honored and cherished the promise of Christ's Body under the presence of bread. Her deep commitment made her feel united to Him in an almost mystical togetherness. She belonged to her Lord and no other. Nothing ever interrupted the oneness she felt in those moments of spiritual food flowing through her body and soul. She often prayed that her nephew would someday reach this same level of faith.

In January of 1952 the Reverend Mother officially opened a Juvenate in Salem, South Dakota. This Juvenate would be more convenient for those who wished to enter the Order and avoided the overcrowding of the facilities at Mt. Alvernia. The Brazilian Province had its own Juvenate which was beginning to attract a greater number of aspirants, especially from the northern part of the country.

"Mother, we have received a letter from the owner of a hospital in Newport

News, Virginia. His father willed it to him and he apparently would like to sell the hospital to us if we have any interest."

"Thank you sister. It looks like the Bernardines are getting a reputation in the medical field," answered the Reverend Mother to her secretary, Sister Chrysostoma.

Before long the evening paper of Newport News reported that negotiations were taking place for the sale of the Elizabeth Buxton Hospital to the Bernardine Sisters. The new name of the 150-bed hospital would be Mary Immaculate. The editor of the paper received a number of letters from residents who objected to the renaming of the hospital. They believed the Elizabeth Buxton Hospital should retain its name. This apparent evidence of anti-Catholic prejudice was quickly overcome by the same paper which featured Dr. Buxton, the previous owner and now chief of staff and surgery as well as chief consultant, and Sister Irena, the first administrator appointed by the Reverend Mother.

In Saginaw, Michigan, the bishop bought a Lutheran hospital, remodeled and prepared it to become the Saint Francis Home for the Aged. He asked the Reverend Mother for her support to have the Bernardines staff the facility. She and the councillors agreed to his invitation and provided seven sisters within the next year to minister to the old people he loved so much. A resident chaplain celebrated Mass every morning and ended the day with Benediction and an evening rosary.

Many duties filled the year 1952, including the appointment of Mother Cantalice as the new head of the province in Brazil. Despite her full schedule, the Reverend Mother wrote a warm letter to Johnny which brought him up to date on her travels during the year.

August 18, 1952

My dearest Johnny,

It is long, so very long, since I have written to you — I mean long for the yearning that I had to write and could not do so. Since July 10th, I have actually lived in my traveling bag. Here's my schedule:

July 10-12 — by car, to and back, Newport News, Va.

July 13-16 — to and back from 1741 Centre Ave., due to Uncle Joe's death.

July 16-28 — to and back, Detroit and Salem, S . D. (returned by car - 1600 miles)

Aug. 9-13 — to and back, Scranton, Buffalo, Detroit and Notre Dame, Ind., by car — to attend the First National Congress for Religious with representatives from Rome presiding.

I should be in N. Y. on August 20th, to attend the True Devotions Conference with the Montfort Fathers, but I just can't. Physically, I'm too exhausted; then, I must have a conference for the sister-retreatants and conduct the Renewal of our Consecration to Mary before they leave on August 25th.

I simply cannot forget Uncle Joe. He was far deeper and of a more sterling character than we could judge. When I think how patiently he bore his physical ailments, I'm blushing for the manner in which I can take the weakness and exhaustion, which is overtaking me. In his last days, his ever present smile and jokes led us into believing that death is not too near. He died without becoming a burden for even one second. Now, I understand that he spent his sleepless nights walking and battling with the thought of near death. He simply expressed this to me on May 30th: "I just can't sleep; I'm worried about the few dollars or even cents that I owe to others. I didn't worry so much before when I owed hundreds." He was just and, doubtless, feared to die owing anyone a penny. He told me that he was on the decline since Christmas.... He made sure that Ciocia was left with not a cent of debt. He emptied his pockets of money on entering the hospital - not keeping a cent for himself. No wonder that he looked so peaceful after death; his sweet smile of the last days lingered in the casket. He lost much weight, but had the appearance of a just man in sleep.

The first few days I knew he was near me. I prayed for him — usually a prayer with him. At the funeral Mass, he suddenly grew distant. From my friends alone, he had received at least 200 Masses. If he isn't in heaven by now, he is near it, I'm sure. I had a strange experience when I rose in the plane at Minneapolis, on July 19th. I always commend my trips to Mother Mary; at times, I can imagine her, in a blue mantle, gliding above the plane, train or car, in which I'm traveling. I prayed, when the plane rose at Chicago, but failed to see Mother Mary. However, at Minneapolis, I saw, with the eyes of my soul, Mother Mary; and suddenly, out of the clouds to her left, came Uncle Joe, serene, dressed in a sport shirt of Her mantle-blue, with an open collar, wafted in the breeze and Uncle said: "Mother, take care of my sister." You can imagine how this affected me. I was filled with joy and gratitude and peace.

Your last three letters convince me that Bozia and Mother Mary are with you; but, the evil spirit is there, too. However, do not fear, Johnny dear. Keep close to Jesus in the Eucharist and hold tightly to Mother's arms. All will be well! Re-consecrate yourself to Mary — and, then, live on in full confidence in Her. Pray to her often by reciting the efficacious 3 Hail Marys with the ejaculation - "Mary, my good Mother, I place my trust in thee."

I am sending you a few spiritual books. Read them slowly and carefully. Meditate on this text and put into practice all that you can. If you can speak to a priest, do so often. If you can't find one who understands you, write to Father Galligan. He made it a point to meet me at Notre Dame. It was only for a brief space of a few minutes, but long enough to bring us closer to each other spiritually. Would you want me to write to him and advance the thought of an advanced standing college work in Latin I and French I? I wonder if I could help you with this? I touched upon this, when speaking to Father at Notre Dame.

Relative to your difficulties with chastity, don't be surprised. After all, our souls live in bodies, that are cognizant of their natural right to procreation. There is absolutely nothing wrong with this natural privilege of ours. Hence, in our lives for God, it is better to forego the negative aspects of this problem. Look at it from the positive aspect. Johnny dear, by consecrating our bodies to God, to Christ, our Spouse, we become the progenitors of souls - thousands of them. Christ does not demand of us to renounce the right to be fathers and mothers. He elevates this right to the supernatural order. Johnny, by consecrating your body to God, with Christ through the Holy spirit you will bring myriads of souls to the Eternal Father, who will bless you for all eternity. As a priest, a God-fearing and loving priest, in the confessional, in the classroom, on the pulpit, you'll be able to nurture souls, souls and souls - yes, those souls who are so hungry for God today. And, what can we say about the power of a priest at the altar? What can't he do for souls, when Christ in the Eucharist waits for his summons? We can't do much, true, but God is ever ready to aid us. He simply wants us to feel our misery and, then, throw ourselves into His Merciful Love. Do this, through Mary. All will be well now and forever after.

Pray for me, Johnny. I'm on the decline, too. From May 1951 to January 1952 I lost 40 pounds for no reason. With vitamins and good food, I can't regain a pound. Of course, I'm working too hard and traveling too much - but, I did all this before also. (I wasn't 54 years old before! This makes a difference, doesn't it?) This decline doesn't bother me, however, spiritually, I do want to be a giant — and this is not easy for me, as it is so difficult for you. I need your prayers. How vanity and sham are revolting to me! Only God can satisfy the hunger and thirst of my soul.

Louis is doing very well here at the grounds of the orphanage. In the spending of money he is easier to control than you. Of course, he is younger than you, but I still think he is easier to handle than my Johnny was.

God's blessings and Mother Mary's care and love be yours always!

Love In Jesus and Mary,
M. M. Edmunda

Johnny was deeply pleased, as usual, to hear from his aunt. Her description of his Uncle Joe's last days made him wish all the more for some way to return home at least for a visit. Thirty months seemed much too long an absence. His younger brother and sister were growing up so quickly he wondered what they might look like when he finally reached home.

The Reverend Mother, hopeful that she might spend a few months at the motherhouse after the hectic schedule she had been on, received notice that Monsignor Larraona, representative of the Sacred Congregation of Religious had invited all General Superioresses to Rome for a meeting to take place September 11-13. She believed a journey by ship across the Atlantic would be cheaper and more relaxing. Her companion and councillor of the order, Mother Daniela, and she would be able to regain the lost strength and energy from their administrative responsibilities of the year. Of course there was no way she could have refused the invitation. Rome was the Mecca of the Catholic universe dating back to St. Peter.

With so little time to prepare for the journey, their travel agency reserved a flight on TWA. The thought of a boat trip simply would not fade away. At the agency she suddenly discovered that the S. S. United States was scheduled to leave New York City on September 5th with arrival expected on September 10th at LeHavre, France. Mr. Sexton of the Dill Travel Agency accomplished the impossible. He secured their passports in record time and handed them to the Rev. Mother on September 4th. Praying for the blessing of the Sacred Heart of Jesus, after a Mass for a happy trip on the first Friday of September they left Reading and arrived at the pier at 10 A.M. The Reverend Mother's sister-in-law, Cassie, was at the port along with a number of Bernardines to bid them farewell.

In a descriptive report available to the entire community she noted that the S. S. United States was the largest passenger ship ever built in America and the fastest liner in the world. Its maiden voyage, made on July 3rd, 1952, would make its fifth crossing of the Atlantic. Little had she dared to think that in less than three months, the "marvel" which she admired from the windows of Mary Immaculate Hospital would, God willing, take her back to Paray-le-Monial for days of prayer, which was the only wish her heart could cherish. "God is good!" she thought. Should their visit follow the projected schedule, they would go to Paray-le-Monial after the meeting at Rome and spend several days at Rue du Bac, Paris, at the foot of the altar where the Miraculous Medal was revealed to St. Catherine Laboure´. The statue of Our Lady of Victories, where Louis Martin prayed his Little Queen to health, would be the next stop in Paris. Their pilgrimage would close with a few days at Lisieux, from where it was only a short distance to LeHavre.

Their two-passenger cabin with adjoining shower was perfect except for the lack of a porthole from which they might have enjoyed the sight of the ocean day and night. The 1700-passenger list included 450 in the second cabin class. A bishop from the Far East and two Jesuits made themselves known to the Bernardines. The Jesuits had been in Auriesville, N. Y., for a year to make their "Tertian" Novitiate, and their presence made it possible for the nuns to hear two Masses each day. One of the Jesuits, who belonged to the Oriental Byzantine Rite, always served Communion under the two species of bread and wine.

On September 9th, both Jesuits said Mass for the intentions of the entire congregation. The first Mass was said in thanksgiving for all graces received by each sister and to petition blessings necessary for each of them. The second Mass was said in thanksgiving for the singular grace of having been solemnly consecrated as a congregation to the Immaculate Heart of Mary and to request for each one the graces necessary to live this consecration to the best of everyone's ability. The day closed unfavorably as they passed the Irish coast and entered the English channel. The lack of Dramamine had them swaying and rocking as they made their way to the dining room on a higher deck. Thanks to the handrails they reached their table safely, found the menu unappetizing and left within minutes after their meals were served. Mother Daniela surrendered the contents of her stomach over the rail. They retired early. After a 5:30 A.M. Mass they went through the port formalities and were seated in a special train for Paris at 7:30. The gracious French had not even opened their bags.

Within four hours the train reached Paris. The sky was overcast at LeHavre and in Paris it was drizzling. From the "Gare St. Lazare" they were taken by taxi to "Gare des Invalides," a general office for all airlines. Their first French dinner at the station was expensive but most unpalatable. Two Mercy Sisters from Merion, Pa., had flown TWA that day to attend the conference. They were both surprised the Bernardines had been able to travel by ship. At the Rome airport they met the Sisters from St. Mary's Hospital, St. Louis, Mo., the Dominican Sisters from Adrian, Mich., and the Presentation Sisters from San Francisco. When they entered the dining room of the Mariamonte Convent in Rome they met the Loretto Sisters, Nerinx, Ky., and an Immaculate Heart Sister and a Mercy from Los Angeles. The United States representation was numerous. All had flown and all felt it was very unfair to be summoned at such short notice.

Father Larraona, the Secretary of the Congregation of Religious, who represented the congregation at the Notre Dame meeting, was chairman of the Congress at Rome. He had returned from the U.S.A. a changed man. He said on his return he had come from a different world and had seen marvelous things in America. He was determined to learn American English. Father Heston, of the Holy Cross Fathers, who acted as the English interpreter told them that Father Larraona was favorable to all that is American. He marveled at the various orders' progress in all lines and could now understand how the apparently easygoing American could also be deep spiritually. He hoped to make the nuns of Italy as he found the nuns in America.

The Reverend Mother and Mother Daniela were housed at the Marymount Convent of Rome for the Congress. Marymount was built in the same locality as the home where St. Agnes had lived her short life. Some catacombs can be reached from an entrance in the basement. The street on which St. Agnes walked was the same Via Nomentana as it is today. Along this street St. Agnes had been dragged to the home of the young Roman where she spurned his promises, checked his advances, and won her double crown of virginity and martyrdom. On the feast of St. Agnes, a procession in which a lamb with a white crown and a lamb with a red crown are carried in shallow baskets, in honor of her virginity and martyrdom. Temporarily chloroformed, they often reach for the flowers on the altar when they recover from the sedative, which is always an interesting sidelight of the ceremonies. From their wool, palliums are made for all Archbishops.

The Congress opened at the Institute of Maria Assunta. To accommodate the unexpectedly large number of attendants it was transferred to the Jesuits' Gregorian University. The American sisters were not especially content with the stated themes of the Congress:

1) To form a commission of Mothers General in Rome to act as a liaison between the Sacred Congregation of Religious and congregations around the world, and

2) to found a Pontifical Institute at Rome for Sisters.

The Americans believed most problems were better solved in their own congregations, and there were already national institutes in place which would be more efficacious than Rome-centered, Italian speaking institutes.

The conferences were chiefly in Italian, with one in English, French, Spanish and German. The Reverend Mother found the process trying, since many lasted more than an hour and the mimeographed summaries were entirely too brief. For example, the Bishop Sheen of Italy, Father Lombardi, S. J., gave a 75-minute talk which was reduced to a 19-line resume. Jesuit Father Emile Bergh delivered an excellent conference in French which captured the Reverend Mother's total interest. "Demands of the Life of Perfection in Our Times: an Examination of Conscience." To her the priest's thoughts touched many of the things which had weighed on her day and night for several weeks. She promised her sisters that they would hear of these, God willing, in the near future. She asked them to pray that God's grace be with her and all of the sisters, for only with God's grace can they capture the *spirit of our Holy vocation* and once they are imbued with this spirit they will run, not walk, along the paths of God's Love. With our saintly Archbishop O'Hara, let us take St. Bernard's words "Following Her, you will not go astray," for our motto in this all important duty of our lives, *our sanctification* — for Mary, our Mother, will lead us safely and directly to Her Son, Jesus Christ. When the conference ended Mother Daniela did some sightseeing around Rome. The Reverend Mother, still feeling exhausted from the hectic tenth year of her term in office, spent her time in prayer, writing and resting.

On September 15th an audience with the Holy Father took place at Castel Gondolfo, his summer residence built on the rim of a volcano not far from the Vatican. Pius XII spoke in five languages, thanked all of the sisters for their prayers for his intention and underlined that he needed them badly. After the speech, he stepped down and the siege on the Pope's person began. The Americans were shocked! Words cannot express the picture ... true Italian mob psychology. Because of this the Americans were invited to a separate room where the Holy Father came to have a picture taken. The Holy Father looked well in spite of his age, his worries, and a cold. He was full of energy, vitality and was quick-of-movement as always.

After the audience the Reverend Mother spent time in St. Peter's: went to confession, prayed before the altar tomb of Pope Pius X, the altar of Our Lady of Seven Dolors, and especially in the chapel of the Blessed Sacrament. She commended all the Bernardine sisters and their dear ones to St. Peter, to Blessed Pius X, and to the Eucharistic Lord through the Sorrowful Heart of Mary. Her gift to all was a garland of prayers. She prayed that the Heart of Jesus, through the Heart of Mother Mary grant to every dear sister whatever graces she needed to make her a *Saint. Only this matters.* That her prayers would be found acceptable was her final wish.

On September 16th the American sisters visited Nettuno, the site of the American servicemen's cemetery. There were many improvements from the Reverend Mother's visit two years before. The wooden crosses were replaced by marble ones and the triple chapel for Catholics, Protestants and Jews was half completed. The scene moved everyone to tears. The marking of some of the graves, "Comrade in Arms, Known Only to God" was especially touching. In her report to the community she did not mention that her own nephew, Richard, was buried there. The next day the Reverend Mother and Mother Daniela spent the Feast of the Stigmata of St. Francis at Monte Sacro, in a villa purchased for the Felician Sisters by the Reverend John Mickun. Mother Magdalen, who was the last American Felician to leave Poland and had been refused permission by the communist government to return, told them volumes of stories about life in Poland under that anti-religious regime.

With heartfelt joy they went by bus to Assisi, the small town built against the steep sides of a mountain made forever memorable by the Holy Saint Francis, the spiritual father of all Franciscans. A torrent of rain turned the streets into turbulent mountain streams which did not dampen their spirits.

They spent time at Carceri, the grotto where Francis and his brethren spent their nights in prayer on the summit of the mountain, the room where Francis was born, the store of his father, the prison into which his father had thrown him when he began leading a life of grace. They walked along the street where Francis had walked to and from his family home, visited the cathedral with the same baptismal font where he was baptized, the Basilica of St. Clare, which holds her dark, well preserved body, the skull of her sister, St. Agnes, the habit of St. Francis, the alb made for him as a deacon by St. Clare and the crucifix from which Christ spoke to St. Francis at St. Damiano, "Go, repair my house."

In the San Damiano convent was the window through which St. Francis threw the bag of money by which his father had attempted to seduce him from his pursuit of sanctity; the original chapel which he repaired; the choir, where St. Clare and her daughters-in-religion prayed; the refectory, where she blessed the bread in the presence of St. Francis and a Cardinal, and upon which a cross appeared.

Resting on the roof garden where the Hymn to the Sun was composed by St. Francis, the Reverend Mother was filled with the serenity of complete submission as a spouse to her Lord, Jesus. The convent also contained the dormitory in which St. Clare died, the cell where her sister St. Agnes died, the bell and the breviary used by St. Clare, almost all kept intact from the thirteenth century.

In the grotto of Carceri the Sisters saw the mark on the stone where St. Francis slept with a stone under his head for a pillow. A small monastery had been built there by the Bernardines' own sweet mentor, St. Bernardine, who loved all that was sanctified by his spiritual father, St. Francis. They also prayed at the tomb of St. Francis. The Reverend Mother had Masses said for the Bernardines in all the sacred places visited and prayed that all of her sisters would benefit greatly from them.

A six-hour bus ride from Assisi brought them to Loreto, where the Santa Casa is enshrined in a huge basilica. This sacred house of Our Lady's where she heard the Archangel Gabriel's invitation to become the mother of Jesus, left the Reverend Mother with the feeling she had been in a blessed place. Whatever the traditional folklore regarding the conveyance of this birth house of Mary from Nazareth to the Adriatic Coast, the house became one of the most famous monuments of Christianity. They returned to Rome around midnight.

The Basilica of San Bernardino in L'Aquila was the next and most joyful experience of their pilgrimage. The Franciscan Brother, their guide for the day, coaxed them to have lunch in the sacristy since the original monastery no longer was in Franciscan hands. The Italian government had suppressed the block-long monastery which was now a square of stores and cafes. The luncheon included pasta, eggs, bacon, fruit, a whole loaf of bread, water and wine which he encouraged them to drink. St. Bernardine's cane was shown to them as well as photographs from the 500th anniversary of St. Bernardine's canonization in 1450. He took them to the cell and room where the Saint had died and where his discipline is retained.

The facade of the basilica, built under the direction of St. John Capistrano, and the beautiful marble tomb where the gold casket with St. Bernardine's body is enshrined remained intact. An earthquake had destroyed the ceiling, replaced by a gorgeous new one. The feet and soles of the saint's preserved body were in the best condition. The Reverend Mother noted that the sandy, stony roads which the dear St. Bernardine had to traverse probably influenced God to keep them intact. Marked by characteristic Franciscan cleanliness, the basilica had a spirit of joy, peace, cheer and purity. Brothers cared for an adjoining orphanage with 130 boys.

The good Brother Salvatore went with them to the bus which carried them to the railroad station in the valley. He remained with them until the train left the station. Of all their visits to various basilicas of the Franciscans, this had been the warmest, the most family-like, thanks to the good Brother Salvatore.

In Rome the next day they were introduced to His Excellency Pacelli, the Holy Father's nephew and direct successor of the family titles. He promised to visit them on his next visit to the United States.

A general audience with the Holy Father took place in the afternoon at Castel Gondolfo. Several thousand people from Germany, Italy, Spain, Ireland, the United States and Argentina heard the Pope speak fluently in five languages despite a severe cold. At 3:30 P.M. on Sept. 22nd the Reverend Mother and Mother Daniela left the "*ciampino*" (or airport) for Paris. Two sisters dressed in red habits from Mexico and two in brown habits, cloistered Franciscan Sisters of the Blessed Sacrament from India, were also on the flight. The six formed a family and the four of them who were going to New York City regretted they would not be together for that trip as well.

At 5:30 they were back in Rome because of one engine's power failure. After supper at the restaurant supplied by Pan American Airways, they left Rome at 7:00 only to return 45 minutes later because a motor had died. The captain of the flight refused to fly at night. After a night's stay at a hotel, a new experience for their four new friends who followed them like lambs, they finally took off successfully at nine the next morning. This gave them an opportunity to attend Mass at St. Andrew's Church where St. Theresa had stayed when she was in Rome. About 20 minutes before landing in Paris, one motor had to be stopped. The strato-clipper, the Western Ho, was further scheduled to go to New York. The Reverend Mother and Mother Daniela were happy about their plans to remain in France.

The good Sister Celine, from Manayunk, made room for them at the Nazareth Sisters boarding house when their original reservations with another residence for religious did not meet the Reverend Mother's indispensable need for cleanliness.

After confession in the chapel of the Nazareth Sisters, attendance at Mass, and then having breakfast there, they started with only limited fluency in French into the countryside to the town of Paray-le-Monial. With Mother Daniela enjoying the Reverend Mother's gestures of helplessness, they arrived for a ten-day retreat for which the Reverend Mother had longed since the Jubilee year of 1950. Their room in the Hotel du Sacré Coeur faced the chapel. With the Chapel of Apparitions of the Sacred Heart and the Chapel de la Colombière so close at hand, she believed a taste of Heaven had embraced her.

Days of grace followed. The Sacred Heart was most generous and they spent their days in one or the other of the chapels. Their prayers, insignificant as they might be, were very fervent. In them they remembered all the sisters, their loved ones — living and dead — and all the works of the congregation, with special emphasis on the *grace of graces* that all might become saints and thus comfort the suffering Sacred Heart of Jesus. His Sacred Heart was so near, so indulging, so generous that the Reverend Mother had the audacity to encourage the sisters to fall back on the Merciful Love of His Sweet Heart and beg It for whatever they needed, especially in the spiritual realm, in memory of His loving condescension to us, poor sinners, during the retreat made there.

Masses were offered daily from 6 A.M., as many as 25 on the various altars. Benediction of the Blessed Sacrament with the recitation of the rosary began each afternoon at 5 P.M. In the early evening many adorers came in so quietly after their day's work that not a sound was heard. During most of the day, without regard for the weather, the chapels had some faithful souls. St. Margaret Mary, who lies in a humble side-chapel, was surely the instrument which the Lord wanted to make of her for drawing hearts to His Love. The Reverend Mother prayed that the Bernardine's Customary and Directory would prove to be such an instrument for the congregation. She humbly begged that all the good sisters remember this intention in their prayers.

In the Chapel of Blessed Claude Colombière an exquisite mosaic behind the main altar is a representation of St. Margaret Mary's vision in which she saw the Sacred Heart with Mother Mary and St. Francis de Sales, with many angels holding the Coat of Arms of the Visitandines and Jesuits. The vision portrayed the roles of the two orders, Visitandines and Jesuits, in spreading the cult of the Sacred Heart. The tabernacle of the main altar is a mosaic representation of the Sacred Heart of Jesus with hands extended and pleading for our hearts. The antependium of the altar is a mosaic work representing two harts at the living waters.

After a short visit with the Reverend Mother of the Visitandines and her companion in the same parlor where Blessed Claude interviewed St. Margaret Mary, they returned to Paris. They visited and prayed in the Chapel of the Miraculous Medal, the chapel where the Blessed Mother appeared to St. Catherine Labouré and where her body lies. Of all the shrines the Reverend Mother had visited, this chapel and the chapel where the Sacred Heart appeared to St. Margaret Mary were her favorites. Other shrines were graced with great basilicas; these two were the very spots, the very walls, which the Sacred Heart and Blessed Mother chose to make their sweeping promises to the world.

Unexpectedly they were given the opportunity to return to the United States on October 10th rather than the 24th. A cabin was given to them on the S. S. United States with arrival expected on October 14th. Dr. Zmijewski, the chaplain at Mt. Alvernia, Mother Chrysostoma and Mother Duklane met them at the dock. Her wonderful pilgrimage had come to a beautiful end. The gifts she offered the Bernardines were gifts of lasting spiritual values — her poor prayers with all the important treasure of Masses offered generously at all the shrines for all of the sisters, their loved ones and all their benefactors, living and dead.

CHAPTER SIX

"Finally! Two stripes," Johnny happily told the missionary on a visit one morning soon after he got paid. His promotion was a wonderful way to start the new year.

"I see you brought some chocolate bars for the children," said Father Gaudry. "By the way, I want to introduce you to our new catechist. She has come to us from her home in Tokyo."

"Nice to meet you. I'm sure Father is happy to have you." The young woman bowed politely without saying anything or raising her eyes to see him.

"A catechist is so important for me right now. She will be teaching catechism to her own people in a way I could not since she knows them so well and speaks the language better than I ever will."

Her mother was visiting as well. To Johnny it was obvious they were quite different from the people he normally met in the north. They were wealthy converts from Protestantism and were excellent Catholics. He felt they would put many lifelong Catholics to shame. The missionary's rectory had been completed at a cost of $4,000. The house looked like a dream home compared to other homes in the town. Johnny hoped he could do something to help them in their efforts to build the Catholic Faith in this little town of Misawa.

On his way back to the base he passed by a store which featured Noritaki china. He stopped in to become familiar with the price range. He came away with the feeling he would one day buy a set of china for his mother and the family. He did buy a Sunbeam electric razor for himself at the PX which would be a quick way to shave each day at a seemingly low cost of $19.00.

"I think somebody's going to be sent to Chitose," said their training officer one day after their two-hour session was completed. "They need a skilled operator up there." Anyone interested in skiing would probably appreciate the transfer in the middle of the winter. Johnny hoped that his limited experience made him a safe bet to stay at Misawa. He wanted very much to complete his Psychology course. Another corporal was chosen who had the necessary qualifications.

When Johnny returned to the barracks, Carl Stallings, a Sergeant from Jacksonville, Florida, unexpectedly engaged him in a long talk about the Catholic church. He was expecting to leave for the States within a month.

"Johnny you come across as a good Catholic. My wife is rather religious and has often mentioned the Catholic church in our talks although she is not a Catholic either. How do you think we should look into it?"

"Read all you can, especially books written by Bishop Sheen or Thomas Merton. Talk to a few priests and find one you think you can get to like and go from there."

"Thanks, that's what we'll do."

"By the way, Virginia Mayo has been taking instructions from Bishop Sheen to enter the church. I just read it in *Time* magazine." An unanticipated uplift always occurred when someone approached Johnny on this favorite of all subjects. His new barracks also housed the 3rd Air Sea Rescue and had become quite a place of religious discussion. Many in the barracks were Catholic and four of them attended Mass daily. Communion on Sundays seemed to be a must.

In response to the news that he had finally been promoted, his mother wrote to Johnny that his dad's feelings had changed enough to get serious about straightening himself out with his Creator and his family; more importantly, with himself. A second letter quickly followed expressing grave concern about his sending money to the Society of St. Edmund. She sounded frightened about the whole idea. Why couldn't he simply keep sending money home? He answered the letter immediately.

Mom, can't you realize that I no longer want to be bound by family ties and that this is my life? Sure, we will always love one another because we're part of an association which will always be there for us. I'm 19 now and living in a world where you have to fight for what you believe in and if you want to make something of yourself you have to start young. I think I know what I want out of this life, heartily thank you for the part you've played in it, but I must now strive to attain my goals.

I've been accepted by a group of men who have formed a Society which advocates what I believe in. Do you know what that means? Apparently not. When you bring up petty ideas like lowering a parent's dignity because I choose to make pre-payments on an education you could not provide you didn't consider that a humiliation, did you? Then why should you disagree with my placing money in the hands of the Society which soon will be my life? They are my brothers, and with God's help and consent I shall soon join them to pray, work, and fight for what we believe to be right and the only cure for the troubles of men.

Undoubtedly, you have not taken me seriously. I hope this will set you both straight. This is no innocent dream but something I've been fighting to preserve. It's down to earth, the world with all its trials, errors, corruptions, sin and vanities. It isn't easy to preserve such a high goal and my environment isn't exactly conducive to it. You know I'm no saint. It's rough but I'm willing to try. I want your love, blessings, cooperation - no petty arguments about parental dignity.

My return from the CAA tower test in Tokyo came in today. I passed 4 parts with flying colors and missed only 'Aids to Air Navigation'. I'm glad I missed one. That will get me to Tokyo one more time on TDY.

This morning's work in the tower proved to me that I am ready to take over as head of a shift. The only job I would substitute for this one is that of a pilot. I got some really swell pictures yesterday afternoon of several aircraft taking off; the F-82, F-84, C-47, TWA, C-54.

By the way, the Psychology class has me overflowing with theories and vocabulary. I am sure you would all find the ideas of interest."

Love,
Johnny

"Man, it's cold in here," was everyone's complaint when wintry weather hit with a vengeance. A transformer blew out which killed all heat in the barracks for two days. Fuel was needed for dependent housing where there were young children. Plows began clearing runways in the middle of the night.

"Johnny, you and a few others will be getting a closer look at the GCA operation next week."

"Okay, I hope it warms up before we have to work out there on the field in that trailer."

Fortunately, the weather warmed up enough at the end of January to allow them to throw horse shoes against some pegs near the GCA unit. Those who were not working during the day played some softball.

A new roommate moved into Johnny's room, a Tech Sergeant and new tower chief who expected to make the Air Force a lifetime career. That put him into a whole different category from most of the men Johnny had come to know in the Air Force. So many of them just wanted to serve their four years and get out.

"Johnny, I hope you like to drink," was one of the first comments he made.

"Sure, as long as I'm on break." From then on Johnny almost never had to buy another beer. The Sergeant always had plenty of supply on hand.

In his next letter to his family he told them of the touching talk Father Riley had given at the Sunday five o'clock Mass honoring the young airman who had received his First Holy Communion during the Mass after being baptized into the church earlier that afternoon. Johnny challenged his family to persevere in becoming perfect Christians and then "*all other things would be added unto them.*" The importance is found in the attempt, not necessarily the perfection, he suggested. He also said he had spoken to an airman from the coal regions whose aunt was also a Bernardine named Sister Joanette.

With Psychology finished in January, in which he pulled a "B," he looked forward to the next course, English Composition, beginning later in February. He prayed he would stay in Misawa long enough to complete it. Rotation to Matsushima, 149 miles south, or Chitose on the northern island of Hokaido was always possible, since squadron policy called for transfer to all three air bases during each man's tour of duty at Misawa.

His mother wrote a letter complaining of some ill feeling toward Cassie and Joe. She believed they were able to enjoy life so much more in Reading than she could ever hope to in Shenandoah. Johnny cautioned her that as Christians we are to "*love one another not only those it is easy to love.*" And please say the Family Rosary every night. Dad and Louis, don't be lukewarm. Get red hot for Our Lady and your own souls. He said he would send $60 home to pay Alma's school bills. He also told his mother to tell Louis how unhappy he was with the "F" in conduct. He also included a letter he had received from Father Galligan of the Edmundites which showed that the money he was sending them was being deposited in the "John S. Fund". She had never been too trustful of the funds going directly to the priests. His tax return was sent along for presentation to the tax collector. His letters to the Reverend Mother dwindled to one a month. The letters she did write in return were always appreciated. He knew how busy she was as Superior General of the Order.

"Are you going to Dave Dorsey's party in town?" asked one of his roommates.

"Definitely. I would never miss a party," answered Johnny. "I wonder what his parents think about having a Japanese woman for a daughter-in-law."

"I hear she's well on her way to having that baby. I guess we'll all see just how far along she is."

They had a great time at the house where Dave and his girl had lived for the past year. He always had his room on the base and spent all his free time in town. They would be going back to Maryland in May. A few days after the party all passes were canceled in an attempt to cut down the VD rate. There had been some 100 cases in the first ten days of the month.

"Just how strong are the winds, Johnny?" asked the trick chief.

"I'm getting readings of 60 mph with gusts to 70."

"There won't be much flying around here if this keeps up." March winds swayed the tower just enough to keep the operators inside. Climbing up and down the many steps kept them close to the handrails. A major snow storm hit on March 15th. Forty inches of snow closed the field to aircraft. Again the task of climbing up to or down from the tower became an exciting adventure.

Captain Love, a jet pilot, gave the operators a talk on the operation of an aircraft and the regulations governing their actions with the control tower. One day a week tower operators could receive instructions in a link trainer. This was the closest any of them got to flight school. Johnny found it exciting to actually sit in a mock cockpit and learn to control the plane using the necessary instruments.

Johnny could not dismiss the news that his brother Louie had gotten that "F" in conduct. He decided he'd better write a personal letter to him. He wrote it on the Feast of St. Joseph, March 19th.

Dear Lou,

Just now returned from the English class and decided to write some letters. I have to work the midnight, or the "graveyard shift" as we call it, tonight.

Well you know by now that I've made Corporal, which improved my morale 100%. The next step is Sgt., which shouldn't take too long.

Mom hasn't had too much to say about you lately and the last report card happened a long time ago, so I won't mention it. Try your best, kid; there's too much in life to be careless about it. I want only the best for you.

You mentioned in your last letter about working at Mt. Alvernia this summer. It is a good idea but it won't be easy. You'd get a darn good workout and, if you work for Sister Maxentia, you will find she is not the easiest person to get along with. Whoever you work for, it will do you a lot of good. You are just the right age for some of the guys at the orphanage who may have some of the same interests as yours.

You might also get a liking for the spiritual life. That's where I got my first real taste of true peace and nearness to God.

Have you ever smoked a Phillies cigar or a Royalist? We've been having quite a few passed out now since everybody's been getting promoted. They are really good.

Try your best to get along with this Sister Beatrice Marie although I know that's sometimes impossible. Whatever you do, keep your mouth shut. It never pays to say anything; they always get the last word in anyway.

Guess you're getting in some baseball practice. The fever has hit here too. We get some catchin' in now and then.

I hope you're getting to Mass every morning during Lent. Learn to pray, Louis; it's the mark of a good Catholic. You don't appreciate Faith until you get into the world and see how little other people have.

I'll always pray for you, do the same for me.
Always yours,
Johnny

Letters became the lifeblood of his spirit. These contacts with his family and friends made him feel there was a world outside of Japan. After eight months, with twenty-two more to go, letters from Father Galligan of the Edmundite Fathers, his high school friend Joe, and the Reverend Mother tapped into his spiritual needs and filled him with confidence that the priesthood was not an impossible dream. Patience had become the one virtue he needed more than any other. The chaplain continued to attempt to get his transfer into the chaplain's assistant job. Johnny and Father Riley believed the assignment would help to keep him focused during the remainder of his tour of duty in the Air Force. In the meantime he served Mass a few times, helped out at the Solemn High Mass on Holy Thursday and attended Holy Friday services.

"That was one crazy night in the tower last night. Some joker took off at two in the morning and ended up in the Pacific three miles off shore." That's how Jack Cobb, the on-duty tower operator for the night shift, began his description of the event which caused quite a stir around the base.

"Exactly what happened? Do they know the pilot?" asked a few of the men listening intently to the details of the incident.

"First of all, he took off without clearance from the tower, just made it off the runway and burst into flames when he hit the water. The body still hasn't been found which leaves everyone guessing. They found his jacket, a pair of shoes, and an open parachute just beneath the surface of the water. If he isn't dead he'll probably get 20 years if they ever find him. The duty officer has identified the pilot as a sergeant who worked on the plane on a regular basis."

"I guess he just flipped," concluded Johnny's roommate, the career man whose drinking habit was probably jeopardizing his own status.

A letter from Joe, his high school buddy in the Paulist novitiate, came one day in early April:

Dear John,

There is one difficulty with our correspondence: its reliance on events or incidents that happened too long ago to be of special interest. I suppose that is why we always end up discussing ideas or feelings and people instead of experiences. Perhaps that is best anyway. Being in a place like a novitiate one has many ideas or feelings to describe, but I can sum them all up into one, "trust". That is one I am anxious for you to acquire, isolated as you are over there, just living for the day when you can get away and begin. Archbishop Goodier expresses it perfectly when he says "To know that God, Almighty and All-Loving is behind all, with His hand on every thread, personally interested in all things, in me, in His own great design, and in that portion of it which He had prepared for me." I have gotten great consolation from that sentence, particularly in those days when things seemed much more unsettled than now, when all I could think about was tomorrow or the future, when everything seemed to be dependent on what decisions I made. If nothing else, the novitiate has taught me that I am God's child, picked by Him to do something in life which only He is sure of. How I will get to that something and when is His doing; He pulls the strings — He makes the decisions. I have learned in the novitiate, and only through some bitter moments, that each day is God's day, of which I am only a part. That everyone around me is a part of that day, that we all are part of the plan of that day, and that if we obey the laws of God and His counsels we are playing our part in the day, which in reality is our only reason for existence: to live always to God's purpose, which is personal as well as universal and temporal as well as eternal.

I have gotten long winded in the novitiate, also. I didn't mean to bore you, and if I have chalk it up to that youthful effervescence which people are always laughing at. It seems ages since I have heard from you, although no doubt it was Lent which has stopped the flow of monthly letters from Japan which were beginning to mean so much to me. I am so interested in you John and what you are thinking and feeling that I sometimes feel guilty at the time I spend thinking about you. At the rate time is passing, at least here in Oak Ridge, it will be no time until you are back in the States. I can easily suppose that you have it figured down to the minutes, but it is that spirit which I was trying to break in that first paragraph epistle. Life is so short, and so important, that it is wrong to waste any of it on the thought of the might have been or the possible. Your salvation depends on the kind of soldier (Woops! Airman) you are now. Your vocation depends to a great extent on what kind of life you lead now. You can only realize the full meaning of that statement when you are in the seminary for a while.

The fellow here from whom I got most of my information about the Society of St. Edmund, a former student at St. Michael's College, left last month, so from now on I will have to depend on you and a few press releases. From what I can gather they seem to do wonderful work. You shall have a wonderful life if you enter that society. I saw mention in the "Catholic Standard and Times" the other day of a new hospital in Chester which your aunt's community is taking over and in which she personally is in charge of renovating.

I heard from Anne who will be a registered nurse in the fall. Sonny writes once in a while and Dick is his own silent, prudent self. Four of the guys have been drafted. My brother Raymond has been accepted at the University of Notre Dame, the best Catholic school in the country, all things considered. The retreat silence on Holy Thursday and Good Friday was deafening. It enables one to understand Thomas Merton's new book "The Sign of Jonas," which I recommend for your attentive reading. Looks like the Phillies and Athletics both have good teams this year.

In many ways I envy you over there seeing the Orient and many other things. I have said this so many times before that you may soon begin to doubt my sincerity, but I actually envy your opportunity for doing good in Japan, both for yourself and for your brothers in Christ that are there all around you. It makes me happy to pick up your letters and see what you are able to do with some of the fellows; it makes me jealous. Of course, here in the novitiate I am getting a spiritual foundation that is necessary for true priestly work, but one doesn't have to be a priest to be an apostle which you seem to have realized better than I. Use every opportunity to strengthen God's gift to you. Frequent Mass and Communion are musts, while visits to the Blessed Sacrament can help you to attain union with Christ. I will write again this summer after the novitiate is completed. Until then I remain your devoted friend in Christ, goodbye, and may God bless you. Pray for me; I do for you.

 Joe

"Are you signed up for that Literature course?" asked Major Parker, his commanding officer, who had been taking most of the courses Johnny had taken.

"Yes, I believe it starts on the 28th. I keep hoping I can complete each course before I get transferred out. There are only four of us left from the time I got here at Misawa."

"Johnny, keep getting those 'A's' and I will see what I can do about keeping you here." This was the kind of officer he was happy to serve under.

Khakis were in season again with the heavier Blues put away until September. His Mormon friend Jim Jenson got the station he wanted back in Utah only 80 miles from his hometown. So many of the operators had come and gone in the last eight months he was beginning to feel like a veteran on the base. In the latest letter to his mother and family he told them of the $11.75 the English Literature course would cost. He also told them how pleased he was that his father was finally settling down and promised his mother he would send some money home over the next four months.

"Everyone's restricted to the base. The Commies celebrate May 1st as May Day and no one can be sure Americans are totally safe in town" reiterated the tower chief from the order posted in the AACS office. Johnny didn't care, because the Literature course was very interesting. He expected to enjoy the entire eight weeks with the Ph.D. who was giving the course. He often wished he could be in class six hours a day instead of the two three-hour sessions each week.

Johnny met an ex-seminarian who had been studying to be a Redemptionist but found it wasn't for him. The training he received was reflected in his excellent manners and respect for the Church.

"Johnny, there is an opening in the Chaplain's Section right now. I am attempting to get you transferred," said Father Riley one day when he had attended Mass.

"Father, I still think the idea is a good one. I am not too certain AACS will let me go. This past Monday I went before the squadron board for upgrading to the skilled operator level and I passed with flying colors."

"I will be seeing Major Parker today. We will have the answer shortly."

"Sounds good. I really like being a tower operator and I am on good terms with the C.O. If he agrees I will probably go along with the chaplain's assistant transfer."

On his return to the barracks the guys were talking about an airman whose mother had died. The letter he received was written by a relative outside his immediate family who also indicated his mother had already been buried. He was told he could still have an emergency leave which he declined because he couldn't face his father or other relatives who hadn't had enough sense to send him a telegram or notify the Red Cross. In the next letter to his family, Johnny alerted them to the importance of letting him know immediately if anyone in the family got sick so that he could get home on leave.

With Mother's Day coming up, Johnny sent a personal letter to his mother.

In this letter I will try my best to express in words all that you mean to me. Please try to understand that whatever is here written, is done so with complete sincerity and not just sentimentality befitting this occasion.

It was nineteen years, five months and one day ago that this poor excuse for a human made its entry into the world after nine months in the most precious womb that exists for me. Therefore, I want to thank you, my sweet mother, primarily for taking time and suffering too much that I might have life. For whether I might die tomorrow or live several more decades it will always be said, "I lived." Thanks for giving me this chance. I pray you'll never regret it.

You've had a tough time of it, Mom, and as I have said before, we all love you for it. Too often it didn't seem like we were doing our best toward you because of disobedience, selfishness and lack of genuine appreciation. Nevertheless, we did always love you. We love you now more than ever because we realize that through all our actions you never stop loving us. These nineteen years cannot be lived over again, still, I hope that not another tear or heartpang will be caused by me or the rest of us.

I'd like so much to be near you this day, dear Mom, and will be in spirit if not in body. My Holy Communion will be offered for you and in this way we will be united with that heart of all hearts, Our Lord. God be with you through Jesus in Mary,

> *Your son,*
> *Johnny*

In the control tower weather was always a primary consideration. Winds had been blowing with a fury for almost two days. The weather otherwise would have been perfect except for the cool wind and dust in the air.

"Johnny! Look at that T-7 on the runway. It's sitting there with it's nose down and we have a few jets in the air low on fuel," shouted the trick chief who was handling the "B" position. "You'd better let me have the mike."

"It's yours," answered Johnny, not certain of how the jets could get down safely with the trainer on the runway.

The jets were cleared to land on the right side of the runway while the crews worked on the T-7. Nothing spectacular had happened; just a neat climax to a dreary shift.

"Johnny, you're a trick chief as of today. That means you're top dog in the tower. The job is now your total responsibility. If anything goes wrong while you're on duty you take the blame." Johnny was delighted with this news from his training officer. He looked forward to his next series of shifts where the mike would be his to command.

"There's no job like it in the Air Force," he wrote to his family. "When I am up here in the tower everything I say goes whether it is for better or worse. And believe me there are a dozen situations or more where things are done on my say-so, or else. After a while you get used to it and doesn't mean much until you sit down and think about it. In most other jobs you've always got someone telling you how or when to do something. When you're trick chief here you're on your own. It's a great feeling."

"Johnny, there's too much red tape to try to transfer you to the chaplain's section," Father Riley told him at their next meeting. " Major Parker and I both agreed it wasn't worth the effort."

"That's okay Father. The fact is I like what I'm doing and it would be a little crazy to give it up now that I'm fully trained."

"By the way Johnny, did you get a chance to talk to the Franciscan missionary who was here?"

"Yes Father. He said he was heading to the States for a three-month vacation after working in Okinawa the past three years. He seems to believe there is plenty of promise for the church there. You know, sometimes I think I'm learning more about the church in the Air Force than if I were in a seminary."

"Yes, it's good to see so much work going on for Our Lord and His Holy church."

"Father, did I tell you the squadron contributed another $132 this last month for the Catholic mission in Misawa. Father Gaudry was really pleased to know the conversion into Japanese money amounted to almost 50,000 yen. They had contributed $100 or 36,000 yen the previous month. Major Parker agreed to this 'public relations' effort even though most of the squadron is not Catholic. A roommate and I visited Fr. Gaudry last Sunday. He has fixed up the new rectory western style. His housekeeper enjoyed setting the table for us for some coffee and cake. You know he actually has it pretty good. His new rectory is the best home in town and has a car which is a luxury item to the local farmers. He also has a refrigerator. I doubt the Japanese here have anything like it."

"Well, Johnny, I guess the French Canadians like to be good to their priests, including their missionaries."

"Father, speaking of the French, the Edmundites in Vermont are an American province of a French order. Some of the seminarians go to France to study, especially if they are French Canadian. I think I would like to study at the North American College in Rome if I do any studying in Europe. I also just learned the society's first colored priest has been ordained. He's from San Francisco."

"Johnny, you're a few years away from the Edmundites right now. Just keep doing what you can while you're here and all that will settle out."

During one of their sixty-hour breaks "Red" Crow, whose Kentucky red hair got him the nickname, said to Johnny and other operators, "Let's do some bike riding today and get some sun."

"Sounds great," they all agreed.

The four of them rode the bikes around the small hills, went down to the lake and ended up pedaling through some fairly deep water along the shore. Special Services provided the bikes at no cost. The rides always gave them a chance to get a closer look at the countryside and the people.

"This is really tough duty, isn't it?" they joked. Korea seemed a world away.

Several new C-124's were at the base during this break in the work schedule. Johnny went flying in one of them for a few hours while the plane made a number of "touch and go" landings. The plane was so huge inside he was happy to have the flight end, since the ride was uneventful and rather boring. A better concept of flying came with another session in the Link Trainer. Initially he had fun simply with the idea of being in a cockpit. Once he got a little more serious he was able to control the Link pretty well.

In early July the base newspaper, *The Depot Sun*, was suspended indefinitely due to lack of funds. Johnny had written a few short articles and was expecting to do much more. The Air Force was cutting back on all expenses and that meant an end to unnecessary projects.

"Johnny, you seem to read that *Time* magazine from cover to cover," commented a staff Sergeant who lived in the barracks.

"Well, Rich, I just started receiving it and I find it totally engrossing. They cover so many areas I feel like I am getting an education. You're welcome to read it whenever you wish."

"Perhaps I'll do that once in a while."

Every week, *Time* became his favorite source of information.

July 2nd was his father's birthday. Johnny mentioned in one of his letters to the family that the 12th of July was the Feast of St. John Gaulbert. Since it was the St. John closest to his dad's birthday he could celebrate it as his own feast day as well. Johnny wanted him to know he offered a Mass and Holy Communion for his father's intention, especially for his soul's sanctification. He observed that heaven would be hell if all six family members weren't there. He then challenged them to think seriously about buying a home instead of continuing to rent. He wrote that by the end of December, 1954, he would have at least $2,000 in his savings fund in Vermont which could be used for that purpose since the GI Bill would provide the money needed to cover his college expenses at St. Michael's College. He was sure the additional money needed to buy a house could be borrowed from the government under the same GI Bill. He did not care where the house was located; that choice was up to them. He simply asked them to think about the idea. With his sister Alma's graduation as a laboratory technician, he felt she might be able to help with the home's purchase as well.

"Will you be free to serve Mass at the Confirmation ceremonies next week?" asked Father Abercrombie, who had replaced Father Riley as chaplain.

"Yes, I'm looking forward to meeting a Japanese Bishop."

The Most Reverend Michael Urukawa, the Bishop of Sendai, confirmed twelve people at the service. To Johnny he came across as a very humble servant of his people. His vestments were modest with no pretention in his demeanor or carriage. Later that evening a few families met at Father Abercrombie's house. It was a real pleasure to meet some dependent families who had joined their Air Force husbands and fathers in Japan.

"Captain Hamilton, I'd like you to meet Johnny, who has helped me a great deal at chapel services."

"Good to meet you, Johnny. What do you do?"

"I'm a control tower operator. As a pilot you probably heard me on the mike a few times."

"Any plans for the future?"

"Yes, I hope to go to St. Michael's College in Vermont as a seminarian."

"How about that! I attended St. Michael's and plan to settle in Vermont with my wife when my tour of duty is over. I was very impressed with the priests there. You will enjoy your time at the school."

The meeting with Captain Hamilton made Johnny all the more eager to get on with his life. He wondered just how long it would take to get to St Michael's and the Edmundite Fathers.

"Sausage Check 1, either fuel or smoke is spouting from behind your canopy," stated Johnny in a very measured tone during the take off of two F-84's on his next shift in the tower.

"Roger, tower. Will check," the pilot replied.

"Sausage Check 2, confirm tower observation."

"Sausage Check 1, looks like fuel."

"Thanks. Will return to base."

The tower went into emergency procedures immediately. No other fighters were allowed to take off or land until the distressed plane returned safely to the base. That's what made the position of trick chief always interesting. Anything could happen and often did. Regrettably, a pilot sometimes got killed. A Lieutenant Colonel who was well-liked, and a father of five, died in the crash of his F-84 right after takeoff.

Classes at the University of California, Berkeley, Extension continued during Johnny's stay at Misawa. He took Speech as his latest three-credit course, which he found extremely useful. He believed the delivery he was taught by the tall, personable, attractive-looking professor, gave him greater confidence on the mike in the control tower.

"Johnny I'd like you to prepare a ten-minute speech for the next class. Everyone will give at least one talk during the next few weeks. Make it simple. Tell us about something which is very familiar to you."

Johnny thought about his assignment during the next day. He wondered what he could talk about which might also do some good spiritually. An explanation of the rosary seemed to make some sense. People knew so little about how a rosary should be said.

During the next class Johnny stood in front of the professor and students with a black-beaded rosary in his hands. This was the rosary the Reverend Mother had given to him after her visit to Rome for the Jubilee Year 1950. "Roma" was written across the back of the cross which held the crucified Christ. He explained how the rosary began with the saying of the Apostle's Creed as one held the crucifix between two fingers. This relatively short prayer summarized the basic beliefs of all Christians: the belief in one God the Father Almighty, His only son Jesus who was conceived by the Holy

Ghost and born of the Virgin Mary; that Jesus suffered, died and was buried, descended into hell, rose from the dead and sits at the right hand of the Father. Also how Catholics believed in the Holy Spirit, the Communion of saints, the forgiveness of sins and life everlasting. The Our Father was said on the five large beads, Hail Marys were repeated on the small beads, a tribute to the Trinity was prayed after the three Hail Marys at the beginning of the rosary and after each group of small beads. The essence of a meaningful rosary was the centering of one's mind on the five Joyful Mysteries: the Annunciation, the Visitation of Mary to her cousin Elizabeth, the Nativity, the Presentation in the temple for the rite of circumcision and the Finding in the Temple when Jesus was thirteen years old and wanted to be about His Father's business immediately. Generally, most people who said the rosary limited themselves to one set of mysteries. There were, however, five Sorrowful Mysteries and five Glorious Mysteries.

His commanding officer, Major Parker, followed his speech very carefully. The professor admitted this was the first time he had understood why the rosary was held in such high esteem by many Catholics. In two weeks the speech course came to an abrupt end for Johnny. He had been assigned to Iwakuni AFB on the Inland Sea several hundred miles south of Misawa. The U.S.A.F. was taking over the base from the Australians who were terminating their involvement in occupied Japan. The one person to whom he said a heartfelt goodbye was Major Parker. He thanked him for the financial help he was giving Father Gaudry at the Catholic mission in Misawa.

Two major differences in his new assignment made him wish he had never left Misawa. No California extension courses were available and the Australians had an outdated direction-finding system which required tower operators to man the obsolete equipment in a small facility which was no more than windmill-looking shack painted in large orange and white squares. The control tower located nearby was about twenty feet in height compared to Misawa's much more lofty elevation. Australian officers operated the tower. They were surprised that Americans who were not officers were allowed to hold such a responsible position, especially if some were still in their late teens.

His new tower chief informed Johnny when he arrived at Iwakuni that an Australian corporal would teach him and Norm, who had arrived from Chitose, the details of operating the direction-finding equipment. "With a little luck we will have our own DF system in the control tower before too long," he said.

Johnny had begun to really miss his family, especially with the new assignment. He decided a letter to his sister Alma might help. The date was August 13, 1952.

Dearest Alma,

Letters will be precious to me from now on, more than before, since this latest change in stations. I am now at Iwakuni AFB and working in a D.F. (direction finding) station. I'd give anything to be back at Misawa but that's the way the ball bounces. What makes it more difficult to take is that I could have turned it down. However, I never expected to come this far south or work outside the control tower.

We have an Australian chaplain here which means daily Mass except when he takes off for Korea. Without Mass, I'd go mad. I had this and much more at Misawa but, stupid ass that I am, I thought I'd like to see more of the south and the bigger cities. Hiroshima is not far away so you should be able to locate this place on a map. I'll see if I can get some pictures this Sunday which I will send home.

It's getting tougher by the day to stay away from home. I'd do anything to be with all of you if only for a few days. To think I have a year and a half to go!

I work with an Australian for the time being until I learn to work the set myself. His name is Wilson and a good old boy. He's got a wife and three kids back in Australia and is a buck sergeant after ten years in the service. Rank comes slowly in their Armed Forces. He is a real career man. His personal interest in his work is the only thing which has given me any encouragement to hang in.

It does seem strange not to be seeing Uncle Joe again, until eternity anyway. I pray there aren't any more tragic separations before I come home. And only God knows if I ever will.

It is great to see you where you are. As I said once before, everything looks perfect. Mother will appreciate that one-third share of your pay as much as any of us. Things will be easier all the way around. It was a good idea getting Louis to Reading to work at the orphanage. That environment rubs off on you whether you want it to or not. Seriously, that's where I got my start and look forward

hopefully to a successful end elsewhere.
God love you. Please pray for all of us.
Johnny

Corporal Wilson was an excellent instructor. Within a week the two Americans were ready to replace him.

"Now don't forget, tea and biscuits will be brought to you each morning at ten and each afternoon at two as long as the Salvation Army stays on base. That's how they keep up our morale. After a while you'll like it too," Wilson said to Johnny on the day he left to return home. "And bring a book with you to the station. You'll have lots of time to read." He always had a paperback in his trouser pockets. The Australians seemed to be good readers.

Convinced he had to do something about the hours he would be spending in the monastic environment of the D.F. station, Johnny enrolled in a correspondence writing course with the Magazine Institute in Rockefeller Center, New York City. He had seen the ad in the *New Yorker* one day while in the library. He decided a writing course made sense after the two English courses he had had at Misawa. The decision turned out to be one of the best choices he ever made. Writing short stories was much more demanding and complex than answering the "five Ws" of newspaper articles. Who, what, when, where and why seemed like child's play compared to creative writing. His tutor, Frances Goodfellow, made the course challenging in every respect. The swimming pool was of Olympic dimensions. In late summer Johnny found the pool perfect for exercise. In the fall and winter the squash court became a favorite way to pass some leisure time. The movies were free — English productions primarily.

Father Tellefsen, the Australian chaplain, took Johnny and his friend Tienken to the Double Seven Club where he got his first taste of an Australian beer called Ballarath.

"How do you like our Australian beer?" Father asked.

"Father, what is the alcohol content? It tastes like much more than the 3.2 beer we get at the PX."

"I'm not sure. It takes getting used to by you Americans."

"Iwakuni D.F., do you read me?"

"Roger."

"My fuel reserve is low. Cannot find my wing man. Give me a heading to the base."

Johnny realized this was his first 'mayday' situation. He hoped he would get the right heading. The major difficulty was the possibility of giving the pilot a heading 180° opposite of the correct one. He listened intently to the signal from the plane, located the dead zone on the D.F. equipment and gave the pilot the direction he needed to fly to reach the base.

"Thanks, Iwakuni. Listen in for my wing man."

"Roger." No radio messages came in from the other pilot. Air Rescue searched for him the next day.

Johnny felt like he had finally done something worthwhile in this new assignment. Until that time his only experience had been in giving practice headings to planes close to the base.

Norm Tienken, who came down with Johnny from Chitose, a detachment of Misawa's headquarters, had a different perspective on the Iwakini assignment.

"You know, Johnny, this base is so much better than Chitose."

Of course, Norm already had two years of college, so the Berkeley Extension was of little importance to him. He also liked the idea of a warmer winter compared to the island of Hokaido. Before long, he and Norm, a Nebraskan raised on a ranch, became close friends. They both attended Mass together, which helped Norm remain faithful to his girlfriend whom he expected to marry on his return to the States. With a great sense of humor, his jokes and expressions usually reflected his farm background and solid German upbringing.

"Johnny, I'd like you and Norm to help me organize a bus trip to Hiroshima. I want to take some clothes to an orphanage up there run by Japanese nuns."

"Sure, Father. That's something we both missed on our first trip last month," Johnny answered. The bus trip worked out well. Johnny could not go along because of his work schedule. During that first trip, evidence of the devastation which had taken place seven years before, could still be seen. The city sat in a large bowl-like valley dominated almost completely by sizeable hills. From the Atom Bomb Casualty Center located on one of the hills, he and Norm visualized how the Japanese must have felt when the bomb exploded. Streets were still being repaired by men and women working side by side. In many cases the women appeared to outnumber the men. With their white hats and white tops over black pants they all shielded themselves from the warm sun.

"Norm, let's go to the Peace Shrine."

"That's something we've got to see. Let's go."

The partially domed building was expected to remain *in memoriam* of the first A Bomb. Once an Industrial Arts Building, some of its walls, including the iron framework of the dome, remained intact. All the windows had been destroyed. Johnny was certain this was a sight he would never forget. An Atomic Sufferer Shop with the proprietor calling himself the "No. 1 Atomic Bomb Patient" stood nearby. His back portrayed the scorching heat of the bomb and he displayed it willingly. Johnny and Norm took pictures of his back for a donation of 500 yen. A cemetery of the bombs' first victims' cremated remains and a boat house could be viewed near the Peace Shrine. The city must have been beautiful, with a river running through it, before the war experience. They both planned to return as often as possible to Hiroshima, since this had been a brief one-day visit.

In late October Johnny decided the time had come to send his family a set of Noritake chinaware.

"Norm, let's go into town and find that set of china I've been wanting to send my family."

"Won't that cost you a few sides of beef?" cracked Norm.

"Probably. The set will probably last a couple of lifetimes, so I've decided to get it."

A place setting displayed in the store caught Johnny's eye. The white dinner plate had a few randomly placed small carnations with narrow green leaves circled by a gold edge at its rim. The other pieces were decorated in the same pattern.

"How much for that one?" he asked the owner of the store.

"18,000 yen."

"That's more money than I make in a month!"

"For you cost is 16,000 yen."

"Okay! What will it cost to have you mail it to the States?"

"There are 93 pieces. $15 American."

"When can you send it?"

"Tomorrow, or day after."

The deed was done. In American money the cost was $144. Johnny believed this could be the most expensive gift he would ever send home and was certain the dinnerware would be the best Christmas present he could give to the family. The china would be a permanent reminder of his time in Japan.

A letter arrived from the Reverend Mother dated October 7, the Feast of the Holy Rosary. Mailed from Paris, she shared with him the highlights of her European pilgrimage and her continued thoughts of him.

Dearest Johnny,

I have been with you, in spirit, daily, for I have been praying for you very fervently these days and in places sanctified by the actual visits of the Most Sacred Heart of Jesus and Mother Mary: at Paray-le-Monial and in the Chapel of the Miraculous Medal here in Paris. Of course you were remembered at Rome, Assisi, Loreto and Aquila just as well, but at the Chapel of the Apparitions of the Sacred Heart and here, where Mary gave us Her Miraculous Medal our days are one long prayer. Did you feel it? I did pray so fervently that, God willing, you return safely and become His own servant, a saint.

We sailed from N. Y. C. and eventually ended up in Rome for the Congress for Major Superiors held Sept. 11, 12 and 13th. The Congress was of no greater immediate consequences, but much of it is expected in the future — we Americans, pragmatically efficient as we are, were much disappointed. However, for me, this was God's own gift. I did spend five weeks away from all responsibility in deep union with God. I must admit that I was flooded with graces and their source is still generous. Eternity will be too brief to thank God for all that I have received from the Sacred Heart and Its mother — would that I be gratefully docile and cooperative! The Mercies of God are so abundant in our lives! Were we only attuned to them to be responsive with generosity!

Mother Daniela, my companion, visited Rome somewhat. Since I had seen most of it in 1950, I preferred the quiet shadows of the beautiful chapel of the Marymount, where we lived. I did go to Nettuno to visit dear Richard's tomb. The military cemetery there is beautiful, only partly completed. I knelt at Richie's grave on the second month of his Daddy's funeral. Little did I think on July 16th that on September 16th, I'd be with the loved by us, Richard.

We went with Mother Daniela to Assisi, to Loreto and to Aquila. Assisi has all that was dear to the heart of our Holy Father, St. Francis; Aquila much that was loved by St. Bernardine, including his body. At Loreto it was a privilege to stand under the window where the Archangel Gabriel made the Annunciation, to touch the walls which were touched by the Holy Family. We were fortunate to hear Mass in the tiny dwelling of Nazareth. The little house of Jesus is today within a beautiful basilica. We also passed by the Polish Military Cemetery which is on the hillside of Loreto.

After some mechanical problems with the strato-clipper we arrived in Paris from Rome on the 23ʳᵈ. The next day we left for Paray-le-Monial, to make a retreat in the chapel, where St. Margaret Mary received 18 visits from the Sacred Heart and received all those marvelous promises. We also spent quite a good deal of time in the chapel of the Jesuits, where the relics of Blessed Claude de la Colombiere, St. Margaret Mary's spiritual director, are exposed for veneration.

After a spiritual feast of 10 days we returned to Paris and, now, spend our days in the Chapel of the Miraculous Medal. We were given the opportunity to return to the U. S. on the 10ᵗʰ rather than the 24ᵗʰ which will put us in N.Y.C. on the 14ᵗʰ. It will be good to be home again! It will have been the longest month I have lived. If it weren't for these favored chapels, it would be insupportable. But so, it always is. We appreciate home when we're at a distance — don't we!

We had Masses said in all these holy places for all our relatives, and having enjoyed so many graces, I'm almost bold enough in my trust in the Mercy of God, to say: "Johnny, when you are really in need of God's aid, say — Oh, God, whose mercies to Mother Edmunda were so great, I beg you for this generosity of your Heart, grant me this, this or this." He won't refuse you whatever you want. But, ask with deeply loving trust.

Father Galligan gave me detailed instructions to get to St. Edmund's tomb, but the change in our schedule precludes a pilgrimage there. I'm sure that St. Edmund will forgive this second lapse of mine, the first one in 1950. I'm so near to him and yet so far!

I hated to deny myself the visit to Lisieux, but I'm sure St. Therese would do just what I did. I'm waiting for M. Daniela's return to ask her when she expressed my love to her, because while in the chapel of Mother Mary this afternoon, I felt Little Therese very close to myself. Isn't the "Communion of Saints" one of the most consoling articles of our holy faith. The Saints and our beloved dead are so near to us in God, who is everywhere!

How are you? I'm rather selfish I said so much about myself with no concern for you. Things are growing darker on our political horizon. We met an American Felician Sister at Rome who happened to be the last American sister who was tolerated in Poland until last January when she left Poland for Rome with important documents relative to the beatification of their Mother Foundress. Then, on the plane, we met a cloistered sister from India. Both say that the doings of the enemies of God are infernal and not human. Only prayer and penance can save us — and how little of both one generally finds.

I'll be anxiously looking for a letter from you. Perhaps, there is one for me on my desk in Reading?

May the merciful Love of the Sacred Heart and Its Mother be with you to guide, to console and to protect! I remain, dearest Johnny,
In the love of these Sacred Hearts,
M. M. Edmunda

For Johnny this was another of his aunt's incredibly beautiful letters. "How did one develop into a saint when cognizant of so many Adamic frailties?" he asked himself.

CHAPTER SEVEN

A week passed before the Reverend Mother reached her beloved motherhouse after landing in New York. The Sacred Heart convent was deeply embedded in her soul. She greeted her Eucharistic Lord in the beautiful chapel and prayed that she would be worthy of the many graces she had received on this unexpected stay in Italy and France.

The "in" basket on her desk was piled high with correspondence. Three letters from Johnny made it difficult for her to delay opening them. In the letters he regretted the change of assignment to Iwakuni, the inability to continue his courses from Berkeley and the need to work in the direction finding station rather than the control tower. She decided it would be best to answer immediately.

> *Dearest Johnny,*
>
> *We landed in N.Y.C., October 14th, but I have continued on the way for the next seven days. The good Lord always gives us what is best for us even though the best does not always fall in line with our wishes.*
>
> *Thank you for the 3 letters which are before me, and also special thanks for the $5.00 which you sent towards the vacation trip of our 19 Brazilian Missioners. God will reward you a hundredfold. We're already in the swing of making the necessary reservations, etc. I can imagine how elated they are.*
>
> *I haven't heard from any of the family since I returned. I am happy for Alma's job location so close to Reading and I am pleased to know that the stay at Mt. Alvernia had a good effect on Louis. His behavior was excellent in every way. Mother Duklane already told*

him he may return next summer, God willing.

Johnny dear, you must strive for stability. Without it, you'll not find happiness anywhere. You see, every corner here below has its "minuses" and our nature shirks from them. You'll find many reasons for desiring a change when you'll find yourself in a seminary, God willing. We have no lasting city here below, and our hearts are restless until they become the dwelling of the Holy Trinity, in full truth — i.e. that we'll cease to direct our courses permitting God to do as he pleases. Try to preach to yourself; try to reason with yourself. Two years in the Air Force are gone already and what will remain of them with you permanently is what you had accomplished in the realm of your interior life. Try to live from hour to hour in loving God's Holy will of the moment. Don't feed on the past; don't fear the future; love God in the moment that is at hand by loving that which he sends you at the moment of a duty, a prayer, a relaxation, a revulsion, a suffering. All these shades of our daily lives come together to form a beautiful character, a noble soul. Pining weakens us and is a waste of God's precious time. It could have been otherwise but it isn't — so, why waste time in regrets. Pray for strength, for peace, tranquility and stability.

Regarding the Rev. Feeney, yes, we should pity him. However, I can see nothing but pride in his case. He is wrong - even tho morally and theologically his contentions were true, the fact that he does not obey his superiors - diocesan and religious — makes him wrong. Disobedience can never be a virtue, Johnny, and there is no place for considering a disobedient soul a courageous soul. A disobedient soul is a proud soul — and pride is a vice.

Keep praying for me, for us, and for yourself. Be good, cheerful and happy — and live in the present moment. All's well that ends well! Nothing is lost if accepted as the Holy Will of God. Lovingly in Jesus and Mary,

M. M. E.

The year was coming to a close more rapidly than previous ones. The following year would see the completion of the Reverend Mother's eleventh year in office. She sometimes wondered how time could pass so quickly. She was ever thankful to her precious Lord for the many opportunities the Bernardines were continuing to receive in the service of God and His Holy

Church.

Another health service proposal arrived at Mt. Alvernia in early October.

"The archbishop has offered us the ownership of the Sacred Heart Hospital in Chester," reported Mother Chrysostoma to the Reverend Mother shortly after her return.

"From what we know about Chester that may be quite a challenge. We should find out why the other community of sisters decided to leave. Please make arrangements for us to visit the hospital. A close inspection will give us a better understanding of what will be needed if we decide to accept his Eminence's offer."

"Yes Mother, I will do so."

After a thorough examination of the hospital's facilities and probable needs, the Bernardines added this substantial project to the community's health-care apostolate. The Reverend Mother gave much of her time to supervising the rejuvenation of the small maternity hospital.

As always, her thoughts and concerns turned to the Brazilian Province. More than forty American sisters were actively fulfilling the requests of pastors and bishops who were establishing church-related schools to foster the growth of the church. The Brazilian sisters in the province had grown to some sixty professed sisters, novices and postulants as well as twenty-five aspirants. The Reverend Mother's great hope was that the Brazilian Province would one day be composed of all native sisters. She encouraged the American Bernardines to raise as much funds as possible for the Brazilian missions.

In November of 1952 the Reverend Mother prepared a conference for her good sisters for the year 1952-1953. His aunt sent Johnny a copy to give him a more insightful view of the depth of the congregation's consecration as "Adorers of the Sacred Heart of Jesus, In Truth". Another of her beautiful letters explained the reasons for this gift to him.

> *Dearest Johnny,*
>
> *Your last two letters were received — thank you for both. Please ponder over the words of my conference to the sisters since I can't write much at this time. I have been induced to do this by your words, "When are you going to present the world with a literary masterpiece?" The Conference is not a masterpiece. It's the masterpiece that I want Jesus to produce.*
>
> *My ambitions have never been directed towards anything like temporal attainments — there was, is and, I pray, will be only one*

goal before me and that is Sanctity — *This is a masterpiece, but alas, it can't be mine. It must be "Jesus' life" in me. All I must learn to do is be* passive — *to remain fully abandoned to the Holy Will of the Father, for this is sanctity.* Jesus is our sanctity - *When we permit Jesus to live His Life of Love for the Father, for His Mother, and for souls, in ourselves by being fully abandoned to the Will of Jesus' Father, then Jesus produces a masterpiece, a Saint. This is the only masterpiece in which I'm interested; this be your goal too — Pray for me that I remain passive; I'll pray that you have no other desires.*

    Father Galligan gave a retreat to our girls last weekend. He was good! He is easily approached; a perfect gentleman. God love you!

    M. M. E.

Johnny read with great interest the words of the conference his aunt indulgently sent to him. When he finished reading her message to her sisters he wondered if he could ever approach the holiness of his aunt.

In the formula of the Consecration of our Congregation to the Immaculate Heart of Mary, we pray that Mother Mary be our way to the Sacred Heart of Jesus, that Mother Mary deign to mold our souls and form our heart so that we may in Truth be called the "Adorers of the Sacred Heart of Jesus". These are not empty phrases, devoid of meaning; they are not my innovation; they are not some novelty. We are the consecrated children of Mary, because we are the daughters of Mother Veronica, of St. Francis of Assisi; because we are the sisters of the great St. Bernardine of Siena; because we are the chosen spouses of Christ, who consecrated us to His Mother beneath the Calvary Cross. Permit me, dear sisters, to develop these ideas in today's conference that they may have a powerful influence on our spiritual life, growth and development.

With a deeply grateful respect, every one of us today refers more and more often to the merits and work of our revered Mother Foundress, who has not spared herself for the Congregation. She was, indeed, an apostolic soul, as was our Holy Father St. Francis, even though her apostolate has not become renowned. She loved Mother Church and carefully observed her every move; she held the Holy Father in highest respect, because he was to her the Vicar of Christ in every sense, and this respect she made evident in a humble obedience to his every wish; she was a Franciscan and a Bernardine, in every inch of herself, for all the loves of Francis and Bernardine were the silver threads of her spiritual growth and development. Above all, she was a child of Mary; in the shadows of Mary's national shrine at Czestochowa her beautiful soul learned to know Mary and her warm heart was set aglow with love for "*Matuchna*". As a young girl, she listened to the reports of Mary's coming to Bernadette at Lourdes, she rejoiced in Mary's triumph in the Proclamation of the Dogma of the Immaculate Conception; (very much like ourselves listening to reports of Fatima and bubbling with joy because of the Proclamation of the Dogma of the Assumption); from the arms of Mary of Czestochowa, after years of suffering and exile, she passed into the arms of the Sacred Heart of Jesus, when she entered the novitiate of the Bernardine Sisters at Zakliczyn, where the Sacred Heart of Jesus reigned and reigns supreme. From this cradle she transplanted into the soil of her American Foundation this cherished devotion to the Heart of Christ, and with an exultant "Magnificat" lived through the occasion of the solemn Consecration of the Human Race to the Sacred Heart of Jesus, by Pope Leo XIII, in the year of 1900. Doubtless, she was not indifferent to the fact that she was asked to found her new Congregation in the Archdiocese of Philadelphia, which had been solemnly consecrated to the Sacred Heart of Jesus, October 15, in the year 1873, by Bishop Wood, who became the first Archbishop of this See.

On the 8th of December, 1951, we only endorsed solemnly what was, is and will be our Foundress' legacy to us; and we have done it in the spirit which characterized all her actions — namely, in the spirit of childlike docility and humble obedience to the wish of Mother Church. In response to the summons of the Encyclical of our gloriously reigning Pope Pius XII of May 1948, we generously consecrated ourselves personally to the Immaculate Heart of Mary and through her to the Sacred Heart of Jesus, on November 1, 1950; and then, we followed this with act of the Consecration of the entire Congregation, on November 8, 1951.

That these acts of ours may be meaningful, dear Sisters, we must understand them in full, then love them, and knowing and loving them imbue ourselves with their spirit that they may become a fact of our lives. That this may be true, it may be of vital importance that we briefly recall what had taken place at Paray-le Monial and at Fatima.

In the shadows of night, in the depths of the grand silence of the cloister, in the chapel of the Sisters of the Visitation, Our Lord Jesus appears to the lost-in-prayer St. Margaret Mary Alacoque. He stands before her as one cast-down, begging her for sympathy, for consolation, for reparation and expiation for the coldness and indifference of the great majority of souls — but specially of souls consecrated to Him and His work. He begs her for the Communion of Reparation of First Fridays ... and for consecration or a total gift of self, returning love with love....

At Fatima, in 1917, and again in the convent of the St. Dorothy Sisters, at Tuy, Spain, December 10, 1925, Mother Mary appears to Sister Lucy dos Santos ... She stands before her with sadness in her eyes, crushed with pain, suffering because of the ingratitude and blasphemies with which Her Immaculate Heart is nourished by sinners ... and she begs for consolation or reparation ... and not for an hour's vigil (this is too long for the softness of the 20th century) but for a 15 minutes' watch in the Mysteries of Her Rosary, for Communion of Reparation each First Saturday, and for consecration, a total offering of self to Her Immaculate Heart.

Jesus and Mary come to us as beggars? Does this not detract from their dignity? Is not this an affront to the divinity of the Sacred Heart, to the divine Maternity of the Blessed Virgin Mary? The ways of God are not our ways. To the great of this world appeal power, strength, greatness, independence; but hearts are conquered with love, and love knows no power or greatness. The Heart of Jesus and Mary do not come to cast us into the dust of our nothingness, in profound adoration, but to enter us into their arms, that we return love for love. Bethlehem, Nazareth, Calvary and the Tabernacle are the best spokesmen for this. Twice each day our lectors remind us in the dining room that *God is love*, "Deus Caritas est." Indeed, God is such love of humble littleness, such love of humility, that the pride of men cannot understand it, takes scandal, and refuses to accept it. This lowliness of God's Love gave rise to all our heresies — *it is too good to be true*, said and say the heretics in each case. Arius admitted that Christ was a truly noble and great man, but he could not be God, because his pride could not conceive how a God could become a weak infant, live in poverty, die the death of a scoundrel ... and all this for the love of man. For this reason, too, God overlooks the wise and the great of this world; the Sacred Heart of Jesus reveals itself to a humble, hidden, scorned even by her own religious companions, St. Margaret Mary, and the Immaculate Heart of Mary appears to three bare-footed, simple, poor illiterates of Fatima, the shepherds of the 20th century.

Our own saintly Archbishop O'Hara underlined this beautifully in his address at Fatima, on the 23rd of May, of this year, 1952, when he said, that this spot "is the sanctuary of God's Will, which Mary revealed to the world through the mouths of three little children. This sanctuary is Mary's one-room schoolhouse, to which she brought her three barefoot pupils, Lucia, Francisco, and Jacinta, and taught them the mysteries of God's ways and, as well, the mysteries of the Immaculate Heart." Does this not appall the worldly wise? Further, continues our Arch-shepherd, that "Mary has not brought Lucia, Francisco and Jacinta here for themselves but for the whole of mankind." She adds, "Unless we become as little as they were, with the mind and heart of little children, we will not learn a thing even at Fatima's shrine." To the wise and great, Fatima will ever remain a closed book, a hilly and sandy countryside of Portugal. In these dark days, Mary seeks children who believe what she reveals; Mary needs children who hope in what she promises; Mary needs children who love what she loves. Mary needs children who in their simplicity of mind and conformity of will, go away from her feet to teach to the world "the deep things of God," which the world of itself can neither see, nor trust, nor treasure. Let us not be surprised, dear Sisters, when we meet with souls who question the consecration, belittle the message of Fatima, and treat the "true devotion" with scorn ... Indeed let us rather rejoice and thank God that we have the privilege to find among our contemporaries souls as great as Our Holy Father, Pope Pius XII, and our saintly Archbishop O'Hara, who accepted the message of the barefooted illiterates and live to fulfill the wishes of the Queen of Heaven. Let us rejoice that we are members of the Congregation, founded by Mother Veronica, who bequeathed to us not the wisdom and greatness of the world, but the humility, simplicity and littleness of God's children... not the spirit of independence and mental haughtiness, but the spirit of delicate docility and blind obedience, which spiritual treasures make us delicately attuned to every call from the Vatican and the Dioceson Authority.

As children of Mother Veronica, the Adorers of the Sacred Heart of Jesus through the Immaculate Heart of Mary, let us try to approach as closely as we can to the Heart of Christ at Paray-le-Monial and the Immaculate Heart of Mary at Fatima, that we may leave this Retreat, enriched with the Wisdom of the Eternal God, all aglow with the love of the Heart of the Master, that we may understand the mission to be carried away from these schools of humility and littleness, that we may requite love for love, that by means of the sacrifice of our lives we may rejoice what has undergone corruption in the Mystical Body of Christ.

Today, neither Jesus nor Mary can suffer in their glorified bodies ... yet, the Sacred Heart of Jesus and the Immaculate Heart of Mary stand before us sorrowful and suffering, begging for consolation and sympathy, presenting to us a program of reparation, whereby their love that is scorned and reviled may be expiated. How are we to understand this?

The death of Christ on the Cross has been as it were the beginning of the end in our redemption — that is, that this redemption in its effects is to last to the end of the world, to the moment, when the last of the elect will be saved — as Saint Therese has expressed it so beautifully, when she spoke of her mission which was to begin with the grave: *"No, there cannot be any rest for me till the end of the world — till the angel shall have said, 'Time is no more' then I shall take my rest, then I shall be able to rejoice, because the number of the elect will be complete."* St. Therese fully and well understood the role and meaning of the church, the Mystical Body of Christ ... just like our Holy Father St. Francis who would not rise from the feet of Mother Mary, until she obtained for him the great grace of a plenary indulgence which could be obtained by all souls who visited his Portiuncula ... and not once only, not for a limited time, but as often as the chapel was visited until the end of time.

This Mystical Body, our Holy Church, is a mystical organism, whose Head is Christ, whose Heart is Mary, and whose members are we. If we understand the construction of our bodies and the functioning of every smallest cell in this body, we understand that the activity of one cell affects all other cells favorably or unfavorably — e.g. if our stomachs function properly, all the cells of our bodies are affected favorably; when one appears before a physician and complains of a weakness and exhaustion of a general nature, the physician orders blood tests, because very frequently this general state of being drained of energy and strength is due to poor blood. Once the blood is enriched, improved, the general weakness disappears and the whole body enjoys new vim, vigor and vitality.

The same may be said of the Mystical Body of Christ ..when the cells of the members are sick , the Head suffers ... and, lo, we find the Sacred Heart of Jesus appearing to St. Margaret Mary and complaining that it suffers. Suffers? Yes, in its Mystical Body. When Mother Mary stands before the three shepherds at Fatima and complains, she complains because she, the Heart of the Mystical Body, the Mother of the Head of this Body suffers, because the ill health of the members affects the Head as well as the heart.

Let us contemplate in short the apparitions of Paray-le-Monial and of Fatima, that the conditions of time, the symbols and the words may help us to understand our responsibility with respect to the existing aches and pains in the Mystical Body, that our spiritual well-being and health may improve this health and increase the strength of the needy members. Let us not forget for one moment that Jesus at Paray-le-Monial and Mother Mary at Fatima came to me, to you, my dear Sisters, as our Archbishop O'Hara stated. Fatima, in a special manner, should be always present to us, because we belong to the era of Fatima; Lucy is our contemporary, is our co-religious. To the extent to which we understand our mission and to the extent to which we are impressed with our responsibility with respect to the sick members of the Mystical Body, our consecration will not be empty words but life-giving realities.

The *Sacred Heart of Jesus* appears surrounded with thorns, with a cross in the midst of the outbursting of flames, with the wound of a lance; the *Immaculate Heart of Mary* appears surrounded with thorns, and is ordinarily represented as transfixed with the sword as Her Heart appeared to Saint Catherine Labour on the Miraculous Medal (although at Fatima did not see the sword). The 17th century, in which St. Margaret Mary lived were the days of Jansenism, which originated in the bosom of the Church, from an unfounded fear before the magnitude of God's holiness, and which caused a chill and coldness — hence, the Sacred Heart comes with outbursting flames and with the instruments of His Passion near the opened wound of His Heart, that we may be convinced, that He is all love, that He invites us to enter His opened wound that we may be set on fire with love for Him ... His Heart calls out to us: *I Love You*; love Me, for I have loved you unto death and death on the cross.

The era of Fatima, our days ... as the days of *materialism*, communism ... they are an era of evil, which originated outside of the church but which is out to contract, to smother, to wither the Mystical Body by preventing its free growth and development ... people are occupied with things of this world, they have no time for God ... they do not deny His existence, but they strenuously object that He in any way interfere with their mode of life. *Mary, through Her Heart* calls to us: I am the Mother of your Head, I am the heart of His Body ... love the Head, my son, through me; permit me to give you my love and through it to give you life, health ... that I may form of you my sons, the brothers of Jesus ... Yes, *"Other Christs"*.

The Heart of Jesus and the Immaculate Heart of Mary prescribe for us methods of curing the evil of our days ... Both of these programs resemble each other very closely: *Communion of Reparation* on First Fridays, that in receiving the rejected Love we may grow warm and make reparation for all those who do not want to believe in the love of Jesus; *Communion of Reparation* on First Saturdays, that we may make reparation for the indifference of people, that we may aid Mary to rid hearts of their material preoccupations, that Jesus may reign in them.

The Holy Hour on Thursdays before the First Fridays, that we may contemplate the Passion of our Lord, the limitless ocean of His love for men, that we may be the Angels of Consolation of the Garden of Olives for the suffering Jesus; that by inflaming our hearts in the contemplation of the Passion we may share this warmth with the souls that are dying of chills and cold, a *quarter hour* of meditation on the Mysteries of the Rosary on First Saturdays, that in this contemplation of the antidote for the indifference of materialism we may help men to return to the true values of life, which are taught to us in the Rosary:

The *Joyful Mysteries* teach us to love manual labor and the hidden life of the family ... family Rosary; both are scorned today;

The *Sorrowful Mysteries* teach us to love and to understand the meaning of suffering in our lives, in our growth in holiness, and in salvation in general; everybody loves pleasure today and uses every measure to escape pain;

The *Glorius Mysteries* teach us to believe in life-hereafter, in eternal rewards and punishments ... today, people live only for material values; who believes in eternity?

The Hearts of Jesus and Mary beg for our Consecration, or the gift of self, the giving of love for love ... from the Consecration of Saint Margaret Mary and Blessed Claude Colombiere to Leo XIII ... form the barefooted trio of Fatima to Pius XII. They beg for *Reparation*, or the reconstruction of the damaged cells of the Mystical Body, the return of love for love, the wounded love, by prayer, work, suffering, sacrifices, and especially by the fulfillment of God's Holy Will in the performing of our duties, our responsibilities, the demands of our state of life. Yes, *True Devotion* is, in the words of St. Thomas: "an act of the will by which man subjects himself to God's Will" through Mary. It is living God's will, Mary's "Fiat," and not a sentimental feeling.

All these are part and parcel of our religious life, as we find it defined in our *Rules, Constitutions* and *Customs*. Let us only be mindful of all; let us be faithful in the making of our morning intentions, whereby each day we offer all our works, prayers, sufferings, etc. as a form of reparation to the Sacred Heart of Jesus and to the Immaculate Heart of Mary. We promise to do this in the formula of our Consecration of the Congregation; let us fulfill this sweet duty with generosity and with love, that our consecration may be not only some devotion, but a living for the Sacred Heart of Jesus through the Immaculate Heart of Mary.

Should the Consecration be to us Franciscans and Bernardines a special way of living, a way distinctly ours? Absolutely so! Our Patron Saint Bernardine had offered himself as a slave to Mary from his very early days. His slavery was a *true consecration*, for he lived for Mary alone, and through her, for Jesus. But, was the devotion to the Immaculate Heart of Mary known to St. Bernardine? Indeed it was. In fact, St. Bernardine's sermon for the Feast of the Visitation, July 2nd, was devoted to Her Immaculate Heart in its entirety ... so much so, that the Congregations, founded by St. John Eudes, the Apostle of the Hearts of Jesus and Mary, use this sermon in the second Nocturn's Lessons for the Feast of the Heart of Mary, which in these Congregations is celebrated on February 8th. In this sermon, our St. Bernardine sings praises to the love of Mary's Heart as it has poured forth in her seven series of words, which we find recorded in the Gospels:

two to the Archangel Gabriel at the Annunciation: "How shall this happen, since I do not know man." And "Behold the handmaid of the Lord; be it done to me according to thy word."

two to St. Elizabeth: Greeting Elizabeth and The Magnificat

two to Jesus: "Son, why hast thou done so to us? Behold, in sorrow thy Father and I have been seeking thee."

"They have no wine."

one to the servants at Cana: "Do whatever He tells you." These last words sum our True Devotion.

Our saintly brother, St. Bernardine, justly remarks that all the words of Mary, uttered to men, are *brief* ... only the Magnificat, the outpouring of her heart to God, is long. There is a wonderful moral for us in this wisdom of Mary ... let us speak briefly to people, but with God, let us not mark time.

Our Holy Father Saint Francis, who received his mission at the foot of the Cross at St. Damian's, "Francis, repair my church" ... Reparation ... misunderstood the meaning of these words until he captured the meaning of his mystical mission in the chapel of Mary of the Angels ... where, too, he not only deeded himself to her entirely, but also consecrated totally all his three orders. His biographers tell us that he vested every new member in the holy Habit of his Order in this chapel, for where he became Christ's slave through Mary, he also wished that every new member received the same life there from Mary. *(Postulants receive veils in Audience Hall.)* To this chapel, he repaired immediately on returning from his missionary trips ... there he spent nights in prayer; in honor of his heavenly Mother, he composed beautiful hymns and prayers; in the Office in honor of Christ's Passion which he composed, every hour begins and ends with an anthem to Mary ... Legend tells us that Francis' mother, Pica, while praying in this dilapidated chapel, received word from heaven that she would be a mother of a son, who will repair the church. In the shadow of this chapel, St. Francis wished to die ... and there he did, brought by his brothers from a great distance, after sundown, Saturday, October 3... there his beautiful soul returned to Jesus, through Mary's hands ... Isn't it providential that we celebrate the feast of St. Therese on October 3? Among all the saints, SS. Francis and Therese best understood the spirit of the Gospel, the spirit of spiritual childhood and littleness....

Should not our Audience Hall be to us what the Portiuncula was to Saint Francis? Should we not be followers and lovers of the two Saints who so resemble each other, and who so well understood their mission with respect to the Mystical Body?

But, let us proceed with the understanding of our Consecration, that we may love it and cherish it above all other treasures. Let us try to understand it in the light of the Calvary Drama; this is beautifully presented in the little book, which I presented to each of the houses — "With Mary Our Mother" by Father Endler. Father calls it the *Consecration of St. John* ....

Solemn High Mass was going on in the sanctuary of Calvary. Silence fell on all creation, for it was consecration time. Sacrificial death was slowly separating the Precious Blood from the Sacred Body of Christ on the altar of the cross. St. John, the "Beloved Disciple", who monopolized the Sacred Heart at the Last Supper, was serving. Mary, the new Eve of the human race, by her immaculateness, supplied the spotless linens, and her tears the water that must be mixed with wine, her Heart the Paten. As the server at Mass represents the entire congregation present, so St. John, standing at the foot of the Altery-cross, represented each one of the elect, each member of the Mystical Body of Christ till the end of time. Now in solemn tones the Divine celebrant speaks: "Behold they Son" ... "Behold thy Mother" ... Jesus wished to give His Mother a last gift before leaving her, a last token of His great and tender life-long love, and He could think of nothing more suitable and precious than an immortal soul, a soul that had three characteristics very dear to Him, namely:

a — great love of charity

b — great love of his Eucharistic Heart

c — *true filial love* for her

By these momentous words our dying Savior signified to his brokenhearted Mother who was about to lose Him by the separation of death, that He wished

Her henceforth to lavish on this particular soul all the maternal sweetness she had ever given Him during all the 33 years, and treasure it with an especial affection and care and above that afforded all her second-born. And this tie of the holy intimacy was to last eternally.

And to John, the Master intimated that he, the chosen beloved disciple, was henceforth to take this gentle Mother "to his own" in a most special way and ever give her a full measure of *filial love,* make her a vital part of his daily life, in a word, live everywhere and at all times in her Heart.

Mary understands, and while she feels the greatest gratitude to her Divine Son for His last gift (given when His Sacred heart was about to break through a love It could no longer hold within Its narrow walls), her Heart goes out to John with a new feeling of maternal tenderness. John, henceforth, will be to her not only a son but a very favorite son, and will so remain for all eternity. John, likewise understands, and from that moment he regards Mary not only as a personal mother, but a very dearly beloved mother. Looking up, as His Master requested, John reads in her tear-drenched eyes a new look of maternal graciousness and love he had never perceived before. She has now become soul of his soul, life of his life.

But are there no other disciples whom the Master loves especially, whom He wishes to bless with this priceless Consecration? *You may become another John to Mary* if you only humbly and earnestly ask Our Lord for the favor and render yourself worthy to receive it by duplicating in your personal life St. John's three outstanding characteristics, the things that will induce the dying Mass-victim to repeat what He once did at the first Mass on Calvary.

My dear Sisters, we are those Johns, those privileged souls, whom Jesus has solemnly consecrated to His Mother on Calvary. But that we may prove worthy of this inestimable grace, Mary must be our life, our soul, our heart. Our souls must be characterized by the loves which were John's:

a — We must possess the *love of reparation* towards our fellow men, those co- members of ours in the Mystical Body of Christ; we must consider their spiritual weaknesses and needs as our own and make just returns to the wounded love of Christ; we must love them in a divine way, in Mary's way, for John's love was the love which he found in the Heart of Jesus while his heart and head rested on the breast of Christ at the Last Supper; his love was the love of Mary which he imbued from the intimacy of his home which became Mary's; we must love our neighbor *sincerely* and cordially, remembering that our love in the first place must consider the soul of our neighbor.

b — We are to be characterized by a deep love for our Eucharistic Guest in the Tabernacles of our chapels; the Tabernacle is to be our *ALL*; Holy Hours, when possible, but certainly frequent visits to this heaven on earth should be our *ALL*, our greatest treasure; at the foot of the tabernacle we should find answers to all our problems; there we should share all our joys and sorrows; these especially we should seek strength and courage when in difficulties and in sufferings.

c — Mary is to be the soul of our souls, the life of our lives; our Consecration must be a living and not only a formula, or some devotion ... it is *to be Mary's life of the will of God*, as Archbishop O'Hara defined it; it is to be a *life of obedience* to the commandments of God, to our Rules, Constitutions and Customs, our Superiors; it is to be a life of sacrifice where on the altar of victimhood our I goes through a slow death by self-denial; where the ego is substituted inch by inch by Christ, where the selfish man of sin is changing into "another Christ"; it is to be a life of the *Ecce*, as Jesus has come upon this earth with the answer "*Ecce venio*" to His Father's wishes, and Mary has entered upon this path of co-redemption with her "*Ecce ancilla Domini*" ... "*Ecce* should be our ever ready answer to all vicissitudes of life, to all calls to duty.

We must, however, never forget that our *Consecration took place on Calvary*, under the cross. If St. John were not present, as the other Apostles, he would not be so highly privileged. He accepted the sorrow and pain of Calvary; in return, he was consecrated to Mary. So, too, our Holy Father St. Francis found his mission at the foot of St. Damian's cross, and to the cross he kept returning with his *reparatory love*, whence he exclaimed "Love is not loved" ... and at Mary of the Angels he found the fulfillment, the realization of this love. *This is the will of God for us.* To Father Olier, the founder of the Sulpicians, Christ once said, "Before I begin reigning in you through Mary, I must reign there through my cross." How true, Sisters! Did you truly consecrate yourselves to Mary? If so, you must be treading the path of thorns from day to day.

And so it must be, for the *end of our* consecration is the formation of *another Christ* in us; it is the transformation of us into children of God ... where "I" reigns, there is no place for Christ, and Mary's role is limited ... and, yet, she is to be the sole life and soul of every consecrated soul. Mary foretold this truth to Bernadette at Lourdes and to the three children at Fatima; she prepared them for a life of great sufferings, telling them this directly, without consideration for their youth and sensitiveness. *Let us also be prepared* for suffering, for persecutions by people and the evil spirit, for the cross. And the more sincere you will be, my dear Sisters, in this *gift of self to Jesus through Mary*, be prepared for greater and almost constant suffering ... but don't become disheartened, you are not alone ... *Mary is with you*. Accept the sufferings as a token of Mary's kind consideration of your gift ... She is letting you know that you are her privileged child ... and through tears and storms, keep repeating:

"Mary, my Mother, I am your child; reign in me through the cross at the foot of which I have been solemnly consecrated to you by the Agonizing Heart of Jesus."

Perhaps, one or another of you is tempted to say at this moment, " This is not my life; I am very sinful; I fear suffering; in fact, I don't want it ... this may be all good and fine for the highly developed spiritually" ... Mary Magdalen, the sinner, was at the foot of the cross and was consecrated to Mary with John.

No, Sisters, the *life of consecration* is not a reward for sanctity; it is *the way of sanctity*. Don't we all want to become Saints? Is not this the primary reason why you and I followed our vocation? Now, the way of consecration is the shortest, the safest, the most certain, and the most direct way to sanctity, for nobody knows and loves Jesus more than Mary, and no one can teach us this knowledge and love of Jesus better than Mary, His Mother, our Mother. Let us permit Mother to guide us; let us be docile; let us place our hand in hers and follow her blindly ... yes, blindly, for we cannot see where she leads us, and we cannot understand ... but theirs is the path of Mary's love to Jesus.

Through the Immaculate Heart of Mary to the Sacred heart of Jesus - this is the mother of the daughters of Mother Veronica, "the Adorers of the Sacred Heart of Jesus, in truth."

"Have we received any news from Mother Benjamina? Has she decided how many of our American sisters we can expect to arrive back from the Brazilian mission for their first visit home?"

"Yes, Reverend Mother, there will be around twenty this time. We can expect them about a week before Christmas," responded Mother Chrysostoma.

"That will be a joyful time for all of us as well as their families. Let us pray they all arrive safely."

CHAPTER EIGHT

The sun over southern Japan, completing its December descent, lazily slipped behind the mountain range west of the air base. The AACS jeep sped along the ashen road, across the taxi strip to the direction finding station about 200 yards off the runway. Johnny leaped from the front seat, walked quickly up the three concrete steps, entered the station and greeted the Australian on duty.

"Well, Wilson, I guess you won't be here much longer."

"We'll be out of here next month. It's been a long four years. I guess this D.F. station must be damned boring to you compared to the control tower."

"With a little luck I'll be heading back to the tower when more Americans are transferred to Iwakuni."

Cpl. Wilson rode off on his bike with a paperback book sticking out of his back pocket. Reading had become the Aussie's favorite pastime. Soon another boringly lazy shift came to an end. Johnny had sent a payment of $115 to the Magazine Institute in New York with the great hope that the writing lessons would help replace the Berkeley Extension courses.

The next day the tower chief presented him with some good news. "I'm putting you in for promotion to Airman First Class. Under the old system that would have made you a sergeant. If it goes through, you'll have that third stripe and a raise in pay."

"Thanks. I need that right now."

"And you'll be going to Itami AFB, near Osaka for your tower physical. The three-day TDY will give you time to visit Osaka and Kyoto."

The three days at Squadron Headquarters aided considerably in breaking the monotony at Iwakuni.

"I think I'll visit Kyoto today. Anybody else interested in going along?" asked Johnny.

"No, we've been there. You'll enjoy it. Perhaps you'll meet someone at the train station going the same way."

Two marines on R & R from Korea were at the station. With greetings quickly exchanged, they invited Johnny to join them.

"Where are you from?" he asked them.

"I'm from Pennsylvania and my buddy's from New Jersey."

"Any chance you may know any marines from my hometown in Shenandoah, Pennsylvania?"

"No, I don't think so."

Around 3 P.M. they arrived in Kyoto. They headed immediately to see the Emperor's former palace and coronation hall where a Japanese guide took them on a 30-minute tour of the grounds.

"These are the first color shots I've taken with my camera," Johnny told his two companions. "I hope they come out all right." The late December afternoon was quickly fading into an early evening grayness, which made him wonder if the light was adequate.

"Let's go to a really good restaurant before we head back to the base."

"Okay," said Johnny. "Any ideas?

"I've heard the Kyoto Prunier is one of the best."

The Prunier was about the classiest in the city. The exchange rate made the restaurant's prices well within the affordability of most servicemen. With two marines out for rest and recreation, they wanted only the best before heading back to Korea.

"You know, this is like eating at the Stork Club in New York," said the New Jersey marine. They all had a drink before the meal. Johnny had his first "Old Fashioned," which he enjoyed. Scotch was out of the question for him after his last episode with the drink.

Johnny passed his control tower physical with little trouble; drawing blood from his arm usually the most uncomfortable part. He returned to Iwakuni by train with thoughts about his aunt's last letter and the conference message to her beloved Bernardines. As much as he wanted to devote his life to the priesthood, he knew he could never be one unless he devoted himself totally to Christ, to the exclusion of all material and worldly desires. In his senior year in high school Sister Marie Eymard had read so eloquently the words of Francis Thompson's "The Hound of Heaven" in which the poet flees from Christ in every possible way, only to find that the Lord is the unperturbed, unhurrying pursuer from whose love he can never totally withdraw. To Johnny, Thompson's line: "Lest, having Him I must have naught instead" was nothing less than a call to sainthood of the highest order. He felt he had only begun to live and to know the world outside of his small coal region town. There had to be so many paths he wanted to be free to explore, that to restrict oneself to one love which demanded so much of that freedom, seemed too much of a burden. He knew too well Christ's promise that His burden was light and His yoke was not heavy. Perhaps if he prayed enough, followed the requests of Our Lord and His mother regarding the first Fridays and Saturdays, went to Mass as often as possible, went to Confession regularly and shared his Catholic Faith with anyone who showed any interest, he might be on his way to a total commitment to the paths of the saints. He also knew the environment he had been thrust into in Japan: the tempting prostitutes who lined the streets with the threat of venereal disease always a possibility; the many friends or fellow airmen who were often indifferent to religion often out of complete ignorance and with little desire to explore the spiritual side of life.

Reading became a habit with him, a love. Evelyn Waugh, Thomas Merton, A. J. Cronin, the intelligible James Joyce, along with the New Testament, deepened his desire to know the really important aspects of life. His present assignment allowed for more use of the base library and meditation. His creative writing was still in the incipient stage and had not yet resulted in any notable work. His meditation centered around Catholicism, its truth and possibilities. A book on Martin Luther titled, "Here I Stand," brought new insight into the reasons for Luther's positions. He also casually read a book on the stock market.

"Johnny, I hear it's your birthday tomorrow. Any plans?"

"Haven't made any," he replied to his friend, Norm Tienken.

"We've decided to have a party for you in town."

The next day Johnny went off with six of his friends into one of the bars where they often hung out. They had gotten to know a few of the girls who were there on a regular basis.

"Jane, today is Johnny's 20th birthday. Tell the girls," said Norm to the girl who had always danced with Johnny when he was in town.

"I tell band to play Happy Birthday! Then everybody knows." The chorus rang out twice in congratulations.

"How many year?" Jane asked Johnny.

"Twenty."

"OK. I smack rear end 20 times. Our custom." Several other girls repeated the custom. Johnny began to feel like an old 20-year-old. At last he was out of his teenage years.

"I hear you a 'Goshu killer,'" one of the girls said to Johnny. The Japanese called Australians Goshus.

One night earlier in the week A/1C Moore and Johnny had walked peacefully through the gate of the air base and had begun the mile-long trek to their quarters when an Australian Corporal, accompanied by several Air Police, approached them. The Aussie was pointing to Johnny and swearing unequivocally that he was one of the American airmen who had just beaten him up.

"I don't know what he is talking about. I don't know anything about a fight," he told the APs.

"This guy swears you were one of them. Your friend was probably one of them also. Report to the station tomorrow morning at 8 A.M., both of you," as they were booked.

The next morning they were instructed that they did not need to say anything on the grounds of possible self incrimination.

"Why is this guy so sure you were involved in the attack on him?"

"We have no idea." A few more questions followed. The Aussie then admitted he couldn't identify either of them. Nothing more happened. Word had gotten around and the girls found out about it. The whole incident helped to break the tedium of daily routines.

He wrote home about the large light fixture which came close to falling on him on his birthday. As he moved back on the food line to get some potatoes which had been placed in another location the light shade dropped some twenty feet and smashed into a thousand pieces to the left of his foot at that very moment. He took the whole incident rather calmly. Others talked about it all day.

In early December Johnny began working in the control tower again. He made another trip to Hiroshima on one of his free days. He visited an orphanage run by Japanese nuns since he had missed this on his earlier trip.

"*Ohayougozaimasu*," Johnny said to the nun who appeared at the entrance to the orphanage. He had wished her a good morning.

"*Ohayougozaimasu*," she answered.

"*Nihongo hanashimosuku?*" Do you speak English? he asked.

"*Iie, gomenasai*," No, sorry.

She graciously motioned him to come inside. Some of the children were huddled around charcoal-burning hibachis. The December cold had the room feeling like a frosty 50-60 degrees. The 70 children, ranging from 2 to 12 years of age, were very pleasant despite the uncomfortable temperature. Johnny left 2000 yen with the nun; not a very large sum, but it eased his conscience. He bought a few inexpensive souvenirs as presents for some of his friends and relatives in the States.

Back in Iwakuni he picked up some Christmas cards featuring the Kintai Kyo Bridge located in West Iwakuni about two miles from the main gate of the air base. Built in the 17th century, the bridge expands or contracts in proportion to the weight load expended by the pedestrian traffic. The Japanese were very proud of this very unique-looking bridge with its five arches.

Johnny's mother wrote to him that she was looking for a new house as he had suggested. She had also decided to purchase a silverware set to go with the china, which they all loved. Alma was beginning to "stray," as she described it, from the spiritual directions she had been carefully taught at school and in the home. Some heavy arguments had taken place. His mother prayed she would not fall into any serious problems after her difficult years in the hospital.

A combination birthday and Christmas package which included a box of molasses-cocoanut patties arrived a week before Christmas and was devoured by his friends in about four hours. A Christmas party scheduled for the afternoon and night of the 25th began to look like an event they all wanted to attend.

"Will you be able to get to the party?" asked Norm.

"I will be working at night," said Johnny, "I'll be there in the afternoon."

"Let's get a holiday picture of the group," the tower chief suggested when everyone was still sober.

They had been joined at the party by seven sailors from the naval air base nearby and about ten girls. The picture showed a group of very happy servicemen happily enjoying Christmas; a world away from the war in Korea.

The Reverend Mother sent a package of chocolates, Hershey kisses, nuts, Life Savers and cookies. Another Bernardine, Sister Wilhelmina, sent a letter with her card and stated that his aunt was in great shape despite all the years as head of the order. A letter from his friend Joe ended the year on a happy note:

Feast of the Holy Innocents
Dear John,
12/52

I won't bother to wish you a Merry Christmas, because by the time you get this letter Christmas, 1952, will be only a memory. I would like to have been able to send you season's greetings, but in religious life we act not when the spirit moves us but when it affects the superiors. In any event, I know that this present letter will make up for any disappointment I might have caused you in not writing earlier.

Christmas in the novitiate was a wonderful experience. In fact, it was only this year that the significance of God's Incarnation came to me. This alone was worth the separation from my family and the old hometown. Of course the great time I have had with all my fellow novices has not been without its pleasure also. Yes, I can say that this was my first real Christmas and that should convey to you all what I am trying to say.

And how about you, John? This was your second Christmas away from home. Way over there in Japan. But it is almost over, John. It won't be long until you are an American again. My former roommate, who spent two years in Japan, left us last November, so I don't have anyone to interest in your impressions of the Japanese countryside now. Speaking of November, you don't know how happy your letters made me. You are the only one of the old gang to write until last week when Richard wrote an interesting letter about his scholastic difficulties. I am pleased to know that your plans for a religious vacation have not gone the way of all flesh. (No, I didn't say surprised.) It makes me happy to even contemplate the thought of someday being a colleague of yours in the conversion of our country. I have heard some things about the Edmundite Fathers and the wonderful work they are doing along these lines. Stay with it, John. Never fail to judge any of your present actions by your ambitions. This will be an excellent means of keeping you on Christ's side in this battle against the evil of the world.

I won't try to describe the novitiate to you, although I feel that you would like me to. I have not the ability to put happiness into words. Let it suffice for me to say that here I have found contentment or at least near contentment. I am convinced that God wants me to be a Paulist. Now I can devote all my energies to that goal. We have the opportunities here to make ourselves men of God in order to do the work of God. That is what the novitiate seems to have as its purpose; to get to know Christ, our best friend. We have two hours of spiritual reading each day. Our novice master, a true priest, gives us a daily conference, and we have an hour's meditation along with periodic visits to the Blessed Sacrament. Silence is in force for about eighty percent of the day, and this has yet to bother me which just shows you how much I can now boast of liking the novitiate. Actually, I should not have claimed contentment above. I am less contented than ever before. But it is a holy discontent, if such a quality exists. More than anything else the novitiate has made me aware of my deficiencies, and knowing me so well you must then have some idea of my lack of content.

Our own Catholic High School won two games this year. Amazing, the most successful year since 1948. And it took our brothers to do it. Your brother Lou must be quite a drop kicker. Ray tells me he can kick them across the goal post from forty yards out. And his two passes which almost beat Scranton Catholic was quite a feat for a halfback.

How much longer have you in the service, John? I seem to have lost count somewhere along the line...I didn't miss going home for Christmas as much as I thought I would ... the novitiate is where God wants me to be. The novitiate and religious life, what I have seen of it, is wonderful. Don't let anything short of God's will deter you from it. Aim at it in all you do now. You have a wonderful chance over there to do a lot of good for Christ's cause, both by works and especially by example. Take advantage of all these opportunities, and get close to Christ — your closest friend.

What else can I say but thanks for your letters and prayers. We need them so badly. Please remember that my letters may be infrequent, remembrances in my thoughts and especially in prayers and Masses will never be lacking. Take care of yourself and keep on God's good side, never forgetting the wonderful, gratuitous gift that is yours. Goodbye, God bless you always, and please pray for me; I do for you.

Your friend in Christ, Joe

CHAPTER NINE

The Reverend Mother faced a major unprovidential development early in the next year of her administration. The recently appointed provincial superior in Brazil was not well.

"Reverend Mother, Mother Contalice may have leukemia," said Sister Imelda to her one morning after Mass.

"Dear Sister, how could this have happened so quickly after only six months in Brazil?"

"It is really unfortunate. Mother Contalice is brokenhearted over the turn of events."

"I will talk to the council and determine our next move."

The council decided to have Mother Contalice flown back to the United States to receive the best medical treatments available with great hope for a full recovery.

"Mother Chrysostoma, please make the necessary arrangements for her return," concluded the Reverend Mother at the end of the meeting. The first provincial in Brazil had been in office for twelve years. A replacement would be needed if Mother Cantelice's health could not be restored.

A letter from Johnny told her he would be a godfather, for the second time, to a tall Texan engaged to a Catholic girl in Houston. He also mentioned receipt of the medical certificate from the Civil Aeronautics Administration in Washington which indicated his medical eligibility to operate a civilian control tower. As usual she responded without delay.

D.M. et O.
January, 1953
Dearest Johnny;

Thank you for the letter. You soared high. Would that you keep close to Christ when darkness sometimes prevails. You know by now that we zigzag between light and shadows. Every special outpour of light is God's grace, but God feeds only the hungry and the thirsty. To enjoy food and to find it truly nourishing we must experience hunger. The same is true in spiritual life and God, the best Master, knows that if we be flooded with light at all times, we should soon tire of it and not appreciate God's gift — hence, the hours and days of darkness. When these come, tell the Lord you believe in His Love, in spite of all, and that your soul seeks only Him as her food and drink. Keep repeating this, with a plenitude of faith and trust, until the light appears again. What counts in your life is not the light but the darkness. When there's light, we become debtors of God; when there's darkness and we remain faithful, God is our debtor — and what returns He'll make! God love you! Mary hold you close to Her Heart!

M. M. E.

Another of the Reverend Mother's many trips away from the motherhouse became necessary when some serious administrative difficulties emerged at one of the hospitals in the Midwest.

St. Francis Hospital in Osceola, Nebraska had been opened at the request and suggestion of some former pupils working in the area. The small town had one Catholic family and very few doctors who wished to serve the medical needs of the thinly populated area composed mostly of Lutherans and Masons. The sisters gradually won the support of the population, however, the absence of any qualified medical personnel meant she needed to determine if the small hospital warranted continued operation by the Bernardines.

"Sister, from everything you have told me, I am going to recommend to the councillors that this operation should not continue. Our sisters are really needed in other facilities."

"Thank you, Reverend Mother, I had hoped you would reach that decision. We have tried in the short time we have been here to improve the needs of the people. There simply are no doctors who wish to commit to the poor prospects here."

The Reverend Mother's willingness to accept the administration of a few small hospitals had given the medical technicians and nursing staff the experience they would need in future assignments. In her next letter to Johnny she mentioned the smooth, relaxing ride she had on the new diesel train called the "Lincoln Zephyr" out of Chicago to Nebraska.

> *D. M. et O.*
> *March 10, 1953*
> *Dearest Johnny,*
> *Thank you for the letter of the 29th. The lapses between the exchange of missives are growing in length.*
>
> *Our Brazilian sisters flew back February 20th. Of the 19 who visited only 10 returned. The others remained for further studying and will return in separate contingents, if I may call them so. One remained for courses in violin, piano, organ, voice and public speaking; another for all departments of art. Then, our sisters were asked to take the management of a federal 170 bed hospital — hence there are sisters preparing for the administrator, X-ray technician, and one is trying to complete her B. S. in Nursing Education. Two of the native Brazilians are taking courses towards a B. S. in Education. One is sick still; she underwent an operation and, then, developed phlebitis. The first three to return are scheduled for August.*
>
> *Then to add to our troubles, the new Mother Provincial in Brazil had to be flown back. She is still hospitalized at Hazleton. For three years we had very few deaths, but 1953 may be a record-making year.*
>
> *So, you see nothing but troubles and many more, of which I do not wish to write.*
>
> *Congratulations on the new son in God! Just a few days ago, a one-year convert asked for admission into our Order. She's only 18 years of age, a Jr. College student, who wanted to be a sister before she came into the Church. Two of her friends are postulants in another congregation.*
>
> *About two weeks ago, when attending the funeral of our Brazilian sister's mother I saw mother. She was very hopeful that dad would get a job elsewhere. I was pleased to find her with this outlook, because I feared to find depression. I saw Sylvia, but missed Louis and your father.*

The "flu" is taking its toll here. Under some form it clutched me and, as yet, didn't say a final farewell. With the continuous "gallivanting", as Father Szal puts it, it isn't easy to rid oneself of a cold. I made a Midwest trip recently; then, went back to Pittsburgh to Mother Duklane's mother's funeral ... She was 79 years old.
    God's blessings and Mother Mary's tender love be yours always!
Lovingly in J & M,
M. M. E.

The Reverend Mother's interest next turned to the new retreat house in the Pocono Mountains of Pennsylvania. The Superior of Saint Francis Province in Scranton told her of a hotel for sale at a very reasonable price. The purchase had been made, after approval by the councillors, in December. By February the Bernardines took possession of the ninety-room hotel and began transforming it into a retreat house for women. The hotel had been built in the opulent twenties located only two miles from the railroad station. A bus station nearby would enable retreatants to reach this house of prayer and reflection with ease. She looked forward to the expected dedication by the Bishop of Scranton in the spring.

CHAPTER TEN

"Man, it's going to be good to get home again," exclaimed Johnny to his new godson, John Eggert, who slept in the bunk bed next to his.

"How much longer do you have over here?"

"Eighteen months have gone by. If I can't get an early release to enter the seminary, that leaves a year to go. And I'm becoming convinced that early release is not going to happen. By the way, when do you expect to receive your First Communion? I expect to serve Mass this coming Sunday. It would be good to see you at the Communion rail."

"Father Whiting has suggested I go to Confession this Saturday and receive Communion Sunday. I'm probably going to follow up on the general confession idea, which will not be easy for me, and start being a decent Catholic."

"I'm sure he'll be a good confessor. Just go ahead and do it. You'll be amazed at how good you feel afterward." Johnny felt a special obligation to Eggert because he had initially wanted Don to be his godfather since Don, also a convert, had shared his own feelings about his decision to become a Catholic before his marriage to a Catholic girl back in Missouri, despite strong opposition from his family. Don had been faithful to his wife during his eighteen-month tour, and everyone respected him for it. Father Whiting had recommended that Johnny become John's godfather because of his aspirations to enter the priesthood.

With his father about to lose his job at the coal mine, Johnny's mother wrote a letter which reflected her deep concerns about the future. Of course, his father had never written to him. Johnny decided to answer with a forceful letter explaining his own feelings about the matter.

184

JMJ

Dear Mom, Dad and all,

Your reasoning is difficult to follow. I neither understand nor like it. The mine closes March 15th; Dad is out of work. Your words: "Until March 15th its no use to worry and then see what will be what." What do you mean? The facts are staring you in the face. Why shouldn't you know what's coming? Yet you refuse to make any plans.

What are Dad's chances of getting another job? Have you any idea how long he will be idle? We're not powerless to act. The future is for those who plan for it. You can't sit around twiddling your thumbs to 'see what will be what.' At 53 Dad's future is non-existent. He is now living in the future he planned for himself and us.

Unsuccessful? We'll let God and Dad determine that. I refuse to judge.

This whole thing has been coming for a long time. You've seen it coming. It's happened before — three times as you say. Are you going to permit it to happen again? Remember, it's not just Dad and you anymore. You have a 22-year-old daughter and a son of 20. We must consider what can be done and how soon. Don't wait until March 15th, think about it today. No one wants to see you worry, but you can't go on blindly. Face the facts, see what can be done, and do it; even if it means leaving the old home town. It takes guts, I know. You said something about 'this will be taken care of by the good Lord." Well, the good Lord takes care of those who care for themselves. He'll help you, but you've got to take the initiative yourself.

All my heart and money are yours. Still, my heart must be in the venture and my money must be invested wisely.

As for the insurance policy, I don't want any part of it. Somebody in town dies and you get all jittery. Why? Do you fear death so much? I'll take care of you, Mom, should anything happen. I love Dad, if for no other reason than that he is my father. Did you ask him if you could or should take out that policy? Can't you see it's like blood money? The very act of getting another policy implies too many things. Is that all his death means? Another $500. Tear that disgusting piece of "security" into a thousand pieces. You can still get rid of it. If ever I send money home don't ever use it to keep that policy from lapsing. You're expecting a rough time ahead and what do you do?

Create another bill to pay. It's as if you'd be waiting for Dad to die just to collect a few dirty dollars.

I'm sorry to be so rude, Mom. I love you, remember that always. Please use some common sense.

You've probably received my income tax return and noticed the Social Security no. is missing. My card was taken with the wallet last year at Misawa. Please send for a new one and correct any mistakes which may have been made on the form.

Dad can expect a letter from me in the near future. I'd appreciate it if you let him read it first. I'm also writing to Alma to see what can be done.

Tomorrow I'll see what I can do about getting a Class Q allotment. With Dad out of work you'll be eligible as a dependent. If the allotment is approved you'll get $140 a month — $77 from the government and $60 from me. I'll still draw about $70 across the board. You can have 40 of that if necessary. Whatever I can do is irrelevant. All I ask is that you analyze the situation, consider the possibilities, and, by God, act. Don't allow circumstances to rule you, be the master of every situation.

God be with you,
Johnny

"Johnny, did you hear the news about our Group Commander? He cracked up a C-54 at Hong Kong, down there with six other ranking officers without authorization. I bet you he killed his chances for promotion to brigadier general if nothing else."

"Well Norm, it certainly doesn't affect us in any way. That's his own personal problem. By the way, the lieutenant is throwing a little party at his home tonight with some help from the outfit. It's a welcome party for his wife who just came over from the States."

"That'll be a nice change of pace. I hear four others are waiting for their wives as well."

A touching Valentine arrived from Johnny's older sister Alma. She told him how much she loved and respected him for all the help he had given the family during his long absence from home.

"Mom is really hurting! She misses you very much. I think you should be more sympathetic to her feelings in your future letters. I know you want the best for all of us but remember the suggestions you are making seem almost impossible for her. And Dad thinks you're just a dreamer. He says you have all these ideas because you don't know what real life is all about."

Johnny decided to write a letter to his family in response to his sister's remarks:

I can't apologize for anything I said in the last letter, however, I do feel better that it was said and now that it is off my mind you may find me a bit more reasonable. Since Dad's job has struck a productive coal vein I guess you can breathe easily for another month anyway....

It's very doubtful that Class Q allotment will be approved so the most you can count on me for is $100 a month. How much pension will Dad draw while he's without work? We will get along, but I don't want to be putting money into a blank wall where little hope exists. I happen to be selfish. Let's get that straight before we go any further. I joined the Air Force because there was little else for me to do. During my second year in the AF I saved $500 and expected to come home with $1,600. That isn't a lot of money, but for me it is. I intend to enter a certain college and expect to pay my own way. I also expect to buy a car for my last year in the service. Is that asking so much? I'm willing to send money home to you since you need it. I still want to see something happening, not just a day-to-day existence of barely hanging on.

You're probably thinking: what are we to do? I know what I'd like to see you do; I doubt you would do it.

Received a Valentine and letter from Alma today. What she had to say touched me deeply. I know it's rough on you, Mom, but remember there are a half million homes suffering the same absence of loved ones. May whatever suffering you are caused by my absence bring you closer to God, the only love worth attaining. All other loves must acknowledge the primacy of His love through which their own existence is made possible. I offered today's Mass and Holy Communion for our happiness; make use of it. Eleven months from now I will be leaving Japan. That's a lot less than the 30 months I once had to do.

I am happy to hear Louis made the Honor Roll at school.

Always, Johnny

"Johnny, how would you like to do some work at the radio station in your spare time?" asked the program director at the Iwakuni Armed Forces Radio Station. Sgt. Glen and he had met at the latest party given by the outfit for another Staff Sgt.'s wife who had recently arrived from the States.

"That sounds interesting. The switch from a control tower mike to one in the radio station shouldn't be too difficult."

"OK, come in Monday if you're free and we'll have you sit in the broadcasting room with the announcer."

Johnny spent that Monday and a few other days of "sitting in" before he got a chance to operate the technical equipment needed to do a short stint of announcing. Before long he became a volunteer announcer at the station.

Spring weather came to southern Japan, with a special festival held in Iwakuni each year at cherry blossom time.

"Anyone planning to attend the festival at the Kintai Kyo?"

"When is it?" Johnny asked a few guys in the one large room they now occupied in a quadrangle built by the Japanese for their own armed forces.

"All week probably, although the big festival is this weekend."

"I'll be going," said his friend Tienkin; "Red" Crow said he would go too.

All three headed for West Iwakuni about two miles from the gate, the following Sunday. Many Japanese had arrived with their picnic baskets and sat close to the bridge. The calm, reserved composure of each of the groups was impressive. Rarely would anyone intrude on these family gatherings. Eye contact almost never happened, especially with strangers.

"The cherry blossoms are in full bloom today. No wonder the Japanese love this place so much. Look how carefully they walk over the arches of the bridge."

"Johnny, I'm glad we came. By the way, did you notice the Japanese priest over there?"

"Why don't we introduce ourselves? He looks like he may not mind talking to us. I wonder if he speaks English."

"Good afternoon, Father," each greeted him and Tienken asked if he spoke English.

"Yes, and German too," he answered in a friendly welcoming manner. " I am a Jesuit who studied in Germany for the priesthood." They spent about an hour with Father Sahada. "Conversions are steady," he said. "Of course we could use money to build a rectory which would leave the building we now use as a church totally for that purpose. I use part of it as my home."

"Father, I'd like to come in town to see you one of these days. There is something I would like to talk to you about. When would you be free to have me visit?" asked Johnny, whose aspirations as a writer were growing with each lesson he completed in his writing course with the magazine institute.

"I will be free this Sunday after Mass. If you like you can attend Mass with my parishioners."

"Father, that would be great, I'll see you on Sunday."

The Mass took place on the second floor of the church building. Father occupied the first floor. With no chairs or kneelers used in the chapel, the Japanese Catholics sat in native fashion on the floor. The very relaxed way the Japanese assumed these positions on the floor made Johnny believe he could do the same. As much as he tried, he could not do it with any ease. He simply decided to kneel or stand during the service. The reverence of the Japanese and the devoted manner of Father Sahada made him happy to see how universal the church had become.

After Mass, Father Sahada invited Johnny to have some rice cakes and tea with him. When finished with the refreshments Johnny asked Father if he knew of anyone who might be willing to rent a room to him where he would have the privacy to write more seriously than he could in his barracks.

"Johnny, let me talk to some people I know and see if any of them have a room you could use. Come back to see me next week."

Father Sahada had a German motorcycle to help him reach his scattered congregation in the farms around the town. He offered to take Johnny back to the base.

"Where did you get the motorcycle?" asked Johnny.

"Some friends in Germany sent it to me and the bike has been a great help in getting around. Perhaps one day I will take you on a tour of the farms around Iwakuni."

"Thanks for the ride and thank you for your efforts in finding a room for me. See you soon."

"Sayonara, Johnny."

At the 9:00 A.M. Mass on Easter Sunday Bishop Heenan of Leeds, England spoke to the congregation for a few minutes and imparted the papal blessing authorized by Pius XII for all the servicemen the Bishop met in the Far East. This "Fulton Sheen of England," on his way to Australia to attend a Eucharistic Congress commemorating the 150th anniversary of the first Mass said on Australian soil, promised he would send a letter to the families of servicemen that he had met.

As a holiday treat T/Sgt. Stodgell invited three of them to dinner. Steak and chicken at the same meal made them have seconds more than once as a tribute to his wife's cooking. The three Stodgell kids were all of over them, which made the evening perfect.

Raymond Burr headed a show in Iwakuni which had to be the best Johnny had seen in Japan. The actor did everything including taking a cream pie in the face.

"I guess you have all heard the C.O. has been promoted to Captain. We will have a party for him next week. Johnny, I would like you and Tienken to make all the arrangements," said the control tower chief to all those in the barracks. The two-man committee followed through, with another great party quickly organized. Several times each month a party for one reason or another kept up the detachment's morale.

Johnny sent one of his few letters to his younger sister, Sylvia, later that day with some thoughts about her coming grade school graduation and entrance into the ninth grade at high school.

> ... *No doubt you're preparing to enroll at Shenandoah Catholic. Alma mentioned the possibility of you going to Mt. Alvernia for your high school years although that could mean entering the juvenate as a candidate for entering the Bernardines. Let us know what your ideas are on the matter and we'll ensure the fulfillment of your desires. If you have any doubts about going away to school I'd suggest you remain in the old home town and attend S. C. H. S. A finer school is difficult to find.*
>
> *A great deal of pressure, or none, may be exerted to influence your decisions during the coming months. All I can say, Sylvia, is pray and pray seriously. Above all, listen to your own heart, your own conscience, no matter what is said to you through others. I want to see you happy. You alone can determine the amount of happiness you will get out of life. I expect to be very happy in this life and the next because I know what I want in life and intend to work to reach that goal. You can do the same. Take your time in making important decisions. You still have four years to prepare, plan, and consider your life's work.*

Be good, sweetheart, and pray for me,   God love you,
Johnny

"I see our orders are here for us to take the unpassed phases of the CAA tower exams," Johnny said to Al Depaulo and his friend Tienken. "I have just one phase to pass. I hope I can do it this time."

"Let's see if we can get a plane ride to squadron headquarters in Itazuki," suggested Tienken. Successful in their request, they flew south for the hour-long flight in a C-45, a small two-engine job.

"This will be a good time to test my new Contessa camera and see if it is worth the $88 I paid for it at the PX."

"Johnny, you know the Germans make the best cameras. That would have cost twice as much in a retail store," commented Tienken. At least a dozen pictures were taken by Johnny which he hoped would give his family and friends a good idea of Japan as seen from a few thousand feet up.

Soon after he returned to Iwakuni Johnny visited Father Sahada to see if anyone had found a room for him.

"A room in a private home fairly close to the church has been offered to you. A former naval officer, employed by the government-controlled electric company, would first like to meet you. He does not speak English. I will go with you to his home."

A few days later Johnny and his Jesuit friend went to the executive's house at the foot of a small hill. They removed their shoes, placed them in a wooden rack outside the sliding doorway, and waited for a house-servant who greeted them and led them to a fairly large, sparsely furnished room with a very low rectangular table at one end. Dressed in a lounging robe, their host greeted them with a respectful bow. His wife, standing at his left side and slightly behind him, bowed to them as well.

Invited to sit at the table across from their hosts, Johnny entered into the private world of the Japanese for the first time since his arrival in the country. No discussions took place until everyone had sipped some hot, fishy-tasting tea. Father Sahada explained Johnny's desire to have a quiet place to pursue his writing interests for, perhaps, two days a week. Johnny searched the man's slanted, nearly invisible, eyes to determine his reaction to the priest's words. His eyes could not be penetrated and his bodily demeanor gave no hint of acceptance or rejection.

Shortly afterward, however, the man took them to a room Johnny could use at a cost of 3,000 yen a month. At nine dollars American he happily showed his acceptance.

"Arigato gozaimasu!" is all Johnny could say. This Japanese "thank you" brought a smile to his newest Japanese acquaintances.

"Thank you, Father. I hope this gives me additional incentive to do some serious writing," Johnny said when they left the house.

"I'm glad you like the room. Not too many Japanese families would do this for an American."

In his enthusiasm to become a writer, Johnny wrote to the Mazagine Institute's Executive Editor, Frances Goodfellow, of his decision to write a novel based on a short story he had written about going "Native for Love." Her response made him reconsider the idea.

Your most recent letter crossed my report to you, which included the answers in advance. Doesn't it seem you are premature in your plans for a book at this time? Judging from what I have seen of your writing, you need a great deal more spadework before you attempt any ambitious project. You have plenty of the future in which to work hard at the writing itself and your book will be more likely to be worthwhile if you buckle down to the chores of learning how to write good prose first.

As I said in my report, there is a story in the babysan situation, but you have not scratched the surface. Your characters are not thought out sufficiently in advance, for one thing. Since the success of a story on this topic depends very greatly on the full-dimensional treatment of characters, this is an obstacle which must be worked through before you can write a worthwhile story. Your best plan at this stage would be to concentrate on characterization and write one full character sketch daily, for practice. Afterwards, take the characters who appear in "I Went Native..." and work out a complete reconstruction of each, for your own guidance. After this we can tackle *scenes* ... you are going to need many thousands of words back of you before your writing has any substantial merit. All these items can be taken care of if you will settle down and do some hard, possibly tiresome, work. Do believe please, that I am willing and eager to help in any way I can. But you do have a great deal of hard work ahead of you before I can.

And congratulations on the good work, "Front-page Johnny." Your articles in the *Iwakuni Sun* are very interesting to me. Please continue to send them. Your articles in the *Sun* and your work on Lessons 10-A and 11-A cause me to suggest an experiment in feature-length nonfiction, for which you may have a flair. For instance, a human interest story on the Kintai Bridge could be carved out of the information available to you. The small portion of this I saw in the *Sun* leads me to think this could be developed very interestingly.

Always my best wishes for your success."

"Are you going to the train station to see Don leave for the States this afternoon?"

"Wouldn't miss it," answered Johnny to one of his newer friends, Howard, who came from Michigan.

"Eighteen months must be so much easier to do. I guess that's one of the benefits of being married."

"Now that I am down to my last eight months, my thirty-months tour is getting more tolerable," added Johnny.

"You mean you have been here almost two years? Your family won't know you when you get back."

"Yes, especially my younger brother and sister. They are teenagers now. I feel I've missed seeing them grow up."

About fifteen airmen went to the railroad station, called the RTO by Americans, to see Don off. He could not have been happier. Johnny took some pictures with his new camera, always trying to read the built-in light meter as accurately as possible. The manual adjustments became easier with every experience; speed is what he hoped to achieve.

In early May, a dynamic Jesuit "stripped naked the soul" with his booming voice and exposed it to the blinking light of eternal truths. Father St. John, S. J., terminated the five days of the mission with a renewal of the Baptismal vows, frightening to Johnny in their reality. All present renounced the devil, the flesh, and the world — with the help of God. "Not to be a saint or never to attempt sainthood had to be simple stupidity," thought Johnny. No one may be perfect, still, the potential power to gain perfection could not be ignored. He wondered how much effort he had put forth thus far in his life. He wrote an article on the mission for the base newspaper.

"Howard, I bought that used bike for $16 in yen. The radio station and my room in town will be easier to reach from now on." Johnny's voluntary broadcasting days each week expended about three hours; his trips to the room in town became very sporadic. Within sixty days he found both too time consuming. The warmer weather made swimming a priority and he enjoyed the softball games played by the AACS unit.

When Johnny learned his family finally had a telephone, he made arrangements to call them. Not every call got through. After two calls were cancelled by the telephone company he received a call from the overseas telephone office telling him the call would get through in half an hour. At $4 a minute he knew he wanted to keep the call to about five minutes.

"Hi Mom, how are you doing?"

"Johnny, is that you? When will you be coming home? You've been away forever!"

"It won't be long anymore. Six, or seven months, at the latest. Is everyone at home? I'd like to hear all your voices."

"Everyone but Louis. Here, I'll put Alma on."

"Johnny, how we all miss you. Please don't let anything happen to you. Do you think you will be home for Christmas?"

"I don't know. My thirty months end in January. How are you?"

"I'm okay. The job is going well and I've made some friends at work. Here's Dad, he wants to get on."

"Johnny, how are you? When will we see you again? Are you sure you're in Japan. Sounds like you're next door. We all miss you. Sylvia wants to talk to you right now."

"Hi Johnny! I graduate next month from St. Casimir's. Then on to high school."

"That's great, Syl, I can't believe I missed both your and Louie's graduations from the eighth grade."

"We love your letters. But you sound so different; not like I remember your voice."

"Well, maybe I've been around these English films, and the Australians, too long. You sound so grown up I probably won't know you when I get home. Better let me talk to Mom again."

"Mom, you haven't been writing very much lately. Please tell me you're okay."

"Johnny, the furnace has broken and they won't fix it. We will keep trying to find another house. I wish you were here. I miss you so much."

"I know Mom, I miss you all too. I am going to end the call now. Say a prayer for me, Sayonara."

Johnny loved the short time he had spent with the family. He began to think more and more about his return to the States.

In his next letter to them he wrote how good their voices sounded on the phone; sorry he had missed Lou and promised that the next few months would fly. They would finally be able to see one another. He also wanted to clear up some comment from his mother in her last letter about his "looking no further than his own nose."

Your latest letter arrived yesterday and in the noon mail today my first Kodachrome pictures came.

I wanted to let this camera business pass without explanation; however, if I can show you that it is you who refuses to "look beyond your own nose" I feel something will have been accomplished.

The camera cost $88 in the P.X, tax free. What made you think I bought it second-hand? I intend to do a lot of traveling in my years, and a camera is a necessity, especially after you've acquired the hobby of photography. And when a person travels he doesn't have a cheap Brownie strapped about him; no, he has an $88 Contessa — $215 in the States, and look up the price if you don't believe me — or any one of the more expensive cameras around.

One more thing; he doesn't take black and white shots, he takes color shots and has slides made which can be projected on a screen for everyone's enjoyment. Of course if you don't care for such entertainment there is nothing I can do but offer it to you. After you've seen some color slides, black and white looks hopeless. I'll send two packages of slides and a hand viewer to you next month to give you an idea of what I'm talking about. The remaining slides I will take of Japan, the Pacific Ocean, the West Coast and other parts of the U. S. I will show you in person with some commentary.

Who is it who is looking "no further than his nose"? All you see is the $88, and the $2.70 it costs for a roll of Kodachrome film. You don't see the pleasure of taking a great picture or the pleasure of entertaining friends in a way they have seldom been entertained. Don't worry, you'll have plenty of money at your service when I do come home, but until then I ask you merely to trust me.

Many spend their money on cigarettes, a "good time" and women — I'm spending mine in a useful way whether you consider it so or not.

God bless you!

Johnny's interest in the *Iwakuni Depot Sun* occupied much of his free time. Many of his articles made the front page after he became the AACS representative to the paper.

"Anyone else going to see the movie tonight?" Johnny asked a couple of his friends.

"Yes, I think I will be going," answered Tienken.

"You know, last week *Time* reported June Haver's decision to enter a convent. The *Daughter of Rosie O'Grady*, is her final picture. I don't think too many actresses became nuns. By the way, *Quo Vadis* plays tomorrow. I don't want to miss that either."

At the end of May John received a letter from Father Galligan, S.S.E., who had stayed in contact with him during his many months in Japan.

> *It's been a long time this time. Your Easter Week letter has been here but yours truly has been away most of the time. The school year is almost over and it's hard to believe that a year could go by so fast. All life is speeding away. It must be up to us to accomplish the most good while we can.*
>
> *I enjoyed your letter, John, and hope you're getting some writing done along with your other duties. Your rotation date will be easy for me to remember. It's my birthday. Wish you could be with our new group this fall, but 1954 will be here before you know it.*
>
> *Everything is fine at St. Michael's. The spring is marvelous though a little wet. Our commencement is Monday when another two hundred Michaelmen will start to make their way in life. I am going to a Mission Exhibit in New York this week. You will have to see one of these exhibitions when you return to the States.*
>
> *Let's hear from you again, John. I hope you are well and doing your utmost to grow in the love of God monthly. A continued special remembrance in my Mass each day is for you that God will make your desire to become an Edmundite grow stronger.*
>
> *Sincerely in St. Edmund*

A memo from Frances Goodfellow arrived at the same time:

> *Thank you for your letter and the copy of the Depot Sun, including your article on the Mission. This seems to give the salient points in*

compact form, and you have combined the facts in good proportion, so that the program of the Mission is outlined; the personality and background of the Jesuit, Father St. John, are touched on; and the highlights of the sermon condensed, with emphasis on outstanding points.

I shall be looking for the various manuscripts, discussion letters, etc. that you mention. Your plans for "The Second Summons" are ambitious, and I am sincerely hoping that you are going to back these up with careful work.

My best wishes for your success.

Faithfully yours...

Rain came in torrents to southern Japan in early June. The drenching rains continued throughout the month. The major advantage of having a control tower much smaller than the one at Misawa meant the operators could climb the steps in thirty seconds rather than three minutes.

Johnny had planned to attend a Confirmation ceremony in Father Sahada's church in Iwakuni during the month. The rain came down for three days forming streams out of the town's roads. His bicycle could not have made it to the church, and he believed the color pictures he had hoped to take would not be that good. He still would have liked to be in the presence of a Japanese bishop once again.

The Air Force began to paint every building and to methodically rejuvenate the base. Fewer Australians could be seen as more Americans came to replace them. Each month that passed made Johnny feel that much closer to home. He would not see another June in the Far East. Saint Michael's College in Vermont had become a reality he could more readily imagine. He sent another $100 to Father Galligan towards his tuition.

A brief note arrived from the Reverend Mother, followed by a letter written in answer to one of his he had mailed to her in May.

Dearest Johnny,

"Just a brief note. Your letter of May 8ᵗʰ came in a few days ago. Your spiritual life seems to be progressing. By the way, I'm taking the "Sign of Jonas" along with me on the trip I am taking tomorrow, that I may gradually complete reading it. I do like Merton's company — esp. in this book, where he is so intimately himself. How much alike are we all!

Did you read the criticism, a pointedly sharp one of this book by a famous Benedictine author? The criticism is directed at Merton and his abbot — of course, we who know religious life can appreciate the value of this humiliation and I pray that Merton's spiritual stamina measures up to God's grace of the moment — God love you!

M. M. E.

The letter brought him up to date on his aunt's busy schedule.

Dearest Johnny,

Your front page debut in the base paper makes me honestly believe you did well and I think you should continue. I can imagine what a wholesome task the writing of these articles are to you. It nourishes your mind and soul with food that must be conducive to health and strength and helps to keep away the undesirable.

Your control tower work must be interesting. Having been in airports and having watched the smooth operations there I can surmise what it's all about. God bless your efforts and your work. May all tend to bring Him glory and praise! After all, only this matters.

I am continuing to read "The Sign of Jonas." I liked your wise reflection that "Adverse criticism never hurt any true soul of God." Would that you act accordingly at all times! If God has fashioned you for greater heights you will be fashioned by the chisel of criticism in the hands of the Divine sculptor. It's the instrument he delights to use. Merton must be God's darling child, since He permitted such a nationwide questioning of his works. But, of course, only a nationwide criticism could have meaning when the subject is an international figure. I noticed a recent Polish translation of his "Seeds of Contemplation" is on the London market.

Our June retreat will open this Saturday and the school students will be here on the 22nd. It was only yesterday that they left for their respective missions. His Excellency, the Archbishop, will, God willing, preside at our Reception this year. If all persevere, there will be 27 vested with the holy habit.

The next year's group of aspirants is not too promising. About eight I expect to enter in September. These with 14 juvenists, who will graduate July 31ˢᵗ, will form the nucleus of the 1954 Band. There may be additional ones entering in February.

Our Juvenate, however, is very promising. If those who are aligning themselves come, there will be more than 50 juvenists in the 3 years of high school. This is better than our best years in the twenties and thirties. I did hope that Sylvia would come to take my place when I'm gone — but it seems that God wills otherwise.

I may be at Ringtown next Sunday for the dedication of the new church. If I go, I'll drop in to see Mother. Perhaps, Ciocia Cassie will go, too.

Our new Villa of Our Lady of the Poconos was dedicated May 31ˢᵗ by Bishop Hafey. Please say a prayer that it's a success as a retreat house for women.

In July (12th-16th), I expect to attend the Fatima Congress at Plainfield, N.J., the birthplace of the Blue Army. It will be a four-days' series of talks about Mother Mary, consecration, reparation, rosary, etc.

God's blessings and Mother Mary's tender love be yours always!
Love in Jesus and Mary,
Mother M. Edmunda

In July of 1953, twenty-four sisters in temporary vows prepared to take their final vows under the direction of Sister Justine. At their first practice session, one of the sisters failed to attend.

"Where is Sister Dominico?" asked Sister Justine.

"She's packing to leave. She has decided not to stay," answered one of the group rather hesitantly.

"Sisters, please remain in the chapel. I will have to tell Mother Edmunda right away."

"Sister, you mean you had no indication of her intentions until today? Please have each of the sisters in the group come to my office immediately!" The one thing Mother Edmunda never tolerated was the spiritual indecisiveness of any member of the order.

"Zostajesz, czy idziesz?" she asked each of the young sisters as they entered her office.

Five of the sisters, all of them from the Indian orphanage, answered, "Ide."

The Reverend Mother, stunned by their decisions, wondered if she had acted somewhat hastily. In her prayers that evening she asked the Holy Spirit to guide those who left the Bernardines, who had so generously prepared them for life in the United States, and hoped they would not forget their years with the order. She spoke to no one about the affair.

Johnny's admiration for his incredible aunt, who took the time to inform him of her thoughts and responsibilities as the Reverend Mother, as well as her constant loyalty to see him progress spiritually, encouraged him to attempt to inspire his own family to succeed as well. His next letter to them reflected this.

Tomorrow will be an important day in the month — the twenty-second month of my arrival in Japan; however, I am happy for many reasons.

I finished a writing assignment for the Magazine Institute which had troubled me for three weeks. Now that I have completed it I feel well satisfied. Your son will be a writer yet, and all my efforts I want consecrated to the glory of God. The spiritual life has captured me. I am in love; in love with the God of Hosts especially. Why do people receive Communion so infrequently? Now that you and Dad are alone for the summer, I'd like to picture you both at the altar rail at least every week, and perhaps, every day. Become saints, I beg of you!

Enclosed is a copy of the Depot Sun with the "Mission" article. I read it over and find it good. When you've written something, read it about six weeks later, and still like it, the writing must be good. I still don't know if the Jesuit priest, Father St. John, is aware of the article.

The base commander has reached the decision to end all "common law" relationships. We have seventeen and eighteen-year-old kids, and worse, married men, keeping Japanese women. Naturally, I've known about it, and have been to parties in their houses, but never have kept one myself. The people at home couldn't even begin to imagine what's been going on over here. It's a different world entirely.

I am writing this in the control tower with another midnight shift coming to an end. The overcast lies low over the field and, along with the rain and ground fog, traffic is limited to the scheduled couriers. Yesterday a C-124 crashed in Tachikawa with 129 men on board. Good Lord, that's a lot of men. The list of casualties should come through today.

The pastor at Ringtown must be winning a few converts among the farmers since his progress indicates a zealous character. The Church is growing everywhere. In Monrovia, California the Catholics are building an addition to seat 1,000 more people, according to a home-town paper one of our guys receives.

I think I've said enough. Please write soon.
God bless and love you,
Johnny

A letter from Father Galligan, S. S. E., informed Johnny his $100 had been received. The savings account now amounted to more than $600 and, he added, that he appreciated Johnny's trust in saving this way with someone he had never met. In a Father's Day letter to his dad, he encouraged him to write and hoped they could one day develop a healthy mutual respect for each other, especially since he had reached his 54th birthday.

Bill Romano, a Californian, replaced one of the tower operators rotated back to the States. Johnny and Bill became friends almost immediately.

"Bill, Father Sahada, the Jesuit in town, will have Mass on First Friday evening. I'd like you to meet him. Care to go?"

"Very definitely. I never realized there were any Japanese Catholics around."

Rain showers fell about four times on Friday. They decided not to walk the two miles to the Church.

"Let's take a ricksha," suggested Johnny. "I haven't been on one lately."

The ricksha drivers always amazed Johnny with their ease in pulling passengers along the street. He and Bill climbed aboard the two-wheeled "chariot" as the middle-aged Japanese owner smiled appreciatively for the business.

"Where you go?"

"Catholic Church by the hill."

"Okay."

Rice paddies and wooden-roofed houses were passed on the way to a relatively narrow road leading to the church. "Bill, there's Father Sahada getting off his motorcycle." With rimmed glasses and his usual French beret, the priest impressed Bill as a young, dynamic leader.

"Father, I would like you to meet my friend, Bill Romano. He is one of our new tower operators."

"Bill, nice to meet you. How do you like Japan?"

"Father, it's a beautiful country. The Inland Sea, so close by, makes me happy to be in Iwakuni."

"Will you be staying for Mass?"

"Yes, Father. This will be a new experience for me."

Very fervent at Mass, the women wore white veils and almost everyone received Communion. They returned to the base after Mass, inspired by the love the Japanese exhibited for the Holy Eucharist and their priest.

In mid July, Johnny's friend, Joe, sent a letter from the Paulist Fathers' Novitiate on the feast day of St. Bonaventure.

> *The obligation to write has again devolved unto me, and thanks to the cooperation of my superior, I can fulfill it, late and tardy but sincerely hopeful of arousing your interest in the doings of a novice at Oak Ridge, from whom you have heard nothing these last three months. I am still here, happy and hopeful of taking my first promises in two months to this very day and at long last becoming a Paulist, if indeed only a temporary one. By temporary, I mean only officially and for the record, of course. If it is up to me the matter of being permanently settled has been taken care of this year, thanks to the goodness of God's grace. But what about you, John? It seems ages since I heard from you last. I know that you are still alive; recent letters from the boys have told me that you must still be a Catholic; those chaplains would see to that. The only thing I can figure is that you got tired of writing in this one-sided correspondence game and decided to wait for word from the wilderness. Well, here it is, as usual sounding complaints and requests, but only those of sincere interest in your welfare, plans, and dreams. I always find such interest in your letters that I realize how much they mean to me when I no longer receive them. But perhaps the slow boat is going to Japan this year and not to China.*
>
> *A check of dates and I see you must now be counting the days as well as the months and weeks until you leave for the States. Why that big day isn't far off now when you get a chance to see your homeland and I get a chance to see you — I hope. And how is our Bohemian coming? I got such a big kick out of your news about renting a room in the city to "study life" that I almost cried in the altar wine from not getting a chance to write and comment on it. But seriously, John,*

how are you doing as a writer? I can't tell you how happy I was to see you begin to study it seriously, not only from the point of view of using all that free time profitably, but also from the viewpoint of one who has realized recently the great need the Church in this country has of writers, both lay and cleric, to present to our people the truth which alone can make them truly happy.

Which is a neat way of getting around to what must need be the main theme of any letter I write to you: you and a religious vocation. If I told you again to keep up the good work and be a missionary there in Japan while I languish away here in my mountain home, you might either put this down as the impractical ramblings of an impractical hermit, or else give up in discouragement at the obstacles to being an apostle which the limitation of your training, nature and your environment place upon such noble dreams. When I stop to think of the problems and difficulties my hopes for the priesthood caused me in those years, I have to shake my head a little and wonder at the way you have continued to talk vocation when your whole environment contradicted it on every side. I admire this, John, and my admiration turns to happiness when I realize that you have meant what you said, that you weren't just talking to be heard, but to be helped; and that is why I have tried to help you with my prayers and masses and words of encouragement. I feel there has been a tendency on your part to go on from month to month now, seriously considering the priesthood without ever having sat down and said, "Do I want to be a priest?" I feel it will help your peace of mind to come to some sort of finality even now while you are in Japan. Of course, you might feel it too early to do so; that a lot of time remains before you have to give the final word. To come to certainty now would enable you to point all your actions towards that goal and consequently keep you from doing things which might injure your vocation. Once you have decided finally on the priesthood, you can devote all your energies to strengthening and protecting God's greatest gift. And believe me, John, it is a great gift.

In religious orders, a novice can look at that vocation in all its beauty and awful majesty. He can look at himself in comparison with that vocation and he shudders at his inadequacy and unworthiness. The novitiate is the place where he first realizes what terms he has heard all his life really mean; like sanctifying grace, the spiritual life, the Holy Ghost dwelling in the soul; in short, the novitiate is a place where he begins to realize things he has always known. And that is its value; it is a year of realization: of one's own worthlessness and God's greatness. Once that is realized, what knowledge remains or what else matters? That is why the religious life, for its novitiate year alone, is such a supplement to the priesthood. So pray hard; no, harder than you have been doing. Decide as best you can, in your surroundings, on a community or at least a field. And then let God's grace carry you over the next few months.

Enclosed find "Paulist propaganda" meant primarily as educational for you. Paulist work is the conversion of our country and I know you are interested in that in any form. I am particularly proud of the Catholic World, which I think is the best Catholic monthly publication. Simply place these items on a rack for others to read. In the diocesan weeklies of Philadelphia and Scranton I have seen much mention of your aunt's order and of her own personal activities. She must be a wonderful woman to accomplish all that she does. I would like to meet her someday.

Dick and Sonny keep promising they will visit me this summer. I will be surprised if they do arrive. I never cease to marvel, and rejoice, at the continuance of our friendship over this three-year period. I pray that it can continue. I don't suppose there is a better way to end this note than to tell you how eagerly I look forward to seeing you on your return. It is almost exactly two years since I saw you last, which is a long time in our short lives, and I count the days until I do have the chance to talk with you and see you. Until then, write as often as you can and oftener than you wish. I strongly recommend frequent visits to the Blessed Sacrament and the acquiring of the habit of mental prayer, as necessary to a life, really Catholic. Get to weekday Mass as often as possible and to communion as well; frequent Communion means an infrequent sinner and an infrequent sinner is God's own holy temple. Pray for me as I do you.

Yours in Christ,

Joe

After reading this "epistle" from Joe, Johnny wished he could assure his friend of his ongoing hope to become a priest despite a continuous curiosity with other facets of life and the recent quick decision to "study life" in some way other than renting a room in town. After the first two months, Johnny found the room idea not working very well. The June rains made the narrow roadways nearly impossible to pedal his bicycle to the house and other interests took away much of his free time.

"Father, I wish you would please tell your friend I will not be using the room anymore," he said to Father Sahada the next time they met.

"Johnny, that will not be a problem. I will tell him."

Less than a month later a diphtheria epidemic hit Japan, with the papers reporting that in central Honshu more than a thousand people had died of the disease.

"All leaves are canceled. No one is to leave the base until further notice," announced the tower chief on July 15th. "The epidemic has affected a large number of indigents in Iwakuni."

"How will we know if any of us has been infected?" asked several of the operators.

"I am told that children between the ages of 2 to 6 are mostly at risk. So far no cases have been reported on the base. If you develop chills, a fever, sore throat or headache and have difficulty breathing, you probably have it."

"Can it be treated?" asked another operator.

"Isolation, strict bed rest along with an antitoxin will hopefully cure it. Frankly, I wouldn't worry about it too much. Just stay on the base."

Johnny felt doubly thankful about his decision to give up the room.

The Korean War officially ended with a truce at the end of July.

"I guess all of the Australians will be out of here within three months. At least that's what I heard the other day on the radio," said Johnny to his friends who sat down at the Airmen's Club for one of their late day snacks of pork and beans on rye toast. The Australians had introduced them to the dish and they liked it.

"That means we won't be seeing any more Arthur Rank films from England. I actually got to like them," as the conversation continued.

"Did you hear about the two Americans who were killed Sunday night at the rail crossing in town?"

"Yes, I hear one of them was decapitated and the other one left a bloody mess."

"That accident has shaken up quite a few people."

"That's a hell of a way to go!"

"Looks like we'll be working more shifts with all the rotations back to the States going on."

"As long as I can do some swimming this month," said Johnny, "I'll be happy."

"I'm leaving for Tokyo tomorrow at five in the morning," said Bill Romano. "I hope that typhoon doesn't strike while I'm there. I've heard it is supposed to hit tomorrow or the next day."

"Good luck," said Howard. "Except for that slight earthquake the other day, Iwakuni has been fortunate."

"By the way, what's this about the tour of duty being extended to 36 months? I'm glad I'm scheduled to go back to the States in January," said Johnny.

A letter from the Reverend Mother in early August kept Johnny's spirits high. His thoughts focused almost totally on his return home, news of her many responsibilities as head of the order always pleased him.

Dearest Johnny

By whatever means I can manage to obtain, I want to clear my desk of all letters, unanswered for so long a time. Yours is among them. I am not so busy; it's the continuous trips that sap every bit of energy and shatter the nerves. I'm still on the road most of the time and, then, it takes much time to gain equilibrium, physically, mentally and spiritually.

I attended a 5-days Fatima Congress at Plainfield, N. J., the headquarters of the Blue Army. Every minute was a treat. I'm enclosing a scapular touched to the Pilgrim Virgin and a remnant of the tree upon which Our Lady appeared at Fatima. The scapular is washable. I need not repeat to you that Our Lady promised to all who die clothed with it, eternal salvation. And, then, the Sabbatine Privilege - that all, who die clothed with it, will be released from Purgatory the first Saturday after their death - provided that they:

1 - Are validly clothed with it

2 - Wear it regularly

3 - Preserve chastity according to their state of life

4 - Recite the office of the Blessed Virgin Mary daily, or have this substituted with a daily rosary by permission of a priest who has faculties for this commutation

5 - The clothing with the scapular is to be considered a Consecration to Mother Mary.

(The last condition is not always mentioned but always understood. We must be Mother Mary's children.)

At the Congress we were addressed by 4 bishops (one from India), several monsignors and priests, and several lay persons. The last mentioned, with one exception, were excellent. Mary certainly does have many apostles among the laity.

Last week again, I attended an Institute on Vocations, at Fordham University. Of the four sessions, only one was satisfactory — even though the matter was not new. It dealt with Psychometrics, as a very useful tool in deciding upon candidates for the priesthood and the religious life. We are using them to some extent; yearly we are improving and adding. They are not infallible, of course, but they do tell a story.

As yet, I have not seen Louis. The desire to speak to him is present, but my absence and then the subsequent rush prevent all personal pleasures.

The next ten days are very busy — all ceremonies, departure of sisters, etc. His Excellency, the Archbishop, will preside at the reception of the Holy Habit. This will be the first time this privilege will be ours. I began with the His Eminence, the late Cardinal, at the election — and, now, the last Reception will be graced with the Archbishop's presence. Another signal grace to the myriads I have already received.

God's blessings and Mother Mary's love be yours always!
Lovingly in J. & M.,
M. M. E.

Johnny wore the scapular she sent to him and prayed that somehow he could be worthy of being saved despite his many faults. He knew the sacrament of Confession forgave his infractions against grace; what he could not understand is how his promises to truly repent never quite took hold for any great length of time.

One of his mother's letters, lately more infrequent, arrived stating her desire to enroll Lou and Sylvia in the public high school as well as her disappointment in Alma's refusal to contribute any of her earnings to the family's needs. Johnny replied that the cost of education could not be measured solely by cost; the Catholic high school gave a well balanced diet of academic and spiritual subjects which prepared students primarily for college and the world. He told his mother to send the bills to him — Louis would finish at SCHS and Sylvia would enter as a freshman in September. As for Alma, he suggested she could not be pushed for funds otherwise she might rebel. Whatever money she would give had to come from the heart; otherwise, there is only bitterness.

"You have been a beautiful, unselfish and usually wise mother who, unfortunately, married someone who cared nothing about money. Speculating about the family's possibilities if money were available would do none of them any good. The best they could do is finance their own ways through life."

Johnny's young sister Sylvia wrote a letter telling him about her summer job in the same institution as their sister Alma. They both had gone to see Louis pitch a baseball game in the top city league in Reading. Though the youngest player, his coach believed the major leagues would sign him in a few years.

Johnny went to the chapel, as he often did, to say some night prayers. On his way back to the barracks a drunken soldier called out, "Help me out, please!"

"Sure, what do you need?" Johnny answered in the same English accent used by the soldier.

"Are you a Canadian?"

The question pleased Johnny because it proved he had learned something from the Australians. "No," he answered, "American."

"Some Americans got me drunk," he said, "and I can't seem to find my way to our quarters."

Impossible to give understandable instructions to the fellow, Johnny said, "I'll walk you to the transient billets where the Australians generally stay."

"Thanks, mate."

The billets were only about a block away and the soldier suddenly recognized his own quarters.

"Thanks again. This is where I'm staying tonight."

After Johnny took him inside he felt like a boy scout doing his good deed for the day, especially when he learned the man had been a POW in Korea for three years and his plane would leave for Singapore the next morning on his way back to England. Most of the British Commonwealth ex-POW's came through Iwakuni, their main base in Japan. Iwakuni served as an international airport for planes leaving for Hong Kong, Manilla, Guam, Okinawa and sometimes Formosa.

A cool north wind blew through the open windows of the control tower and the temperature stood at a comfortable 70 degrees. Johnny slept through the first half of the midnight-to-seven shift, at least when he could keep his exposed arm free of mosquito attacks. Finally, he decided to read the rare letter he had received from his brother Lou.

August 29, 1953
Dear John,

It seems I just never feel like sitting down and writing a letter. I don't seem to get anything out of it. I know I should just for brotherly sake. I'm writing just before going to a vital game in our quest for the flag. We're playing in the final round of the playoffs. I haven't done too well in this league because its composed of ex-minor league players and almost all ex-American Legion players. The competition is really great. My log so far is 3 wins, 2 losses plus about 15 innings of relief work. I have 65 strike outs in 50 innings. It's not too bad considering I am, by far, the youngest player in the league.

I'm getting away with a lot of loafing here at the orphanage in Mt. Alvernia. When I feel like working I work like a mule, but when I'm lazy I just sit around. By next year I should own this place. I hope to be doing a lot of driving and that will make work much nicer. I've done a lot of work here because I'm the only worker they have. Maybe the orphanage grounds aren't too large. I still have to try to keep going to keep them in shape. I'm also doing a little carpentry work. I've fixed some chairs, tables, doors, etc.

I'll be going home next week for good and I can't wait until that time comes. I haven't been home for three weeks and you get tired of being away too long. I was trying to get in shape for football, but there's nothing like practicing with the old bunch. "Happy" Cook is going to enroll at Malvern Prep this fall so there goes my competition for left halfback. I don't think we'll have too good a football team this year because it's too small. We'll have a good backfield but no line. I hope someone turns up to fill out that line. And please stop praising me because I might get a swelled head.

I should go home with over $200 but I don't know how much I spent on baseball shoes, etc. It's a nice feeling to know you've saved something.

So long for now.
Your admiring brother,
Lou

In a return letter to his brother Lou, Johnny updated him on some of his latest adventures in the tower.

Dear Lou,

Well all I can say is: thanks one hell of a lot for the letter. I enjoyed it immensely. I'd just as soon not write letters either; however, when your morale depends somewhat on mail, especially now when so little time remains, I know well that to receive mail you must send some in the opposite direction. Keep me posted on your football activities once or twice a month.

The last two day shifts have been thrillers. Yesterday I worked a mess of close traffic, and today we had two F-80's land with about three minutes of fuel left. And just before those two shifts I had a ringside seat listening to the accidental destruction of three F-86's. A low overcast prevented a flight of five from any visual contact with the ground. They were trying to get into Tsuiki Air Base and got lost in the process.

"My radio compass just went out!" shouted one of the pilots.

When a radio compass ceases to function, Lou, it means the pilot is unable to use any radio assistance such as "homers," radio beacons, broadcasting stations, etc. to determine his location. He began calling any direction-finding station who could hear him and yelled for a steer. By now he and the flight were running low on fuel. Then we heard, "Bail out, bail out, bail out!" Two 86's had just collided — one had a busted canopy and the other apparently was burning — and the pilot of one shouted to the other to bail out.

Then another pilot shouted: "Mayday, Mayday, Mayday!" That's the international distress voice signal. Very low on fuel, he had to land somewhere or else bail out. No D. F. station could give him a satisfactory steer so he finally bailed out too.

"Mayday, Mayday, Mayday! Any tower reading Jet 586 give me

a call, give me a call!"

"586, this is Iwakuni tower, over?" I answered.

"Iwakuni, can you give me a steer? I'm low on fuel. I'm down to 500 lbs."

I sent him to our D. F. station on 121.50, the international distress frequency. Misawa tower had direction-finding equipment. The Iwakuni had none. Well, it turned out he had to bail out also.

The Russian MIGs couldn't knock out that many aircraft in one day during the entire Korean War. In all, six jets were lost and one pilot is still missing.

And please, start thinking about college. If you don't get a scholarship elsewhere I'd like to see you at St. Michael's for at least two years. Then you'll be mature enough for the major leagues or the service, if you have to serve.

Whatever you do, keep your marks in the 90's. I know you can do it if you try. Study just one hour every night and you'll be well on your way to honors. Undivided attention in class is most important.

From your letter I know you liked working at Mt. Alvernia and are already looking forward to next year. Your life is well organized and you're not losing any time. That's important. Time is much too important to waste. But that's enough pedagoguery. (Look it up.)

Good to know you have left-half sewed up. I'd give anything to see you play. By the way, how tall are you? I hope you reach six feet. I certainly don't want you to be a runt like me at five-eight.

And the women. I suppose they're all desperately in love in Junior year, but is there anyone special? I must have been interested in about ten in Junior year.

Continue living a full life, Lou; stay close to Our Lord, and give everything you do everything you've got.

Be good,
Your brother, Johnny

Father Galligan's letter arrived confirming the last check Johnny had sent toward his college expenses at St. Michael's. The total in the account had reached $900.00. The Vocation Director added some guidance as well.

No matter what we decide to do in life, there will be difficulties and plenty of them. However, stability, whether married or religious, will help us to overcome these difficulties.... Doubts arise because sometimes we look for the kind of surety of our vocation that St. Paul had. We don't have it because we are not recipient of divine intervention. At the same time, we don't need that surety he was given. We have moral certitude which is more than sufficient in God's plan. He gives us the tools and it's up to our free will to decide how we're going to use them. A vocation is a voluntary thing. If there is a shortage, it's only because not enough people are responding to the call. It's not easy, but what in life that is worthwhile is easy?

Continued falls dull our sense of sin, and make it far more difficult to do good. Fortunately for us we have hope. God is good and asks only that we put forth our best for which he always supplies the grace. What's past is past in God's work. Our present and future resolutions are important. A live prayer life and a realization of what the sacraments can do for us if we are positively sincere makes us strong. Temptations of all kinds don't necessarily lessen in strength through the years, but a developed strong will makes it easier to overcome them. Try to develop in yourself a proper balance in all things. Sex, of course, instead of being treated as one of many problems facing young people, has been completely overplayed. It has been taken out of its sacred content and so it's not difficult to understand what happens when it is presented without any spiritual foundation.

Thank God for everything and in return give him the best you've got. That is what He wants and expects from every one of us. Classes are on again. Fine group of junior seminarians this fall.

Sincerely in St. Edmund,
Father Galligan, SSE

"The Air Force Far East tour has been cut to 24 months. All you single guys may be home sooner than you had expected," announced the tower chief to those attending his weekly session.

"Does that mean some of us may get home for Christmas?" asked Johnny, who expected to leave Japan in January.

"Who knows? Things change all the time. One thing is sure, this change will boost morale."

"I'll be directing traffic for the air show on Sunday. Anything special I need to know?" asked Johnny.

"Nothing that I can think of. Just hope there won't be any accidents."

On Sunday the air show went well. When an F-86 broke the sound barrier, a whip-like explosion cracked the air. The spectators loved this demonstration of jet power for many of them clapped their approval.

Two friends went with Johnny into Iwakuni the next Sunday, hoping to get some pictures of a parade celebrating harvest-time, or some other yearly event.

"Look at that giant 'dragon' leading the parade!" About a dozen young men had the green and yellow dragon dancing in the street. Many floats followed this dazzling display, carried by men in colorful matching clothes. Headbands of one distinct color, differentiated each group.

"That float looks like a Japanese hunter ready to do some serious hunting." A bear's head perched on the front of the float directly in front of the mannequin-hunter. A beautifully colored pheasant stood to his left and some dozen deer antlers completed the display.

"Let's get a picture of those three Mamasans over there," said Johnny. The three older Japanese women, in their black kimonos, posed for them. They all felt a greater kinship to the people of the town after the parade ended, especially after they had taken the picture of a Buddhist priest dressed for the festive occasion.

A letter from Johnny's friend, Joe, detailed the eventful and thrilling week when he and twenty others became members of the Paulist community.

> *Dear John,*
>
> *I have been planning to write this letter since I left the novitiate last Tuesday and began my career as a Paulist, but the absorbing features of the new routine here at St. Peter's College in Baltimore occupied and absorbed me for a few days. The library, with its many magazines and newspapers and all those things which unfortunately still interest me, I find myself in little mood for any kind of mental discipline. Cosmology, metaphysics and all the rest will swamp me soon enough.*
>
> *On September 8th, the feast of Our Lady's Nativity, our Superior General described the reception of the habit as a foretaste of that greatest happiness, ordination. My parents and brother as well as Monsignor O'Brien, in all his ecclesiastical purple, lent dignity and*

honor to the occasion. *Allowed one night at home, I met a few of our school friends; most of the others, however, were away. A real surprise came shortly after my return to Baltimore. Sonny, who often had promised to visit, greeted me with the news of his impending marriage to a girl who had entered the Church at the age of 15 entirely on her own. They had found happiness together, he for his loneliness, so far away in San Francisco, and she for her insecurity due to her parents' marriage problems. I am sure he has matured faster than most of us. He hoped that his marriage would help him in his studies and his moral life. I did not discourage the step; pray that he is doing the right thing. And please, pass along any information you may hear about his plans, the next time the airplanes stop buzzing around your tower long enough for you to write.*

With your approaching return to this country nearing the realm of discussion now, we all, and me especially, are wondering what is going to happen to you and through you. I can't wait to see you and talk with you. In fact, it would probably end up as the major disappointment of the year if you did not find it possible to visit here next winter on your return. But of course, that is only a subtle way of reminding you of your promise. You see, in this discussion we have almost reached the point where letters can be dangerous as well as beneficial. It has been a long time since we met, and we both have changed so much. Actually we no longer know each other, in a sense. That's why I hesitate to advise you. To suggest decisions when you might react in a way entirely different than I expect. Now, that's not so silly as it sounds. Take the last letter in which you talked about acting, and writing and teaching. Those are noble ambitions, some of the highest. Of course, you were only thinking out loud; but I had never heard you think that way before. And I don't want to tell you not to become a writer or an actor, since I don't know how those talents have developed in you in two years and whether your character is of the nature now where you are stable enough to devote your life to one of dedication to art, without the grace and stability religious life gives you in its demands for dedication of your whole *being, with all its talents and ambition and time. The religious life, the life of a missionary, is a glorious life, a full one. But it is an exacting one and one that requires you to be all priest and all missionary. Now, as I say, I don't know whether you are at the point* now of wanting, or being able to give your life up to something, wholly and entirely. That is what a religious life requires: dedication. If you are willing to and ready to dedicate, then now is the time to educate, your mind and your soul, particularly your soul. Prepare for the grace of stability which God will send you, if He has given you a religious vocation, prepare for the grace of perseverence He will send you with that vocation. Prepare your soul to cooperate and recognize those graces by educating it in the ways of Christian living. In other words, John, if you have a vocation then live in mortal fear of losing it, and pray as through you had no hope of being strong enough to live only for it. I can promise you that God will do the rest.

All of which comes down substantially to a repeat of my last letter, i.e., make a decision of some kind and gear the whole of your life to it whatever it may be. If it be writing, then study writing and the difficulties involved in being a success. If it be teaching, then again I say look at its demands of almost total dedication, and weigh them against your character. And if it be the priesthood, which is my earnest hope and fervent prayer, then I say, "Put everything else in its proper perspective and live only for your goal in life. But John, get a goal. Without one you are lost, mentally and perhaps spiritually. Those are strong words I know. But I feel they are true and cogent. To use a hackneyed metaphor, an aimless man is like a rudderless ship. And there are too many dangers in this sea, many of which you have already met and perhaps been swamped by, for a rudderless ship to escape. So at the risk of boring you, I urge you again, to make a decision and let it color your life, which it will with all the brilliance of God's glory, especially if it be a decision for the missionary priesthood.

My brother Ray begins school at Notre Dame today. He tells me your brother should be a star of the football team at S.C.H.S. Until next time, may God and His Immaculate Mother give the grace, guidance, and goodness necessary to determine your vocation and live up to its important preparation. Pray often for me; I do for you.

Your friend in Christ

Joe

Johnny said a special prayer for Joe after reading the letter and hoped he would someday decide what to do with his life.

"Johnny, that's quite a story you have written." Chiz, the librarian, whom Johnny had gotten to know after his many trips to the base library, thanked him for the opportunity to read the 6,000-word love story he had written about an airman who had fallen in love with a Japanese girl and married her despite the objections of his commanding officer. His girl had become pregnant, botched an attempted self-induced abortion, and, seven months into the pregnancy, sailed with him to the States.

"Thanks, that's the first story I've done for the Magazine Institute with that many words."

"By the way, I showed the story to a friend of mine who is a Fine Arts graduate of Yale. He would like to talk to you about it. Apparently he liked it."

"That's great, maybe I've got a chance to end up as a writer after all."

"Johnny, I know you enjoy serious reading. I have an extra copy of fifty paperback books — published by the University of Chicago." Johnny relished this wonderful gift covering all the great books from Homer to Aristotle, Augustine, Aquinas, Dante, Shakespeare, Galileo, Adam Smith, Tolstoy, Dostoevsky, and Freud. He realized these paperbacks were merely a brief exposition into logic, metaphysics, God, aristocracy, beauty, and astronomy, as well as many other concepts, which philosophers had delved into over the centuries. His amazement at how little the mind of man had changed from the days of Plato and Aristotle made him wonder if humanity would ever finally resolve to educate each generation in the way needed to build properly on the past. He felt he had been given insights into Western thought which would surely help him to become as well educated as possible.

During a visit to Father Sahada, the priest asked Johnny if he had visited Yamaguchi.

"Johnny, Yamaguchi is one place you don't want to miss. St. Francis Xavier won thousands of converts and established a flourishing church which never lost its faith even during the persecutions which followed Japan's total dedication to a closed society."

"Father, I will go there before I leave for home."

The following week Johnny asked his friends if anyone wanted to accompany him to visit the church in Yamaguchi. He did not want to postpone the trip too long.

"I'll go with you. How far is it from Iwakuni?" asked one of his friends.

"About 50 miles west. We can take the train."

The train ride on the September day they made their small pilgrimage to Xavier's church could not have been more pleasant and whenever Johnny had an opportunity to mix with the native population he felt a kinship he could never experience on the base.

"Let's take a taxi to the church. I believe that's one over there." The driver carefully whisked off the smallest amount of dust while waiting for his next passengers. The age of the car did not matter.

"Catholic church," said Johnny to the driver.

The man nodded that he understood where they wanted to go. The church stood on a small hill, with the grounds well maintained.

"It certainly looks like a Spanish church, doesn't it?" They both agreed the architecture reflected a Spanish influence.

A priest in black cassock greeted them shortly after they entered the church. In a brief conversation in very broken English the dark haired Jesuit missionary from Spain told them the new church had been built to commemorate the 500th anniversary of St. Francis Xavier's introduction of Christianity to Japan.

"How appropriate that Spanish Jesuits are here in Yamaguchi to carry on Francies Xavier's mission started so many years ago."

"Yes, Johnny, I'm glad you invited me to come along."

"I will have to thank Father Sahada for reminding us to make this visit."

A letter from Father Galligan arrived in response to Johnny's latest letter which questioned the administration of the church.

> *Dear John:*
>
> *Yours of September 22nd was here on my desk when I returned Sunday night. At the risk of monotonous repetition, let me say I always enjoy hearing from you. I nod agreement when you imply that environment of study, prayer, and hard work will determine the necessary stability of your vocation.*
>
> *I read your comments on the administration and authority of the Church with keen interest. I would suspect, John, that you will be a very good student. The desire to learn is a marvelous quality which does not in any way subtract from the ideal of obedience. The expression 'totalitarian' implies a depriving of right which the church does not do. Then again, in discussions of this kind, one is apt to*

lose sight of the true nature of the Church, which is divine. The human element is naturally present and as a result, human defection is always possible. But remember, the soul of the church is the Third Person of the Blessed Trinity. I am not trying to imply that these few lines are at all an adequate answer to your inquiry. They do, however, give a little food for thought.

I will look up and attempt to locate Father Murray's "Theological Studies" for you. Father Murray is currently teaching at Yale.

Here's hoping we have the good fortune to get together before many more months pass. I do hope you will be home by Christmas. St. Michael's has an undefeated season in football with the last game against the University of Vermont this week.

Write again, John. I will be praying for you that God will continue to give you the necessary graces to lead you in the right direction.

Sincerely,

Father Galligan, SSE

Johnny, as always, felt that the introduction to Father Galligan by the Reverend Mother gave him the support he needed to pursue his goal to the priesthood.

"Who's going into town to catch the Sumo wrestlers? asked Johnny.

"I don't know, what time?" answered Howard who was becoming a really close friend.

"Early afternoon, I believe. We could go in around one."

"Okay, that's something I've never even heard of before. Any idea what goes on?"

"All I know is the wrestlers are a special physical breed, developed from the time they are very young."

Johnny and Howard made their way into town on the warm, pleasant October day to West Iwakuni near the Kintai Kyo bridge. A large crowd circled a slightly raised arena where oversized Japanese contenders prepared to wrestle each other outside the ring. A referee introduced them in their apron-like tsunas, which covered them from the waist down. Silk loin cloths alone remained once the tsunas were discarded. The sheer size of the wrestlers, so different from the average Japanese male, impressed John and his friend. After a greeting of bows, the wrestlers reached for each other in what seemed like lumbering movements, until one of them was forced outside the 20-foot diameter ring. Some matches lasted a few minutes; ten minutes constituted a longer battle. The crowd appeared enthralled by the sight of these huge wrestlers who came from all over Japan to entertain them. After about an hour Johnny and Howard returned to the base.

"By the way, John, I guess you know Charlie and I have enrolled in a course of instruction preparatory to entering the Catholic church. Thanks to you our interest increased as we listened to your enthusiastic explanations of what the church is all about."

"Howard, that's great!"

In a letter to his family, Johnny commented on this news regarding his friends: "Whether I have been the chief instrument of their decision is questionable, but the wonderful point of it is that I have the satisfaction of witnessing the fulfillment of their own, and perhaps, others' desires. Within a few months, God willing, we will be brothers in Christ and two individuals closer to our goal of one fold and one shepherd."

A squadron party in town the following weekend to which Johnny invited a base school teacher, Jo Guernsey, turned into one the best parties the AACS personnel had had in some time. He had wanted to take his librarian friend; unfortunately she had a previous engagement.

A letter from the Reverend Mother arrived informing him of her recent activities.

Dearest Johnny,

The Statler Hotel stationery tells the story that your aunt is still on the merry-go-round of conventions. This was a Conference for Major Superiors sponsored by the Catholic Hospital Association. I promised myself that this was the last that I attended ... and the promise should not be difficult to materialize in view of the fact that July 2, 1954 is so near.

I have been out for the greater part of the last six weeks. At first, it was my private retreat; then, a visitation at Newport News, Va., and the Conference at Washington, D. C. Now, I do hope to remain at Mt. Alvernia for the balance of this scholastic year.

My retreat was again a series of God's graces. The good Lord must find me very incapable, so He does the work for me. Woe to me, if I let these singular graces pass by.

We have a Pilgrim Virgin for Reading and one for each of the Provinces. Mine made her trip to Virginia and now she will begin her tour of the houses here at Mount Alvernia. It was a true consolation to see the Sisters so happy because of her coming to Mary Immaculate Hospital. We renewed our Consecration quite solemnly.

Penance and mortification advisable? No, just as important as prayer. In the last Encyclical, of September 8, 1953, our Holy Father says: For the effect of devotion to prayer is this: 'The soul is sustained, is prepared for arduous deeds and ascends to things divine. The effect of penance is that we control ourselves, especially our body, the greatest enemy because of original sin, by reason and by the law of the Gospel. It's clear that these two virtues are intimately connected, help one another, and combine to withdraw man who was born for Heaven, from transitory things, and all but carries him to heavenly intimacy with God.'"

If you consider mortification, which is nothing but self-denial, as only advisable, your prayer-life will not continue. Passions, urges, wishes, etc. cause havoc in our souls; prayer to be prayer must be an exchange of words between God and the soul; how can God speak to the soul when it is disturbed? The Holy Spirit speaks to us in a breeze, a gentle breeze — and to hear Him, our hearts must be calm. Only self-discipline can create order in our fallen nature. Hence, don't place mortification among the advisable ... some spiritual writers speak of our spiritual development as a flight on two wings - - of these, one is prayer and the other is mortification. Have you ever seen a bird fly while using only one wing?

May you soon come back to the States and as soon as possible join the ranks of those whose hearts and souls belong solely to God.

Recently, through no intention of mine, I received a copy of William Barrett's "The Left Hand of God." I enjoyed it thoroughly. I can imagine that "In the Shadows of the Images" is equally delectable. I have never heard of him before, but, then, I know so little about the world outside of my four walls. Somebody should give me a test on the present makings of the mind of any ordinary woman of the world; I know that I would fail miserably.

Mother is just a trifle too early with my feast day. It comes in November and not in October. She sent her greetings the other day. Since Louis left, I have not heard from or about him. I suppose it's the same Louis, all-engrossed in his sports.

November is fast approaching and with it will come the retreats of the girls. I presume that Sylvia will not be here this year. We have some 500 applicants, which is the highest ever.

May God bless and love you. May Mother Mary guide you along the paths to her Son's Heart!

Love in the Two Hearts
Mother Mary Edmunda

All of his days now centered on the assignment he would get when he returned to the States.

"Johnny, I"m hoping to get stationed in Texas next year. How about you?" asked Johnny Eggert one day as they relaxed in the barracks.

"Anywhere in the East will be fine with me."

"By the way, will you be going to the Thanksgiving Dinner at the Wachman's?"

"Yes, I'm sure it will be better than the Mess Hall."

And it was. The meal was the focal point of the day. Turkey, mashed potatoes, cranberry sauce, peas, corn, beets, dressing, ham, pickles, sweet potatoes, pumpkin pie; along with ambrosia, cake, coffee and plenty of drinks. The major negative on Thanksgiving Day — no definite date when he could expect to sail from Japan.

A letter from his now totally spiritual friend, Joe, arrived late in November.

Dear John,

Tomorrow is Thanksgiving Day and a welcome respite for all us philosophers.... I suppose that you are looking forward to spending next Thanksgiving at home. You must really be looking forward to packing your bags and saying goodbye to the perfumed scents of the Orient. I will not write to you again, as you have suggested, since you may be on your way Stateside in short order. The preparatory college here in Baltimore has been wonderful but I languish for Washington and the Catholic University atmosphere. St. Paul's, the Paulist College on the University grounds, is my fondest wish for the coming year. Actually, I guess it does not really matter where you are, as long as Jesus is with you, and I do feel His presence strongly here, although not nearly so strongly as in the novitiate. That was really a great year, and I hope with all my heart that you may someday have the opportunity to look at yourself and at Christ as only you can do in the novitiate. In fact John, I can say that is now one of the fondest hopes of my heart. This country needs Catholicism so badly; without it there can be no tomorrow. But to give Christ to our country we must first give ourselves to Christ. I hope you can do this yourself, preferably in the religious life , but if not, then in the lay life, as an apostle of the good news of Christianity which man needs to hear so badly today.

I have again resolved to refrain from offering my brilliant, little trinkets of vocational advice. It's about time I realized my limitations. Simply let me say that the religious life is truly a sharing in this life of the beatitude of heaven. Order your whole life, from now on, to attaining it. With all my limitations I can truly say that it is worth the effort.

News about mutuals is slower than ever. Jack H. is on the staff at Stars and Stripes in Germany. Rich still seems kind of lost, or perhaps he only gives that appearance. Sonny hasn't written and is probably a pleasant phase of the past, which is now over. Please visit him in San Francisco on your return.

Give my best to your family, especially Alma. Until the next time or on your hoped for visit to St. Peter's in Baltimore, I remain, as ever your friend in Christ Jesus Our Lord. May He ever guide you and bless you in all that you think or do. Pray for the conversion of our country.

Joe

Johnny did pray for the religious unification of all Christ-centered believers. He realized also that for America to become predominantly Catholic, with acceptance of the Pope as the successor to St. Peter, a thorough conversion to Christian principles by those who called themselves Catholics was essential. His favorite brief prayer: "Come Holy spirit, fill the hearts of Thy faithful and kindle in them the fire of Thy divine love. Send forth Thy Spirit and they shall be created, and Thou shalt renew the face of the earth." He believed that indifferent, spiritless, sacrament-starved Catholics, unconscious of the almost irreparable damage they are doing to the church and the will of God is the pathetically wretched instrument which slows us in the march toward the triumph of truths and the establishment of the kingdom of God upon this earth.

He also found, in a beautiful account of the testimony of Lillian Roth, a

Jewish nightclub singer, renewed hope for the acceptance of Christ by American Jews as the true messiah promised the Jews of the Old Testament.

"I'm a Catholic and I'm a Jew. I love them both — my religion and my race." In a rather shattering book, *I'll Cry Tomorrow*, she set out to prove that a human being, with God's help, can rise out of complete degradation. The book apparently impressed Catholic and non-Catholic critics. She believed that a natural bridge exists between Judaism and the Catholic Church. Yes, there was bigotry. But for "every one of those Catholics who thoughtlessly discriminated against Jews she had met hundreds that were wonderful."

Two days before his 21st birthday he wrote one of his happiest letters to his family.

> *Dearest Mom, Dad & all:*
>
> *Man, am I happy!!! Guess where I'm going? Columbia, South Carolina. I'm in the library now finding out just how fortunate I am. The more I read the more enthused I become.*
>
> *Shaw AFB is just outside Columbia, smack in the center of the state. I'll be able to look the entire state over and branch into Georgia, North Carolina; not far down the Georgia coast is Florida. Just think of it. I'll get to know the Southeast in no time.*
>
> *The University of South Carolina is in Columbia — summer sessions and all. I'll probably be forced to remain in the Air Force until later in the summer. I may even get in some night courses until then. What's more important, I'll get to know the southern college students' viewpoint on many subjects. What an adventure!!*
>
> *The Atlantic seaboard is only about 100 miles from the base. Three lakes are nearby. The scenery must be great. My color shots will let you in on it all. Any place is a photographer's paradise, at least for a while.*
>
> *Also comes newspaper work. The base probably has a paper and I'd like to do some work for a paper in Columbia.*
>
> *Of course, you might as well know it now, I'll need a car. The way I feel now I don't ever want to settle down. I just want to write, do things, see places, and live life fully. Of course reality challenges me to pursue a more stable goal and I don't intend to let my vocation in life be dissipated by any nonsense. This coming year, however, I want no barriers in my pursuit of education and writing experience. I want to get to know southerners like I know the old home town and*

its people. It's going to take a lot of tact, confidence, guts and know-how. But I'm going to love every minute of it.

Please try to understand me. You can't be tight with money, brains, heart, or love if you expect to live well. You get out of life what you put into it. I have an opportunity to discover the Southeast and I'm going to do it. Please, please, try to understand. We'll have plenty to talk about when I reach home. I doubt very much that I'll be home for Christmas.

Well, as you can readily see, this assignment has buoyed me up to feverish excitement. I'm completely satisfied with the Air Force. These four years have done me no harm and certainly a great deal of good.

My godson, Johnny Eggert, is going to Eglin AFB in Florida. We should be able to get together. Pray that I continue to learn well. God be with you.

Johnny

"So what do you have planned for your 21st birthday?" asked his friends.

"I don't know. Do any of you have any ideas?" Johnny answered.

"The Hirobessu in Hiroshima is exactly where we should go. If you haven't been there, you haven't lived." Howard's opinions usually proved true, so Johnny agreed.

On this final trip to Hiroshima in early December the sun over southern Japan warmed Johnny and his two friends as they hopped on the bus in Iwakuni. Although Iwakuni was the terminal point of this particular run, the bus stopped only long enough to pick up waiting passengers. The time schedule always ruled the Japanese transportation systems.

Before long they headed north along a road which followed faithfully the curving contour of the coastline. Eastwards, the waters of the Inland Sea quietly besieged its natural boundaries of the shore or man-made retainers. Mountains rose up in peremptory fashion for apparently no other reason than to support their scraggy pine covering. To the west mountains also crowded the scene.

Indigents, in other words, the local Japanese, shuffled on and off at various points with their ever-present briefcases or kerchief-wrapped possessions eliciting odors easily sensed by their foreign nostrils. The wind, gratifying at times, could also serve notice of some freshly filled "honeybuckets" with their human waste fertilizer, plots of enriched soil, a rayon factory or rice paddy, with choking suddenness.

"There's Hiroshima," said one of his friends as he sighted the city on the northeastern shore. Rows of heavily rusted dock cranes lent evidence to his remark.

"Yes, no doubt we'll be there in *shkoshi* time."

In the city's center they got off the bus, walked through the streets until they reached the Hirobessu. Young women, dressed in evening gowns, smiled to them invitingly. Each one, more attractive than the other, stood on either side of the cement walkway into the nightclub.

"Take your pick," said Howard. "If she likes you, she will be your guest for the night."

"Sounds good. What's the price tag?"

"Don't worry about it. If you run low on cash we'll take care of it," Howard assured him. The choice was not easily made. Johnny looked over the twenty or so girls, hoping for some clue as to whom to choose. Finally he saw the one he believed would be a pleasant date for the night.

"Hello! My name is John. You speak English?"

"Yes, I do." Her smile indicated she liked him.

"Great. Join me for the night?"

"OK. My name is Masako." Johnny could not have been happier. His two friends also made their selections. A live band played inside the club; many of the guests were having dinner and cocktails. The host seated them at a table for six.

"Are we ready for dinner or would you like to dance a while?"

"Well, let's order now and dance until the food arrives."

The waiter explained anything they did not recognize on the menu. The girls helped as well.

"Tabako?" said one of the girls at the table.

"Tabako?" asked Howard. All the girls accepted his cigarettes as they warmed up to us.

"Beer anyone, or should we stay with hot saki tonight?" asked Johnny. Asahi beer satisfied them before the meal with plenty of hot saki afterward.

Around ten o'clock Howard explained the time had come for hot baths, a massage, and whatever else we wanted.

Johnny and Masako decided to do it all. Soaking in the hot bath came after a young woman attendant bathed him with plenty of soap and water as he sat on a small stool at the side of the tub.

"Preeze," she said, and handed him a cloth to wash his private parts. No one went into the tub with soap still on the body. Then came the entrance into the hot tub. His skin reddened from the clean, overly warm water. Patiently she motioned him to stay with the temporary discomfort. After five minutes she indicated he could come out for a much cooler rinsing with relatively warm water.

Next came the steam cupboard which covered Johnny up to his neck. Masako occupied the cupboard next to him. Ten minutes into the treatment he motioned his wish to get out. She seemed prepared to stay longer. Into the room came a masseuse who appeared somewhat lightweight to effect a thorough massage. What a surprise when she walked on top of him as he lay flat on his stomach. The rest of the massage went uneventfully after that.

What happens now? thought Johnny. *This is my 21st birthday. I will be in Japan for another month, why not enjoy this last fling?*

"Come," said Masako, as she led him to a bedroom close by. When he laid down next to her, the alcohol, the hot bath and the long evening reduced Johnny to a limp rag. What a waste, he thought; here is this beautiful girl, as clean as he was, and all he wanted to do was sleep.

"In the morning, maybe, we can make love," is all he said to her and collapsed into oblivion.

She was gone when he awoke.

Johnny and his friends had breakfast and returned to the airbase. They all agreed the evening had been a blast.

A letter from his sister Alma arrived on the 26th of December. An immediate answer might help her to resolve her frustration with the family's financial situation.

> *Dearest Alma,*
>
> *Sweetheart, you're a jewel. What fire! What excellent presentation! I love you.*
>
> *But reality, when acknowledged, must be viewed analytically. The status quo exists. Why does it exist? Is there any reason to believe personal intervention, or lack of it, has fostered it? And if the present position is unfavorable what can be done about progressing to a more agreeable status?*
>
> *We are against a brick wall. You and I had nothing to do with the present crisis. We were born into a family destined by circumstance and apparent lack of initiative to reach the inevitable stage we now call reality.*

Humility I pray, will one day be mine. I admit to many lapses in the pursuit of virtue. However, never confuse humility with resignation to one's position in life.

"Know thyself" is synonymous with humility. Know where you stand and why you are there. (That's not so simple to do as it seems.) Then ask whether the result brings satisfaction, and if not, why not?

I am dissatisfied with the dead end to which those responsible have brought themselves and us. Indirectly, and directly if we choose, we too must share that dead end, for those same individuals are very near and dear to us for many reasons.

Especially are they important for the role they played in the life we possess. Life is an opportunity, a challenge. Their co-habitation has made life a reality to us as individuals, and for the experience I am grateful.

You have been directly affected by the situation and I thank you for helping Mom and Dad with their problems. If you did not, I would have to do so. I would not be particularly happy about it. You are not satisfied to expend financial gains in a project which exhibits few signs of hope and success. I can't blame you.

Poverty I do not detest. But resignation to a situation, I passionately hate. Especially when the situation can be altered by bold initiative and the true humility which seeks advancement and perfection.

I have been away from home a long time and have lost touch with facts. From Mom's letters, however, I've been able to uncover a few references to the dominant attitudes prevailing in the atmosphere you term: "it". These attitudes are the same as when I left. I can discover very little or no improvement.

With the grace of God and trust in His mercy I expect to enter the seminary in September. With like trust I might very well marry in September. I've done a good deal I think in helping our parents to "get along" a little more easily. I carried papers, worked at Sam's, Reading and the convent. I wasn't too disagreeable to live with during those years. At least I don't think so. I didn't badger them about not having a car, a larger home, etc. Or did I? I wanted to attend college, instead entered the Air Force. There are other things I prefer not to mention.

Now I am in a position to live my own life with a fair amount of ease and independence. Maybe I'm wrong, I don't know. Perhaps independence and ease aren't mine to possess. Christ Himself was born in a stable. But that life is mine so long as God wills and I would like to accomplish a few things.

I mentioned before that the situation is far from hopeless. Radical action is necessary, and only if action is taken, will I be willing to invest in the project called family life.

What action is necessary we can discuss when I return. If you understand my proposition then attempt to explain the same to them. I advise you to talk things over with Dad and Mom.

Christmas brought deep peace and a stability I have not known in the past. Nothing passionate or sensational, only the truly wonderful peace which told me Our Lord is not too dissatisfied with me. All I want to do now is finish my term in the Air Force, enter the Edmundite Order, and if possible become a priest and saint. I may waiver in the future, I don't know, but the important thing is the way I feel today. Tomorrow will take care of itself.

Granted, a 1954 DeSoto is an extravagance. You can forget about it. Perhaps someday it will be different. I'm very happy. We'll discuss the family problems when I reach home. I refuse to worry about them anymore.

A friend of mine from the Midwest is well on his way to Baptism in the Church. He'll be a great asset to the church and vice-versa. Too bad I'm leaving so soon. I'd give anything to be with him on that day.

Definite word came in last week; I report to Fuchu, the replacement depot near Tokyo on January 13th. This means I'll be seeing you, possibly for our birthday, in February. Two of my friends left for Fuchu last night.

I had Christmas dinner at Greg Wachman's and spent the afternoon there with Howard and Moore. The meal was delicious. The dependents' wives certainly take care of us in AACS.

Today I received a card and note from Roger Lacharite, a future brother in Christ, who is studying in Rome. This past summer he spent a month in England, a month in Germany, and one in France. The Edmundites are definitely international. I look forward to becoming one of them with enthusiasm. Fr. Galligan has been helpful during the past two years. It will be good to meet him.

All my love, Johnny

The time to leave Iwakuni had arrived. A half dozen of his friends saw Johnny off at the train station.

"Don't forget us," one of them shouted as the train pulled away.

During a day of picture-taking in Tokyo an offer of $250 in American dollars made him think seriously of giving up his Zeiss Ikon camera since he had paid only $88 for it. The complications of dealing with a black market transaction convinced him to turn the offer down. American script is all a serviceman could use in Japan. Any dollars found on the final inspection before leaving would be confiscated and a possible lowering in grade could happen. At least he now knew just how valuable his purchase had been. When he reached Inchu, Johnny learned he would not be sailing on the 15th of January.

"How do you like that? Hurry up and wait," he said to another airman. After several days of ten hours sleep and three meals, orders come regarding their departure on the 19th on the U. S. N. Freeman for Seattle, Washington.

"Well, that will be a new experience. I was sure we were heading for San Francisco," which is where Johnny wanted to go in order to visit his old friend Sonny and his wife. A final physical check and transfer of military script took place on the afternoon before they arose that final morning at 4 a.m. turned in their bedding, ate and went through a customs check at 7.

The day he sailed from the port of Yokohama, with a band playing and some flags waving, Johnny could not believe the feeling of nostalgia which overcame him. Ecstatic about heading home, he realized he had also learned to love this country where he celebrated his last three birthdays. This land of beautiful coastlines, terraced rice paddies, incredible sunrises and sunsets seen so many times from the control tower, and the people he had met, who would be treated as totally foreign by most Americans, yet to him had become so familiar. He had learned and experienced so much in thirty months he knew he had grown in many ways. He would never be the same again.

"This January weather will keep me below decks; better get used to a lot of reading and card playing," he thought on the first day out.

"Let's find a few pinochle players," Johnny said to another airman who had a bunk nearby.

"I think we'll find them. I don't think everybody wants to play poker." In short time they found a number of willing players who never seemed to tire of the game.

"I really wish I had the guts to get in on a poker game," he said to one of the guys he had seen playing the game.

"Hey, give it a try. Some of the games are pretty tame, you know; nickel, dime, quarter; three raises."

"Well, maybe I will." He never did, however, since he wanted to make certain he had enough money to enjoy his ten-day leave. The sail back to the States was uneventful. He did show a few airmen the short story he had written.

"That's exactly the way it was," remarked one of the readers. The comment pleased him. Maybe he would enter it into one of those magazine contests his instructor at the Magazine Institute had suggested.

On February 2nd they arrived at the Strait of Juan de Fuca with Canada's Vancouver Island to the north and the State of Washington to the south. Seattle looked like the cleanest city he had ever visited. The next day he flew to Philadelphia on Northwest Airlines, took a train to Pottsville and ended his trip to his hometown on a bus. The train had stopped its passenger service to Shenandoah years before.

When he arrived at his parents' apartment with his duffle bag and three-striped blue uniform, he could not believe how small the rooms looked. Everybody was out at the time. No key ever locked the door, which gave him access to his old homestead. His mother arrived from the grocery store, fell into his arms and thanked God he had finally arrived home safely after all that time away from them.

"Johnny, Johnny, Johnny," is all she could say, with tears streaming down her face.

"Mom, I'm home. How are you? It's so good to be back in the old U. S. A.!"

"I am so sorry nobody was here when you arrived. Louie and Sylvia are still at school and Dad is at the mine. Alma will come home for the weekend from her job in Hamburg. How long can you stay home?"

" They gave me a ten-day leave. Then I go to Shaw AFB in South Carolina probably for the rest of my enlistment in the Air Force."

"Johnny, you look so good. We painted two of the rooms for your homecoming."

"Mom, the rooms look so small to me. And Alma told me the furnace doesn't work anymore. How do you stay warm? You know, we must get out of this house, and probably out of this town."

"How am I going to get your father to move? This town is all he has ever really known. The Maple Hill mine closes in March. After that we will somehow scrape through."

"I don't know. I don't like it. We need to do something. By the way, where are the packages I sent before I left Japan? I want to show some of the picture I have taken over there. I think you will all like them."

"I have kept them in our bedroom closet. They should be okay."

Soon the rest of the family arrived. Everybody looked him over to see if he was the same Johnny who had left so many months ago.

"You look good in that uniform, Johnny," said his brother. Lou looked the picture of health with his rosy cheeks and athletic body.

"You look pretty good yourself. Do you still have that paper route?"

"No, I gave it up last summer before I left for Reading. Sylvia took the summer job in Hamburg, so we decided to give it to a friend."

"Well, Johnny, you look good, but pretty skinny as always," added his father.

"So Dad, how are you these days?"

"Not so bad, except for the cold nights at home since the furnace gave out. I think I had some pneumonia last month."

"That should convince you, we have to get out of here."

"Sylvia, looks like you've put on some weight and you've grown about six inches." Johnny felt he had missed much of her growing-up years.

"Johnny, you sound so different. It is like you've taken speech lessons, or something." Delighted at having her brother home, she listened carefully to everything he had to say.

"Johnny, we are going to have T-bone steaks for dinner. How does that sound?" asked his mother.

"Great. Do you still smother the steak in butter and fried onions?"

"Whatever you want."

The meal seemed like those he remembered, with everyone around the kitchen table and his father measuring out each portion of the steak.

"Today we'll give you most of the filet. Lord, it's good to have you with us again even if you don't sound like a hometown boy anymore and not Polish either."

"Dad, how long do you have to live in America before you're an American, not some hyphenated ethnic type? In Japan I was an American GI, period."

"Well, I'm always going to be a Polak, no matter what you say."

His mother had baked some bread, baked an apple pie and prepared some fresh coffee in the drip pot. The next day his older sister Alma arrived home.

"Johnny, I thought we'd never see you again. I wish I could stay home with you for the week."

"Hi, Sis, it is good to see you. How's everything going?"

"Not too bad. I have a new friend I'd like you to meet sometime. We both work at the state hospital. Maybe you could visit next week and see Mother Edmunda as well."

"Okay, I'll see what I can arrange. Without a car it's not too easy to get around."

"Now that Alma's home I'd like to show you some of those color slides I took recently."

The slides of Tokyo, Hiroshima and Iwakuni kept everyone's interest. One shot, with Johnny standing in the train station, brought the following comment from his father.

"There, I always knew you were not quite right, with all that talk about getting me to straighten out. You're probably screwed up yourself." Johnny took a closer look at the slide to see what his father had noticed. The only thing he could see – a certain bent of his head beneath his military cap – had aroused this unexpected comment. Whatever it was, Johnny cut up the slide and threw it away. He might have lost respect for his father, still he didn't want anyone else getting the same impression.

The ten-day leave could have been shortened to three days as far as Johnny was concerned. He found the town even duller than when he had left, and his parents hadn't changed at all. He just wanted to get back to the Air Force, especially with a new airfield at Shaw available for him to direct traffic. He never did get to visit the Reverend Mother who had a private retreat in progress. He did stop off in Baltimore to see his friend Joe who had recently written to him. The letter reflected the closer friendship they had developed since their high school years.

> *Dear John,*
>
> *I eagerly await your visit – more than that; I can't wait. When I stop to realize how long it's been since last we met, I wonder if we will even recognize each other. Thank heaven for the letters.*
>
> *The weekend is the best time to visit me at St. Peters. South Chapelgate Lane is easy to find. Until we have the good fortune to see each other, John, goodbye, and be assured of continual remembrance in my prayers.*
>
> *Yours in Our Lord,*
>
> *Joe*

Johnny and his seminarian friend, dressed in a black cassock, rejoiced at their meeting after such a long absence.

"Joe, you look like a priest."

"Well John, you look like a real airman in that blue uniform."

"Yes, I've always liked these Air Force blues."

Johnny looked at his friend more closely and found he had developed into an even more enthusiastic, smiling personality than in their high school days. With that kind of vigor and welcoming exterior, he would surely become a successful preacher and missionary for the faith.

"John, I'd like to take you around the college and introduce you to some of the seminarians and staff."

"Father, meet my friend John who has recently returned from thirty months in Japan," Joe said to a professor who stood just inside the main building.

"Father, a pleasure to meet you. If I weren't committed to entering the Edmundites I think the Paulists would be a good order to join."

"Well, with Joe already with us, the Spirit may move you to reconsider your decision. Anyway, good luck, a real pleasure to meet you."

"Have you had lunch? If not, please join us," said Joe as they neared the refectory.

"No, I haven't eaten yet. I will be happy to join you."

As they ate Johnny could see the contentment in many of the seminarians' faces. He believed he would fit in well in such an atmosphere. After lunch he informed Joe of his need to catch the bus for Shaw AFB around 2:00 P.M.

"John, I wish we could have had more time, but it's been so great to see you. Take care of yourself."

They shook hands enthusiastically and promised the next visit would be a longer one.

As attractive as he had hoped for, Shaw AFB made for an easy adjustment to the States. The other control tower operators, GCA staff, and radio personnel related well to one another. He and another northerner had the only colored airman in the detachment assigned to their room. A/1C Johnson could have probably roomed well with anyone; the commander decided to entrust two northern Catholics to the situation. Sullivan, from Michigan, and Johnny got along with their roommate without any problems.

The control tower shifts, very much like the ones in Japan, usually allowed for a 48-hour break from duty after four rounds in the tower. Ed Turner, an

Airman First Class like himself, lived off base with his wife, Lovelene. Johnny smiled at the name, Lovelene. Where else would a girl be named Lovelene except in the South? He and Ed became friends shortly after they shared a round of shifts in the control tower. One of the longer night shifts, without much traffic, became a sounding board for each of them to discuss some details of their personal lives, particularly what they would do after leaving the Air Force.

"Well, all I have ever wanted to do is get a college education. I did get about 15 credits while in Japan. Right now it looks like I'll be heading for the seminary."

"No kidding! You know Lovelene and I are the only Catholics in each of our families. Her Southern Baptist sister is sure we are going to hell. I came into the church first. She followed soon after. So tell me about this priesthood idea. Do you think you can be a celibate?"

"Ed, you know, I really don't know. That's what the seminary training is all about, I guess. It's just a matter of taking one step at a time and seeing where it leads. I know one thing, I can't do it without a lot of prayer and grace."

"Which seminary are you going to?"

"I've been accepted by the Society of St. Edmund into their college in Vermont as a student-seminarian. With some luck I'll be there in September. From what I hear the Air Force may let us out a few months early if we are accepted by a college."

"Well, I hope you get to be a priest. The short time I have known you makes me think you might be a good one. I'd like you to have lunch or dinner with Lovelene and me. It may help her if she gets to meet more Catholics. You know there aren't that many of us down here."

The following week he met Ed's wife who had cooked a southern-fried chicken dinner which Johnny relished. "Lovelene, I can't believe chicken can taste this good!"

"I'm glad you like it. Eat as much as you wish," she replied. Her long, soft blond hair and blue eyes made her the perfect southern young wife.

"Ed, you didn't tell me just how beautiful a wife you have. You should have some great-looking kids."

"Johnny, Ed tells me you may become a priest. Does that mean you're willing to be a bachelor the rest of your life? You don't look like the bachelor-type to me."

"You're right. That's a big part of the final decision. Only time will tell if

I will be able to do it. In a religious order, like the Society of St. Edmund, obedience and poverty become important as well. I have been in touch with them the last two years and can enter their college if I am discharged in September."

"Let's hope that happens. Ed tells me you have talked a lot about it in the tower."

"Yes it's been good to have Ed around. I'm glad we met so soon after I came to Shaw."

The next day, Johnny learned more about Southern prejudice, in a barbershop operated on the base by civilian barbers, than he had expected to find on an Air Force base. As part of his latest assignment with the Magazine Institute, he wrote the feelings he had experienced when a colored airman rose from his chair to get a haircut from one of the barbers. He titled the brief essay, "Incident in a Barbershop."

Hope struggled then strangled and died; I sat in my chair and watched.

Justice turned its face and cried; I sat in my chair and watched.

Faith longed to linger and lost; I sat in my chair and watched.

Charity screamed in desire then wept; I sat in my chair and watched.

Human dignity blushed. I sat in my chair and watched.

Six barbers — five white and one colored — performed the barber's rituals on six white servicemen in the Post Exchange Barbershop of an Air Force base in South Carolina. Two men sat in red leather upholstered, chrome chairs awaiting their turn. Both were young. One was white, the other colored.

"Next," said a barber as he finished with a customer. The white serviceman rose and took the empty chair.

Another barber finished.

"Next," he said. The colored serviceman rose and headed indifferently toward the chair.

Two steps from the chair he was stopped. Stopped by the same voice that had said "Next." It now coldly said, "He'll take care of you," indicting the colored barber who was attending to a white serviceman.

His dignity lashed by a whip against which he could not retaliate — the voice echoing the heart of a fellow human being — the young man with a skin pigmentation he didn't ask to possess walked self-consciously back to his seat.

The pages of a magazine he had already read became his defense. His eyes looked at the print and pictures he didn't really want to see. He was dazed.

Shoulders and back thrust forward over the magazine in an attempt to recover composure. Elbows on knees supported the weight of a crushed heart.

Hope struggled to remain alive then died in the wry smile of bewilderment and embarrassment which soon dominated his features.

That day in the barbershop humanity bled in defeat. I saw it die.

And the simple barber who became a murderer of humanity sat contentedly in his barber's chair. He was proud of his achievement.

Perhaps someday someone will tell him of the day he murdered his brother. Of course, he won't understand.

A copy of his short poem-essay received some favorable comment from his editor at the Magazine Institute with an inquiry if he intended to continue with the course since he had not submitted at least four assignments or used a number of optional manuscripts. Johnny replied that his return to the States had diminished his interest in completing the course. Writing would always be of interest to him; he simply could not dedicate his time to any serious pursuit of much beyond feature articles for the base newspaper. His main focus was gaining entrance into a college in September.

Two letters from his sister Alma in early March shattered some of his hopes for getting the family moved to another house. He had really trusted that she would do a great deal to turn the dream into a reality.

> *My dearest Johnny,*
>
> *Please forgive me for not writing sooner!! You have been in my mind constantly. I cannot forget what a dear brother you are — and that I love you very much.*
>
> *This Saturday I hope to get married. I'm pretty sure that Earl loves me enough, not to make my life hell on earth. I think I love him right now, but I don't know what I'll feel like in a year or so, because I'm still not sure about him — I think he might let me down. If he does not prove to be a spendthrift then I shall have a happy married life.*

I feel fine and look okay, but to me I feel as if I'm showing a mile because I know about it. Mom still doesn't know I'm pregnant. She only knows I am getting married outside the Church to a divorced man. Whatever you told them at home you did it well. When I called the other day Mom seemed to hurt badly. One thing she said, and I don't know where she ever got the idea, was, "Did I make you do this?" She said I'm over 21 and ought to know what I'm doing. And I said, "Believe me mother, I do." And all I kept saying was "don't be mad at me." She ended by saying she would not be angry at me.

Daddy is finished at the colliery. The miners refused to work for three weeks to prevent the shutdown of the mine, but the company won't care about that. Mother is still working at the sewing factory.

The next time you hear from me I'll probably be married. Please write soon and thank you for all you've done for me mentally and materially.

Love Always, Alma

Alma's next letter expressed her disappointment that Johnny had changed his views about her impending marriage outside the Church.

I am disappointed yet I am pleased, because your views are the ones of a good Catholic and the only ones, except for the marriage to the first party — which is out of the question — that are right.

But I have to have this baby — true I can have it unwed and keep it, but I won't do it that way. I do love Earl, if only for the fact that he's marrying me, even though I'm carrying another man's child. And if he disappoints me later on, so be it.

It is a shame that this has happened at all — but it is my fault, my fault, my most grievous fault. And if there is mental stress because of having left the church that too will be a bitter pill to swallow. And because you love me, because you are my brother, I suppose I cannot stop you from the pain of knowing that I am in a state of excommunication. As I write this the tears stream down my face, not for myself, but for you, dear brother, and for my dear sweet mother who I shall be hurting terribly.

Perhaps the Grace of God is not too close to me — or else I would abide by what is right and proper. And if God should decide to take me from this earth before my mistake is corrected, either by

237

being able to marry Earl properly or by leaving him after I marry him, then I shall deserve His Justice, as well as His Mercy.

The only thing that bothers me is will this have any effect on your entering the seminary? I certainly hope not, and if it does, you shall have all the more reason to hate me.

As much as I love you I dislike the pride in you, and the ambition to get ahead. I sometimes think your real disappointment in me is that now I will not be able to help you in these things.

I do hope I haven't hurt you tremendously. After all, it is myself I shall be hurting most of all. Just try to forget what I have done and what I will do. I expect to get married legally this Saturday in Elkton, Maryland and I doubt if I shall have the courage to go home.

Remember Esther, the girl in the lab who has a friend in New York with Fairchild Publications. She has invited us to go to New York to meet him. It would be especially well for you to make his acquaintance. He is Irish and a Catholic.

Dear Johnny, forgive me for having hurt you so much. I hope you won't hate me for refusing to do as you now wish. Still, I'm glad you wrote as you did, because if anything goes wrong, you will at least know that you did your duty.

All my Love, Alma

Johnny felt his hopes for the family's progress shattered by his sister's unfortunate dilemma. He lost himself in his work in the control tower, the McCarthy hearings on television which he found totally engrossing, his new friends, and the Mass. The Holy Eucharist had become the highlight of his day. He attended Mass at the Catholic chapel when possible. His prayer life became more intense. Often when he walked out of the chapel he could feel a lightness, a renewed confidence, that all would be well in ways he had no way of predicting.

The McCarthy hearings took on the atmosphere of a theatrical soap opera. The Senator had a way of bullying witnesses, slurring associates, and making the television screen alive with the sinister spectacle of an unrelenting judge demanding the termination of anyone remotely friendly to the Communist cause. Any witnesses unwilling to answer questions, or who ducked behind the 5th Amendment, looked like traitors to the Senator and his staff. Television viewing had not been available in Japan, which added to his pleasure in watching the proceedings.

An unexpected letter from his friend Howard arrived in late March.

Dear John,

I imagine you have given me up for dead. I'm sorry it has taken me so long to answer your wonderful letter. First of all I wish to thank you for calling my parents. They were thrilled to death just to talk to anyone who knew their son. I'm afraid you completely shocked them with your statement that I was now a Catholic. They knew I was taking lessons but this was something new. If they sounded upset I'm sure you will understand. They now know I am still taking lessons but have not taken the big step. I still have many doubts, and questions which may take some time to iron out. I've got to be absolutely sure of such a step because I know once I take it there is no turning back. Father Chris, of course, can't understand such an attitude. I believe he referred to it as dilly-dallying around. Doesn't it sound exactly like him? Speaking of Father, every day my opinion of him plunges. I'm beginning to believe you were correct about him from the start. Honestly John, he doesn't even seem like a Christian to me. God forgive me but I cannot help it. He is putting many doubts in my mind instead of helping me. If I can't make up my mind I plan to wait until I get home and start from scratch. He swears, drinks, and God knows what all. I'll admit my thoughts are as anti-Christian as you can get, but I do know that he isn't any example for me to follow. To be converted under such circumstances is indeed a task, and one I have not been capable of. The other day I was in his office and this will give you an idea of what I hear. We now have an Australian priest and if you think the Korean was bad you should see this battle. The fumigators were coming and he told them "to be sure and have the damned Aussie's desk fumigated." Such an attitude coming from a priest I can't understand. Jesus taught love and understanding, can you see how I feel? You know how he drinks; I've gone in many days for a lesson when all I could smell was liquor. Well enough of my troubles, here is the news.

There is hardly any of the old boys here now. I miss DePaulo terribly, you know how wonderful he was when you were down in the dumps. He could charm the devil out of hell. Coin left two nights ago. They had quite a party for him. I've never seen so many drunks in all my days. It was really terrible. I think Coin really hated to leave O'Neil. We have so many new boys in the squadron you wouldn't know the old place. They are all a little dull and not ready for a good time like the old boys.

Last month I had seven wonderful days in Tokyo. Mom and Dad sent me $500 so I would have enough. (Ha) I took four pictures of Mt. Fuji. I saw The Robe which I thought was out of this world. Please write when you have time.

As ever, Howard

How ironic that a Franciscan priest named after St. John Chrysostom, a 4th century doctor of the church, had undone whatever small influence Johnny had had on his friend. His one hope that Howard would find the right priest to lead him by example and proper instruction into the Church relieved him of any resentment he had against the priest he called "The Forsaken Franciscan" in some of his notes.

"Have you thought about joining the Knights of Columbus?" asked Ed one day in the tower.

"Well I do like their ads in newspapers and magazines inviting people to take a correspondence course discussing various truths of the Catholic Church. If it doesn't cost too much I would consider it."

"A friend of mine from the parish in Sumter will be joining next month. He asked me to join with him. I told him I would invite you also. I can't recall the exact cost of membership. It can't be too much."

The next month the three of them drove to Charleston to become members. Johnny considered the trip a good way to see more of South Carolina. Columbia, some 35 miles west of Shaw AFB, could not compare to the coastal city of Charleston, famous for its Fort Sumter National Monument commemorating the first shot of the Civil War.

The Knights owned the building where the proceedings took place. Johnny felt the Knights represented the best of Catholic laymen organized to support one another and evangelize anyone they might attract by advertising and their own good example. He gladly took his oath of membership. On the return trip to Sumter Johnny noticed a sign for Moncks Corner.

"Let's stop in to see the Trappist Monastery on the Mepkin Plantation. I understand it is very near Moncks Corner."

"Johnny, sounds like a good idea but we have to get back home to take care of some things," replied Ed.

"Okay. Now that I know the plantation is really not that far from the base I'll probably find a way to get down."

"Perhaps you need to buy a car if you want to get around. My uncle has an old Packard he keeps in his garage since he can't drive anymore," said Ed's friend.

"Sounds like a chance to do something I've been thinking about for a while. Trouble is I can't drive."

"I'll give you a few lessons. You'll be ready to take a test in no time."

"Thanks Ed. Perhaps I could see the car in the next couple of days."

The Packard looked like a small tank to Johnny when he saw it the following week. He wondered how the neighbors back in his hometown would react when he drove it home.

"How much will this cost me?"

"My uncle says you can have it for $600 cash."

Johnny thought about the money he had saved for his college expenses. Perhaps he could use some of it to purchase the car.

"Sounds like a good price." He hadn't really investigated car prices since his return from Japan. He only knew Packards were one of the top models.

"Ed, do you think we could start a few driving lessons?"

"Okay, I'll see you in a couple of days and we'll see how you do."

Johnny's excitement at the possibility that he might actually drive a car home on his next visit overcame his concerns that the money really should be put to better use like that house he wanted his parents to buy or the college expenses which could begin as early as September.

"Today's the day, Johnny; are you ready to drive this thing?"

"Sure, let's get started."

Ed carefully explained the various gadgets on the huge dashboard, showed him how to depress the clutch while shifting gears, how to release the brake, turn the lights on, and how to start the engine. After a few hair-raising sessions Ed decided he did not want to endanger his life, especially after Johnny had come close to smashing into a truck.

"Ed, I'm just going to have to wait until I'm ready for this idea of owning a car. There are too many things I may need the money for and, I believe, it's made me pretty nervous."

"Probably, not a bad idea. My friend will not be happy about your decision, but that's his problem."

On the Feast of St. Vincent Ferrer Johnny received a letter from Joe.

This little note is not a cheap attempt to get another letter from you. The main reason for writing now is to pass on some information regarding some Paulist activities. Each Sunday afternoon during April two Paulists are presenting a pulpit dialogue on T.V. for the Catholic Hour. In typical fashion, the dialogues are directed at the non-Catholic but certainly any Catholic can learn much about his faith apologetically and otherwise by watching. The television station in Columbia, S.C. is carrying the show live on Sundays at 1:30 P.M.

Your friend Turner must be quite a zealous Catholic; the kind so necessary for winning our country to the faith. Give him my own personal regards and promises of prayers. There is much you can learn about the objections non-Catholics have to the faith and the means of answering them from Fathers Finley and Reynolds (giving the dialogues) who have had much experience in working with new Catholics.

Have you gotten over to the Trappists yet? Paul Comber whom you met here (tall, thin, blond, from Philly who sat with us at supper that night) has a brother there. His name in religion is Brother Dennis and you might look him up if it's allowed and if you care to. Also, if you get over to see Dale Francis in Charlotte tell him how much all of us here with the Paulists admire the work he is doing and the sacrifice he is making for God and for His church.

I can hardly believe it's six weeks since you were here last. I hope it won't be too long until you can make your way here again. Take advantage of these last few weeks of Lent and get close to Our Lord. Be good; be better; be holy, friend, and please pray often for me.

Yours in Our Lord, Joe

Joe's mention of the Trappists finalized Johnny's decision to visit the monastery at the Mepkin Plantation near Moncks Corner during the final week of Lent. He decided he could hitchhike the sixty or so miles in a reasonable amount of time, especially if he wore his summer Air Force uniform. After ten pickups from people who were traveling just a few miles each time, he found himself walking along the road to the monastery. After a very short time a pickup truck stopped next to him on the very narrow road.

"Where are you going? Perhaps I can take you there. I am Brother Sam from the monastery."

"Good morning, Brother; I am hoping to spend some time at the monastery today. You're a Godsend. I had no idea how far the monastery was from the main road."

Brother Sam looked totally contented and at peace with the world. He gave Brother Sam his name and happily shook hands. Johnny wondered why he was allowed to drive outside the grounds.

"Johnny, I am the extern for the monastery. This allows me to travel into town for any of our needs and, if necessary, to pick up visitors who have no transportation into the plantation."

"Brother, if you don't mind telling me, how did you decide to become a monk?"

"Well, I was a Jewish businessman in Chicago until I was forty. Somehow I began to read Thomas Merton's books, especially *The Seven Story Mountain,* which described his own conversion to the Church, and before long I found myself following in his footsteps all the way to Louisville and Our Lady of Gethsemani monastery nearby. With the monastery growing very rapidly the Immaculate Heart Monastery at Mepkin Plantation was founded in 1949. We are considered a daughter-house of Our Lady of Gethsemani. We have been here a little over four years."

"What a great pleasure to meet you! By the way, the moss on the trees has me totally mesmerized. Is it always on the trees? Almost makes me think of the Civil War."

"Yes, that's part of southern plantation life, especially in South Carolina. Well we're here. Just ring the bell and a brother will let you in."

The visit to the monastery began with a small dinner of fresh baked bread and soup. Lenten regulations meant Johnny could walk around the grounds but would have no other contact with the monks. The atmosphere enveloped him. Huge trees dripping with moss surrounded him in every direction. A path led to the cemetery where Clare Boothe Luce's daughter was buried after an automobile accident. The Mepkin Plantation had been the Luce's home which they donated to the Trappists. He had begun to wonder how he would get to the main highway or bus stop when Brother Sam appeared and offered to take him there. The visit to the monastery made his Lent complete. A letter from the Reverend Mother served notice that she had become concerned about his steadfastness regarding life in general.

D.M.et O.
April 13ᵗʰ
Dearest Johnny,
*   You're living in the clouds most of the time; perhaps, a little realism is what you need to see life face to face.*

*   Home is not any different now than when you were there. And, don't mind when I remind you of the times when I tried to see fault with your keeping late hours and too easy spending of money. "We just can't have it and squander it at the same time" – is what I kept saying. You found me too exacting, too serious; didn't you? The fact that you saved $1,200.00 gives me hopes that you learned something. If you did, perhaps, Louis, who is so pliable, can be taught by his older brother. You love each other, this should make teaching easy.*

*   Alma? Your mother mentioned it to me at our Mother Frances' funeral who was one of our co-foundresses and died at the age of 85. I don't know whether I was shocked or not. Perhaps, I'm too realistic? This doesn't mean that I'm not hurt; I expected more from one who went through a Catholic H.S. As yet, she didn't write to me – so, I'm silent, too. I don't know the facts, so I have little to say. She definitely knew better.*

*   Humility of mind and heart is the only foundation upon which we may safely build our structure of perfection – It is only heart-breaks that can open our eyes to our own poverty and the nothingness of life in general. May you begin wisely under the direction of your good chaplain. But, don't be too wise. And step down from the clouds.*

*   Your desires to change things at home are excellent! How I bemoaned and still bemoan what is! One can say little - at least, I can say little. See what you can do for my heart's best wishes and prayers are with you.*
*   Love in J & M.*
*   M.M.E.*

Johnny requested a second leave to see if he could do anything more about his family's financial situation. When he returned to Shaw AFB a letter from Bill Romano, another one of his friends at Iwakuni, arrived in the mail.

Dear John,

14 April 54

The last time I saw you, I promised to write when I reached the States. If you passed it off as just another parting word from one of the boys, then this letter will come as a surprise.

I can remember your station assignment gave me quite a chuckle, but I guess the loudest and last laugh is on "yours truly."

My state-side orders came through on January 30th while I was still at Iwakuni. Someone, somewhere had marked me for Del Rio Texas. So here I am at last in the Mexican border town of Del Rio, far removed from Mitchell Field in New York and McChord in the state of Washington – my first two "choices."

I left Japan aboard the Simon Buckner on February 12th and arrived in Seattle on the 22nd. That's about the fastest time one can make I guess. Aside from the garbage detail I was called upon to perform, the whole trip was satisfying – good weather and no sea-sickness.

I sincerely hope you enjoyed your leave at home and were able to smooth out some of the financial worries that were bothering you.

As for me – I was glad to be home again, though it seemed strange in a way. I still can't get used to the idea quite yet. I knew I'd changed naturally, being away, but only now realize the extent. I feel now that my future plans call for revision somewhere down the line.

This, actually, more than anything else prompted my letter, although I would have written in any case.

I have a problem! Tell me John, do you still have the ambition for a priestly life as you did in Japan?

Sad to say – I never felt the same as you about the priesthood. I never wanted to instruct and convert souls or cultivate the mission fields. Into the bargain I'm a poor practicing Catholic.

Despite this, is it possible I could have a vocation? Not many years ago I "thought" I did.

You see, ever since my trouble in Japan I've rather feared married life – for obvious reasons. I have a scrupulous conscience – not a delicate one ... a scrupulous conscience – and I'm unable to laugh away the matter like others have done; therefore, I want seriously to reconsider my chances for a religious life.

I grant my motive is shallow and selfish, but it's ground to start from. Am I wrong in thinking this way?

I haven't discussed this with anyone. I don't even want to bring up the issue before my father or my few Jesuit friends for two reasons – first, it might raise false hopes – second, my trouble in Japan.

Right now I feel like a dog that's been chasing its tail in circles for a lifetime – confused and nearly worn out.

I don't know what you thought of me in Japan, maybe only a loud-mouthed bag of hot air – certainly not your intellectual equal, but I respected your opinion on most matters.

I can read books, pray night and day, and frequent the sacraments. At this stage though I need some helpful advice and hope I can turn to you. I would appreciate very greatly, if you'd take a little time, analyze my situation and give me your views on the subject. When I started to write this letter, I intended to draw a clear complete picture of my present dilemma (or dillema, or dillemma). I hope it hasn't been misleading. If I have the slightest grounds to pursue this thing – tell me. You've come a long way searching out a vocation and the last time I saw you I thought you had it licked. I believe you can help me in a way. I wish you'd try.

Well John, this has been a difficult letter to write. I'm afraid I can't improve on it – I've tried the past four days – so I'll let it go as is. Waiting to hear from you.

Your good friend
Bill -

Bill's letter demanded an immediate response. Johnny hoped his thoughts might help his friend.

Dear Bill:

Your letter was waiting for me the day I returned from my second leave. I had thought of you several times and wondered if you would write. The surprise was a pleasant one.

I didn't make too much of a hit with my family during my first leave.

In Japan when you mentioned the possibility of a vocation I was not too surprised but I did not take you seriously. Now it seems you are very serious. I pray the following words may help you find a solution.

The difficulties involved in attempting to analyze one's spiritual condition, possibilities and hopes for the future, is readily appreciated. I attempted the same several times with a knowledge that the finished product was obviously incomplete. Perhaps the most successful vocation directors are those who can perceive the full picture aided by their own experience and early gropings, intuition or the grace of God – and lead us to a vantage point from which we can see the complete picture ourselves. After that we're more or less on our own.

A true vocation to the religious life necessarily implies a deep love of God and, or, the desire to eventually love Him well.

That you feel disposed to reading books, praying without ceasing, and frequenting the sacraments is a good indication you want to know His will. And if we are to love Him well it is easily seen that we would do so only in the life He wishes us to embrace.

Of course, Our Lord is no dictator or tyrant. He offers us love, peace of soul, everlasting life. Never does He say we must take these gifts. Yet, as rational creatures, we realize the utter foolishness of refusing them.

Likewise, when we feel compelled to make a decision concerning the religious life, it is utterly foolish to say "No" when for some unknown reason (a vocation perhaps) we'd like very much to say "Yes". That "Yes" may need to be said many times after the initial one and; a few "No's " may ring out dramatically, demanding to be heard.

But with me, as well as you perhaps, it's getting later in the game than we'd like to think. Why go on frustrating an apparent desire and continue living in a world of distractions?

As for the religious life itself. The thought of all that obedience, the sometimes petty rules, etc. used to repel me. Now, all I ask is that I be free to kneel before the Blessed Sacrament whenever the opportunity presents itself, that I be free to meditate 24 hrs. a day on the goodness of God and His mercies to me, and that I be free to love Him completely with no reservations. (Thank heavens, we can do these things to a certain extent anywhere, or else I'd be miserable.)

So long as we keep before our eyes the goal of living every day given us as close to God as possible all the little tedious tasks and details which manage to become part of religious life will melt into nothingness or at most a slight irritation which can be erased with a sense of humor.

I think I know how you feel about the very real lack of desire to "instruct and convert souls or cultivate the mission fields." Although I've now reached a point where I feel I would be willing to do any type of work my superiors decided I should do, for the longest time I had a definite repugnance toward the duties of a parish priest. I still would not be a secular priest for more serious reasons.

Just yesterday I finished reading Newman's, "Apologia Pro Vita Sua". Perhaps, Bill, you're in a position slightly similar to his but of a different nature. During the course of his conversion to the Church there was a period when many asked if they should go over to Rome. He had not yet made up his mind as to whether he should go himself, although he felt his sympathies were in that direction and, on the basis of sympathies alone would not counsel others to go where he could not in conscience trod. Many went without him anyway. This he did not oppose completely, however, because every man is responsible for his own soul. Nevertheless, he was called a hypocrite and a few other things besides, for holding such a position.

This period he considered a time of " Physician heal thyself". Perhaps, Bill, after you have been healed of all doubts and have approached closer to Our Lord your attitudes toward helping others may possibly change.

But not necessarily. Of course, you will want to help others, but not in those specific ways. Perhaps you have a vocation to the contemplative life. In the near future, God willing, you may find out where you stand.

So you see, I at least, do not consider your motives completely shallow or selfish. In fact you're most generous to consider abstinence from the sex act to protect yourself and others from further possible consequences. You recognize the religious life as a way to put this sacrifice to its greatest use and hope to pursue this reasoning, with the grace of God, to a satisfactory conclusion. No, I cannot consider this shallow or selfish whether you ascribe it to a scrupulous conscience or not. There is no reason to believe that from this perhaps imperfect beginning you cannot reach more ideal motives.

Our Lord has been most generous to me in many ways. I've deserved far less from Him for many reasons. Believe me, I've had to say "Yes" to my vocation hundreds of times in the course of these years in the Air Force. I only pray, and hope you will too, that the final "Yes" will come soon if it has not already been uttered. During my first leave I was very unsettled and confused. I met a recent convert here, Ed Turner, who bolstered my faith when I needed it most. I'll write more fully next time.

And enjoy Del Rio, Texas – sounds fascinatingly immoral.
Sincerely in Christ,
John

Johnny's friend Ed wrote to him using a Pennsylvania address with only the name of the town and no home address showing. His mother sent the letter to him at Shaw. Ed's talent at making signs for grocery stores and other enterprises had given him the idea he might make it a career after the Air Force.

Dear John,

May I have the juvenile pleasure of inserting a pun? Here goes, "This is my first 'Dear John' letter." - Thanx!

Look, fellow, what makes you so doggone nice, I mean, whatever it is, don't let it go, your interest shown for us since you have been on leave simply overwhelms us.

I don't know of anything we could have appreciated more than the 'Sacred Heart' pictures. They are really beautiful and will have a special meaning when we see them, that you gave them to us.

What have you done exciting since you have been home? You seem to be getting around to all the places. What have you found out about entering school? I am very anxious to hear all about that. Have you seen your friends that are in school? What about the "Mother General"?

About all I have been doing is hammering and sawing, (a little shoveling too). This park is really going to be nice, but o'boy, what work trying to complete it.

John, I am really enthused about the sign enterprise, although the initial investment has me worried more than anything else. Even with a G.I. loan it sometimes takes ages to get them through, and do you think I could get enough from them to start?

Lovelene has been doing very well since she has been home. It's the baby's first trip home and the baby has been doing very well also, hasn't even cried once!

Doesn't this make you wish you were already out of service? I have been working hard since I have been home but the freedom is wonderful, I like the wide open spaces where there are no jets, stripes or bars.

May I ask a question, thank you! – Have you wrecked any trucks since you have been home? – O.K., that was poor taste, but now I've said it and I'm glad!

When are you going back to the base, I think I will go Monday (26th) – I need an extension, I may get one, do you still plan to?

Say, John, look at all the questions I've asked, now it's imperative that you answer them, I'll be waiting for your reply.

I want to say again how much we appreciate the pictures and the information about the signs. We'll go over it thoroughly in Sumter. Your friend Joe must be a very nice man. When you become one of the bishops of Penna., I am coming to visit you both.

Our regards from us both.
Your friend,
Edwin

The thoughts expressed in the letter from Ed gave Johnny the feeling of true friendship with his friend from North Carolina. He believed southerners like Ed and his wife were gifts to the Church with great hope for the future.

Joe wrote a letter to Johnny in late April which made him believe the Paulists just might be a better order to join. His long connection with the Edmundites' vocation director made any change of plans unlikely. The letter, written on the Saturday after Easter, gave him much to think about.

April 24, 1954
Easter Saturday
I hoped to have heard from you by this time, John, but if I put off writing to some other time, I don't know when that other time will ever come around. We began school after our Easter vacation on Thursday, but have had it easy the last three days since our philosophy teacher is in Milwaukee for the philosophical convention. So this is probably the best chance I will have to write for some time, since things will be mighty busy during the next month I am sure. This is

no complaint now, I know you have been busy yourself, what with being home for Easter and all, and after getting those two letters in two days I really have no grounds for complaint. But do write when you can; your letters are always more than welcome.

Easter was wonderful. We had a retreat from Wednesday night until Holy Saturday which was one of the best retreats yet. Then the folks were down for two days after that. We had a great visit. Ray is doing well at Notre Dame, really likes it now and is doing quite well in his studies. They didn't have much news about home; in fact, it would be more accurate to say that they didn't have any. There haven't even been any deaths of interest lately.

I got an Easter card from Sonny yesterday, filled with writing on all its available space. I was beginning to get worried when four days went by after Easter, since he never misses the holidays (actually, the holidays are the only times when he writes). But the news was well worth the delay. He sounds and claims to be happy; says there is nothing like married life to settle one down. His wife Charlotte is expecting a baby, some time in July, I believe. Naturally this has our friend mighty excited, and he succeeded in communicating some of that happiness to me. I guess it must be one of the greatest expectations known to man. He had other good news. He hopes to be sent to Baltimore when he enters the army this summer for his schooling. I believe he thinks I will be here myself next year, but since Washington is not too far away, it will be almost as good. He asked for you John; said I will have to tell him all about you when I write. I will too; but you yourself could do a much better job of it. Why don't you?

Richard has not written at all since January. I answered his letter in early February but haven't heard since. Of course, he has been silent for long intervals before, so perhaps he will come through with some communication soon, if it's only an invitation to his graduation. Did you ever write to him?

Your two letters were extremely interesting, and is probably in expectation of more of the same that I write this to you. Your friend Turner sounds like a wonderful person. Each of you should be able to benefit from the other. As I have said so many times before, John, I really envy you and your opportunities in the service. Of course, I realize that if I were there, I would kick them just as I kick my jobs and assignments and spiritual life here. But it is good to dream anyway. I have been thinking some more about conversions lately, and although I hesitate to subject someone like yourself who has had actual experience to the advice of a theorist, I would like to pass my thoughts along to you for what they are worth. It seems for one thing that we are still too defensive in talking about the Church. Too apologetic in our apologetics. We act as though we needed to defend when actually what we need to do is expose. Your friend Turner had an interesting point when he said after baptism, "He felt he had been a Catholic all his life". What he was stating was simply that the church was made for him. Like it is made for all men. We forget this in spending all our time talking about the Reformation and defending the Papacy. We don't convey the fact the Church is primarily a means to union with God, not an organization. In talking about the Church, we must spend more time and thought on showing its interior side, showing that the Catholic Church is actually the best means, the only means, for people to fulfill the needs and aspirations of their nature. This was Father Hecker's idea; less stress on the external, which of course can never be excluded entirely, and more on the internal. The Church is not an organization of bishops and priests, the Church is not simply a law-maker, the Church is nothing but people, held together by the presence of the Holy Spirit, living their lives of grace in Christ as His Mystical Body. We must convey to others this inner bond, this life of grace which makes the Church. I don't really have any suggestions for doing this. I realize that most of your opening to non-Catholics come as a result of questions that most often deal with the external organization of the Church. But if I were you, I would read the epistles of St. Paul and get some of the feeling he had about the Church. Then perhaps you can convey some of the inner spirit of the Church in your discussion, realizing that since the Reformation we have been on the defensive but that the time has come for that to end. Let us show to our fellow-countrymen that the Catholic Church has the answers to their problems. That the Catholic Church has the means of making them happy here on earth as well as in heaven. That the Catholic Church is their means for satisfying their desire for security and peace. Americans are starved spiritually. Those who never go to Church certainly, and those who do as well, by their one-day-a-week religion.

Show them as often as you can the way Catholicism encompasses their whole life, demands their whole life, gives them a whole new life – the life of God living in their souls, nourished by the sacraments, restored when lost through our weakness by the sacraments, making them more than just men, but in a very real sense, supermen, men of supernatural life.

Of course, John, you can convey this spirit, only if you grasped it yourself. You can grasp it only by prayer and meditation. Therefore, I urge you to get to pray as often as possible - oftener. You want the life of an apostle. No, you have been made an apostle, because you have made a Catholic and given the privilege of being an apostle. But an apostle is one sent. That is one who is on his own, free from minute guidance and direction of his protector. You are in the world and must bring Christ to that world. As a Catholic you possess Christ; He lives in you. Naturally you can be aware of the presence and then communicate it to others, only if you are pure of heart. Now that doesn't only mean free from sins of impurity. It means one whose heart is cleansed and free from the dirt and scum of all that is not Christ. Free from the world is what it means. You can attain this state of purity only by prayers and deliberate breaking from the world about you, which calls you and lures, you, which woos you and wins you. You can't do this on your own; you can't do it by ordinary means either. It takes courage and heroism. It takes work and it takes sacrifice. Give them.

I am sorry for sounding off like this, John, I realize that I have no right to preach to you at all. Certainly you know me too well. But you will forgive me, because this is something so close to my heart that it almost chokes me when I try to talk about it and my fingers just stumble when I try to put it down on paper. I want you to be holy, to give Christ, not because you're you, but because of what is in you and in all of us which we seldom see. Try, John, resolve, fully completely, entirely, and then try – and succeed!

I have sent along some magazines to you which you may be able to use. They are completely at your disposal, for work or waste it's up to you. I am sorry for sending so many at once, but I have to or these things never get done at all. I am also enclosing a pamphlet which I know you will be interested in. You might let your friend Turner read it too, as well as anyone else who might be interested –

there must *be others.*

No more, John, although I am really wound up. Besides I would just get repetitious and I don't suppose you would be able to stand that at this point. Write when you can, John, and tell me as much as you feel free to. Always be assured of my interest. Get closer to Christ, John. Goodbye for now and be good – be better – be holy!

Yours in Christ

Letters between the Reverend Mother and Johnny became more sporadic. The latest message from his aunt showed again how much she continued to care about his mother and the family.

Deus Meus et Omnia!
April 29, 1954
My dearest Johnny,

With your letter of yesterday, came in one from mother. Sylvia was disappointed in not finding help wanted at Hamburg. With your letter, I began wondering whether this was the complete story.

We tried here, with Sr. Imelda calling up our old friend, to obtain a job for her. The answer came: more yes than no*; hence, we are hopeful that she will find something to do at the Reading Hospital. I asked mother to write to Ciocia Cassie about keeping her during the summer. If she gets the job, remains docile to Cassie, begins thinking seriously about thrift, etc.; I'm sure that she will be able to save a nice sum of money between the closing and opening of the school door. Write her a loving brother's lecture. Cassie can't say much, because it sounds like interfering. Aunts like in-laws are best when they say the least, but brothers can say all they want.*

Mother Duklane also answered Louis that he may return for the summer. I do not expect to be at Reading after July 2nd, so I will not be keeper of his money ... but, if Louis learned the wisdom of saving during the last two summers, when he proudly returned with $200.00, he should beg Mother Duklane to hold on to his money.

When I progress, who progresses with me? ... Was a rather heart-rending question. I mean that I do understand the pain. Well, there is still time to present to them the folly of living only from day to day, with no thought of the morrow. However, when it comes to money, this cannot be brought into the home of your father, for it is gone before it can be put to good use .... You know what I mean. If there should be someone to control every cent in seeing that it is spent where, when and how it can make the most for the future, all may be fine. Mother doesn't seem to have the power over him; but for peace sake, at times, we must capitulate in matrimonial disputes.

Yes, you cannot do all...With Sylvia doing a little, Louis his share, mother hers and dad his humble bit, all could get somewhere some day. You have my best wishes, dearest Johnny, and my prayers. May you accomplish much, with your good will coupled with God's blessing. Alma could have done much to help you, too ... and, I do understand why you were embittered. If we only were less wise, sought counsel, were more cautious, could say NO to ourselves – what a difference? Following nature, following self is the path of least resistance.... It is the easiest, but the end is REGRET.

This is not preaching, Johnny; this is to offer consolation to your wounded heart. I have lived with these pains the greater part of my life as far as the family goes. In my work, God has given me many joys; an eternal TE DEUM is my task.

In whatever you decide to do, decide and act with prayer.
M. M. E.

"Have you heard from any of the guys who are still back in Japan?" asked Johnny of a few of his friends at the base canteen while they drank beer well into the night.

"Not really, you know how it is, once you're gone, you're gone," agreed the others.

"I guess I've been lucky. I have heard from a few of the guys since getting back. In fact I just got a letter from John Eggert's wife from Florida. She sounds great. He came back to the States soon after I did."

The letter from John's wife made Johnny feel that perhaps he had done some good while over there. He read her letter again when he returned to his room.

Friday 30th, April 1954
Hi there John,
Just in case you're very much confused, I'm the beautiful? one you spoke of in John's letter from you.
John is at work (at the base) right now and doesn't know I'm

writing you. I feel as if I already know you, John has spoken of you so often. My main reason for writing you is to thank you for helping John to become a Catholic. I know it's all your doing that he's one today. I never felt free to say very much to him about becoming a Catholic because I wanted him to become one of his own will, not just because I wanted him to.

Yes, we are married! (Feb.24th)

We are so very happy John. I only hope, if ever you decide to lead a married life that you'll be just half as happy as we are. He is a wonderful husband to me. He helps me so much more than most men do and we have so much fun working together. He's a wonderful guy isn't he John? I'd love to meet you. If you get another chance to travel, pack your swimsuit and please come down. We're right on the water here.

Write to us real soon. I'll see to it John writes to you right away.
Love you,
Margie Eggert

A letter from John arrived the next day.

1. May, '54
Greetings John,

Well! It sure did take you long enough to write, but I guess I'll forgive you. I'm not too awfully good at writing either.

I sure was glad to hear that you were doing so good at your new assignment (Stateside assignment, that is). Really sounds like you've been putting the miles under your feet since you've been back. But, pray tell me, how you managed that extra leave? I've got to rant and rave to get a day off around here.

How's everyone at home? Bet they were sure glad to see you and have you back again.

Yes, Margie and I were married the 24th of Feb. She's down here with me and we're very happy. We've got a nice little place right on the water and are doing fine. And by the way, if you're in Texas around the first of the year I'll let you hold the first Eggert offspring. Better make it late in Jan. just to make sure. How's that for fast work? We're really thrilled over our blessing.

Everyone at home is doing fine. Mother asked, in a letter, the other day if I had heard from you yet. She's quite anxious to meet you. Guess the meeting is entirely up to you though. I do hope that you'll be down to see us before too many years pass though.

I sure am glad you like Shaw. This place is for the birds. The cost of living is so high that Margie and I are really having to watch our pennies. The country, however, is very beautiful and we are trying to enjoy it just as much as possible. The beaches here are a lot more beautiful than those in Miami. We've both already got good tans and expect to get darker yet.

Well John, I've got to close now. Not only am I running out of paper but I'm taking Margie to our church bazaar.

Write soon John and take good care of yourself.

God Bless You,

Johnny

PS (90% of the people here are Catholic. That's really quite the deal for a city this far south isn't it? There's standing room only at every mass and the church isn't small at all.)

Bill Romano appeared to appreciate Johnny's comments on his dilemma regarding a vocation motivated by an escapade with V.D. in Japan. A letter in early May gave Johnny the feeling that at least he had absorbed some of the wisdom in the letters from the Reverend Mother, the Edmundite's vocation director, his seminarian friend Joe and the books he had read.

May 3, 1954

Dear John,

Your reassuring letter of the twenty-fifth arrived one day last week and brought with it a certain amount of relief.

Your practical view of the situation had been anxiously awaited, and I knew you'd recognize the importance of my predicament enough to "call a spade – a spade." For that reason too, I was afraid you might say my case for a vocation was built on shaky ground, too much so; therefore your answer gives me more reason to think pursuit of a vocation is justified.

I noticed your letter was dated on the feast day of St. Mark, my patron in Confirmation. If I were superstitious, I might construe the coincidence as a favorable omen of some sort.

I'm sorry that your leave at home wasn't all you had hoped for.

Frankly, I was disappointed in mine too. An air of uneasiness prevailed all the while I was home. I felt a definite cleavage between my friends – my father too to a lesser degree.

It seemed no one had changed in two years, though I had, and there was no common ground for us to meet on. I no longer had any particular interest in their interests. Actually, I was glad when it came time to leave home.

After my first letter to you, I read two books – one dealing specifically with vocations, which left me cold. It must have been written for the youngest innocent mind. The second was Fulton Sheen's "Peace of Soul." You may have read this one long before I got around to it.

I undertook this book with one thought in mind, "Does Sheen have something to say to me personally – has he written a passage I can apply to myself?"

Page after page revealed nothing I was looking for, and I began to wonder if my particular problem was so hopeless or remote, that no one had thought to write even a sentence on its part.

Toward the end of the final chapter, the following paragraphs all but rose off the page and smacked me square in the face. They pin-point "me" so well that I want to re-quote them for you.

The chapter dealt with conversions actually; however I'm bound to believe these passages apply to me in at least a narrow sense.

....But there is a third type of conversion caused by a third event. The crisis is physical when it comes through some unexpected catastrophe such as the death of a loved one, a business failure, disease, or some suffering which forces one to ask, "What is the purpose of life? Why am I here? Whither am I going?" So long as there were prosperity and good health, these questions were never in the foreground; the soul which has only external interests does not concern itself with God, anymore than the rich man whose barns were full. But when the barns are burned, the soul is suddenly forced to look inside itself, to examine the roots of its being, and to peer into the abyss of its spirit. This excursion is not the delightful voyage of a summer day, but a tragic inquiry into the possibility that we have neglected to seek for the best wealth, treasures which rust does not consume, moths eat, and thieves break through and steal — treasures which only God can give when hearts are emptier than

any purse. All crises, even those of material disaster, force the soul inward, as the blood is driven back to the heart during some sickness or as a city under attack moves to its inner defenses....

Illness especially, may be a blessed forerunner of the individuals conversion. (OR VOCATION FOR THAT MATTER) Not only does it prevent him from realizing his desires; it even reduces his capacity for sin, his opportunities for vice.

In that enforced detachment from evil, which is a Mercy of God, he has time to enter into himself, to appraise his life, to interpret it in terms of large reality. He considers God, and, at that moment there is a sense of duality, a confronting of personality with Divinity, a comparison of the facts of his life with the ideal form which he fell. The soul is forced to look inside itself, to inquire whether there is not more peace in this suffering than in the sinning. Once a sick man in his passivity begins to ask, "What is the purpose of my life? Why am I here?" the crisis has already begun. Conversion becomes possible the very moment a man ceases to blame God or life for his troubles and begins to blame himself; by so doing he becomes able to distinguish between his sinful barnacles and the ship of his soul.

A crack has appeared in the armour of his egotism; now the sunlight of God's grace can pour in. But until that happens, catastrophe can teach nothing but despair....

Well that's it. There is something concrete on which I can base my future efforts. In Time magazine last week I ran across an article in the ART section regarding the construction of a Benedictine monastery in Minnesota. It seems many many years will pass before it's completely finished. The abbot was asked in so many words, how he felt about the long time in construction as he probably wouldn't live long enough to see the finished product. He answered, "What's a few generations to the Benedictines."

I thought to myself, "What a grip that man has on this life, he really knows how to live it...he hasn't got a care in this world." I'd like to have his same outlook very much.

That's about the end for now John and I will remember you in my prayers, believe me. I hope things come your way a little easier from now on. So till later then, write when you can....

Sincerely,
Your friend Bill –

The letters from John and his wife Margie gave Johnny the courage to write a letter he had thought about ever since his return from his old neighborhood on Carbon Street. A neighbor, whose son Richard and he had become close friends after the death of his young friend Louis, had always treated him with much affection. He had wondered why someone with her generous personality could resist the call of the Catholic church as he had come to know it. The letter had to be written with great care. He hoped he got it right.

> *Dear Mrs. Dower:*
>
> *First, I want to thank you for your charity, kindness and encouragement. Do you remember the day you drew me aside and told me how pleased you were with my plans to buy a house for Mother and the family? Your eyes reddened a little while you spoke. And it humbled me to think you could be so solicitous for a neighbor. Not too many people are like that. Which leads me to say, at last, what I have wanted to say to you for several years.*
>
> *As you know, we live in a predominantly Catholic town and neighborhood. Yet to me, you have always been the most practical Christian among us. You have common sense, and a living charity which springs to the help of anyone in the neighborhood in a time of crisis. You've always been willing to help where others didn't care enough to be troubled.*
>
> *In the service I've learned a great deal about Protestants and Protestantism, I owe to you, however, my warm regard and love for those not of the Faith.*
>
> *I've learned to take each individual for what he is. In other words, if a person claims the name Catholic, he's got to show me that he is everything the name implies. And it doesn't matter to me whether a man is Lutheran, Episcopalian, Mormon or anything else. If, as an individual, he is living up to the creed he believes is true he is held in great respect by me.*
>
> *That doesn't necessarily mean that every religion is just as good as another. Truth is truth whether the subject be science, mathematics or religion. And for this reason I am sending you a small booklet explaining the teachings of the Catholic Church. You may not agree with all the facts presented; however, believe me when I say the*

booklet presents the teachings of Christianity as we Catholics know them without any distortion or pretense. Especially consider the Questions and Answers on pages 4 and 5.

When you have finished reading the booklet consult Rev. Boyd as to what you should do. (Your minister is Rev. Boyd, isn't he?) For if he is a minister intent on following truth regardless of where it may lead he will give you good advice. In fact, I'll enclose another booklet for him. Then you and he can discuss the matter more fully.

I've never met Rev. Boyd but he must be an excellent man to direct so well his congregation which is held in respect by many of the people in town who are intelligent enough to appreciate it. Give him my best regards. I hope someday to meet him.

Well, I'll be discharged in January of 1955, and possibly earlier, and then I can accomplish what I've set out to do. Buy the house, get an education and go into some field of activity where everyday Christianity is a necessity. Thanks for your time. God love you. Pray for me.

Yours sincerely,

John

P.S.: Perhaps your minister would be interested in reading this letter. It would let him know that at least some Catholics of the town are solicitous for more mutual understanding and greater Christian love.

The spring of the year gave Johnny the feeling of better things to come. All the conveniences he had in Japan, no longer available to him, meant a return to shining his own shoes, making up the bunk and helping in keeping their quarters in presentable shape for the usual weekly inspections.

"Man, I miss those Japanese houseboys. They even saw to it that my uniforms were cleaned and pressed along with all the other things they did," Johnny said to his roommate Andy after sweeping out the room.

"Well, I guess this is the real Air Force you now have to deal with."

"Of course I'm getting out later this year and that makes all the difference in my outlook. Who knows, maybe I'll be free of the service in September. Then on to college, somewhere."

"You haven't said too much about your college plans lately. I thought you were pretty sure about that school in Vermont."

"Andy, I'm still kicking it around. My family may soon move to another house and that will probably mean I'll be parting with some of my savings. The GI Bill should take care of college expenses so it doesn't bother me too much. Still, I don't know."

"By the way, have you heard from your Paulist friend lately?"

"Actually, I had a letter last week. I will probably write to him tomorrow."

The letter Johnny wrote to his friend Joe on the Feast of St. Antoninus revealed that a major change had taken place in his thinking.

May 10, 1954
St. Antoninus
Dear Joe,

You're a friend, the sort of friend I am very grateful to possess. I pray I'll never lose your friendship.

You have captured the spirit for which the Church has always hungered. Thanks to the grace of God and the life I have attempted to live I understand your letter fully. It's good to know there's someone like you in the seminary. I pray there are many more future priests with your spirit.

This past First Friday, Joe, something happened. As you may know, you, my aunt and Fr. Galligan know more of my plans for the priesthood than anyone else. A recent letter from my aunt ended with, "In whatever you decide to do, decide and act with prayer." Your own letter mentioned purity of heart and was almost a cry to help restore all things in Christ.

And on Friday I found what I've been looking and groping for these past few years: Faith. Naked, unadulterated Faith.

Both you and my aunt stressed prayer. And pray I did. Not necessarily with more fervor. Because as I may have told you before, I've always found praying easy. I love to pray. But I did ask Our Lord to show me my heart as it is and what He wanted me to do in this life.

The greatest gift He could have given me He gave that day. Faith. Faith as I have never known it. And perhaps this next statement may seem vague and unconvincing. It seems, however, that He wants me to be a priest in every sense of the word except the actual taking of Holy Orders, the absence of vows and superiors. In other words, a priest without a Roman collar.

It's not going to be easy. I expect no glory, no rewards, and have

262

asked Him to save all consolations for eternity except those He feels necessary for my spiritual well-being.

Faith was the object of my search from the very beginning. In my immaturity I translated it in terms of a religious vocation.

The answer He gave was the most improbable I expected. I was so overjoyed, nevertheless, that I told Louis and Sylvia, who answered the phone in lieu of mother's absence since it was a Mother's Day call late Saturday afternoon — I had found what I had been searching for these past few years. I hope someday they'll understand.

Perhaps eventually I shall marry. I am in no hurry to do so, however, and intend to lead as strict a celibate's life as any priest until then. Is it possible? Yes. Throughout the past four years, with the grace of God, prayer, reception of the Eucharist at least four times a week and Confession usually once a week or whenever necessary I have done a fairly successful job of it in some of the most tumultuous years of a young male. The worst is definitely past.

Yesterday I was given the grace and courage to write a letter I've wanted to write for several years now to a Protestant neighbor of ours. To me she was always the most practical Christian in the neighborhood, although strong-headed at times; I've always wanted to tell her this and also give her some literature which would explain to her the truths of the Faith. I'll let you know what comes of it. (The booklet was, The Truth About Catholics *and, I included one for her minister that they might discuss the booklet more fully.) I've also written to CBS in response to a request by Dale Francis in his column which said CBS was considering the telecasting of Pius X's canonization. He asked for about 50,000 letters. Well, at least I know one has been sent.*

Joe, I'm going to need your help. Please, never consider anything you have to say to me as preaching. I welcome as gold all your suggestions, your ideas and advice.

You are right about St. Paul. Overseas I learned to read the Bible. No matter what doubts exist in my mind, I find that fifteen or thirty minutes of the Scriptures clear a great deal of the problems away. Everything becomes lucid.

Purity of heart is absolutely essential. I understand what you mean completely. Yes, it does take " courage and heroism". "It takes work and sacrifice."

You are also right about Catholics being too defensive. It is wishful thinking to say that we have enough – the fact is we have very, very few – laymen who are willing to live their faith in the marketplace. It's a vocation all its own. Often it is more difficult than the actual taking of vows. Someone has to do it if the Church is to be a well rounded organization.

Pius X said the most essential requirement for the growth of the Church is a nucleus of well trained, well educated, apostolic laymen in every parish. Very few parishes and very few towns can boast of that nucleus. Where are we going to find those men?

Thank God our seminaries in America are filling up with possible vocations. Maryknoll ordained forty. I feel almost nostalgic when I see the pictures of those who have reached their goals. Just recently I told you I would feel very downhearted if I were rejected by the Edmundites. Perhaps Our Lord wanted me to reach that stage before He revealed to me my true role in life. For we must not forget that the religious life is always more commendable than the lay.

Yes, I did read an account of the Holy Father's encyclical on virginity. But we cannot afford to overlook the active lay apostolate. More specifically, the spiritually active lay apostolate. I think if we have that, we'll always have enough priests.

Yesterday in the Des Moines Messenger *I read that Fr. Gillis has been accused by Card. Mooney of misinterpreting the Holy Father's stand on the U.N. Fr. Gillis is accused of a lot of things, isn't he?*

In one of your Commonweals *I read John Calley's "Anathema Sit" which revealed to me the plight of the "liberal Catholic." I fully agree with Fr. Gillis's anathemitizing of individuals who are " timid, confused fellows, given to snobbery and religious indifferentism. Who can only with difficulty be distinguished from the non-Catholic." But can you properly use the term "liberal" to describe them accurately?*

Prof. Jerome Kerwin of the Univ. Of Chicago is supposedly one of these liberals. It's difficult for me to see how he can be this kind of individual if he, acc. to J.C., "has probably brought more people into the Church and then led them to the religious life than any five of his critics (The Brooklyn Tablet & Florida Catholic, etc.) and who has kept hundreds of born Catholics from going astray." There's more to it, of course. And it's all very interesting.

Thanks for sending the reading material. I usually devour every Catholic World *I get hold of. If ever I get a more stable address I'm going to subscribe to a half dozen magazines I've been reading. Write soon.*

John

P.S.: Re the letter to CBS and the canonization of Pius X, the "American Pope", I emphasized his closeness to the Catholics in America because he believed American Catholics have utilized his guidance to the fullest extent. He "saw the danger and the need for intelligent instructed Catholics in the crucial decades to come. He worked on the principal that you can't do much with ignorant Catholics. If they don't know their religion, they'll abandon it. If they do know it, they'll respect and love it."

I quoted this from an article in a recent Information *article.*

Johnny tried his best to overcome the betrayal he felt about his sister's pregnancy and unexpected marriage. A letter from Alma arrived telling him she and her husband Earl would not consider his proposal to combine their resources with the rest of the family and find a home, probably in Reading, which they all could share.

Dear Johnny

Your proposal is definitely inconceivable. Earl has had a hard life; a horrible boyhood in Tennessee (5-14 yrs. old) through the hands of his stepmother; a medical discharge after catching malaria on Guadalcanal; a really messed up first marriage to a wife who had a three-month old baby (not his), who ran around with Earl's good friend. Earl left her when he came home and found them together. The same day she bought a fur coat under his name and he had to pay for it. The house they owned was sold and the proceeds divided. He then lost another home and lost that only through keeping a pack of his relatives.

He has been a heavy drinker (only beer), who bought a lot of drinks for others in the bar. He hasn't drunk at all since we've been in Philadelphia, and somehow, I don't think he will. He's too interested in home-life.

Now after all that, already losing two homes, do you think I

want to put a burden like that on his shoulders? We are renting and
expect to for some time. I still have not told Mom about the baby.
   Love always,
   Alma

SUPREME COURT OUTLAWS SCHOOL SEGREGATION headlined the *Columbia Star.*

On May 17, 1954 Chief Justice Earl Warren read the decision of the unanimous Court stating that the doctrine of "separate but equal" had no place in the field of public education. Johnny found the strong reaction of the southern airmen almost unpatriotic.

"Have you guys seen the latest headlines in the Sumter and Columbia papers?" Johnny asked those around him the squadron lounge.

"What did you expect? We Southerners will never go to the same school as blacks," came the unanimous response. "Of course a nigger-lover from the North would never understand how we feel! And we wouldn't share a room with a black either." The remarks made Johnny understand why many of them had kept their distance from him and Sullivan because of their black roommate.

Johnny thought any further discussion would lead nowhere. It did prepare him to comprehend the remarks of South Carolina's Governor James Byrnes who declared he was "shocked to learn that the court reversed itself" with regard to past rulings on the doctrine of separate but equal. "I urge all people, white and colored, to exercise restraint and order." Senator Eastland of Mississippi stated he "will not abide by nor obey this legislative decision by a political court."

Johnny was enmeshed in his own concerns, trying desperately to know which direction to take regarding his educational ambitions now that his vocation to the priesthood seemed less certain, his need to move the family into a more promising environment and his sister Alma's pregnancy and dubious marriage over shadowed the momentous happenings in the country. He wondered what his decision to forego entrance into the seminary would mean to his friends and family. His faithful friend, Joe, wrote a letter expressing his views on the matter.

June 5, 1954
AMDG
Vigil of Pentecost
Dear John,

I don't suppose there is anything more worth beginning this letter with than mention of your late decision. I can't say that I expected it, John, but then I can't say I was overwhelmed by it either. You have been torn between these two lives for some time now and it was evident that God might lead you either way. I pray that you have made the right one. There is no need for me to remind you that in the past you have made some fairly definite decisions about the priesthood; it is possible of course that this too might not be definitive. Understand now, I say this with no trace of reproach, because I realize, in some way at least, that God's grace leads through many strange and often apparently contradictory ways. I will say though that in your letter you seemed to say it with real finality, and if it does turn out to be so, my fervent prayers go with you that you have the courage to abide by it and live with it.

One thing in particular struck me in your letter. You mentioned that you love to pray, that you always have found prayer easy. This is a great gift, John, and if genuine, far from common. Many truly holy people are not blessed with it. But of course it brings with it accompanying responsibilities. One is its frequent use, the other a sincere appreciation of it, and through it, of yourself. It seems that often when God gives us a gift, He also gives us a corresponding trial. For those who " pray well" this trial is often a difficulty in being humble, a difficulty in seeing others and oneself in true perspective. So pray for humility, John. There is no holiness without it. You mentioned this on your visit here and I know you appreciate the problem and its importance. I can only repeat what I said then, "In seeking humility, begin with God and not with your fellow men." It is a great saint who can look at others clearly less talented than himself and say that they are better and greater than he. The saint can do this because when he looks at reality he sees much more than we. But for us to get humility, the foundation of the spiritual life, we must start with our relationship with God; see our insignificance in comparison with Him; see how far away we are from attaining to Him, that attaining which others far less intelligent and gifted than ourselves have achieved. You want to live a life of Christian holiness in the world that God has made and loved which ignores Him. You have taken upon yourself a tremendous responsibility here; you know the truth about reality, how you should live and how you should die to live more fully. You have no excuse now but your own weakness. And that weakness can damn you or save you, save you by giving you humility, for when you begin to realize the grace God has given you in revealing himself to you in prayer and otherwise, and how you have failed to correspond with those graces, thrown them in His face, then you can truly be humble, for then you have seen the truth, which when you come down to it is all humility is: seeing the truth.

And pray for zeal, John, zeal to give men the life that they seek in all their pleasures and plans, in all their search for security. God has given you this life; more than that He has given you some appreciation of it. Give it to others, John, this life that is Christ. They want it, in the very depths of their being they want it and they don't know it. They see it in the Catholics and Catholic Churches all around them. And they reject it. Why? Only because what they see in Catholicism is not the life but the death, not the truth but human additions and trappings which we in our stupidity and weakness have tacked on and inadvertently used to hide the light and the life that is meant for all and for which all are meant, Americans included (or should I say especially; but no, this would necessitate too much of my opinionizing and I do too much of that, for you see, I too seek humility). But I have said too much. I want to thank you, John, for being so faithful in writing. I wish I could promise even a continuation of my now erratic corresponding, but I fear that things may be a bit tighter from now on. But we'll face that when we come to it. Continue to write and be assured I will do the best I can to answer.

That was good news about your being at the university next fall. I sincerely hope you will be able to follow through on it. But if not ... Well, we are old enough now as God's children to know this is His world, not ours. I shall be in Shenandoah for three nights and two full days over this coming weekend, June 11 to June 14. It is unfortunate I couldn't have let you know this earlier, or perhaps you might have been able to arrange a trip home at the same time. But it was impossible with exams and all. By the way, John, when you write next please tell me the story on Alma. I gathered from one of your recent letters that she is married. Is everything all right with the marriage? Please tell me, if you think it advisable.

Anne wrote me last week and said she had just received a letter from you. It seems hard to believe that it is four years since we graduated from high school. I almost choke at saying it, but with God's most provident blessings, the same amount of time, four years from now, will find me receiving the sub-deaconate with the deaconate to follow that fall – in 1958. Pray for me, John, that He does lead me unto His altar, and that He leads me from it to the people who will need me because they need their God, and He will have chosen to come to them through me. Please pray, John.

No more friend. Our summer address is: St. Mary's of the Lake
Paulist Fathers
Lake George, N.Y.
Yours in Our Lord,
Joe
P.S. Pass these prayer leaflets along if you have some already.

Johnny could not believe how wise and perceptive his friend had become. He would continue to pray, and hope to God, that he would remain faithful to his conscience and the grace of the Holy Spirit. As for Joe's mention of Anne, since he believed he would not pursue the priesthood, some connection with the girls he knew back home seemed like a good idea. He had no idea what response his letter to her might bring. The only other girl he had written to, a Marie Tarminas, who had invited him to the prom in high school and had lived along his paper route, already informed him a year ago that she had a marriage proposal which she would accept.

The Air Force had not come through with any directives about early releases, which left Johnny making tentative decisions, with no certainty how the year would progress. Father Galligan's letter gave him hope that at least St. Michael's College would enroll him if he got an early discharge.

June 14, 1954
Dear John:
Before taking off again for a short vacation trip, a few lines in your direction are in order. I received your letter a couple of weeks ago and am glad to hear that all goes well.
I really don't know what the setup is at Catholic University in

regard to gaining admittance for the second semester. My own opinion is that you might be a lot better off at a smaller college., particularly on the undergraduate level. Everyone in my family, except myself, is a graduate of C. U. And that is probably where my opinion has come from. This is where I put a plug in for St. Michael's.

Under separate cover I am sending you a new St. Michael's College catalog. Read it over carefully and I'm sure that you will find in there a challenging program for your college work. Things like the Catholic Evidence Guild I don't believe should motivate your choice of college for the simple reason that participation in such activity is understandably very little if any on the undergraduate level. You see, John, there is always the danger of dreaming great dreams without facing up to the reality that the years of preparation are years of steady, difficult and inconspicuous study. Once we gain a foundation in that way, then we are in a position to do the things we dream about.

This isn't meant to be a speech so I will sign off here for the present, wishing you well at Shaw now that summer is here. Drop us a line when you can and know that your letters are always welcome. God bless you and best wishes,

Sincerely in St. Edmund,
Father Eymard P. Galligan, S. S.E.

Anne wrote a brief note declaring she would surely always be a friend and stated that "this is a difficult time of life for us – trying to find our roots and decide in which way we'll best serve God." His Aunt Catherine wrote to say she had missed not visiting him at Shaw, when coming back from a trip to Florida where her brother, Ziggie, and Martha had bought a home at Riviera Beach. All of her brothers and sisters had moved from the small enclave they had shared in Pennsylvania. The summers he had spent there always remained in his memory. She also mentioned her excitement crossing the new 4-miles-long Chesapeake Bay Bridge. He promised himself he would make certain to cross the bridge someday as well.

Two letters arrived the last week of June. His sister Alma announced that her baby boy, born five weeks prematurely, would not be released from the hospital until he reached a minimum of 5-1/2 pounds. She expected to have him baptized the middle of July and invited Johnny to be his godfather if a furlough could be arranged. The baby, named Gregory Earl, had quickly become an important part of her life. She especially liked his cute little nose which she said looked just like hers. He wished he could be happy about his first nephew. Perhaps, someday, he would be.

The Reverend Mother responded to his news about this faith he had finally discovered which no longer included a call to the priesthood.

> *D.M.et O.*
>
> *Dearest Johnny,*
>
> *Your letter came in this morning. Whatever you may be or whatever you may do – is after all your own responsibility. You are of age; you have the ability to reason and the will to choose; you have faith enough to be convinced that the Almighty governs all and that we, of ourselves, can do nothing – hence, that we must seek light in prayer. Your life will be lived by yourself; you will bear fruit of your acts. I remember you in my prayers. May God and Mary do the rest!*
>
> *With joy, I count the days which separate me from July 2nd. How wise is our holy Mother Church and how considerate to give no laws which terminate what is, at times, so difficult! If these laws didn't exist, one would fear to rejoice, lest one should sin by choosing escapism in preference to God's Holy Will.*
>
> *I do know that I'll not have a third term and I did already inform the delegates that I do not wish to be a member of the Gen. Council. My only reason for this choice is to give perfect freedom to my successor. A living organism undergoes changes; the Mother General must consider these. If a need occurs to change some of my decisions, she could suffer interiorly – fearing to offend me. I had perfect freedom, so I want my successor to have the same.*
>
> *In view of this, I really haven't the slightest idea where I'll be two weeks from today. And, I'm not anxious to know. Whatever the superiors choose for me will be God's Holy Will – and, this is all that I want and seek.*
>
> *I saw Louis on his arrival; since then, I haven't met him. I presume he is doing well on the orphanage grounds.*
>
> *May God bless and love you always! May Mary guide you.*
>
> *Prayerfully yours,*
>
> *M.M.E.*

PART THREE

"he who walks in the dark
does not know where he is going."

JOHN 12:35

CHAPTER ONE

On July 2, 1954 the delegates to the General Chapter elected Mother Mary Chrysostoma to succeed Reverend Mother Edmunda. Despite her request not to have a seat in the General Council, Mother Edmunda became the First Councillor by vote of the delegates, reluctant to have her totally depart from leadership of the Bernardines. They had come to love and respect her depth of spirituality and hard work.

"Mother Edmunda, sorry we could not honor your request. Where else could you better serve the order? We need you," was the common refrain from the sisters.

"Now that I am simply a Mother, perhaps you can treat me as somewhat of a grandmother. I really need to slow down." Members of the general council, and provincial superiors, usually received the acclaim of the other sisters with the title of "Mother".

Mother Edmunda settled happily into the Sacred Heart motherhouse where she could pray, free from the travels and responsibilities of a superior general. After two days of relative tranquility, her successor approached her and said, "How would you like to spend some time in Brazil? You have given yourself so much to the Brazilian Province I believe you would enjoy seeing the fruits of your labor."

"What a wonderful idea! Thank you for your kind consideration. Perhaps I can help the Brazilian sisters with their English proficiency, if nothing else."

"Seven of the sisters will be returning to Brazil with you. Mother Herculane, the new provincial, has asked me to have you accompany them for she wants you to see all the good that has come from your many efforts in promoting the good of the province."

Mother Edmunda spent the 4th of July with Cassie and her sister Mary who had been looking for a home in Reading.

"Mary, I'm so glad you're leaving Shenandoah at last. There really is nothing left of the town, for you or the family. Have you found a home that you like?"

"Yes, we found a house only four blocks away from Cassie and just a block away from Victoria. You know, Johnny always called her Sainksa. And one of the Mihalski girls from the Carbon Street neighborhood lives close by as well. Her husband says he could help with any moving we would need. You probably know that two of her sisters are now with the Bernardines."

"Oh yes, they joined us immediately after their stay at the orphanage. I'm so glad you told us about the family's needs after their mother died. The father must have been totally irresponsible."

"Compared to him, my husband John looks almost good."

"How much are they asking for the house?"

"$5,500 plus some closing costs. I've asked Johnny to send me at least $500 as soon as possible. He said he would. You know he always wanted us to do this and I really don't want to rent another house. We'll get the rest of the money somehow; Cassie said she might help."

"All I can say, Mary, this is certainly good news. I hope everything goes well. When I return from Brazil I'll look forward to seeing it." She hadn't seen her sister look so full of expectation for a better life in many years despite the soul-wrenching marriage of Alma outside the Church.

"Have you seen the baby as yet?"

"We will be going down next week. I still can't believe this has happened. I often wondered if Alma's stiff hip would make any pregnancy difficult for her. She said the baby's face was black and blue. The doctor had a hard time with the delivery. But what can we do about it? Things happen."

"Mary, all we can do is pray. People have to live their own lives. Alma suffered so much in childhood I had hoped she could enjoy her adult years."

After a full dinner and Cassie's apple pie, Mother Edmunda and Sister Imelda, her companion, rode back to the convent with a friendly neighbor.

Mother Edmunda made a private retreat before she and the seven returning sisters left their beloved Sacred Heart Convent for New York to board their freighter for the voyage to Brazil. A freighter, less expensive than a luxury liner, suited the Franciscan sisters because of greater privacy and fewer worldly distractions.

Relatives, friends, and a few Bernardines waved a happy, as well as somber, goodbye to the sisters returning to Brazil. As much as the departing sisters knew they would miss the people they loved, they also knew how committed they had become to the people they served in southern Brazil. Soon after the people on shore became too distant for their eyes they rushed to the other side of the ship to bid farewell to the Statue of Liberty and once again viewed the skyscraper outline of New York City.

"I suggest we get into our staterooms and organize our belongings for the rest of the trip," said Mother Edmunda in her gentle, unassuming voice. A half hour later they were chimed into a neat dining room below and ate heartily despite the luncheon they had eaten earlier in the station.

With their bodily needs satisfied, they gathered on the deck and formed their first choir. Vespers and Compline were recited in common and the Ave Maris Stella sung with unexpected devotion.

"Mother we are all so happy that you are here with us. I pray you stay with us in Brazil for a very long time," commented one of the sisters.

"Whatever our Lord wills," answered Mother Edmunda. "Perhaps we can organize our horarium so that our days are well spent on the ship." Within a short time the following schedule for the coming days was set up.

Rising .... 6.45 A.M. - 7:00 A.M.

Prayers, meditation hours and Ave Maris Stella on deck 7:25

Breakfast.. 8:30

Study ... work ... followed by lunch .... 12:30 P.M.

Vespers, Compline, Prayers for Church in silence 1:10

Study, work, rest, followed by rosary, in common, Matins, Lauds and Angelus and Litany 5:00

Dinner... 6:00
after which, the Ave Maris Stella is sung again ... and Recreation

Evening Prayers in Stateroom No. 2............. ....9:00

"If only we had a priest to share the journey, we could have Mass every day." They all agreed.

The next day, after dinner, they invited the Captain, his nephew, two female passengers and a couple of mates who served them, to join them during recreation. Each day someone joined them for games of scrabble or canasta, usually on deck. Singing often took place, for the sisters were in a joyful mood throughout the trip. A true Franciscan spirit of simplicity and childlike play brought everyone close together. A teacher, although a Methodist, developed a warmth which made her feel as one of the sisters.

Two days later the ship docked in Savannah, Georgia.

"Thank heavens for the breeze. This hot July sun makes the deck feel like a toaster," said Sister Anne.

By noon, with little time wasted, the loading of a great deal of lime, along with other items, took place. The derricks worked in precise, methodical fashion, almost a pleasure to watch. At midnight, more loading took place at another dock, featuring an endless list of John Deere tractors for Santos. The storerooms, truly a marvel to observe, were carefully loaded at the same time. The Mormac Star carried a weight of 100,000 tons which needed to be loaded in a precise manner to assure the proper balance within the ship.

"This is quite a boat," said Mother Edmunda to one of the crew as she observed all that was happening.

"This is *not* a boat. This is a ship. Why do you call it a boat?"

"Well, what is the difference between the two?"

"A ship can carry a boat, but a boat cannot carry a ship. For example, we have two life boats which hold 60 persons each, and they are carried on the ship," he patiently explained.

"Thank you. I will tell the other sisters not to offend your shipmates about traveling on a boat," she laughed.

The first fire drill took place at 3:00 P.M. on the fourth day soon after leaving Savannah. The captain, a congenial, but very strict person where duty is concerned, insisted that all the passengers, including the sisters, had to report to their stations in life preservers. On other trips the sisters could simply carry them along at their sides. The drill was repeated when many of the crew did not answer when their names were called at their specific stations.

"Sisters, the captain informed me at dinner yesterday that the Brazilian government's new regulations regarding food products means we will have to eat all the fruit, cookies, cheese and jam we have brought along. These are no longer permitted at the port of entry."

"Mother, we'd better have them for dinner."

A buffet dinner, with a delicious, large fruit salad prepared by the sisters, and all those cheeses and cookies, made for an unconventional meal. A hearty laughter which accompanied every bite was the dessert.

The ship slowed down one day and kept maneuvering around the island of Curacao. The sisters questioned the reason for the delay. "We cannot dock for refueling since there are other ships at the pipelines. The delay should not be very long," said one of the crew. The delay could not have been more advantageous for the next day was Sunday.

"Sisters, I have arranged taxi service for you at 5:30 tomorrow morning. Enjoy your day in Curacao," the good captain informed them.

At 5:20 they left the ship and, to their great joy, found themselves at the cathedral dedicated to St. Ann, the mother of the Blessed Virgin. The captain had thought of everything. They heard three Masses and, at each, heard much about the Feast of St. Ann which was the very next day. Dominican Fathers serve the Cathedral. One of the priests noticed the sisters, introduced them to the Dominican priest who spoke reasonably good English. He offered to tell them something of the history of the island.

"Father, we know very little about Curacao. The one thing we had heard is that many of Napoleon Bonaparte's Polish veterans came to the island when his armies were disbanded."

"That may be true, sister. There is a Polish church which primarily serves the Polish Catholics here."

"The first thing I'd like you to know is that the island is of volcanic origin, a perfect desert. All the food and crude oil is brought in from South America or the U.S.A. Their furniture, electric appliances and clothes generally come from the U. S.A. And Curacao, a Dutch possession which is 90% Catholic, was discovered early, almost at the same time as El Salvador. Traces of the Spaniards are very strong in the language spoken by many of the people. Curacao became a Portuguese colony and then French, prior to the Dutch takeover. That's why the Portuguese name remains."

"The Catholics here are very faithful to their religious beliefs. The churches are filled every Sunday; thirty Catholic schools operate compared to three public schools; the elementary and high school courses are completed in 13 years. There is a university. Women do not work outside the home because the only industry available is oil refining which pays the workers a fair wage."

"Are there any Communist influences?" asked Mother Edmunda.

"There really is no politics on the island. Queen Juliana visited a few years ago; the residents are all happy with the way they are treated by the Dutch. The Communists would have no impact on them. The island does have its own Senate. The governor is always a Catholic appointed by the Queen for four years."

Always interested in educational data, one of the sisters asked about the length of the school year.

"The children are on vacation from school during the 31 days of August. They really are well educated. By the way, Dutch Franciscans teach at the cathedral's school."

"Thank you, Father, for all your information. We finally know something about Curacao. Please say a prayer for a safe trip to Brazil."

"I will. God bless you all on the rest of your journey and may St. Ann, the patroness of our island, look after you as well."

The next day the sisters celebrated the Feast Day of St. Ann, the patron saint of two of the nuns, with another buffet dinner of the foods they had to eat before reaching Brazil. A very delicious cake, baked by the chef as a token of thanks for the three cases of Coca Cola given to the crew by the sisters who had received them in Savannah from a very good Catholic who had arranged an auto trip around the city. He had also introduced them to some Franciscan sisters who took care of three parishes for Negroes. This introduction to Mr. Chandler by one of the crew had made the sisters' visit to Savannah that much more enjoyable. The cake, served on a music-box dish which chimed away the well known "Happy Feast Day to You," added to the festivities.

"Sisters, how would you like to tour the bridge today?" asked the captain a few days later.

"Captain, after two weeks on the ship that would be a welcome diversion," they all agreed.

His first mate, Mr. Johnson, acted as the guide.

"Earlier today, at exactly 4:36 A.M., we passed the Equator. We know this from some technical evaluations that are made using various maps and other highly technical operations which at times I have difficulty understanding myself."

He went on to explain that the depth of the ocean is sounded by electrons. " How does this differ from the plumbing approach used for so many years?" asked one of the sisters.

"They are surprisingly very accurate. The depths of oceans, bays, etc. are all marked on different maps. So too are the currents and winds that the captain may know just what to expect at the various points and how to counteract or avoid whatever may slow the speed of the ship or endanger it in any way. Some of the currents flow along the surface while others are subsurface and these rock the ships to a fine cradle 'rock-a-by'. One of the most vicious current spots is just at the Panama Canal. If the isthmus did not exist and the current could continue unmolested, its fury would be spent."

"How is the ship steered, given all those possible hindrances?" asked another sister.

"Excellent question. The answer is the gyroscopes or the gyro as we call it. The gyro steers the ship."

"Sisters, do you see the lighthouse? That must be Recife. This is the closest we have been to Brazil," said one of the crewmen to the sisters as they prepared to eat lunch. "The city is the easternmost port of the country. A lot of trade goes on at the site."

"Finally, Brazil, after two weeks at sea." The sisters wondered how much longer before they reached Porto Alegre. They knew a stop at Sao Paulo's port at Santos was necessary, for this cargo ship was too large for the docking facilities at Porto Alegre.

The captain developed a warm friendship with the sisters. During one of their dinners he told them about the Moore McCormick Lines.

"The two founders started from scratch; collected scrap iron initially; bought their first small cargo ship around 1910 in which they carried cargo on the Great Lakes, with their families doing much of the work as stewardesses, cooks, etc. By 1950 the company, headed by Mr. Moore's son, had some 40 cargo ships, a tanker and two passenger ships, the SS Argentine and SS Brazil. They gave a third ship, the SS Uruguay, to the government for various needs during the war. Mr. Moore died suddenly this past year while walking the street near his house; Mr. McCormick is still alive."

The sisters found the story compelling and asked him to go on.

"From everything I know about them they were active all their lives and both remained simple in spite of the wealth they had accumulated. To the very end, they shared one desk; never had private offices, and acted as two young boys when they were together. One an expert in personnel matters, the other a politician and diplomat who knew how to sway high officials of business and government. Each one acknowledge the other's expertise. Jealousy, underhandedness and the like never marred their cooperative effort."

"Since the company has grown so large, what kind of schooling is required of the officers?" asked one of the sisters.

Very simply and humbly, Captain Thomson informed them that in his days the men first became sailors, started from the very bottom and with application and private study made their way to the top the hard way. Today, thanks to the Chrysler family, a merchant marine school now trains officers at a school on Long Island. Prior to that they studied in Key West under the Navy's supervision. "My nephew Garry, whom you met, is a student at the school. As for myself, the Mormac York is my home. I have a sister, Garry's mother."

"Our final Sunday recreation will take place this week. Please join us if you can. And thank you for the stories about the company."

The captain, dressed more casually than usual, with a St. Christopher medal around his neck, arrived on the deck to join in their recreation time.

"I see you're wearing a St. Christopher medal. Is there a story about that too?" asked Mother Edmunda.

'Well, I'm not a Catholic, but a French girl gave it to me during the first World War. I think it helped, and I've worn it ever since."

To the sisters, the captain appeared lonely at times and could detect a tear welling up in his eyes, especially when he spoke of home, a real home he could call his own. When the accordion played and the singing began, the captain confessed he had not sung in a long, long time. His rich, resonant voice joined theirs. His nephew Garry noted that "life at sea was a good-paying job, but very, very lonely."

Mother Edmunda hoped that if the sisters did anything that would resound for God's glory on their trip it was the joy they shared with others, the Franciscan liberty of God's children. She recalled how one of the waiters said to the other: "Their life must be lonely." The other responded: "They don't look as if it were." The two have since repeated that they would miss the sisters very much because they rarely have had so much radiant and buoyant joy onboard.

The Methodist teacher kept asking whether sisters everywhere love themselves as they do; whether they are always so fond of each other's company; whether they are as jubilant, etc.

"The happiness comes from a willingness to share our experiences and to show that a dignified and radiant joy of God's children, with regularity in spiritual exercises, has a powerful influence upon those who come into contact with them," explained Sister Edmunda.

The teacher, who always stayed in their presence, even when they prayed in common, asked one of the sisters, "How can you all be so calm, composed and dignified when you sing, especially the Ave Maris Stella? I keep wiggling continuously."

"What she did not know is that within us is a treasure which motivates all ... and, yet, is so precious that nothing frivolous can mar its sacredness. It is great to be a nun, a true nun ... we are set apart, if we can respect ourselves and respect the treasure placed in our hearts," reflected Mother Edmunda when she heard of the teacher's remark.

The sisters stood on the deck, at all hours, as the ship passed Rio. Some thought they saw the Corcovado Christ which stands majestically above the city. The sky, decked with myriads of stars played "hide-and-seek" for there were so many falling or flying stars. The *Cruzeiro do Sul*, the Southern Cross, could be seen in all its beauty. The four large stars outlining the cross looked incredibly magnificent.

Santos, where the cargo ship docked for partial unloading, finally placed the sisters back in Brazil. A radiogram to Rio, hopefully, would reserve 8 seats on a Pan American flight from Sao Paulo to Porto Alegre. The radio operator received no reply to the request. "This is how they treat Americans; they ignore us whenever they can."

The sisters traveled by bus to Sao Paulo after an unexpected delay at Santos. The dock workers, on strike for three days, kept some 30 ships standing idly in the port. Although 10th in line, Captain Thomson received permission to temporarily enter the harbor to allow the sisters and the other three passengers with their baggage, to land at last in Brazil.

"Sisters, there is no way Pan Am will allow you to take all of your baggage along on the flight to Porto Alegre. Please leave as much as you wish in one of the staterooms and I will transfer it, first chance, to one of our ships going to Porto Alegre."

"Thank you so much," said all of the sisters to the captain. Some gave him a warm Brazilian embrace for all he had done for them on their long return trip to the country which had become a second home.

"I think we should stay at one of the better hotels since we do not have any convents in Sao Paolo."

"Let me check with the tourist official, Mother." Before long they taxied to the Hotel Pao de Aucar.

In the morning the sisters very happily attended two Masses and received *Bozia* at the cathedral, especially since this was the First Friday of August. Without Mass and the Holy Eucharist for so many days, they felt at home again in the world.

They returned to their hotel, really the finest and newest Mother Edmunda had ever experienced. She delighted in its cleanliness compared to the filthy hotels often found in both Brazil and the United States. Although expensive, she decided this would be her special treat to the sisters, despite the knowledge that St. Francis often went to beggars and their pitiable conditions and spent time with them.

"Mother, we are going to do some sightseeing."

"That's fine, enjoy yourselves. Sister Prudentian and I will stay here to make some phone calls and patiently wait for one from Panair. And please don't exchange any of your dollars on the black market. This morning we were offered 64 cruzeiros for a dollar. The poor Brazilians surely do not have a very strong currency."

After several calls to the provincial house and Panair, Mother Edmunda spoke to Sister Prudentian about their voyage and the remarkable captain who had befriended them.

"I just cannot understand how one can make sea-life a career. Imagine those men out there in the open sea waiting for days and days! Captain Thomson seemed tired of it and, with a glistening eye, kept on repeating how lonely he is beginning to feel on the sea. For me the parting on the boat was hard. The officers, and crew, and passengers did knit themselves to us. The officers, including the captain waved 'good-byes' as long as the launch was in sight. The poor captain waived both of his arms; he certainly left his dignity in his suite of rooms. At his last dinner with us he said: 'The uninitiated person imagines that your life is so drab, and yet, how far from the truth this is!'"

"Mother, what you have said must have run through most of our minds as well. At least I hope so! By the way, that stay at the *alfandega*, might have been much longer if the strike had not been settled on Thursday morning."

"Yes, the people at the Customs House had several days work to do because of the strike. I am glad we did not have to stay at Santos overnight."

"We're back, thank heavens. Sister Gaudencia hurt her ankle during our city tour."

"I'll take care of it immediately," said Sister Charles. She bathed, massaged and bandaged it which made the pain easier to bear for her sister in Christ.

Mother Herculane, the superior of the Brazilian province, disappointed that plane reservations had not been obtained, decided to go directly to the Panair office to accelerate the process. Returning to Brazil after attending the General Council with only a year in the new office to which she had been hastily appointed by the then Reverend Mother Edmunda, she had the exuberant personality to charm the most officious ticket agent, even in Brazil. After three hours she returned to the hotel.

"Panair could not accommodate us. They did, however, make four reservations on Varig, the Brazilian airline, for tomorrow morning; the others will follow on a later flight." The whole disconcerting experience, finally resolved, brought songs again to the sisters' lips. They would all be in Porto Alegre for the weekend.

The small convent at Porto Alegre housed only four sisters. Although the new provincial, Mother Herculane, resided there, the majority of the sisters in Rio Grande do Sul lived in Camaqua where the initial Brazilian Provincial house had been since 1943.

"Sorry to arrive here unannounced, sisters. We simply could not reach you by telephone from Sao Paulo or the airport," said Mother Herculane.

"At least you have brought some dry weather with you. The rainy season has been in full swing with 42 consecutive days of rain. The telephone lines were disrupted and some flooding has occurred in parts of the city."

"What a pleasure to have you with us, Mother! I hope you stay a very long time," said one of the sisters to Mother Edmunda.

"Whatever God wills. Our dear Reverend Mother told me to stay in Brazil as long as I wish."

"How would you all like some of our great Brazilian coffee?" The returning nuns happily accepted the offer.

A letter from one of Mother Edmunda's most faithful corespondents, Celia, arrived within a week. Celia and two of her sisters had remained unmarried, aided a brother financially during his seminary years and considered Mother Edmunda a special cousin, blessed by extraordinary grace in her years as a nun. They did everything possible to support the endeavors of the Bernardines, especially during Mother Edmunda's years in office. She replied with her usual warmth which endeared her to Celia and the family.

Deus Meus et Omnia
My dearest Celia,
Let us always bless and love the Holy Will of God! Today, God brought my very dear ones to me, via mail. Your letter came in at noon and Sister Imelda, who always sends a card or letter to greet me wherever I go, had sent a note which arrived last week and only today was handed to me. Thank you, dearest Celia, for your generosity. I certainly do appreciate it and you will be happy to

know I am purchasing a pair of gold vases for the chapel at this new Provincial House, your gift for the altar. I told Sister to purchase two pairs that I could present to Mother Herculane on her Feast day together with a censer and a censer stand – now, one pair will be from me and one from you. God love you for all you do for me and for us. I am happy you enjoyed your trip to Lourdes. We spent three days there. The first day was bliss; there were few people at the grotto and I could pray in peace. Then came the Armada from Spain. We were deluged and I lost all interior joy. Of all the shrines at Fatima I liked best the "4 X 4" chapel of apparition – and when I say 4 X 4, I mean it. Two persons were almost one too many for it. When I prayed there nobody saw me, but Mary – and such prayers give me great happiness. Oceans of heads are perfectly all right and I was swept off my feet with them at St. Peter's, but they do not answer the needs of my soul.

Our trip was exceptionally good ... However the Villa and especially the garden here in Porto Alegre are just beautiful. The steps leading to the convent are somewhat steep, but they do add much to its imposing beauty. The entrance is from a street which runs along a wide river – it reminds me of our Mary Immaculate Hospital at Newport News. Large ships come up this river to the docks of Porto Alegre – among these the smaller ships of the Moore McCormack Lines. Beyond the convent is a rather dense forest, which belongs to the sisters. This is a blessing since wood is the only fuel used at present. Atop the wooded section is a plateau and this the sisters are trying to purchase for their ginasio and college. When you think of us, please pray that we may obtain it. The price is quite high and we still have a debt on the Vila, which became ours, thanks to the generosity of the American sisters and their good friends. From this elevated spot, one can see the large hospital in the city (14 stories) which is supervised by our sisters, another one (smaller) in a nearby town and the school that we have just below the hill. All the sisters need to do is hang out their flags to give messages.

God has been so good, so good to the Bernardines! Everyone just admires what the sisters have accomplished here in the past 16 years. The Rev. Chaplain said that he doubts there is another group of religious that can boast of so many of God's mercies. I tremble when I think of all that we received within the last 15 years ... tremble at the thought that we are not grateful enough, that we do not love the good God enough.

Tomorrow, we plan to visit Camaqua. The postulants, novices, juvenists with a long list of professed sisters live there, where we have an elementary school, a ginasio and a normal school with a rather large boarding school. Then, we shall drop in to see the other houses before I begin to work seriously. I am trying to study my Portuguese anew. I began on the ship and I do hope to gain much once I am settled. Yesterday and today, I spent quietly ... the first days it was sisters and sisters then came the visits to the city, to the officials, etc.

With love to all and with renewed assurances of my daily mementos at Mass and in my prayers and good works.

Devotedly in the Two Hearts,
Sr. M. Edmunda

At every house they visited the sisters thanked Mother Edmunda for all she had done for the Brazilian province.

"Mother, without you we could never have done so much for the people of southern Brazil. The Polish people are especially grateful that the Bernardines came to help keep their faith in the Church alive. The people of Dom Feliciano cannot say enough about us." All of the accolades made her realize how right Mother Angela had been some 18 years before when she had denied her permission to leave for Brazil as a missionary. Her constant zeal while the Reverend Mother energized everything in their Brazilian endeavors.

The first few months in Brazil limited Mother Edmunda's contact with her family. She wondered exactly what her nephew Johnny would decide to do about his college ambitions. Mary's family had moved to Reading in late July which gave much promise for their future economic well-being. She prayed that all would progress smoothly.

CHAPTER TWO

"Johnny, five of us will be going down to the Jacksonville Air Traffic Control center for some orientation about its operations. The captain has arranged everything, including an overnight stay," said his roommate Andrew Sullivan, or Sully – a nickname used by his friends. "He will be going down with us."

"That sounds like a good idea. I've always wondered how they manage to stay on top of all the IFR traffic in their area. I'll also get my first look at northern Florida near the Atlantic."

"The automobile trip will probably take about four to five hours. We will leave at 0800 hours right after breakfast. Everybody have that? See you tomorrow," stated the communications officer.

The Air Traffic Control Center tracked every plane in flight within its area of jurisdiction. The constant flow of information kept the controllers continuously moving slips in metal containers, with specific information, around the open file-boards in front of them.

"How can you be certain that every plane is accounted for?" asked Johnny.

"That's why we have radar screens. Every container represents an individual aircraft we can identify on the screen," answered the controller.

After a thorough orientation, the remainder of the day passed by without incident. The unexpected happened when the captain explained they would have to share two rooms at the motel. He and another airman would have one of the rooms; the rest would have to double up in the two beds in the other room.

A tolerably good dinner and several drinks had Johnny, and the others, tired enough to simply want a place to sleep. He undressed and lay down in one of the beds with no concern as to who might join him; within minutes he fell asleep. At some point during the night he felt an arm around his waist, and a hand apparently reaching for some private territory. He always slept on his side, which allowed him to make a quick motion of refusal and protected both of their integrities. Johnny rolled onto his stomach. The hand quickly withdrew. He then realized the serious occasion of sin he had overcome. Neither one of them mentioned the episode the following day. The closeness of his discharge date kept him from pursuing any assault charges. He remembered the "queer-bait" remark in the early months of his enlistment and let it go at that. The possibility that the other airman might be queer crossed his mind.

A week later notice arrived that the AACS detachment would come under the Wing Commander at Shaw. "Perhaps this will help me get that early release," said Johnny to his communications officer.

"I'll look into it right away, Johnny, and let you know."

The adrenalin began to flow within him. At the next Mass he attended, Johnny asked the Lord of the Eucharist if he was truly meant to be a priest. Suddenly the answer came: *"You are not to become a priest."*

Johnny could not believe the clear conviction of this thought which flooded his mind. He had heard that prayers were often answered, but not with such clarity and the certainty that this came from his Lord. The complete relief he felt when he heard those words filled him with a peace he had not known in a very long time. He felt as if a great weight had been lifted from his shoulders. This answer meant so much because he needed to know which direction he would take when he enrolled into a college.

Things developed very quickly. The captain informed him a discharge would be given as soon as he produced a letter of acceptance from a college.

"Sully, I'm getting that discharge after all. I am sure St. Michael's will send me their acceptance as quickly as possible."

"John, congratulations! Get that degree you have wanted all these years." Sully had become a really good friend. John called Father Galligan immediately.

"Father Galligan, I'm getting out September 10th," he nearly shouted when the vocation director came on the telephone. "Can you send me that application to St. Michael's right away?"

"John, I'm still not certain what direction you want to take with your courses. You could enter as a student seminarian. That will give you a partial scholarship. And you might actually decide to continue. I'll have the registrar's office handle the paperwork."

"Father, I really am not sure about my religious vocation. Perhaps I can give it a try." Johnny disliked taking advantage of the scholarship offered. Still, he needed all the help he could get.

"John, you really should be here by the 13th. Can you do that?"

"I think so, if I get the paperwork done in time. Thanks for all you've done for me these past few years."

Everything proceeded as he had hoped. His family could not believe he would finally come home at last. When he arrived at their new home the shock that he would leave in two days for Vermont stunned all of them.

"Why do you have to go so far away again?" asked his mother.

"Well, Mom, that's the only way I could get an early discharge. St. Michael's has accepted me into the college. It's a good liberal arts school. And it's fairly inexpensive. I will also be a seminarian for the Society of St. Edmund."

"How did you get involved with them anyway? Sister Edmunda had a lot to do with it, didn't she?"

"Mom, she met this priest, Father Galligan, at a conference at Notre Dame. She believed the order had much to offer. That's how it all started."

"Sometimes I wish she wouldn't put all these ideas into your head. When will you be back to see us ?"

"At Christmas. I won't be able to afford a trip on Thanksgiving. Don't worry about anything. It will all work out."

Johnny's brother, Lou, had begun football practice for his final year in high school. His mother had hoped he would drop the sport. She could not dissuade him.

"I tried to stay at S.C.H.S. for my senior year. I really hated to leave after three years in the school, especially since I liked the coach and was sure of playing halfback."

"Lou, you'll be better off here. It's a much bigger school. Knowing you, you will probably play more than you think," Johnny replied. He knew the move had disrupted his young brother's life. His younger sister, a sophomore, would have three years in the same Catholic High School. The adjustment for her would be somewhat easier.

"Johnny, I am helping Cassie's nephew with some painting and other repairs. There is also a small shop close by; just around the corner from the house. I have applied for a job. They said they would call when something opened up," said his dad, who had begun looking much thinner than John had remembered.

"That's great Dad. You will like it here more than you realize right now. I really hate to leave you all so quickly again but you know I've always wanted to get away and go to college."

A train ride to Burlington, Vermont brought Johnny to St. Michael's college by late Monday. He took a taxi to Winooski Park, called Father Galligan's number from the Administration Building and met him a short time later.

"John, after all this time, we finally get to meet!"

Johnny looked at the personable, friendly priest who had stayed in touch for so many months not knowing the final outcome of his efforts. "Father, I can't believe I'm actually here. The Air Force kept holding off on the early discharge for so long I wondered if I really could be in college this fall."

"Well, thank God you're here. Let me take you over to St. Edmund's Hall, where the first-year seminarians live. It's right across the road from the main campus."

In a few minutes they entered a building, which must have been a house at one time, where they met the priest in charge of the residence.

"Father, here's the young airman I've been telling you about. John, this is Father Agnello. He will direct you from here to the rest of the campus tomorrow starting with the Registrar's Office."

"John, good to meet you. The house is pretty small. You will be sharing a room with another seminarian. Would you like anything to drink?"

"Yes, whatever you have will be fine."

"How about you, Father?"

"No thank you. I will be going away tomorrow; have some preparations to make. I will leave you with John. Take good care of him. See you in about a week, John," smiled the priest he believed responsible for his good luck in getting out of the service early.

"Looks like all I have is some Coke."

"That's something I've drunk a lot of in the Air Force. It will be perfect."

"John, let's get you to your room. Your roommate's name is Dick Peladeau. He's just out of high school."

Dick answered the knock on the door, somewhat shyly. The seminary and college experience, no doubt, had put him a little on edge.

"Dick, here's your roommate, John. He has just been discharged from the Air Force. He may help you adjust to college life."

"Hi, John," Dick quickly said with a slight French-sounding accent.

"Dick, one of my best high school friends had the same name. I'm sure we'll get through this first year okay."

"I hope so. I've never been this nervous before in my whole life."

"Dick, all we have to do is hang in and see how it goes."

The next morning John happily found out he had been classified as an advanced freshman. All 15 of his Berkeley credits had been accepted. This allowed him to take a Literature course open to all students including seniors. This gave him at least one class outside the usual freshman schedule. Dr. Jeremiah K. Durick became his favorite professor, and "Major British Writers" his favorite textbook. Latin, French, Logic and Mathematics rounded out the liberal arts requirements. One thing he had not anticipated – each course lasted a year and six credits were obtained. Since 120 credits produced a degree, five courses each year sufficed. Of course one had to stay the entire year.

"So, you're the veteran Father Galligan has been telling me about," said Father Stankiewicz, the bursar. "Your G. I. Bill should cover all your expenses since, as a seminarian, the school will cover the rest. Simply bring the check in when you receive it. I am not sure when the first one will arrive."

"Thank you, Father. You must be one of the few Edmundites with a Polish background. Most of them seem to have Irish or French names."

"Well, if you continue on you'll add to the order's diversity. I hope you do."

Johnny felt like he had made the right decision after all. The totally male school had a little over 800 students, new dormitories in the planning stage, and north of the campus, in the distance, stood snow-covered Mt. Mansfield. The trees had begun to transition to their fall spectacle of color. Maybe it all did make sense, despite the guilt he felt about leaving his family to cope with their new surroundings and their deep disappointment that he would leave them again so soon.

The next day at Mass, Johnny's conscience troubled him regarding his scholarship as a seminarian. The great grace he had received at Shaw while at Mass during the Consecration of the Host made him believe he was acting in direct contradiction to that grace. Could he ever know any kind of emotional or spiritual peace living this subterfuge? He trembled nervously in his disquietude and wondered if the exhilaration at finally attending a college full time had pressured him into a faulty decision. How could he successfully live through the entire school year carrying this burden as well as the guilt of letting down his family struggling in their new surroundings. Why did he find the idea of living at home so undesirable?

"Gene, have you ever heard of the Opus Dei movement?" Johnny asked the one seminarian he found very compatible to himself intellectually.

"No, John, I don't believe I have."

"I know they have a house in Chicago. I think I'm going to write to them. An article in one of the Paulist magazines described the total dedication the members have to the Catholic Church and to the pope."

"Does this mean you will not be staying with us in the seminary?"

"I don't know. I do know I want to decide before too many months go by. Say a prayer for me, if you don't mind."

"Well, I'll pray that you stay."

Johnny wrote a letter to the Opus Dei house on Woodlawn Avenue in Chicago. He received a reply dated September 28th.

Dear John:

Thank you very much for your letter of September 23, concerning your interest in Opus Dei. As you say that you are free to move to another place, we feel that coming to Chicago would be the best way for you to know about our work and our way of life – much more than what we could explain to you by letter.

This house of Opus Dei, Woodlawn Residence, is a house for students doing graduate or undergraduate work in different schools in this area, plus some young instructors. Not all the men here belong to Opus Dei, as also there are quite a number of members who do not live at the house.

I think that staying with us you could find an answer to your questions and attend some university in Chicago at the same time. Perhaps this time of year does not seem the most appropriate for you to make a change; however, for what you say in your letter it seems that you are willing to come as soon as possible. In this case we will be very happy to have you as soon as you can. Please let us know about your arrival.

Sincerely yours,
Sal Ferigle

The quick reply surprised him. The thought of actually leaving St. Michael's jolted him into a sense of reality. Some things needed to be placed on the back burner. Johnny sent a reply thanking Sal for his letter, told him to keep his name on the list for any mailings they might send to prospective candidates and promised he would be in touch the following summer.

The class schedule kept Johnny occupied enough to bring some stability into his anxious mind. The Latin professor, a handsome Italian who spoke with a foreign accent, asked him why he was taking Latin.

"I am a seminarian."

"*You, a seminarian!* I don't know. I don't think that's the right place for you."

Johnny had not expected this sort of comment. The professor also directed the school theatrical productions; maybe he knew more about people than the average instructor. Johnny did not make any reply and smiled with good humor. He suspected that a part would be his in one of the college plays.

Sully, his roommate at Shaw, wrote the first Sunday in October in reply to a letter John had mailed to him in late September.

> *Dear John,*
>
> *I've just returned from Mass and a "whirl" at the cafeteria for coffee and donuts. Your letter was both interesting and gratifying, too, to know you are gradually readjusting.*
>
> *The news from here is dull, drab, uneventful and boring. I talked to Turner the other day as we picked up our pay checks. The talk was of you, of course, and he said a letter from you was still in his mailbox. He did say he had your camera, however, so if you haven't heard from him yet that might relieve your mind.*
>
> *We have three priests here now, one of which I haven't seen. The other besides Fr. Lawler is a likeable Fr. O'Hara – very gentile and seems quite conscientious. The incoming 9th Air Force probably prompted the move. The chapel is as beautiful as ever and I think of you often when I'm there.*
>
> *I ran into a lucky streak the past few weeks – won a grand total of $507 at the poker tables. Still, you know how I hate money and the discussion of it so I'll switch to another subject, if you don't mind.*
>
> *We saw every game of the World Series on a TV they set up at the back of Supply. Everybody just said "to hell with the work," including Sgt. McKinney, who watched throughout. I believe each and every man was saying to himself, "I couldn't care less."*

So things are quite natural in this little "world" of ours, John. I am still utterly disgusted, disgruntled and disappointed, which leaves me just as you left me. I couldn't help thinking of our "corresponding" problems – yours of the priesthood and mine of marriage. Your apparent skepticism is both intelligent and wise in that it reflects a mature depth. Such in any situation should be sincerely appreciated rather than frustrating for, speaking negatively of course, it is only when the world measures up to our ideals and pleases them and us should we become pale with disgust with ourselves.

There is no word from Rita in over six weeks now. I think you realize my position. I've discussed with you many times my outlook of marriage – which I shall never change. This all has probably initiated my disgruntled state. I shall love her always and very, very dearly but it is quite a different matter from swallowing pride when one is asked to relinquish his dignity and the dignity of the relationship. You can see, John, when those means to an end would only prove to be the means of destruction. I would lose her respect as well as her love. It is difficult for women, even my Rita, to see such an evident qualification – nevertheless it could never be sacrificed and still retain a man as its "victim". If this appears hazy you will some day encounter it John, should you leave the seminary and find your woman, for I am sure the caliber of your woman would be such that will necessarily encounter such a problem. I have seen many couples who have never faced it and perhaps, in their bliss, they are so very fortunate. In the least appraisal they are more content, anyway.

So too, with your confusion now. Weigh it all – and weigh it again and again. Seek much advice and the more advice you seek the more disregard in decision you should give it. There is none so wise as the man who uncovers all minds and displays his own. There is no greater fighter than he who knows what he fights. I speak, perhaps, in tones too legalistic. But in law as in each and every other field of life it is the hat that counts. A "Homburg" harbors more thoughts than an average Stetson. Remember, Johnny boy, be the last to take your hat off!! You'll be the first to put it on again!! It's so gratifying to know with even a minimum of finesse you can see the other fellow's hand without ever uncovering your own. In your next letter, if there is one, your literary nature will rebuke me,

no doubt, sharply for those last statements.
Waiting for those rebuttals, I'm still,
Your friend, Sully

Johnny knew his friend, Andrew Sullivan, would one day become a good lawyer. He appreciated all the ideas conveyed in his letter. The very next day a brief letter arrived from Ed Turner.

Dear John,

How are you boy? Well, at least I know by your letter that you really are enrolled and that makes us both happy.

John, I know how surprised you must be to find that most of the boys do not have any apparent outward solemnity for their attendance there. I can say without reservation that you are most prepared and have trained and disciplined yourself to a degree that will take months and probably years for some others to acquire. I wouldn't let that bother me, by your example and others like you, plus their unexcelled instruction it won't take long. I must say, however, some of that, to a degree, is necessary since you'll be coping with people like that in your vocation all your life.

I got your camera for you. I will send it this week, also the check.

We are doing fine and "its" to be in about two and one-half weeks.

Be sure to write us as often as you can and we'll write you as well. You have been a great inspiration and friend to us and our prayers are for you always,

Very sincerely yours,
Ed & Lovelene

The arrival of a baby to another one of his Air Force buddies! This birth meant so much to Ed and Lovelene because they had been trying to conceive a child for at least two years. In his reply he congratulated them for the baby and the friendship they both had shown him during his stay at Shaw.

In a short while, Johnny appeared in the weekly news publication, *The Michaelman*, as a member of the editorial board. The editor of the *Lance*, Dave Essenfeld, invited him to write an essay for the jubilee issue of the school's magazine. A seminarian from San Francisco, Dave, a senior and the only Jewish student on the campus, worked enthusiastically for the success of this literary effort, circulated to a hundred Catholic colleges and universities as well as all the priests and religious in the Burlington Diocese. *The Oxford Isis*, one of the leading college publications in England, had honored the magazine in a recent issue. Johnny used his writing skills to good effect and wrote an essay acceptable to Dave's requirements.

The Society of St. Edmund's connection to Oxford probably stemmed from their patron, St. Edmund of Abingdon, Archbishop of Canterbury, who had studied and taught at Oxford in the 13th C. and whose tomb was rumored to rest beneath one of Oxford's buildings. The French, however, believed his death in France meant his final resting-place on their soil had greater credibility. The Society believed they knew where he had been buried and honored the French claim.

"Gene, I'd like to write a piece about your chess expertise. Didn't that Vancouver paper recently publish a chess problem you had submitted?"

"John, it's really not a big deal. How many people here have any real interest in chess?"

"Well, I'm impressed. Give me some details and I'll make you look like a genius."

The chess puzzle appeared at the top of Johnny's column for the *Michaelman*. Gene believed that his new friend made him look much too good.

Johnny's interest in math had always been marginal. The instructor at St. Michael's explained math in ways he had never experienced in high school. He actually made you believe the subject could be made interesting. The irony was that the instructor also taught French because of his French Canadian background and equal proficiency to teach the language.

On the surface Johnny appeared to function with great confidence. He also managed to live totally celibate for about three months. That discipline faded significantly as he heard and felt his young roommate satisfying his sexual urges in the bunk bed above him. He had never realized that some sexual activity helped him greatly to offset the emotional pressures he began to feel with greater and greater intensity. Finally he decided to talk to the priest in residence who taught Psychology at the college.

"Father, I need to transfer to the regular college. I like St. Michael's but I do not want to continue as a seminarian."

"John, that's a rather hasty change of mind, don't you think? How long have you been with us; two months?" The priest smoked his pipe as he spoke.

Johnny felt the rest of the conversation would not go easily.

"Father, I have begun to believe I do not have a vocation to the priesthood." Johnny had never spoken to anyone about the voice which he had heard in the chapel at Shaw. He did not want to reveal that episode to this priest who looked at him with some condescension.

"Of course you know a move to the regular student body will probably jeopardize any funding you may be receiving. Why don't you stay in this residence until the end of the year?"

"Father, my conscience won't allow it. I will simply risk the consequences of the move."

"John, I am usually not quite this blunt. You strike me as probably being a homosexual." Johnny looked at the priest in complete disbelief. His mind quickly focused on the psychology professor from Berkeley, whom he never quite liked, and remembered the concept of projection. Is it possible he is projecting his own guilt and inferiority? John said nothing. He walked out of the room. This "put-down" very much reminded Johnny of the day the pastor of his high school addressed him as a "skunk" as he gave out the last quarterly report cards. Johnny believed the priest resented Johnny's decision not to enroll in a seminary as expected by the Polish pastor who had paid his yearly tuition. The priest at St. Michael's knew he had lost any chance of keeping Johnny on the path to the priesthood.

"John, report to the Registrar's Office and tell them you're transferring to the main campus. Let *them* find you a room," the priest said to him the next morning after Mass.

"You mean you're leaving the seminary?" asked his friend when he learned John would no longer be with them.

"Gene, I must make the transfer to the main campus. I really should not have come here in the first place."

"Well, if you're leaving I am not sure I want to stay either."

"That's something you have to decide on your own. I'll see you around the campus."

The Registrar told Johnny he could stay in Senior Hall in the old Administration Building until the next semester. After that he would have a room in one of the new dorms. When Father Galligan heard of Johnny's decision, he simply whispered a prayer that no more nephews of nuns would cross his path while he was the director of vocations.

Winter came early in Vermont. By mid November the leaves had fallen and the snow arrived. Johnny's emotions ran rampant a few days after the transfer. He felt guilty as hell about leaving his parents and family. The knowledge that he had not listened to the Spirit – instead, left the Air Force in great haste to fulfill a need he had, with no patience to make the right move with greater care. Suddenly, he simply fell apart. The emotional overload made him feel he was going out of his mind. By some miracle he made his way to the infirmary and collapsed. Two days later a doctor stood by his bed, assured him he would be okay, and told him to take things easy for a while. Johnny believed the doctor knew what he was talking about, returned to his usual activities and looked forward to the end of the term.

A letter from his friend, Joe, arrived at the end of November, written on the Feast of St. John of the Cross.

Dear John,

I am really very sorry for not having answered your letter earlier, especially since you seemed to want a quick reply. But a superior's ways are not our ways and in this life one has to learn to be patient. I hope you won't be too angry with me, for I have remembered you constantly at Mass and in my prayers even more than before since I realized that this was a trying and important period of readjustment for you.

This is a difficult letter to write, John, because it is an answer to a letter obviously written during a period of depression and emotional disturbance which has no doubt changed since then and may very well have been entirely transformed. But since I can only go on what you said in that letter I will try to piece together some coherent words and phrases if not particularly significant ones. In fact it seems that the best way to comment on what you said is to handle it as something entirely past, leaving it up to you to decide if any of the comments have any meaning today, some two months after.

You were obviously let down by St. Michaels, and I can hardly say I am surprised. Your letter didn't state explicitly whether or not you were actually in the seminary department, but I know from some follows who went to St. Michael's as college students that the life of a seminarian there is not much different from that of an ordinary collegian. This meant that you were going right smack into an atmosphere that you were hardly prepared for. Not that you weren't mature enough for it, but on the contrary, you were too mature. You were thrown in with young fellows to whom life was still pretty much of a lark; you had spent four long years wrestling with the problem of your life's work. To them life was still pretty much of a day-to-day proposition; to you life was something to be used and dedicated. I remember myself entering the junior seminary four years ago (I have to pinch myself now to believe it is that long ago and that I am really here). I wanted to be a priest, sure. And yet Sonny, you, Hacker and all the rest were so much more real (and likeable) to me than all these other people. A good time to me meant a lot of laughs and gags; not instructing souls in the truths of Christ. All that has changed now, thank God. But for many, if not most, of the young fellows with whom you were thrown in last September theirs was much the same mentality as mine. And you weren't ready for it, because for you life was important. This month was important, it was a step to your final goal. To you the coming Christmas vacation, the next game, a show, all these things were sidetracks for you. You had made your break. You had come to give your life, and no one seemed to be interested in that.

No wonder you were let down. This wasn't the religious life; it was rah-rah college stuff, kid-stuff, the kind of stuff you had outgrown in Mississippi or Japan. But chances are you were the exception in the group. The community was set up primarily for these boys to whom the priesthood was only a distant vision and not the reality with which you had struggled for many years. Naturally you felt out of place, because in a real way you were out of place, the common good, the good of the many had won out again. But certainly you must have soon seen that it was unfair to judge a school for what it doesn't give to an exception. And even more, you must have soon seen that it was unfair to judge a religious community by its minor seminary. I feel sure that if you had come to our prep sem in Baltimore your reaction would have been much the same. They are geared to boys, not men. It is a difficult problem to train its delayed vocations and its average young ones in the same place and according to the schedule, at least in the beginning. But a community doesn't do its work for Christ in its minor sem and a man doesn't live his religious life in the minor house of studies. Religious life is a lifetime dedication and can't be decided on the basis of a few months, or even a year or two, in a minor house of studies. What I am trying to say here is, "Give the Edmundites a chance." You can't allow yourself to become a religious window-shopper. Not that it would be necessarily wrong for you to change your community. But it certainly seems to be rash to think of doing it soon. However, you have a spiritual director to help you with such decisions and I had best keep my nose out of it. I will add only this. In your letter you remarked on the chance occurrence that brought you to the Society of St. Edmund. I must admit that when I heard of it a few years ago, I thought the same. But I have learned a little since then about the workings of God's grace, and can say that I have heard of many more strange influences leading to a decision. In other words, don't rule out the Edmundites by saying you were simply attracted to them by an emotional experience. It is true that we have to be constantly on our guard against delusions of this kind, some of us more so than others, but it is often very hard to draw the line between grace and gush.

Well, it didn't take me long to lose my impersonal air and launch into my polemical best (or worst). But I am interested in you, John, I feel I have grown with you over the years and do want you to cooperate with God's grace most fully. I know you will forgive me if in any place I have said too much. Naturally I was delighted at your interest in the Paulists. I can't say that I am surprised after the zeal you have manifested for non-Catholic souls these last few years. But as I said above, think much and pray more before you come to any decision. Life in our community, as in any other, can be difficult if God has not called you to it. This next sentence would fit best above, I suppose, but I will add it here; it isn't my own advice but that of a priest friend given some time ago. "Never leave (referring to the community) unless you feel a distinct call to some other life. Never leave just because you don't feel like you belong there. Because there are going to be times in your life that you won't feel right anywhere." And with that I will close. Write and keep me informed about any developments in this regard. If you still feel interested in the Paulists and your spiritual director agrees, I would suggest your writing to the Director of Vocations, Paulist Fathers, 415 W. 59th St. N.Y., N.Y. rather than to Baltimore, You will get fuller information and more direct treatment from him, Father James Powers at the present time.

My father has been very sick with a heart condition. He spent about two months in the hospital, and though home now, must spend the next five weeks in bed. But thanks to the Lord's goodness it looks as though we will have him with us for a while.

That will have to do it for now, I don't write often, but wow! I didn't think I had it in me. Our superior, a wonderful man, is not too free with letter-writing permissions so these epistles won't be so very frequent – can I hear you sighing with relief? I will write you around Christmas time though, so try to have written at least once by then. Forgive me again, friend, if I have said too much. Be assured of frequent remembrance in my prayers. Please do the same for me, especially when you are united with Our Lord in prayer and sacramental communion. Remember He wants you too – no matter in what garb or way of life – He is drawing you to Himself. Your whole life is worked out solely to bring you and those you come in contact with into the arms of our Father. We are made for God – nothing else. Nothing counts or has any meaning except insofar as it takes us to Him or away from Him. Think often about this end, John, for it is only then that you will direct your life according to it. And when those blue days come, as they surely will perhaps more often now than ever again, offer them up for your past sins and for the conversion of some soul to Christ, and above all remember that they always pass away and are part of the divine plan to make you realize the true nature of things – their inability to satisfy our craving for the happiness we will find only with Him. God love you and love God.

Your friend in Christ,
Joe

Johnny appreciated his friend's understanding of the emotional trauma he had experienced. Joe and his aunt had been informed of the breakdown; no one else.

CHAPTER THREE

Mother Edmunda, who had begun to sign her letters as Sister Edmunda, wanted more than ever to entirely enfold herself within the community. She prayed for the humility to accept the will of the new general superior and the decisions of all the councillors whether they agreed with her own ideas or not. Her sole purpose in life as the Reverend Mother had centered on the spiritual progress of each sister. She prayed nothing would change that direction of the community.

The latest letter from her nephew Johnny, who continued to correspond, although with less frequency, made her wonder where his life was heading. She answered in the best spirit she could muster.

> *Porto Alegre, R.G.S.*
> *Deus Meus et Omnia!*
> *My dearest Johnny,*
> *May we always bless and love the Holy Will of God!*
> *Due to the several letters which have never reached me, I was at a loss as to your whereabouts until about two weeks ago.*
>
> *Your letter didn't surprise me. Firstly, I am, perhaps, beyond the stage of being surprised with human frailties and weaknesses and foibles; secondly, I meant what I wrote when I said "get out of your dream world" and I'm sure I also said something like "You are old enough to know what you want." I shall say no more, either now or in the future. I am praying for you recently – that is, since I'm in Brazil, free of the worries of responsibility – more than I ever did. I am begging our good Mother Mary to make her intentions for all those who are dear to me and to present them to Her Son for their*

fulfillment. She knows best and her "omnipotent intercession" is the best I can plead for you.

Whatever the future may be, please be prepared for difficult moments. Every way of life, every career, every profession has its humps ... and, unless we are ready to get over these humps by sheer force of the will, we cannot be successful. Are you giving up all the credit you could earn this semester? This is only a question; it is no suggestion that you continue against the doctor's orders.

It is growing rather warm here, but, the evenings and nights are rather pleasant – so one cannot complain about the weather as we do in the States. Yesterday, I made the visits to the Marian churches of Porto Alegre. We visited 15 of them, in honor of the 15 mysteries, and returned home very tired – yet, very happy and full of joy. It was one of the very happy days of my life. I am well; the weather, the food, etc. is giving me no trouble of acclimatization. I am a citizen of the world rather than of the U.S.A.

May the Holy Infant and Its Mother bless you always! May you find the New Year replete with heaven's benedictions. As far as I am concerned, please do not think for a minute that I am disappointed in any way or that anything else would give me more pleasure. God's Holy Will is all I want. Pray that you follow it, for only this matters.

Devotedly in the Two Hearts,
Sr. M. Edmunda

Summer had arrived in southern Brazil, especially in the state of Rio Grande do Sul, which borders Uruguay and Argentina. Mother Edmunda, although first councillor of the community, relaxed as much as possible in her distant position from the decisions undoubtedly occurring in the motherhouse in Reading. She trusted in the loyalty of the other councillors and the commitment of her successor regarding the good of the order. The pleasant weather near the coast freed her from any anxiety which might have begun to develop.

A continuous problem with the directions she had left at the motherhouse meant some of her letters did not reach her until months after they had been sent. A wrenching letter she had received from her nephew Johnny in January forced her to reply in full to his observations about his decision to leave the seminary and the disillusion he had felt from his Christmas vacation visit to the family. As usual, he thanked her in his heart for her constant support and prayers.

Feast of the Five Protomartyrs of the
Franciscan Order, Jan. 16, 1955
May the Holy Will of God be blessed and loved always!
My dearest Johnny,

Your letter of October 11th, forwarded to me, via Mount Alvernia, reached me January 14th. I can see why and how. Since the date of my return to the States was not settled and since I requested Rev. Mother not to forward to me letters, more or less of business or simply charitable nature, it was placed on the shelf with all others that were considered of no immediate importance. On January 9th, Mother Duklane sent me many belated ones, among which she slipped yours, too. This is our human explanation, but I am certain that the Lord has His own love in the matter. Perhaps, I could not take it at the time it came. You know that Mother's of a similar note was lost. The good God never asks us to carry a burden beyond our strength. This is just another proof of His solicitude for us his weak children. May His Will be blessed!

Mother Duklane mentioned to me in her letter about your visit and that you did not look too well. Of course, you are not what Louis is; hence, aside of him, your indisposition must have been accentuated. I am happy that you paid Mother a visit; she was always so very good to you both, esp. to Louis.

How are you feeling at present? How were the exams? I presume that they are a fact of the past by now. Did you receive my answer to your Thanksgiving letter? Had I your letter of October 11 this latter one would have been more intelligible to me. However, here again, let me underline my faith in God's Holy Will. Perhaps, just now, I am better prepared to answer it.

Johnny darling, I understand you fully. You are trying to carry the burdens of the whole family and they are stupendous in some ways – esp. because of your father's irresponsibility. He is good but he is too weak to forget self-satisfaction and sacrifice the required self-denial upon the altar of a father's duties. Your mother deserves your full love, Johnny. She is not perfect – just another mortal being with her pluses and minuses – but let us be fair. In spite of manifold difficulties: her own illnesses, Alma's troubles, no work, no income, etc., she alone carried the burden of home-making and keeping. Christian life? She never neglected the Church, she gave all of you a Catholic education for twelve years, which is denied to other children, whose parents are blessed in a material way. All this was not easy. Please just stop and think. The Sisters of the Parish always assured me that every one of you was well-dressed and clean; you did not show poor nutrition – you excepted, of course, but it was not due to food or lack of it.

Now, Johnny, as I told you at Reading, the purchasing of a house at a rather low price, I agree, but very high for her own hands, was a rather great burden. She is doing her best as far as I can judge from one of her letters. In the first very trying months she told me that she paid the quarterly interest on the mortgage and paid for the stove ($215.00). This I don't think that even I could do with the administrative abilities, which others think that I possess. It is easy to be a good administrator when income can be multiplied, but when only expenses are to our credit, it is a sheer miracle to make ends meet. That you feel your responsibility with respect to this, I can fully understand and I respect you for it. As far as I can judge humanly, God would not demand from you an immediate answer to His call at the present moment. Your duties to a needy mother must be considered. But, if you do, please do not act as Alma did. I know that you have already proved your worth like few boys do, but continue in the same vein. God has many ways and paths for us and He certainly will reward your sacrifices for His love. The peace and security of a community life is a great reward for our sacrifices; perhaps, He wants you to prove that you are worthy of them. If He has other paths for you, we must simply bow our heads and say "Thy holy Will be done!" If your plans are to complete the freshman year at St. Michael's, good and well. Mother will be able, I hope, to continue with the interest on the mortgage and perhaps even to pay off a little; then, with your added help she will begin to throw off the principal. Did you obtain the government help for your education? If not, with working hours, you perhaps could manage to continue your schooling at Albright at a slower pace, it is true, but still not giving up the one great desire of your heart, a college education.

But, please show your mother that she and her needs are your concern. She needs this affection and this understanding for her all-out efforts. You will bring sunshine into her life and God will reward you a hundredfold. Ciocia Cassie? Well, it is hard for me to judge just what lies underneath their relationship. You know it began at least 35 years ago. Let us not even try to solve the puzzle. Both mean well. I certainly do love Cassie. She has been a real mother to me and she has treated you all rather well. Now, there may be a streak of jealousy and there are reasons for it. You see, Ciocia has a beautiful home, well-furnished; she is provided for financially to the end of her days. All this must be hard for mother to accept when she has only debts to see and when she must deny herself the possession of many things. Let us be considerate and have understanding. If I were you, I should try not to discuss Ciocia at all. I would show interest and love for the one whom God gave me as my mother; who day by day did her best for you and who is in dire need of help, who is hungry for a little recognition of her worthy efforts. Get all that is noble in yourself, Johnny my boy, and be to her all that she is craving for. You'll be happy and she will bless you forever and God will shower His precious gifts upon you for all the days of your life. Just imagine how much joy you would bring her, if being with her and trying to help her with the standing debts, you would still from time to time save a little on what is given you as spending money to buy her a surprise. You like to do this, I know. You did it while being in Japan. With what pride, she showed me the dishes you sent her!

Have conditions changed any? Did you notice any improvement while home for the Christmas vacation?

Did Mother Duklane present you boys with neck-scarfs? I asked her to do so; I had some in my trunk and I asked her to send them to you. Of course, she is so busy with the big house that she might have not found time for the searching of my trunk.

As to the Edmundites, Johnny, I think I need to give you an explanation. When you prayed to the Blessed Mother, as you wrote me, I was doing the same. You see I did not like the unwholesome indecision that I noticed in you and I wanted to put an end to it by prayers and otherwise. While in Buffalo (I think it was from there that I wrote to you), I casually heard that the Edmundites opened a high school, or rather were given charge of a new high school by the Bishop. You said that you wanted to do home-missionary work, then you spoke of teaching ... so this report gave me suddenly light that perhaps the Edmundites could satisfy your desires in whatever direction they went. I prayed and felt that I should try to settle that indecision of yours. I have no doubts that the Blessed Mother was in the case, since both of us prayed for the same cause ... even if the solution was only a temporary one. As I have written in my last letter, you will not disappoint me if you do not become a priest at all. It is your life, dearest child, and you chose what you think will give you joy and happiness. I love my Patron-saint, but I have no ties with the Edmundites. I do not know the Community; I simply thought that in this particular community, you could do work in the home missions and at the same time find an outlet for other work as teaching in high schools and colleges.

You are in my daily specially fervent prayers. Until I hear from you, may God bless you and Mary hold you close to her Immaculate Heart and my good St. Edmund make you a good brother to your sister and brother as he was to his.

Devotedly in J. & M.
Sr. M. Edmunda

Mail during the Christmas season – December through January – often arrived at the provincial house on an irregular basis.

"I haven't heard from quite a few of my most faithful friends and relatives. I am beginning to wonder if they are okay or if they are having some health problems."

"Mother, with a little patience, I believe you will receive your Christmas greetings from all of them," replied Mother Herculane to Mother Edmunda's worrisome comment. " By the way, I do hope they send any monetary gifts with personal or bank checks. We have had reports that mail is sometimes opened at the post office in search of cash. When no cash is found the mail is often destroyed."

"Thank you. I'll watch for any tampering of any mail I do receive."

On January 21st, a letter from her dear friend and distant cousin Celia arrived. In the letter Celia spoke of a card and check; neither had arrived. In her reply Mother Edmunda expressed her fear that illness or some other trouble had disheartened her and other members of the family to the point of silence. She continued:

"Father Ignatius's letter lightened the weight of fears somewhat when he wrote about his holiday visit to the family. Still, I couldn't make out the cause of the silence – the first at Christmas time within the last 30 or more years. As for the missing check please stop payment and replace it with a duplicate. Thank you for your unfailing thoughtfulness."

After a lengthy letter she closed with the prayer that God would bless and Mary would love her until they met again.

Sister Baptist cashed or deposited many of the checks at a New York City bank with offices in Porto Alegre. During their hour of recreation she told Mother Edmunda about the banker and his family.

"We are fortunate to have an American Director at the bank," noted Sister Baptist to Mother Edmunda. "They all know Mother Herculane and myself, so they ignore all the formalities attached to cashing checks. They will even cash your checks without a personal appearance by you when I take them in. I do not need to present a passport or other identification, simply your signed check. Last Thanksgiving Day the wife of the Director brought us a turkey and at Christmas time two of their boys came to spend the afternoon with us; one brought a case of soda, the other, a large beautifully decorated cake. There are so few Americans in this part of Brazil they feel we are all family."

Sister Inez came into the recreation room to tell all of them that she could now drive the convent's Ford in Brazil.

"After payment of the absurd duty of $500.00 and some reconditioning by the bank director's chauffeur I have finally been given a certificate of good behavior by the police and have passed their driver's test."

"So apparently your American driver's license meant nothing to them. How upright they pretend to be despite so much official depravity! Well, as enigmatic as their world may be I still like the Brazilians and Brazil!" commented Mother Edmunda.

A three-day retreat for the sisters in Porto Alegre, Camaqua and Dom Feliciano took place shortly after the Christmas holidays. The young Jesuit retreat master had spent a year in Indiana and spoke English very well. Mother Edmunda found his conferences in Portuguese almost as easy to understand as the English sermons. Still, she gained so much more from private retreats she intended to beg her superiors, if necessary, for permission to do that in the future. Always, of course, if God spared her to continue to serve Him.

"Mother, I'd like you to receive the twelve Brazilian postulants into the order next week."

"Mother Herculane, you are the provincial! I would not want to take this great honor from you."

"I will be here, God willing, for many more years. You would do me a great honor to preside at the ceremony, standing at the side of our dear Archbishop, as the postulants receive their holy habits. Please say yes."

"As you wish. I will be most grateful to perform this sacred function for what I am certain will be the last time. This is something I had not expected to do during my time here."

Mother Edmunda prayed with great humility that these newest Bernardines would help to carry the Brazilian province to greater heights of holiness and service to Christ.

"The number of sisters continue to grow," remarked Mother Herculane later that day. "We have four postulants at Camaqua which by February will increase to 15. Almost miraculously, these four were brought to us by a young priest from Ceara, a northern state of Brazil, over 3,000 kilometers from Porto Alegre. As a seminary student in this Archdiocese he spent about five summers at Canela where we have a school and a hospital. He could not return home for the summer vacations because of the expense. He became a loyal friend to us. He is now the rector of the minor seminary in his own diocese and made himself almost an outcast for the vocation work he is directing towards us. He brought us his sister, his cousin, and two others – all rather well educated and promising as future members. We pray that they persevere for they are so badly needed! On his way to the Eucharistic Congress in Rio, he hopes to bring four more. Recently, he said very humbly, 'When I bring 70 girls will I have the pleasure of getting Bernardines to my parish?'"

"He has a widowed mother," she continued. "He is hoping to have a parish where she could live with him. He is good to the core."

During a visit to Camaqua this young patron of the Bernardines had explained to them how life in Ceara differed from that in Rio grande do Sul.

"The people are good church-goers and lead a rather intensive spiritual life. In Fortaleza, the capital of the state, in one area of the city, out of 700 girls in the parishes, some 300 make a daily meditation, are present at Mass each day, receive Communion and often make closed retreats. The girls who have joined you had to rise at 5:30 to attend the 6 o'clock Mass and, then, report to work on time."

"Little wonder that vocations are coming from Ceara," thought most of his listeners.

"Some priests are almost fanatical about their dress requirements," he continued; "e.g. a girl not having a full length sleeve will not receive absolution at confession or be allowed to receive holy communion."

"I have tried to break some of these extremes, but I am meeting a great deal of opposition. While a rector I also directed a college for girls where I also served as chaplain. A summer camp for girls seemed like a good idea so I opened one for the students of the college where they could enjoy their vacation in Catholic surroundings and atmosphere. Singing, dancing and acting were added to the program. All of this scandalized the traditionalists and I had to resign from my college posts."

"Are there any other priests who feel the same way you do?" asked one of the Bernardines.

"Some of the younger priests, understanding my American-like ideas, are moving ahead courageously. We all look to Americans like you to help us bring about the changes."

"Father, let us hope you adopt only the best ideas. Not all things of America are good."

In late January news arrived about the death of Mother Angela. Sister Edmunda, who had loved and respected this wonderful friend of hers when she served as Secretary General of the order, prayed the Bernardines would follow in the steps of this loyal, true, devoted, upright, pious and Franciscanly simple woman who had served as the Reverend Mother prior to Sister Edmunda's tenure in office.

"Mother Angela; how fortunate I was to have her on the council for my 12 years as Superior General. A genuine Nathaniel of the Gospel best describes her," said Sister Edmunda to the other sisters during their recreation period.

"And she died at a relatively young age. I don't believe she had quite reached her 60th birthday."

"You are probably correct. She really hadn't been in perfect health during her second six-year term," answered Sister Edmunda. "She and Sister Imelda were my special blessings all those years."

With Mother Angela's passing into eternity, Sister Edmunda began to meditate on her own death and entrance into everlasting life. She also began to wonder when the Reverend Mother would have her return to the States. Perhaps when one of the sisters in Brazil left for a summer session at Villanova she would be asked to accompany her.

In February the "Carnival" days arrived. The residents of Camaqua, very much like all the towns of any size in Brazil, noisily played their music and sang their songs in street parades sometimes well into the night. To Sister Edmunda the music seemed to have only 2 or 3 measures and reflected the noise of a primitive people.

"I understand their night clubs are in full swing until the dawn. You can just imagine their state of inebriation when they leave these *clubes*," said one of the sisters.

"Some of the saints - e.g. St. Margaret Mary suffered very much in the days of the Carnival, imagining the perversion of many of the participants," noted Sister Edmunda. She never really wished to judge others – it all appeared so obvious during these days. The summer heat seemed to add to the frenzy.

"The Felician Sisters from Rio will be our guests at the end of the month. Your room will be needed to help accommodate them. Please return to Porto Alegre," said Mother Herculane to Sister Edmunda during a brief telephone conversation. Mother Herculane, as provincial, had also been preparing for the opening of the new school year on March 1st. She always had a great appreciation of Sister Edmunda's thoughtful conversations and suggestions.

Another letter from Celia arrived in the middle of March. Neither of the monetary gifts she had sent had been received, including the duplicate check of $17. She suggested to Celia that she follow her bank cashier's advice and send the checks to the New York City Bank in Porto Alegre. American dollars went a long way at the time for a dollar which once brought in less than 20 cruzieros now converted at 87 cruzieros. What once cost 5 cents, now is just a trifle more than a penny.

A letter from Johnny finally arrived in April. As usual, she replied immediately, especially since he again appeared unsure of which direction to go with his life.

> *D.M. et O.*
> *April 16, 1955*
> *May we bless and love the Holy Will of God!*
> *Dearest Johnny,*
>
> *You almost received no answer to your letter of April 7, which arrived yesterday. Why? Because I could not recall your address. "Winooski" isn't a name to hang on the tip of our tongues. I'm still wondering whether I am correct. You see we have a Catholic Directory at the Novitiate House, but not here; hence, I have no reference.*
>
> *Thank you for the letter. Did you receive my other two letters? You never acknowledged their receipt. So many letters are being lost or discarded by some unscrupulous soul, that I wonder how many of mine reach the persons addressed. There's one advantage*

to being prompt in answering. Few persons blame you for not doing it. I have thus far answered many letters; hence, I can freely say: "If I received your letter, it was answered." This is a true consolation in a situation as ours. Mother Provincial lost her father, March 1ˢᵗ; the family wrote five letters describing the last days; Rev. Mother wrote a letter to the same effect; not until the last week did she receive word of the exact date of death, etc. This was too much, so we are taking the case up with the American Consulate. Our reports to the chief of the P. O. Department brought no results. Nearly all our letters, if they do reach us, are re-sealed. We need not fear unjust accusations; the purpose of this must be search for the American dollars. Ever so often, the contents of the letter states: we are enclosing you ? dollars – but none are found.

You said nothing about your school work – excepting the mention that you are majoring in Philosophy. And, you are still unsettled? Why don't you decide definitely and stick to your guns, regardless. I am not for Albright College, but I thought that you were certain of your future plans and here, you're fumbling as in the past. Perhaps, the best thing for Louis is to get work and help mother. How can she carry the whole burden, esp. of the mortgage? I have no objections to baseball, but many have been disappointed there as elsewhere. Then there's the army service not far away.

I don't think that God expects more from us than He permits us to understand. This holds good in religion as elsewhere. I think those at home are doing their level best: they attend church, say their prayers, receive the sacraments and all of you, in spite of great difficulties, received and are receiving a Catholic education. What else is essentially wanting? Aunt Cassie is doing more of praying, but she is drawn to this, has the time, and need not worry about financial obligations. Have understanding, Johnny. Sympathy is a beautiful trait and it means nothing else but placing yourself in the position of another as it actually is and not as we should like it to be. Don't mind my frankness.

May God bless you and Mother Mary hold you close to her Immaculate Heart!

Devotedly yours in the Hearts of Jesus & Mary,
Sr. M. Edmund

A new generalate had become a priority for the council and Mother Chrysostoma for the Sacred Heart Convent, which had been the motherhouse during Sister Edmunda's life as a Bernardine, appeared no longer able to adequately serve the needs of the order. A large estate in Villanova, just an hour away by car, had become available for sale.

"I really believe we should buy the Perot estate before Mother Edmunda returns from Brazil," said Mother Cantalice to the other councillors and Mother Chrysostoma. "You know how reluctant she will be to change the location of the motherhouse."

"Well, you know we likely have three votes, including mine, to institute any changes we feel are needed. Edmunda will simply have to accede to the majority opinion."

"That may be true, Rev. Mother. You know she will not go down without a serious fight for her position, I am sure."

"From what I understand she is still writing her version of our Directory and Customary. A labor of love is how she terms the project. Perhaps if those are accepted by us she will be content," noted Mother Duklane.

After some tearful farewells to many of her sisters in Christ, Sister Edmunda returned to the States, as directed by Mother Chrysostoma, accompanied by a young sister who would continue her studies for a degree in nursing.

Sister Edmunda entered her beloved convent in Mt. Alvernia and went directly to the chapel to thank her Lord for her safe return and for the many graces the Bernardines had been blessed with in Brazil. The next day the councillors met to make a final decision regarding the purchase of the new motherhouse in Villanova.

"To bring everyone up to date, the estate in Villanova has passed inspection and we can proceed with its purchase."

"Reverend Mother, how much will we pay for the property?" asked Sister Edmunda.

"Our bid is $120,000; an absolute bargain I understand."

And how large is the lot?"

"Around ten acres I believe."

"What will it take to furnish the house?"

"Well, as you know, institutional prices are usually quite reasonable. Perhaps $20,000 should cover all of our additional expenses."

"I really cannot see the need to move the motherhouse to another location.

Mt. Alvernia has become such an integral part of the Bernardine spirit, even our dear foundress would find the idea something of an outrage."

"My dear Mother Edmunda, can't you see the decision had already been decided upon while you were away?" asked the Reverend Mother.

"That's very apparent," she responded, with a discouraged look of betrayal she could not hide. "When can we expect to make this dramatic move?"

"October is the most likely date."

"Shall we vote on the purchase of the estate?"

The four to one vote left little doubt that Sister Edmunda held little power in the new administration.

CHAPTER FOUR

Johnny's return to St. Michael's after the semester break found him with a new roommate in a recently constructed dorm. A letter from Bill Romano arrived a few days later.

1/19/55

Dear John,

Excuse the steno-paper – my meager veterans allowance doesn't permit the extravagance of tailored stationery.

I was happy to receive your letter some days ago and wasn't too surprised to learn you were attacking St. Michaels with typical freshman enthusiasm.

Aside from regular classroom study – your extra activity program appears an ambitious undertaking alone. More power to the person who can maintain the grind of both.

You never disclosed the results of your debating ventures, but I'm almost sure, won or lost, you had the last word. Seriously speaking, I hope you'll have as much success and enjoyment in the coming term.

I submitted an application for admission to Univ. of Santa Clara and was told to get lost in a Jr. coll until such time as my grades met their standards. I will start there on the 31st.

I received a Christmas card from John Eggert with a note enclosed. They were particularly concerned as to your whereabouts, and also proud to announce the birth of a baby girl named Luanne, born early in December.

I think I told you I visited them in Houston some months ago.

Believe me John, Mrs. Eggert is every bit the woman you saw in John E's photographs, if you remember. In case you've misplaced their address this is it – 7518 Dixie Drive, Houston.

I hope I'm not trespassing on private private ground, but a question that comes to my mind once in a great while is, "whatever became of Marie?" I'm almost sure that was the girl's name. I'd seen her picture, heard you speak of her, and knew you were quite fond of her. Frankly it's none of my business, because I didn't really know you that well. It's not the kind of question that demands answering, but sometimes when I think of old faces and places, that name provokes a little wonderment.

Well amigo, you're a busy boy, and I'll be busy myself soon, but I trust that over the year one of us will take time out to dash off a few lines, letting the other know he's still alive. Until I hear from you again – or you from me – I remain
    Your friend
    Bill

Happy that the military service part of his life had ended, Johnny continued to appreciate letters from his friends and to know his own somewhat haphazard future had begun to unfold. He felt some regret that he had not visited the Eggerts during his stay in South Carolina.

The breath-freezing weather of the Vermont winter made Pennsylvania look good by comparison. Perhaps he could accommodate the family's needs and his own ambitions by enrolling at Albright College in a pre-law course. He wrote to the college and received a reply from the Assistant to the President, Samuel Shirk, who informed him that the political science and history department kept close contact with the requirements of the law schools and constantly provided the most practical routes of training. One graduate had recently passed the State Bar Examinations, had been first in his class at Penn Law School and had been on the staff of the Law Review. Two other graduates had begun work at the University of Michigan Law School and Emory University in Georgia. An application blank enclosed in the letter made Johnny think seriously of enrolling for the fall semester.

Meanwhile, the school year sped by. Worrying about the future dissipated with each busy day. He concentrated totally on the challenges and opportunities as they developed. His hard work on the school paper promised him the editorship the next year. A vote for the school council gave him a seat on that as well. An all "A" student, except for Latin, made him believe he had found a school in which he could excel. He began to look forward to the summer vacation knowing he would return to St. Michael's.

Two experiences in the classroom had impressed him. Doctor Durick, in his late sixties, always quoted eloquently from Shakespeare. One day he spoke dramatically regarding Macbeth's concept of human limitations after he learns of the queen's death.

> *"...To-morrow, and to-morrow, and to-morrow,/ Creeps in this petty pace from day to   day/ To the last syllable of recorded time;/ And all our yesterdays have lighted fools/ The day to dusty death. Out, out, brief candle!/ Life's but a walking shadow, a poor player/ That struts and frets his hour upon the stage/ And then is heard no more. It is a tale/ Told by an idiot, full of sound and fury/ Signifying nothing."*

In his Logic class a discussion took place regarding time and eternity.

"Isn't it possible that if we believe in eternity we are already in that state of being?"

"John, you are the only one who has thought through to this philosophical concept and brought it to the class's attention. This is the kind of inventive thinking I like to see developed in my Logic classes. Thank you."

In March and again in April Ed Turner wrote to Johnny about his experiences as a Catholic. The April letter made him feel he had perhaps done some good at Shaw AFB.

> *Dear John,*
>
> *I imagine at this time you are still celebrating your spring holidays. I hope you are, since you will get to be home at Easter.*
>
> *We are being very calm and only pacing the floor and watching the calendar until I can get out from under the thumb of my rich uncle. We have about 80 more days to go, I think.*
>
> *Are you studying hard at school? I know you are. I imagine it is hard to start really concentrating on studies after such a long " vacation" from that sort of thing.*
>
> *I have some news that I am sure will be of interest to you. We are going to build a grade school at St. Anne's.*

I think the initial cost is approximately $60,000.00. We are getting pledges from each family and also held a St. Patrick's Day Dinner. There seems to be much interest and I believe everything will go through just fine. I had gathered previously, by Father Doyle's mercenary way, that he was here on some type mission. He really is doing a fine job. I have changed my opinion of him immensely since I first met him.

John, I can well imagine how you must feel when your classmates classify you as a convert to the Church.

Let me tell you of some events that prove it takes "one" to appreciate it.

I asked some of the Catholic boys at the base to buy some of the tickets to the dinner (St. Patrick's). They didn't even seem to take interest in the project of building the school in this predominately Protestant country and section. One of them did. I sold two tickets to a devout Lutheran and two to another devout and fanatical Baptist, another to a devout Protestant of some type that is also trying to raise money for their Sunday school, – and– a non-denominational type sect woman offered to give $1.00 toward the fund. If my thanksgiving of the adherents had not overcome the laxity of the other, I might have lost some friends and wouldn't have particularly cared, either.

We'll make a Union-Confederate proposition, you keep the North revived with the Spirit of the Church and I will here in Dixieland -- (prayerfully, of course).

I think your choice of studying law is very wise. I think you will certainly succeed and do the profession justice by serving in it.

The family is fine and we grow a little more devoted every day. Our sweet baby daughter, Paula Frances, is now four months old. She has her mother's blonde hair and blue eyes.

We love to hear from you and hope to do same real soon.

When are we ever going to see each other again?

Keep up your good work.

Your friend,

Edwin

In May a letter arrived from Philadelphia where another of his high school buddies currently lived with his wife and two young kiddies. The old ties always seemed more binding and the letters bonded them more closely together.

> *25 May 1955*
> *4503 Comly Street*
> *Philadelphia, Pa.*
> *Dear John,*
> *I certainly was glad to hear from you after the Easter holidays. I'd been wondering what had happened concerning that last minute note I sent you. Anyway, without attempting to appear noble or anything, I'm forced to admit that it was my fault that things didn't turn out as they could have. If I hadn't forgotten to answer your initial correspondence, we could have easily made contact while you were down here. We mustn't be dismayed, I guess, although I surely was looking forward to that "exchange of ideas." I somehow don't feel that we actually met that first time, John, and I certainly believe there's more to our friendship than that first meeting indicated. Frankly, it left me sort of cold, and I'm sure it had much the same effect on you. In addition, I felt sort of obligated to show Charlotte an "extra special" good time, since I'd told her so often there was no place like Shenandoah during the Christmas holidays. Anyway, I know it didn't measure up to the expectations of either one of us.*
> *I'm sure things will be different from now on, John. It's pretty certain that I'll be permanently stationed in Philadelphia at the above address for my remaining thirteen months in the Army. So before I go any further, I'd like to point out that you'd be more than welcome any time you decided to pay us a visit. In fact, I'd be greatly disappointed if you were in the area and didn't drop in to say hello. It's a little harder to move around for old Roland, what with having a wife and kiddies. I still can't believe I've grown roots so fast, but I'm grudgingly resigning myself to it. Once I'm out of the service, it will just be a matter of finding a decent place not too far removed from Shenandoah, to plant those roots. As of now, I'm definitely not pro-Philadelphia.*
> *It looks as though you'll be in Winooski, Vermont, for a while, huh? So it will just be a matter of letting me know a little beforehand*

when you're coming down next. Needless to say, I'll answer promptly in the future. We can then plan things accordingly to make room for lots of time to talk over old times and how the world has changed – and I'm sure it has for you also, John, although probably not as drastically. If time permits, we can visit Joe or tie in with some of the old gang that may be around.

I'm trying to avoid getting sentimental or philosophizing or rehashing things in my distantly spaced letters, because I feel there's plenty of time for that when we meet. Besides, I'm sure you'll agree it saves precious time. It's difficult enough just keeping in contact and exchanging bits of information. I use to enjoy doing it in the old days when we were fresh out of high school because I had the time and I was still searching, as you are now! Once you are married, your life follows a definite pattern and your work is cut out for you. We'll chop it off there, John, because that's one subject I can really get involved in – I've thought about it enough! In short, I guess I mean to be practical in writing and to save the deeper subjects until there can be a mutual, intelligent discussion of the matter. Letters are sometimes a little too one sided. I guess I need someone to help me rise above that certain ordinary, everyday plane that the majority of the world seems to be engulfed in. I guess we all need to back away from life every once in a while and watch the mad whirl continue without us. Yeh, it's been a good long time since I questioned life in detail or speculated about some of its oddities. I guess intelligent discussions are almost a necessity at times to help a person regain the proper perspective. Therein lies the worth of a good confessor! Must stop – hate to – but I must – for the time being, anyway.

With that I'll sign off rather abruptly, John, as it's getting late. You mentioned something about getting here in June – write me about it and we'll get together. Forgive this crazy, mixed up letter, John, I'll make more sense next time I see you. I almost hate to write anymore – I make such little sense. Try to understand, John. Write soon.

> *Sincerely,*
> *Sonny*

Search for a decent-paying summer job dominated Johnny's thoughts when he reached home. The Reading Railroad often hired college students to work on special projects. Their personnel office, within walking distance of the house, made it easy for him to inquire about any positions which might be open.

"Any jobs for college students?" he asked the personnel clerk.

"Well, you're in luck, we have quite a few this year. The company is upgrading about thirty miles of track northeast of the city. The work will be manual labor which means you will have to pass a physical."

"Sounds like something I would like to do. When can I take the test?"

"First of all fill out this application, and we'll see about the physical."

Everything went well. His veteran status helped and Johnny happily reported to the family that he had a perfect job for the summer. He could not only contribute to the needs of the house but also save for his sophomore year at St. Michael's where he had decided he would stay as a pre-law major. Johnny began to like the house, the row of townhouses, and the neighborhood in general.

After a few weeks Johnny suggested the living room needed a new 21" television set.

"We have some other things to do before we can spend money on a 21" TV," said his mother.

"With everybody working I think we should have something at home to entertain us. This old set seems pretty dated."

"Mom, a 21" TV would be fun!" Louis and Sylvia almost shouted.

"OK, maybe we can buy one on credit. See if you can find one you like."

A week later a new Zenith 21" TV console costing $20 a month for one year, purchased in his father's name, sat at one end of the living room. Everybody loved seeing it there. Bishop Sheen's "Life Is Worth Living," became one of the family's favorite programs.

Work on the railroad gave Johnny the perfect outlet for physical labor and meeting other college students. In upgrading the railroad tracks, all of the wooden ties had to be replaced with new ones which had been treated with a preservative coating. The iron rails, for the most part still very usable, were raised to allow the new ties to slide beneath them. One of the other students and Johnny became fairly close friends because of their mutual interest in things Catholic.

"Ted, it's good to know someone else who takes his religion seriously."

"Yes, for some reason not too many of us like to get into the religious aspects of our lives. I'm glad we've made a connection," answered Ted Radomski, a medical student at Jefferson in Philadelphia. "If you're interested,

I usually attend a meeting in West Philly with a group of Catholic students who discuss ways of making the Church a more dynamic part of our lives."

"Sounds good. Of course, I don't have a car yet. If we could ride down together in yours I'll be happy to go along."

Johnny attended a couple of meetings, found them reasonably interesting, then decided not to get too involved since most of his next year would be spent in Vermont.

Lou had a tryout with the Phillies baseball team that summer. Although they liked him, they really wanted tall southpaws. Lou's five-ten height and right handedness didn't meet those qualifications. He took a job with a shoe factory. After one day he told them he would not be back.

"That machine I was working on slammed down so quickly I thought I'd lose a finger. I'll just find something else to do."

Johnny's mother worked at a local hospital stripping beds and cleaning rooms. She really had no other qualifications regarding employment possibilities. His father did get a job at the small industrial plant for which he had applied the year before. He rarely complained, had a few beers with some men from the parish who lived in the same area of town. They all liked his company and his gift of story-telling.

On one late Saturday afternoon Johnny sat reading *Man and Superman* by George Bernard Shaw when his father returned from the neighborhood bar and said to him, "Johnny, when are you going to go out and have some fun?"

"Dad, I am having fun. This writer has a lot to say. I enjoy it."

"Hell, at your age I was out all the time. How are you going to meet any girls sitting around reading?"

"Look, you know I have to save every penny I can for college. If I spend it, will you give me any?"

"Ah, forget it! I just want to see you have more fun in life."

"I *am* having fun. I like my work on the railroad. And it's good to be home for a while. Your kind of fun will come later."

"And when are you going to get some fat and muscle on those bones of yours?"

"Who knows? I can handle things on the job. Nobody worries about how skinny I am. Don't worry about me. By the way, you're looking pretty thin yourself these days. Are you sure you're all right? Maybe you should see a doctor."

"I don't bother with doctors."

On July 2nd Johnny's father celebrated his 56th birthday. On August 20th he died. An autopsy showed his lowest spinal vertebrae had deteriorated so badly the nerves no longer functioned, which is why his father never complained of pain despite a continuous loss of weight and low energy level. Johnny had insisted he go to an internist rather than a general practitioner about two weeks before he died. The doctor placed him in the same hospital where their mother worked. This allowed her to see him frequently during the day. Johnny never went to visit him. He had liked his father for a number of reasons; he never really loved or respected him.

Mary took his passing very hard. Their marital problems always took second place to the committed love they had for one another. Sylvia had spoken to her one day about her father's drunken condition at one of Lou's American Legion baseball games where he had become a spectacle with his off-color remarks about the umpire.

"Don't ever talk about your father like that! He told me the other day he looked forward to the day you graduated from high school. He always loved all of you."

"Have you made any arrangements for the funeral?" asked Johnny.

"Yes. Sister Edmunda told me they always use the Kopicki Funeral Home when one of the sisters dies. It's on the south end of town."

"Mom, do we have enough money to pay for the funeral?"

"Johnny, you know I cashed in all of the life insurance policies to help with the move. We'll just have to do what we can do with the money we have."

"Well, I guess you can have some of the money I've saved for college," he said, knowing the added sacrifices he would need to make throughout the year. He knew one thing; with Louie out of high school, the family would have to survive without him. He had to return to St. Michael's no matter what.

Sister Edmunda visited the family almost every day before the funeral, scheduled the same day as Lou's birthday on the 23rd.

"Mary, I know this must be a heavy cross for you to bear. Trust in Our Lord and everything will work out. You have the children, and Sylvia will get some income from Social Security until she is 18. Did you know about that?"

"I don't know much about anything anymore. Maybe we shouldn't have left Shenandoah, after all," as her tears fell into her handkerchief.

"And Johnny's home now. Maybe he can enroll in a school closer to

Reading."

"He said he wants to go back to Vermont, he likes it there. I don't know what I'm going to do when he leaves," she said despondently.

At the viewing of the body Johnny could not shed a tear. When the services ended he said to Lou, "Perhaps we can do something to make him proud that he had us. Whatever else he was, he was there for us, in his own way."

"Yeah, I guess so."

Aunt Helen, his father's only sister, and the other members of the family could not believe a burial plot had been purchased in a city he had lived in just one year.

"Mary, why wasn't he buried back home?" asked Helen.

"Helen, I know there are some plots up there. Maybe one of you can use them some day. The kids wanted him here. Besides, our two lots are next to my brother Joe's."

"Well, I know he's not happy about it, wherever he is."

"He's in a better place, probably purgatory, I hope. He did have the last rites in the hospital, I saw to that. He looked at peace after the priest blessed him and he received Communion. Thank God I worked there."

Two weeks after the funeral Sister Edmunda visited the house to see how things were going.

"The Social Security checks for Sylvia will start coming in next month. Louis is working for a plumber now and I guess I will keep my job at the hospital. Johnny has his job at the railroad until school begins."

"Let me talk to him, perhaps this weekend."

When Johnny learned his aunt wanted to see him, he just knew what she had in mind. He went up to the convent to visit her.

"Johnny, how are you doing? Your mother is almost sick about your leaving home now that your Dad has died. Maybe you could put off school again for a while and help her to get her bearings. I know that's a lot to ask especially since you seem very happy at St. Michael's."

"Well, they're expecting me to edit the paper when I return and I'll be on the student council as well. If I don't go back I wonder if I'll ever get that opportunity again," answered Johnny, trying to convince himself that nothing would keep him from that college degree he had always wanted. He could not believe another delay had developed in his plans.

"God has a way of testing us, doesn't He? And always remember that when we give of ourselves unselfishly we usually get repaid a hundredfold. He pays us back in ways we cannot even imagine."

"You may be right. Still, I've been hoping Louis could help over the next few years, if he finds a job he can stay with for a while. Sylvia can work part time while in school and Mom will be better off if she continues to work. The Social Security check will help also. I don't know why they couldn't do it," Johnny said, as his emotions slipped slowly into the terror of having to live his life looking for a challenging career without a degree to get him through the door.

"Well, you have about three weeks before the next semester begins. Perhaps by then you will be able to reach the right decision." The frustration she could feel coming from her nephew she had shared so much with over the last few years penetrated her own heart more deeply than she had expected. She wondered when he would finally be free to follow his dreams.

"That's what I'll do. I'll see how things develop over the next couple of weeks. In the meantime, I have my job on the railroad."

One week later his mother fell into a mood of despair so deep she could not leave the house to go to work. She looked at her oldest son as the only one who could save her from this newest crisis in her life. "I really don't want to keep you from going to college, but do you have to go back to St. Michael's?"

"Mom, one thing is sure, if you can't find the energy to go back to work someone is going to have to work to pay off the mortgage to this house and keep us together. Let me talk to the personnel office at the railroad and see if I can stay on there. Don't worry about me. Somehow I'll get that degree I've been after for so long." He wanted to take her in his arms and assure her of his loyalty. He could not. As much as he wished to love her unconditionally he wanted his freedom even more, and sometime in the future, perhaps that day would come.

When Johnny finished his day's work out in the hot August sun he called the personnel office for an appointment to see the manager. Mr. Yoder told him to stop by on his way home.

"Mr. Yoder, as you know, my father passed away and it looks like I'm not going to return to college this year. Any chance I can stay on when the summer job ends?"

"The outside project will definitely end soon. Perhaps you could work here in personnel. I need someone to file and do other office work. You will not be paid as much, of course. Does that interest you?"

"Right now, that sounds okay with me."

"See me when the outside rail job is done, and it will be good to have you on board," said Mr. Yoder, who now seemed friendlier than the first time he had met him. A bachelor, who had worked for the railroad for many years, Mr. Yoder had an immediate affection for his new assistant soon after he began work in the office.

A brief note to Johnny's friend, Joe, brought the following reply:

October 11, 1955
Maternity of the B.V.M.
Dear John,

The news about your father's death and the resultant disorder in your life was a surprise and something of a shock to me. I am sorry for not writing earlier, I planned to, but ... There is no need to say more now that I am back at the typewriter.

I have prayed for your father and for you. I had only met him in passing a few times but I know that you will miss him. Your own troubles were even more of a surprise to me since I had thought you were set at St. Michael's for the next few years. There isn't much for me to say on those lines until I learn more of your plans, so I will let it go at that.

It would be wonderful to have you and your brother come to see me here. I don't suppose I have seen him since that day I made a decision which cost his team a baseball game (and gave it to my brother's team). I can still hear him saying to me, "And you're going for a priest!" Well, bring him along if he feels he can talk to me by now.

I hope it won't be too long before you can come, although I don't want in any way to put you on the spot since things are no doubt still mixed up for you.

How is Alma, John? Has anything happened there? Do you think she would mind getting a letter from me? If you think it would do any good please give me some of the background and I shall write.

Had a pleasant surprise about three weeks ago. Our old friend Richard dropped in to see me. He was working in a town in Maryland as a chemist and dropped down before going into the Army. He hasn't written to me since but I presume he is with the colors by now. He looks and acts a lot older, but is essentially the same old Dick.

Things here are wonderful. With each passing year, and they are

*passing quickly – this is the sixth, the life gets better and better. I am
in theology now and feel all the closer for that. The studies are not
bad this year, but with so many extra things buzzing around in my
head, the time becomes no more plentiful. God certainly has been
good to me. I shall never understand why. Even if I had to leave
tomorrow, I should have to be eternally grateful for His blessings
over the last five years, especially the last three.*

*I guess that will do it for now, friend. Please write soon and tell
me what is happening with you. Remember always that God does
have a place for you in this life. That place may change from one
day to the next for a long time, but He is always watching and guiding
you to Him. Cooperate, listen, move at His touch and that is where
you will end – with Him.*

*The most consoling dogma of our religion is the Divine
Indwelling in our souls – God is with us. He has come to us who are
lost, who are weak, come to us to strengthen us and guide us. The
way to happiness is to let Him be our impulse, let Him be our
inspiration. Goodbye now and please pray for me; I do for you.
Regards to all.*

Yours in Our Lord,
Joe

Ever grateful for the friendship his seminarian buddy continued to show
him, Johnny became certain Joe would become one of the Paulist Fathers'
most dynamic members. He prayed once again that he would one day see Joe
ordained to the priesthood. Mother Edmunda prayed that the future held
greater promise for her nephew than he imagined possible. Sylvia and Louis
felt relieved that their older brother was home to stay. Sylvia transferred to
the commercial course curriculum at the high school after a couple of failures
in Algebra and Latin. Lou managed to stay at his latest job of delivering fuel
tanks to various businesses.

"Johnny, how about stopping by my house to fix a water heater in the
basement?"

"Mr. Yoder, I'm not sure I can be of any help. That's not something I've
done very much of," answered Johnny, who suspected the manager had other
ideas as well.

"That's too bad. It might have given us a chance to get to know each other better."

Within a week Johnny received notice that the job had been terminated. With no regrets Johnny thanked his boss for the extra weeks of work he had given him and soon after took a Christmas season job at Pomeroy's, one of the town's better department stores. He knew he wouldn't be there long. He did wonder exactly where he might work the following year.

"Mom, I see there's an ad in the help wanted section for an assistant buyer's position with IGA. That sounds like something I might enjoy doing."

"Good luck, son. I hope you can get it," his mother replied, with a voice that could no longer hide the deep malaise becoming entrenched in her whole being.

"Mom, you have to start believing we're all going to make it. Soon you may want to begin working again. Until then just take care of things at home." His words of confidence bolstered his own hopes that he could stay resilient himself.

Early the next day Johnny called the Independent Grocers Association and made an appointment to interview for the job.

"I see you've done some college work. Any reason why you're not continuing on?" asked Mr. Overley, the regional owner.

"Yes, my father died last summer. The two jobs I've had since then were only temporary. I would like to think I can make a career of this position."

"Well, it certainly looks like you have the qualifications. When can you start?"

"Whenever you wish."

"Come in for an orientation tomorrow morning at eight. Will that be okay?"

"I'll be here. Is there a dress code I need to follow?"

"A shirt and tie will be fine."

Happily, he reported to his mother, brother and sister, that he had found a job he might actually like. He also told his cousin Larry, an engineer at Western Electric, and the only other Scislowicz in town. Impressed by this former bombardier, who served in the Pacific during World War II, and his loving wife Mary, Johnny sometimes wondered if he too could do something in the engineering field, or some technical field related to it.

"Johnny, now that you have a permanent job, I guess you'll forget about college."

"Larry, I'm going to get a degree one way or the other. I just haven't figured out exactly how. At least I have two years in."

"Just don't drop the idea of a degree. Engineering's a tough course. Have you ever thought about becoming a metallurgist or chemist?"

"Not really. You know I was in the seminary one semester at St. Michael's and liberal arts seem to be my strong points. Before my Dad died, I wanted to return and continue on as a pre-law student. In the Air Force I tested well for technical skills. Maybe I shouldn't close that door completely."

"Well Johnny, have a beer and celebrate your new job."

"Johnny, have you talked to Sister Edmunda lately?" asked Mary in her usual jaunty voice.

"Yes, we all went down to the Villanova to visit her in the new motherhouse at Christmas. Mom's not too happy that she is no longer here in Reading. I'm glad I picked up that used Chevy in November and finally got licensed to drive. She wasn't too happy about my spending money on the car. Now, we need it just to see her. Mom needs that contact with Sister since Dad died."

"Johnny, you know we feel badly about not having any children, especially since Larry has a really good job. A baby is exactly what we need right now. When we saw Sister Edmunda at your Dad's funeral she promised to pray to Saint Philomena and asked us to pray to her as well. So far – no luck."

"Mary, if Sister Edmunda prays for you, something good will happen. By the way, I'm enjoying that job at IGA. Placing orders with the sales reps of different food companies, supervising and sometimes helping the grocers with their orders and keeping track of inventory make for a busy day. So far, at least, it's not too boring."

"How's your mother holding up?" asked Larry.

"Well, each day I keep hoping she'll snap out of her depressed mood. She may have to see a psychiatrist if things don't change for the better."

Two months into his job as an assistant buyer, Johnny felt trapped in the monotonous daily routine. At night he tossed in his bed, thought the world had come to an end for him, and searched for an escape into a more exciting future. "Maybe Larry's ideas about metallurgy made some sense," he thought. Perhaps he could find an inexpensive school and see if he had the ability to be come a metallurgist.

CHAPTER FIVE

At the motherhouse in Villanova, Sister Edmunda continued her adjustment to the new reality which deprived her of the familiar grounds of Mt. Alvernia. She had not taught any college level courses since the late 1930s and diligently mastered her newest challenge in teaching junior sisters Latin and Algebra. As always, the patience and persistence she had invariably had in the past made her a popular instructor. In response to a letter from Celia in April, 1956 she discussed her sister Mary and her nephew, Johnny.

May we always bless and love the Holy Will of God. Thank you for the letters of February 19 and March 5 and for the donation too. Mary was here with Johnny and Sylvia to give us a helping hand last Saturday. Johnny did outside work while Mary and Sylvia cleaned the windows of the first floor. Mary is still buried in her depression. I'm concerned about her, but I promised the good God that to prove my living faith and trust in His Merciful Love I would not worry, so I'm not worrying, but praying and trusting. Please say a prayer for her when you remember her. Her case is becoming serious and will tend to aggravate unless she snaps out of it.

Johnny is a great consolation to her, but he does want to take advantage of the standing $3,000 on the G.I. help for his education. I'm for it, too. At present, he finally is decided upon metallurgical engineering. He matured emotionally and otherwise. As always, the Cross of Christ has always only our good as its aim. This cross of his mother's emotional instability has thrown the responsibility upon his shoulders and, as far as I can see, he is progressing admirably. There are no true and permanent values here below, but those that *blossom and fruit in suffering. He hopes to go to Belmont College (a Benedictine school) in North Carolina next Sept. (year). Belmont College has an affiliation, or something of this sort, whereby the students do their basic work at Belmont and, then, complete the course at the State University of No. Carolina or at Notre Dame. This is, of course, heaven for Johnny. If only Mary could muster enough unselfish courage to go along with the poor boy and help him! They are to come to me with his papers, etc. this Sunday, God willing.*

Rev. Mother is progressing with her visitations, so, even though she writes nothing about the return date, we expect her before Easter.

I am so happy about our new Holy Week Liturgy. It will bring us so much closer to Christ's Passion, I think. Aren't we Catholics becoming a very closely woven family? God, how grateful we should be for the great grace of being born and raised Catholics!

"Maryview" is putting on its spring look. In a few days, it will be singing its solemn canticles of praise to its Lord and Creator. Our "Alex" remains the same unfriendly master of his domain. In fact, he bit our Reading chauffeur after he tore his trousers. We had to take him for a distemper injection.

In union of prayer and with love, I am ever yours in the Two Hearts,

Sr. M. Edmunda

Sister Edmunda attempted to eliminate her sister Mary's depressed state from her mind without much success. On the next visit from Johnny she asked him, "Is there a mental health professional your mother could see?"

"Dr. Allen has an office nearby on 5th Street. Perhaps he could be of some help."

"Why don't you make an appointment to see him. There may be some medication she could take. I know this is another burden for you. Pray that we may all be able to see her through these black days."

CHAPTER SIX

One afternoon, after he had returned from work, his mother sat across the kitchen table from him, her eyes swollen from crying. Black marks appeared below her eyes, her hair uncombed, and a smell of depression surrounded her very presence. She looked at him with desperation.

"Johnny, women like me shouldn't have children."

"Mom, why are you saying that?"

"I'm too much of a problem, to myself and to all of you. I'm not the kind of mother I wanted to be."

"Oh God, Mom, if only perfect people had children there wouldn't be very many people around. You've given us everything you could."

"I don't know. Look at Alma. She has two boys and a third baby on the way in just three years. I don't know how she can handle all of that. And we can't do much to help, with her in Philadelphia. You want to go away to college again, and this time to North Carolina. I can't help with that either."

"Maybe we can go to see Dr. Allen. He's not that far away. If he can make you feel better about yourself you'll be able to go on."

"I don't know. Can we afford the medical bills?"

"Mom, we have to try this. I'll call him tomorrow?"

"Okay, son. Thank you. And Jesus help us," she whispered through lips reddened all around by a constant sucking to relieve the torment within her clouded mind.

The next day Johnny called Dr. Allen's office from his desk at work.

"How badly does your mother feel?" the receptionist asked.

"She can't bring herself to leave the house. I'm getting concerned about letting her stay alone during the day when we are away. We must have her see the doctor as soon as possible. We live very close by on Church Street."

"Let me talk to him. He's finishing a session right about now." After a few minutes she said, "Bring her in at noon today. The doctor will see her then."

"Thank you. Thanks a lot. I really appreciate this," answered Johnny, relieved that some professional help would enter the picture.

"Mr. Overley, I'd like to take some extra time off at lunch today. My mother has a doctor's appointment at noon. It is something of an emergency."

"Okay, take as much time as you need." He had a Wall Street Journal in front of him, which Johnny noticed he usually had on his desk each day.

When Johnny reached home his mother could barely pull herself out of the living room chair she often sat in during the day. He got her into a sweater to keep her warm during the short walk to Dr. Allen's office. The receptionist took some information into the doctor before they proceeded into his comfortable-looking surroundings.

"Let me talk to your mother privately if you don't mind," said the doctor after he had shaken Johnny's hand.

"Certainly." Johnny liked the doctor immediately. His friendly air made him seem like someone who could be trusted to do the right thing.

After two weeks of a strong antidepressant medication, his mother showed little sign of recovery. The doctor recommended an electro-convulsive therapy as a way to relieve his mother of her depression. The therapy worked. Within a week she said to her children that she really wanted to return to work at the hospital to help pay the bills.

In August Johnny notified the owner of the company that he had decided to return to college.

"I wish you had told me earlier. You could have helped train your replacement." He was not too pleased with Johnny's early departure from the position. He had liked all of Johnny's qualities and would have enjoyed watching him grow in the company.

"Well, everybody, I'm sorry to leave you all again. Belmont Abbey College did accept me in their metallurgical engineering program. It's a Benedictine school and really not that far away. I'll miss you while I'm away. I'm sure I'll be home for Thanksgiving. The car is yours, Lou, while I'm away. Enjoy it."

When Johnny arrived at Belmont he found how close the school was to Charlotte and Gastonia. And directly across the highway a beautiful academy run by the Sisters of the Sacred Heart sat within walking distance. This totally

Catholic atmosphere made him feel the church had made some inroads in North Carolina, a seemingly total Baptist state.

His roommates at the college were something else again. One fellow, a veteran, obviously older than the average student, seemed bent on knocking some normality into his apparently demented head by throwing himself against one of the walls of the room. Within a few days the administration had him removed from the school. Johnny knew nothing about what finally happened to him. The other roommate, a rather reserved, quiet oriental, and Johnny easily adapted to each other, especially when he found out Johnny had spent 30 months in Japan. Not that Chen cared that much about the Japanese, however, that an oriental face was not an obstacle to Johnny as it was to many Americans.

A new roommate assigned to them came from Florida; highly energetic, good looking and excited about life in general. His name was John. All three of them, delighted that they had somehow found the right combination of personalities and interests, settled in for the semester.

Another shock soon hit Johnny. Tentative, at best, that he could actually pass the science and math courses required for an engineering degree, the Physics instructor, hired to teach the course, never showed up. A gentleman with fractured English arrived to take his place.

"I guess you only get what you pay for," Johnny said to his roommates as three weeks passed by. Frustrated by this development, he did his best in the Physics course, pursued the other subjects with some interest, and hoped the semester would come to a quick end.

"Johnny, I can't get interested in any of my subjects either. Let's rent a car and travel around the state. I have a few friends here, a girlfriend at Queens College in Charlotte, and some family friends. Maybe we'll get some southern fried chicken at the Sims. Their son and I knew each other at the other Benedictine school I attended back in Florida. Of course you will have to rent the car in your name since I'm not 21 yet. We'll split the cost."

"Why not? I'm game. We really should keep it to long weekends."

A letter dated September 17th arrived from his aunt, Sister Edmunda, with the "Maryview" letterhead, from Villanova.

> *Dearest Johnny,*
> *I have been looking for a letter from you, although I thought you would like to tell me something about the school proper and this would not be earlier than Friday; hence, this morning's letter was a*

surprise.

So, Father Bernard thought more of your credits than I? I couldn't see you any lower than sophomore at Belmont and he placed you as a junior? God be blessed for this, although the placement itself is not the important thing; it's the goal and the path that will lead to it that is all important. To be ranked among the juniors must have been a pleasant surprise to you?

However, Johnny, please watch out for the courses you have taken and will take. Are they in line with your basic preparation for a major in Metallurgy? What will you take this year? What are the other schools that have the course in Metallurigcal Engineering? You mention a transfer in January? Does this mean that you would go to N. D. in February?

Father Brooks is at N. D. You remember him from Reading? I could write to him although I don't know how much good this would do. Perhaps, asking Father Leichner would be excellent. He may have friends among the Holy Cross Fathers. But I am willing to write to Father Brooks.

This difficulty of being settled in a college is nothing new to me. All of our Sisters find so much red tape, so many cross-stitches, that if they do not flounder, I'd wonder what's the matter. Although, Johnny dear, it is best to decide on something and then push the cart in one direction, without any discouragement. You decided on Metallurgy, so one decision has been made – as to where you'll take the degree, decide now. Father Bernard, doubtless, has a list of colleges where the double degree does not hold. Perhaps, with another summer school, you could graduate in 1958, from one of these – and, then, find further opportunities opened. All will depend upon what courses are needed for the degree in Metallurgy. Make a thorough study of all this – Please let me know what courses you must have for this degree? And what courses are you taking now? 17 s.h. is not too great of a load unless you'll take more than one science. With all this before us, I'm very much interested and I'll be waiting for further news from you.

Don't let any of the problems upset you. Believe me that this is the regular thing. If it was otherwise, I'd be much surprised. I'm making a novena to our Lady of Mercy; it's main intention will be your failing.

You'll like Belmont? You like it! Excellent! This is saying much, indeed!

Alma wrote immediately after your departure. She told me how happy she was to hear of Louis' Drafting course. Would that he continue! As yet, I haven't heard from Reading. I am waiting anxiously for news about Louis.

God be with you! May Mary guide and keep you safe!
Love in the Two Hearts,
Sr. M. Edmunda

Sobered by his aunt's observations, Johnny thanked her for her realistic understanding of what he faced in pursuing a goal which just might be beyond his capabilities even under the best of circumstances. He prayed in the beautiful abbey church for the gift of perseverance.

"Hey, old buddy, Let's get that car we talked about and scout around," called his friend John with great eagerness after their last class on Friday afternoon.

"John, you know I just realized my insurance on my car back home may not cover me here at school."

"Well let's check it out.

At the car rental agency in Belmont they asked for the driver's licenses of both of them, and said nothing about insurance. Johnny decided to take a chance that his coverage back home would cover them.

"Let's toss a coin to see who drives."

"It's in my name. I want first crack at it," answered Johnny, pleased to have a better car to drive than his old Chevy. "Let's drive over to the academy first and see if we can get a look at some of the girls," he added.

"You realize you're a little old for those high school girls, don't you?"

"At five-eight and 140 pounds I don't think I'm going to look too ominous to them."

The drive into the expansive, beautifully landscaped grounds of the academy reflected the affluence of the girls who attended the school administered by an order of nuns who in many cases came from the same kind of background.

"Beautiful place, isn't it?"

"The nuns probably have some strict rules about dating, no doubt."

As they neared the entrance to the main building Johnny noticed a girl who certainly looked Japanese.

"How about that? A girl just for me."

"Johnny, I bet you couldn't get a date with her, no matter how cute you think you are."

"Well, let's see. Bet you a beer," he laughed.

He stopped the car, parked about 20 feet from where she stood and approached with one of his usual friendly smiles. "Hi! My name is John, a student at the abbey. May I ask you a question?"

"Hi! Yes, sure. I'm new here. What would you like to know?" she asked, her "d" sounding somewhat like those he had heard in Japan. Her "l" sounded much more American.

"I know we just met, but after spending thirty months in Japan I feel I'd like to get to know you since our schools are so close together. May I ask your name?"

"My name is Masako Hinata. The Korean war, is that why you were in Japan?"

"Yes, I served in the Air Force near Hiroshima and also at Misawa in northern Honshu."

"My family came from Tokyo. I was never in Misawa."

"Masako, what a coincidence, I knew a wonderful girl in Japan by that name."

"John, maybe we could spend some time at the Friday night dances we have here at the academy. We could get to know each other better. And you could invite your friend as well."

"That sounds great. His name is John too. Maybe you could invite one of your friends to meet him."

"Okay. See you next Friday."

John returned to the car and said, "You owe me a beer!"

"Did you actually get a date? No way!"

"I got you one too. We will meet them at the school dance next Friday."

"Johnny, I'm starting to believe in you. I think we're both going to have some fun this semester."

Happy and carefree in the company of his new friend, Johnny also felt totally guilty about the failure he felt descending upon him regarding this latest attempt at settling into a serious career effort. Math at this level proved almost impossible to master. Physics totally uninteresting, and chemistry at least doable. His spiritual life also seemed at a dead end. He went to Mass, and Benediction on some evenings. A letter to his aunt brought a response written on the feast of St. Teresa in early October.

Dearest Johnny,

No, I didn't suspect anything of what you wrote. My faith and confidence in God's Merciful Love precludes these dark thoughts. I accept, or try to accept, all shadows as His love, but I do know that He does not try us forever.

I suppose the basic work for a degree in metallurgical engineering would demand chemistry as a major. How do you like your courses? How are you faring out in mathematics? You were not too certain here. It is good to know that if conditions demanded, you could end at Albright, but let us hope that all will go well and end as you planned. Have you heard anything about the transfer to Notre Dame? Keep metallurgy as your goal; don't swerve from the path leading to it.

What did you mean by "continued reasons" for not being interested in you? Johnny, I always was and will be. I'll continue being, perhaps, painfully frank, but this is my policy and I don't intend to change it. I just cannot digest duplicity; double-dealings are beyond me. Then, too, I'm practical and realistic; I cannot follow dreams. Hence, I'll surprise you with jolts, but this is only to bring you back to solid thoughts. It's not a waning interest at any time.

How is life at Belmont? What is the enrollment? Have you made any friendships? What are your extracurricular interests or activities? Do you find individual interest in the professors? Who are your professors – chiefly Benedictines? Do you correspond with the nurse-friend at Reading?

We began our courses with the Junior professed. I am enjoying the College Algebra and Coll. Latin I assigned to me – but to open one's books after 33 years is not a simple matter. Age and the accumulated rust are challenging opponents. How differently one feels at the turn of 60!! The spirit is young; but the mental tools are on the decline.

I am praying that Lou's job will continue; but if he lost it, may he find another. I also pray that he continue his course. Mother wrote almost 3 weeks ago; she's apparently feeling well. May God keep her so! Sylvia was to contact the Sisters at Darby, relative to her acceptance after graduation, but I haven't heard whether she did or did not.

I sent Alma's new baby a complete set – i.e. sweater, cap and

booties – all the work of good Sr. Imelda. Alma was pleased. Little
Theresa is to be baptized on the 21ˢᵗ.
    God bless and love you! In His Heart, I remain -
Affectionately,
Sr. M. Edmund
Are you a daily communicant? Pray for me, please.

The Friday night dance at the academy made Johnny realize he had walked into a world different from this own social background. Monitors made certain the dances never escalated to any kind of foreplay by more adventurous dancers.

"John, I am enjoying Masako, but have you seen those Cuban girls?"

"Johnny, don't let the low-cut dresses give you any ideas. That's the way they dress. It's a culture thing."

The following week they talked about possibly meeting some nursing students in Charlotte. John had an old girlfriend at one of the colleges. He believed she might be able to help them get introduced to a few of them.

After he had informed Sister Edmunda about his decision to drop the physics course Johnny received a letter dated in late October.

Dearest Johnny,

Your letter of the 17ᵗʰ arrived just as I was preparing to leave for Washington, D.C., where the St. Jude school and convent were to be blessed on Sunday - We made the trip by car – 5 hours each way – (Our Sisters teach there.) All went well, but I'm still dizzy; traveling is too taxing for me.

Johnny, if I were writing the letter that you sent me, it would run like this: – "I found physics too much for the load that I'm carrying, so I dropped it. I'll go on a straight chemistry course." Don't you think it would sound more like a man?

Perhaps, it isn't only perseverance that accounts for your inability to swing two sciences and a math course? But, if you think you do need perseverance, please don't introspect and project – and waste more time – but apply yourself to the tasks at hand. After all, straight chemistry is something. It will get you places with effort and application.

What did you mean by "continued reasons"? If I wrote that, it certainly did not refer to you, but to myself; even if I can't recall the context, I'm sure of this, because my trust in you has not waned, so I could not have you in mind. One year away from school is not so important. I closed my books 33 years ago; I'm nearing 60, after a very strenuous life – and I still can pick up the threads where I left them. True that I must prepare when I want to enter the classroom, but I'm enjoying the preparation immediately. Hours just fly and I forget all my worries and aches. The hours of actual class work are hours of bliss. If any good students enjoy the minutes 1/10 as much as I do, I'm sure that their days are happy ones, too. They appear satisfied, even if college algebra is not too easy and the Latin vocabulary and syntax not too inviting. Come! Tell me that you're in love with calculus and chemistry; you'll fall in love as soon as you give your time to both generously. It's fun once we forget time and ourselves.

If you attend daily Mass, why not receive daily, with the permission of your confessor? You need light and strength. Why not meet the Source of Light and Strength each morning and beg for both? Try and you'll find life so different.

Mother planned to visit me on the way to or from the christening of little Therese, but I called her up Friday night to tell her that I wouldn't be home Sunday. I surely would have enjoyed her more than the visit to D.C., but Superiors willed it otherwise. She told me that Louis continued on the R.R. job at Birdsboro.

Until I hear again, I'm with you in the Two Hearts – prayerfully and devotedly,

S. M. Edmunda

Johnny attempted again to immerse himself in his studies. Maybe he *could* salvage the semester and continue with his studies in metallurgy. Another letter from his aunt arrived bolstering his new-found determination. He had also told her of a chance meeting he had with a sociology professor at the college.

Dearest Johnny,
May the Holy Will of God and Father be blessed, loved and praised by all!

Your letter of "Christ the King" was long in coming. It arrived this morning, but the posting date explained the delay. Thank you!

Your meeting of Mrs. Gwyn was a grace, indeed. How much we learn from others!! With Faith we can overcome all difficulties. Think of her when your faith in God and in His loving help for you is low. Learn that only difficulties make us "men", make us individuals of character. Not ease, not wealth, not prosperity.

You'll never know how much joy I found in your statement: "I have committed myself to metallurgy and there is no turning back." Will you try to hold on to this determination as to an anchor? It will get you far! Easy work, studies easily mastered, get us nowhere, believe me, Johnny. Genius, or success – call it what you will – is application to work to the nth degree. And, as you write about calculus, you will write about physics, chemistry, etc. The more inertia we overcome, the more sweat and grease we put into them, the more we shall learn to like them. Changing from one task to another, just because the former appears more fascinating and easier than the other, simply undermines our will power and perseverance. When you just can't seem to find any logic in the work, when all is dark as to the next step to be taken, etc., drop the book and pencil and take a stroll to the chapel and there beg for will-power, for light, for help. It will come miraculously.

What will happen to the Physics you dropped? Can you make it up somehow?

I have never lost faith in your abilities, Johnny. But, I was many a time disappointed in your lack of will power to make the best of them. Won't you pray to be able to overcome what is distasteful in hard mental work and then resolve to stick to your guns regardless the cost? Just be severe to yourself and chain yourself to this difficult task and in a short while you'll like it. Don't change; don't drop anything you begin. What are your chances of being accepted in Sept. 1957 in the Jr. year in Metallurgy, if your physics is not made up?

Bishop Sheen was on twice thus far - I think. We couldn't find him this week. But, he was far below his best when we did have him. If he continued in the telling of stories, as he began, he'll drop in his reputation, I think. Or did he reach his peak and is on the decline now!

We still don't know who won at the polls yesterday. Whether it's Eisenhower or Stevenson, he needs our prayers, indeed. God bless and love you always!

In His Love, I remain

Sr. M. Edmunda

After a careful reading of the letter, Johnny wondered how he had come to deserve the care and love of this extraordinary aunt of his. He knew that all she ever wanted, a saintly and disciplined life, in which he would fulfill all of the talents he undoubtedly had. He went to the chapel and prayed that somehow he would reach some kind of conclusion about how to proceed with his life which seemed to be continuously derailed.

At the end of November Johnny received another letter – this time without a letter from him.

Sunday

My dearest Johnny,

May we bless and love the Holy Will of God!

I have been thinking of you more than you could guess ever since you wrote about the dropping of the "all-important" physics, but since yesterday, I am almost sick over it. Sick for more reasons than one. Would that I could take it for you!! Would that I could change this and that.

Today, before I packed the catalog to return it to the good secretary at the Penn State U. Centre, at Pottsville, I studied the Metallurgy course. The Junior and Senior years' work is most interesting. The basic courses are exacting and taxing. They are stiff – but, the technical work, properly speaking – appears very inviting. I can see why your heart is set on it. This second semester the physics will certainly get you over the bridge. It will be the end of Mathematics and the basic sciences.

As I studied the years of your Metallurgy, I noticed that Anal. Geom. is given in the 1ˢᵗ semester of the Freshman year - Therefore, definitely you couldn't take it at Penn State and again that would be trouble. Couldn't you possibly, Johnny, approach your Dean and ask to have something done about the physics? But, let me put it the other way, do you see that with effort to a higher degree you could conquer the apparently impossible to take the Physics I before

February? You don't need the Sociology, so even if you dropped it, you wouldn't suffer any consequences. Of course, I don't want you to drop it – If you present the matter humbly, admit your hastiness, discuss the financial impossibility of a 5-year program, present the needs of the family, etc. – perhaps, they could do something in the line of permitting you to re-enter the course and to do extra work after class or so. Maybe you could spend the Xmas vacation at Belmont working on physics alone, even if this would entail an extra expense. If Mother couldn't see her way financially, perhaps, I could find someone to borrow you the money, which you could gradually return by working during the summer – What about trying? Perhaps, one of the students who is good in physics could be your monitor with a fee of some sort between now and Christmas – or now and February. Perhaps, you could even work up at home during the Xmas holy days, if you got a good start now.

But, Johnny, if this should be absolutely beyond your mental or physical strength, then, by all means: No. You and your health are more important to me and us than the courses. But, I saw that your heart is in the work, so I'm thinking and advising. This plan came to my mind and heart while I tearfully prayed for you today – I'll continue to pray for light for you.

There are some courses that I'm sure you could take by correspondence during the summer while you'd work and this would make you a full-fledged junior by Sept. 1957. It's only the physics, but let's try, if your health permits. It will call for a giving up of some time of leisure and pleasure – but what is this compared to the returns?

I'll be waiting for your answer.

In union of prayer, I am, lovingly yours sincerely in the Master's Heart. May He and His Mother bless you!

Sr. M. Edmunda

On the last day of November his aunt replied to a letter he had sent in response to her latest request to answer her suggestion about spending Christmas in Belmont to save the semester from complete disaster.

My dearest Johnny,

May we always bless and love the Holy Will of God!

Your letter came in today. I shall desist from making any comments. Perhaps, we have done too much doubting our own judgment; therefore, Johnny, please make a very good preparation before the Feast of the Im. Conception and for that of Christmas, with the intention that through Mary the Holy Will of God may be made known to us at the time of your Christmas vacation. Make a good Triduum before the 8th and a Novena before the 25th. Could you receive Holy Communion during these days of preparation and speak directly to Jesus in your heart with Mary at your side?

Johnny, as to me – all I can say is, that a college education is no essential factor to happiness in my opinion. It's a goal attained and as such gives us a grain of satisfaction, but, I am certain that there are many more people happily settled in life without it. The big thing is to do what God wants us to do. However, may I ask you once again to forego introspection and projection. These lead us nowhere. We (supposedly) cry over the spilled milk because others upset the bowl – the better thing is to try to see what God wills for us, accept this will ungrudgingly and, then, roll up our sleeves and get down to the job before us.

Johnny, as never before, I shall pray for you between now and Christmas – I am already in special prayers for you in the Novena which began yesterday (29th) – Until you come however, forget all, but the prayerful union with God in your intention to know your future, and plunge into your school work full-heartedly. This is His Will for you now, *so do it with a generous heart.*

Until I write again, my prayers and love are yours in the Hearts of Jesus & Mary,

Sr. M. Edmunda

The fall semester at Belmont Abbey fell into a kind of oblivion for Johnny. During the winter break, spent at home, he became convinced that he had to end this venture into a field for which he had no genuine interest or capability.

"Mom, I am going back to college to finish the semester. After that I'll be home for good."

"Johnny, what can I say? Sometimes we try to do more than we can. Maybe you'll be able to finish college some day."

"I don't know what made me think I could be an engineer like Larry. Whistling in the wind, I guess, trying to take on subjects I thought I could pass. Now I know better," he said resignedly.

"If you're going back by train maybe Louie can drive you to Harrisburg."

"Okay. He seems to be enjoying the car. I will leave on the Saturday after New Year. That way he won't miss any time off from work."

After a trip to Philly to see his sister Alma, her husband Earl and three children, he prepared for his return to North Carolina.

"Johnny, I'll be glad when you get back home. As soon as you find a job I'm going into the Air Force. My baseball prospects don't look that great and I can't seem to find any kind of work I like."

"Lou, you'll like the Air Force. I hope you get an assignment overseas during your enlistment. Those two and one-half years I spent in Japan made me feel like a man of the world."

"Syl, thanks for all the help you've been to Mom. In June you'll be finished with school. With the three of us working we should finish off the mortgage in no time."

On the way to Harrisburg a light snow began to fall. "Lou, I hope you will be extra careful when you drive back home," Johnny cautioned his brother as he enjoyed the drive to the train station. Their mother rode along for a final farewell.

"Johnny," his mother said in a worried tone,"be careful, take care of yourself, until we see you again."

"Mom, the next few weeks will go by quickly and I'll be home." His young brother stood by without saying very much. They shook hands warmly and exchanged farewells.

"Mom, let's get going. We still have to drive home," Louis said to his mother as they waved goodbye to Johnny as he boarded the train.

On the return trip they suddenly found themselves on a fairly steep hill with cars parked on both edges of the road waiting for better traction. Lou decided the old Chevy could easily descend with very little trouble. As they reached part of the way down the road another driver had turned onto the highway, intending to drive up the hill without checking the center of the highway for any traffic. Louis could not stop the Chevy. He slid gently into the oncoming car which had no chance to get out of the way. The car they hit slid backward, all the way down the hill as Louis kept bumping him further down.

"O' Jezusa, Matka Boska Czestohowa!" his mother kept screaming at every bump, certain that they would not make it home without serious injury. Her Polish prayers always surfaced in times of stress.

"Mom, don't worry, we're not going very fast. If he just lets his car drift backward we'll be okay." At the same time, he hoped nothing would happen to the Chevy. He knew Johnny would not be too happy about that. When they finally reached the bottom of the hill Louis and the other driver checked over each other's cars, found no real damage, and went on their way.

Soon after Johnny returned to Belmont Abbey he wrote to Sister Edmunda, told her of his decision to leave college, perhaps enroll at Penn's Wharton Extension in Reading and settle for a degree in accounting by attending evening sessions. He also mentioned Emily, a nurse he had dated a few times during his year in Reading. Sylvia had told Emily about her brother and they began a brief courtship which ended abruptly when he returned to college. She had the sweetest kiss Johnny had ever experienced; he wondered if they could date again when he returned home. Sister Edmunda's reply showed again the loving care she had for him and the family.

> *My dear Johnny,*
>
> *I was interested in what you have sent me. Wharton seems to fall into the picture excellently, but I desist from any remarks – leaving all in the merciful hands of God. Please pray for light that you may do what He wills. Perhaps, all that you have attempted was not in His designs for you. Perhaps, what you choose now is your pattern for life.*
>
> *There's this to remember, however, Johnny, that you are leaving college not because of home but because you will it. Please understand this statement. It was not until you faced the stark truth of having closed the future in metallurgy, by dropping physics, that you began to seek avenues of defense. Why am I so emphatic about this? You are too prone to project. Projection is always detrimental to our interior peace, without which little can be done. As long as we blame others for our mistakes and deficiencies, we can never make headway in any form of success. Will you please close this chapter of your past life forever, regardless how strong the temptation to continue to project may be? It's always unwholesome for our spiritual, moral, and character development and growth. Concentrate*

on each day's duties, chances, opportunities and snatch at them.

Now, the truth. College education, a degree, are not essential to our peace and contentment. There are many very noble and truly happy and successful people without it. The thing is to fulfill God's Holy Will wherever and however He wills it. Am I opposed to a degree; no! I would have been the happiest woman if you ended with one and you know that I did my best to convince mother to give you the chance you so well deserved. Is the degree episode closed? No! There are many people who receive degrees at 50 and even 60 – a degree opens the door for many opportunities, I agree – But, for the time being, let's forget it since you have decided to drop. At the moment, it seems to be logical.

That mother needs you now with Louis's behavior, I fully agree. She cannot go on and surely after June would find it absolutely impossible. If Louis had some sense of responsibility and love for the family, things would be different. Sylvia does deserve at least a year's course to see herself prepared for the problems of life. You found your line of work, it seems, to me – so, now, it's only steadfast "stick-to-itness" and all will begin rolling in the right direction. You'll be happy in the happiness of others. This noble thread of your soul and heart is too evident not to be appreciated. Then, too, Johnny, Mother seems to fall back upon you with almost childlike trust; she is your mother in God's designs, so our first duty is towards her. Make her happy now as you made her happy in all the days gone by and God's blessings will be with you. Do you realize fully what a mother's blessing means?!! "Whatever happens I want to be self respecting and conscience free" – says the author of "Myself" – you'll be conscience free when you'll be able to look into mother's sparkling eyes – eyes that will sing with pride in you – conscience free, when you'll see Sylvia's way paved – conscience free, when you'll see the home in proper condition with no fears for the future.

If you consider Emily your true choice, keep loyally to her and when things become cleared and happily shaped do marry. This will add another stroke of steadfastness. With all this, continue your studies. It will give you intellectual joy and satisfaction and, I am still hopeful, you will one day rejoice in being a degreed accountant or whatever God wills!

My fervent prayers are yours! Be happy, cheerful and trustful in

God's merciful love.
  All your in the loving Hearts of Jesus & Mary,
  Sr. M. Edmunda

"John, it's been great knowing you these past few months. The best part of my stay at Belmont Abbey has been our friendship."

"Johnny, you know I'm leaving too. I never write letters, but maybe we'll cross paths somewhere down the line. Have you said goodbye to Masako?"

"Yes, last night. We also don't know what the future holds for us. She promised to keep in touch when she returns to Connecticut. Her mother lives with a family in Greenwich – in some guest quarters."

"Are you going to Benediction tonight? Sometimes I think you still believe you are still in a seminary."

"Yes, why don't you come along, as a final farewell to the Abbey?"

"Sure, why not." John tucked his shirt carefully into his pants, checked his appearance in the mirror and apparently decided he looked ready to take on the world when he left North Carolina. That's what Johnny had always liked about his friend John, the great sense of self confidence and a stride to his walk which made him look taller than he was. Johnny hoped he could emulate his friend's approach to life.

As the Benedictine priest blessed the worshipers with the gold monstrance holding the blessed host, Johnny felt free once again. He knew the decision to return home and assure the success of the family's relocation to a large new city would bring him success as well. He did not know the details of how this would all develop, he just knew the best lay head. He thanked his Lord for being there, as always, in this special way.

Within two weeks of his searching through the help wanted section of the daily newspaper Johnny found one ad which looked worth pursuing; a brokerage house needed a trainee for the business. He called the listed number, set up an appointment for the next day, and after an interview with Mr. Bickel, the manager, returned home to tell the family he had a job he could really get excited about.

"Johnny, how can you become a stockbroker? You don't know anybody."

"Mom, I'll get to know them. The manager wants me to work in the office for a few months, start taking some correspondence courses from an institute in New York and eventually become registered as a New York Stock Exchange representative."

"How much does this job pay?"

"Not much to begin with. Fifty dollars a week to start."

"Johnny, you made more than that on your summer job with the railroad. I wonder if you're just dreaming again."

"Well, whatever it is, I'm going to give it five years and see what happens."

Entranced by the future possibilities of this new career he called his friend Sonny in Philadelphia to share his good fortune.

"Sonny, I'd like to visit all of you and get to see Charlotte and the kids. Is it true baby number three is on the way?"

"Johnny, how great of you to call. I've been hoping to get in touch before we return to California. My Army service is just about over. The baby is due in July and I told Charlotte I'd like to have you as the godfather."

"Just give me the date and I'll be there."

"We'll set the date for the christening as soon as the baby arrives. In the meantime come on down, maybe we can do some swimming in one of the pools nearby."

"Sounds good. I'll be there on Sunday."

Within a month Johnny became a godfather again. This time to a beautiful baby girl named Catherine. What a great way to bind a friendship which they all hoped would last a lifetime.

As part of his training at the brokerage house Johnny posted the prices of various New York Stock Exchange stocks as they passed on a tape projected about five feet above customers who came into the office to place orders or simply sit in the theatre-like chairs facing the tape. A humble way to begin an exciting career, the postings helped him learn the symbols of the Dow Jones and a hundred other stocks rather quickly. Johnny decided he would do whatever needed to be done to advance to a commissioned broker position with the firm.

"Johnny, I've enrolled you in a course which will give you a history of the New York Stock Exchange and explain the basics of investment trading."

"Thanks, Mr. Bickel, I guess I'm in a hurry to fill that chair next to Mr. Thomas."

"Johnny, you can call me Russ. By the way, how do you like this new office? We had been on that second floor office at least twenty-five years."

"I'm sure the customers appreciate not having to climb those stairs. Looks like I've come into the business at a good time."

"Well, it's good to have you. Some of my customers tell me you already have a professional air. Just stay with the program, be patient and you'll probably do very well." Johnny liked his manager and his calm mannerisms.

Within a year Johnny completed the two required courses, passed the Registered Representative examination, and enrolled in two evening courses at Villanova University with a degree in accounting as his major. He also joined the Toastmasters, the Junior Chamber of Commerce and stayed in close touch with his cousin Larry and his wife. Larry helped him immensely by recommending him to other employees at Western Electric. Many of them sold their holdings in AT &T, which owned Western Electric, for various reasons, and sometimes became regular clients for other transactions as well.

"Aunt Mary, I got a call from Sister Edmunda telling me to expect a call from a nun at their hospital in Chester," said Mary on a call to their home one evening. " You know, she's been praying that Larry and I will be able to find a baby to adopt."

"That's a good sign."

"You know, we went to Catholic Charities last year and they told us we would have to adopt an older child because Larry is almost forty. We really would rather have a baby."

"Mary, their hospital in Chester is strictly a maternity hospital. They must have a baby the mother cannot afford to raise and would rather adopt it out."

"I really hope so. I've been praying to St. Philmomena like Sister Edmunda suggested the last time we met."

"Well, let's hope for the best. Let me know what happens."

"I sure will."

The next day Mary received a call from Sister Dorothy, an administrator at the Sacred Heart Hospital in Chester.

"We may have some good news for you in the next few days. We have a woman who needs to give her baby up for adoption. I understand the state has already interviewed you and your husband to assure us you would be responsible parents. Of course Sister Edmunda has spoken highly of you. Let's hope the delivery goes well."

"Thank you, Sister. I'll be here waiting."

Larry, at school in North Carolina for the company, assured Mary he would return home on the weekend. On Thursday, a doctor called to let Mary know they had a baby boy.

"Larry, we have a boy. How soon can you get home?"

"I'll be there Friday night."

"Be careful, honey, I want you home safely."

On Saturday, they met Sister Dorothy at the hospital. Told they could not take the baby home for two weeks, they got their first glimpse of him in the nursery.

"He's ours," is all they could think and say.

Larry returned to North Carolina to complete his seminar. Mary purchased all the baby things, crib, etc. The happiest day of their lives occurred when they brought their son home. Sister Edmunda delighted in their joy.

In October, 1956, the Hungarian uprising resulted in 200,000 Hungarians seeking refuge in other countries when their revolution failed. A number of American agencies, including Catholic Charities, joined in the effort to place some 80,000 refugees who had been accepted by the United States. In the spring of 1957 Johnny read an advertisement placed by Catholic Charities in the Philadelphia Diocesan paper, "The Catholic Standard and Times", seeking sponsors for those who had not yet been placed with anyone.

"Mom, why don't we let Catholic Charities know we have room for at least one Hungarian refugee. With Lou in the Air Force, those two rooms on the third floor should be enough to accommodate someone looking for a home. What do you think?"

"You know, we have just the one bathroom, and getting to the third floor would mean going through your room. You'd better think about all that before you make any phone calls."

"Sylvia, how do you feel about it?"

"I guess we could give it a try. Maybe we would be able to get something for room and board. What if the person doesn't know any English?"

"Well, I guess we could teach English to whoever arrives. Let me think about it for a few days." Open and adventurous, Johnny called Catholic Charities in New York the next day to let them know of their willingness to become part of the placement effort.

"Thank you very much for calling. We really don't have any single Hungarians looking for accommodation, but we do have a young Dutch fellow who indicated he would like to live in the Pennsylvania Dutch country. His family left Indonesia because the nationalist movement under Sukarno was on the brink of expelling the Dutch. His father did not want to expose the family to any more threats against Dutch residents even though he had married an Indonesian woman. What do you think?"

"Well, you know we really aren't Dutch. The Pennsylvania Dutch are actually of German descent. If you explain that to him and he still wants to come I have no objections to having him."

"Okay, I'll explain that to him. By the way, he is an auto mechanic and speaks English. He should have no trouble getting a job. We'll be in touch shortly, and thanks again for your offer to take someone into your home."

The next weekend Jan arrived at the Reading Railroad station about three blocks from the house. Johnny greeted him enthusiastically, walked him down a short hill to the car and drove him to the house to meet his mother and sister. Jan's black hair and dark brown eyes gave him a decidedly non-Scandinavian look. Around five-ten in height, perhaps 160 pounds in weight, he carried himself like the son of a Dutch colonial with a somewhat superior attitude. Johnny wondered if the family's modest home would satisfy his expectations of America.

"Jan, here's where we live. I hope you'll like it."

"I will like it."

"Mom, this is Jan. Say hello while I take his bag up to his room."

"Hello Jan. Your name sounds like John in Polish."

"Yes, my name would be called John in America. Good to meet you and have me in your house," answered Jan as he bowed slightly toward her. Later he met Sylvia who viewed him somewhat cautiously.

Johnny set up an appointment for him at the local VW dealership where Jan worked for the six months he stayed with them. A fellow mechanic drove him to and from work. He had hoped Jan and his daughter would be attracted to each other and possibly marry. Instead, Jan met a slightly older divorcee with one child who invited him to go to Florida with her and marry. All three members of the family wished they had taken in a Hungarian as originally planned.

With his continuous reading of *Time* magazine, Johnny learned something about sex in the medical section he had not anticipated. Sex researchers cited that the risk of getting cervical cancer increased for women whose partners had not been circumcised. Since he intended to marry as soon as his income improved, he wanted to prepare himself for the event, especially since he had noticed a small polyp on the inside of his foreskin. The growth developed during his stay in Japan. He checked the yellow pages for a doctor who sounded Jewish and made an appointment to see Doctor Wisawitz, a family doctor with an office in town.

"Hello, my nurse tells me you want your foreskin cleared of some kind of growth. Lower your pants and let's take a look." Johnny liked his professional approach and receptive manner. He decided he would do whatever the doctor recommended.

"The best approach would be a circumcision, although I could remove it by cutting away part of the foreskin. That would reduce part of the foreskin so why not go the whole way. Are you planning to get married?"

"Not right away. Does that mean a trip to the hospital?"

"No, I could do it in the office."

"Okay. Whatever you suggest."

The half-arousal he felt for seven days and nights after the operation made Johnny realize what priapism might feel like. Glad to get this concern out of his mind, he came to understand the cleanliness he felt without the foreskin. He would have liked to tell his father he had become even more of a Jew.

A letter from Joe dated Good Friday, 1958, confirmed the good news that he would be ordained a priest on the first week in May in New York. He included a reserved ticket for the ordination in St. Paul the Apostle Church in Manhattan. He also informed Johnny that in Sonny's last letter he had sounded happier and more content and expected #4 in August. As the H.S. class president he hoped to come East from San Francisco in the summer and arrange a class reunion for 1960. His last paragraph described the seminarians' efforts on Good Friday in downtown Washington.

I won't say much about Good Friday. We are going downtown to preach from twelve to three on the street corner – seven of us each take two stations of the cross and preach on them. I know what my reaction will be – a numb acceptance of the really shocking fact that for so few people does the death of Christ really mean anything in their lives. It is hard to believe that Christ could really have a higher purpose in mind in letting things go this way – so little attention paid to the world's most important day. If only we could get men to realize what Christ has done for them, what it means to live a new life with Him through the power of His Cross and Resurrection. We must make them realize it – and to do it as Catholics I think we have got to stop preaching the Church to non-Catholics and just preach Christ. The Church has meaning only after they first see and appreciate Christ. And is perhaps the cause of our failure the fact that we don't really appreciate Him either? Well, anyway, we try, try very hard. Pray for me; I do for you.

Sincerely in Him,
Joe
P.S. Thought you might like the enclosed picture of Father Hecker.
You are going to be hearing more and more of him in the future, as
we become more aware of the breadth of his ideals and vision.

Delighted that Joe would soon be a priest in one of the finest American orders in the church, Johnny looked forward to that day in May when Joe would realize his dream. He decided to take Sylvia along with him to New York as a kind of reward for her faithfulness to the family.

The next few years quickly passed. Johnny's career stayed on track, slowly and methodically. He appreciated the opportunity to get to know more and more people in the community. Graham and Dodd's, *Security Analysis* text prepared him to analyze companies independently. The guaranteed draw paid each week, and the commission check at the end of the month gave him the feeling he could control his own destiny. The mortgage, extinguished after five years, gave his mother a security she had not known during her married years.

"If only people I lent money to paid off as diligently as you have there would be no risk in the business," Mr. Grim said to his mother when she gave him the last payment.

"Our thanks goes to you for your willingness to lend to us. We could not have bought the house through a bank."

Sylvia worked as a typist for a car dealership after her graduation from the Catholic high school. Lou finished his four years in the Air Force without any overseas duty and enrolled in a local college as an art major thanks to his athletic ability and sports contracts. He also lived at home.

CHAPTER SEVEN

In Sister Edmunda's fourth year as first councillor under Reverend Mother Chrysostoma, frictions developed between them concerning the direction of the community. Discussions took place regarding the Constitutions and Customary to which Sister Edmunda had devoted much of her energies over the years.

"Prayer is such an important part of our spiritual life I can't think of a greater mistake than to reduce our prayer practices to anything less than we now have," commented Sister Edmunda at one of the council meetings.

"You must admit, Sister, that the community is involved in activities and professions which limit the number of hours in the day which can be sacrificed simply to prayer."

"Reverend Mother, isn't that lack of prayer time a way of giving greater significance to the things of this earth. We need to engender in all of our sisters, and ourselves, the primary reasons why we are involved in all those activities. I can see us falling victims to the prudent of the world and widening the gate through which we hope to attain sanctification."

"Sister, please try to understand that not all the sisters have the endurance to devote themselves, as you do, to all of our present ideals," noted one the councillors.

"Please, I am the least worthy of any of you. My only desire is to live a life as close to that of St. Francis, our Seraphic Father, otherwise, of what use has my life been."

At prayer, in her room, Sister Edmunda agonized over what she sensed as a departure from the Franciscan ideals she had worked so consistently to engender in the congregation. "Sincerity and simplicity alone would lead her 'little- sisters' to the Heart of Jesus, with a sincere prayer life an absolute essential requirement in that pursuit," had motivated her years as Reverend Mother.

"Dear Lord, help me to understand this change the council appears intent on making. Can't they know that every step away from the spiritual is an invitation for earthly delights to creep in?"

A few days later the Reverend Mother approached Sister Edmunda about the possibility of Sister writing a history of the order.

"I am sorry, but I must defer on your request. So much of the order's development and growth centered around my own, that it would include too much of myself. I don't want to do that. And I am really not a good writer."

"Sister, you are an excellent writer. Anyway, if you won't do it, I'll commission a professional to write the story," she answered in exasperation.

"Incidently, Mother, have you given any thought to setting up a small cloister at Mt. Alvernia? I would certainly be happy to join a few devoted Bernardines who would pray for the order and all its undertakings."

"Sister, I need everyone to fill the expansion I envision for the order in the teaching field. As you know, we are now concentrating on education as our primary focus. I trust that meets with your approval."

"Reverend Mother, you're in charge. Whatever you wish." Sister Edmunda had thought about the opening of a small cloister for she loved to pray and spend hours before her Lord in the Blessed Sacrament. If the prayer life of the community diminished, perhaps a few cloistered sisters could return some balance to the congregation.

In July, 1960, a general chapter re-elected Mother Chrysostoma as the Reverend Mother. Sister Edmunda became the second councillor, much to her dismay. She had really prayed that she might somehow return to Mt. Alvernia in some capacity and leave the lavish estates in Villanova. With the central novitiate moved to the generalate, a second estate had been purchased nearby and became the new "Maryview". The mansion, beautifully furnished, and the antithesis of their sacred vow of poverty, created an additional anguish in Sister Edmunda: obedience to a superior who appeared destined to lead the community away from the things of heaven for the things of earth. Sister Edmunda meditated on the thoughts of St. Clare, the beloved disciple of St. Francis.

"Our labor here is brief, but the reward is eternal. Do not be disturbed by the clamor of the world, which passes like a shadow. Do not let false delights of a deceptive world deceive you. Close your ears to the whisperings of hell and bravely oppose its onslaughts. Gladly endure whatever goes against you and do not let good fortune lift you up: for these things destroy faith, while the others demand it. Offer faithfully what you have vowed to God and He shall reward you."

Little wonder that St. Clare's memory would live forever. In the mystery of God's Providence, Sister Edmund, also a stable, translucent symbol of the vision of St. Francis of Assisi wished only to: "Leave the things of time for those of eternity, to choose the things of heaven for the things of earth, to receive the hundred-fold in place of one, and to possess a blessed and eternal life." These are the reasons Sister Edmunda humbly held inside her soul and had dedicated her life as a Spouse of Christ.

Changes came very quickly during her first few months as second councillor. The nuns eliminated the heavily starched headgear surrounding their faces; a smaller veil now covered their heads. Other accoutrements also disappeared: the large rosary, the four-inch long crucifix made smaller, and the length of the wool habit reduced. Annual two-week vacations replaced the more restricted vacation of one-week every three years. Articles in the Constitutions and Customary were eliminated and the prayer program modified. Sister Edmunda privately confronted the Reverend Mother with the betrayal she felt regarding these changes.

"Where do you think the community is heading? Are these just the beginning of a decline into a mediocre spiritual life?"

"Sister, when will you finally realize things are changing. Frankly, your opposition to my ideas have reached a point where I believe either: YOU SHOULD GO, OR I WILL GO," an exasperated Reverend Mother blurted out.

Stunned by the vehemence of her superior, Sister Edmunda decided her conscience could no longer submit to the vow of obedience. Not certain exactly what course she should take, she humbly walked to her room and read again a short profile of her patron saint, Edmund of Abingdon, who had died in the year 1240.

Born in 1175 at Abingdon, Berkshire, England, Edmund Rich attended Oxford and the Sorbonne; taught philosophy and mathematics for about eight years at Oxford. Then taught theology while obtaining his Ph.D. in that subject. In 1222, he was appointed Treasurer of Salisbury Cathedral, and promoted to the See of Canterbury in 1234. During the contest between King Henry III and his Barons, Edmund favored the party which aimed at securing national independence from the domination of Henry's foreign favorites. He also endeavored to suppress many corrupt practices in the Church and, to this end, his Constitutions were issued in 1236. The resentment he incurred led him to visit Pope Gregory IX who failed to support him. Feeling his position to be intolerable, he retired to Pontigny's Cistercian Abbey in France, where he died in 1240. The memory of his pure and holy life attracted many worshippers to the shrine which still marks the last resting place of St. Edmund in Pontigny. He was canonized in 1247.

Sister Edmunda prayed to St. Edmund for some guidance. Should she leave her precious Bernardines and enter a cloistered monastery as he had done? How ironic that she had been given a name in religion after a saint who also faced conditions he had also found intolerable.

"Reverend Mother, I have decided that I will leave you in peace. My decision has been made to enter a cloister as soon as the administrative details can be handled."

"Sister, don't you think that is somewhat extreme? You have been a pillar of the community. What will the sisters say?"

"I really don't think there is any other choice, at least for now."

"You understand that if you leave I will do everything to erase the memory of you as a Bernardine. I will forbid anyone to write to you."

"Do what you will."

Nailed to her cross by a successor incapable of understanding the depths of Sister Edmunda's spirituality, she left the motherhouse for a Franciscan cloister in southern Ohio not knowing if she would ever return.

* * * * *